LORD SWINTON

Lord Swinton in 1936, when Minister for Air
(*BBC Hulton Picture Library*)

LORD SWINTON

J. A. CROSS

CLARENDON PRESS · OXFORD
1982

941.082092 SWI
CRO

Oxford University Press, Walton Street, Oxford OX2 6DP

London Glasgow New York Toronto
Delhi Bombay Calcutta Madras Karachi
Kuala Lumpur Singapore Hong Kong Tokyo
Nairobi Dar es Salaam Cape Town
Melbourne Auckland
and associates in
Beirut Berlin Ibadan Mexico City Nicosia

Published in the United States by
Oxford University Press, New York

British Library Cataloguing in Publication Data

Cross, J. A.
 Lord Swinton.
 1. Swinton, Philip Cunliffe — Lister, Earl of
 2. Statesmen—Great Britain—Biography
 I. Title
 941.082'092'4   DA566.9.S/
 ISBN 0-19-822602-0

Library of Congress Cataloging in Publication Data

Cross, J. A.
 Lord Swinton.
 Bibliography: p.
 Includes index.
 1. Swinton, Philip Cunliffe-Lister, Earl of, 1884–1972.   2. Great Britain—
 Politics and government—20th century.   3. Statesmen—Great Britain—
 Biography.   I. Title.
 DA566.9.S77C76 1983   941.08'092'4 [B] 82-8093
 ISBN 0-19-822602-0   AACR2

Typeset by Graphic Services, Oxford
Printed in Great Britain
at the University Press, Oxford
by Eric Buckley
Printer to the University

Preface

THERE can have been few longer or more varied ministerial
careers in modern British politics than that of the man who
was born Philip Lloyd-Greame, changed his name to Cunliffe-
Lister in 1924 (when his wife inherited the great Swinton
estate at Masham in Yorkshire), and became Lord Swinton in
1935. A junior minister under Lloyd George, he first entered
the Cabinet under Bonar Law in 1922, at the age of thirty-
eight. From then until 1938 he was almost continuously in
high office in Conservative and National Governments: as
President of the Board of Trade at a time when Britain was
reversing its long-standing commitment to free trade; as
Colonial Secretary; and, from 1935 to 1938, as the Air Minister who more than any other ensured that the RAF was prepared for the exigencies of war. From this last office he had
to resign in circumstances which suggested failure rather than
the outstanding success which, it has since been recognized,
he achieved at the Air Ministry in those vital years. The war
led to a renewed call for his services, first in non-ministerial
appointments concerned with the economic blockade of
Germany and the co-ordination of Britain's security services,
and then as Resident Minister in West Africa, followed by
service as the first Minister of Civil Aviation. A member of
the Conservative Shadow Cabinet throughout the first post-
war Labour Government, he played a leading role in the Conservative Government from 1951, retiring (as Secretary of
State for Commonwealth Relations) with Churchill in April
1955. From then until his death at an advanced age in 1972
he remained close to the centre of Conservative politics, a
confidant of the party's leaders and elder statesman extraordinary.

vi *Preface*

Until now there has been no biographical study of Swinton, apart from an unpublished 1961 graduate thesis by Alan Earl, who was not able to make use of the relevant public records and was concerned with his career only before 1938. Swinton himself published a volume of memoirs in 1948, and a second volume, containing reminiscences of prime ministers from Balfour to Douglas-Home, in 1966. Unfortunately his writings provide disappointingly few insights, being often inaccurate in detail and both reticent and selective about important phases of what was, by any standards, a remarkable career in politics.

The present volume attempts to fill this gap. In the necessarily limited space available its main emphasis is on Swinton the Minister, for it is in this capacity that solid political achievement can most readily be discerned. And within this ministerial career the decisive years at the Air Ministry must take pride of place. The principal primary sources have been Cabinet and departmental records, the Swinton Papers at Churchill College, Cambridge, and several other collections of private papers (see Note on Unpublished Sources), as well as interviews with many who worked alongside Swinton in government or party.

I have incurred numerous debts of gratitude, among which I would particularly like to mention those to the present Earl of Swinton (with whose authority I undertook the biography and who allowed me the complete freedom of his grandfather's papers), the Countess of Swinton (Lady Masham), Mr and Mrs Nicholas Cunliffe-Lister, Mr Paul Adorian, the late Viscount Amory, the late Lord Armstrong of Sanderstead, Mr A. J. L. Barnes, Mr R. H. Belcher, Mr G. D. M. Block, Lord Brooke of Cumnor, the late Sir Alan Burns, the late Lord Butler of Saffron Walden, Mr F. H. Butters, Sir Sydney Caine, Sir Fife Clark, Mr D. K. Clarke, Mr D. J. C. Crawley, Lord Diplock, Mr G. R. Downes, Mr Alan Earl, Lord Fraser of Kilmorack, Mr Malcolm Frost, Mr Robert Rhodes James, Mr Francis Johnson, Sir Stephen Luke, Mr Harold Macmillan, Sir Frederick Pedler, Dr K. E. Robinson, Mr Richard Scrope, and Dr Anthony Seldon. I am most grateful to the British Academy and the Small Grants Research Fund for financing my research; to the staffs of the Churchill Archive Centre, the Public Record Office, and a number of other libraries and repositories of research material; and to my publishers, Oxford University Press. My greatest debt, however, is owed to Sir Folliott Sandford, who first suggested I write the Swinton biography and upon whose advice and unique information about his former chief I have been able to call at every stage of its preparation.

J. A. Cross

Contents

CHAPTER 1

Career Foundations

THE future first Earl of Swinton was born Philip Lloyd-Greame on 1 May 1884, the scion of generations of considerable York-shire landowners. His paternal great grandfather, George Lloyd, had married Alicia Greame (pronounced Graham) who, on the death of her brother, inherited the large Sewerby estate of the Greame family near Bridlington in the East Riding. On her death, in 1867, the estate passed to her younger son, the Revd Yarburgh Gamaliel Lloyd, who adopted the additional surname of Greame to mark his succession to Sewerby. When he died, in 1890, the property passed to his only son, Yarburgh George Lloyd-Greame, who in 1867 had married Dora Letitia O'Brien, daughter of the Irish Anglican Bishop of Ossory. Of the five children of the marriage three survived into adult life: Yarburgh (1872-1965), Dora (who became Mrs Hannay), and Philip.

Philip Lloyd-Greame was six when his father inherited Sewerby House and its estate. He had in fact been born in the North Riding, at the Lodge, East Ayton, in the Vale of Picker-ing near Scarborough. But it was in the graceful environment of Sewerby that the chief part of his childhood and early man-hood was spent. Sewerby House is an elegant mansion in the early Georgian style, dating from 1714–20 although incor-porating certain features of earlier houses on the same site. Extensions at the beginning and in the middle of the nineteenth century were executed in the same style. Attractive and well appointed as the house undoubtedly is, however, it yields in charm to the park which surrounds it, with natural woodland, walled gardens, and lawns dipping down to the cliffs over-looking Bridlington Bay.[1] Growing up in such a milieu could hardly fail to instil a love of nature and country pursuits; and Lord Swinton remained very much a countryman through all the shifts and changes of his long career.

His relationship with his father was warm. 'Blessed is the son whose father is his closest friend,' he wrote in his memoirs. 'That was my good fortune.' He emphasized, too, the value to their local community of men like his father, who (materially assisted, no doubt, by the possession of independent means) 'in a long tradition of service do a hundred and one tasks'.[2] Among the tasks Yarburgh Lloyd-Greame undertook were those of magistrate, commander of the Yorkshire Artillery Militia (retiring as honorary Lieutenant-Colonel in 1886), chairman of the Bridlington Board of Guardians, member of the Harbour Commissioners, and president of a Bridlington hospital endowed by his family. He was also active for many years on Bridlington Rural District Council and East Riding County Council, and while neither local authority would have exhibited much of the cut and thrust of partisan political debate, his service on them doubtless provided an additional element of political training for Lloyd-Greame's younger son, the future Cabinet Minister.

Colonel Lloyd-Greame lived long enough to see that son well advanced in his political career—he died in November 1928, at the age of eighty-eight. Lord Swinton has not recorded any references to his relations with his mother, and his private papers do little to remedy the deficiency. For her part Mrs Lloyd-Greame seemed entirely satisfied with her son's filial devotion, telling him on the occasion of his engagement to marry that 'You . . . have been a source of joy and hope and thankfulness ever since the day of your birth.'[3] She died in March 1922.

After prep school the Lloyd-Greames sent Philip to Winchester (his elder brother had gone to Eton), where his five years—from 1897 to 1902—were reasonably successful but did little to suggest an exceptional subsequent career. His particular academic skills were in classics and modern languages (French and German); an early mathematical ability apparently being dissipated by bad and eccentric teaching. He played cricket and soccer for his house and rose to the ranks of house and school prefect. He essayed amateur theatricals but on both the occasions which have been recorded was left to take a female part, a thankless task for a strapping six-footer with a voice in no sense lacking masculinity. It was no wonder that his Nerissa in *The Merchant of Venice* was, according to a contemporary source, 'too inaccurate and too little vivacious'.[4]

In reply to the charge that public schools of his time were too stereotyped in the education they provided, Lloyd-Greame was later to write that 'A certain routine is necessary in education to inculcate steadfastness and thoroughness, to teach us to surmount difficulties and to plod through dull routine'; and that at Winchester this was combined with encouragement to follow one's own bent.[5] His own success in taking advantage of the latter may be gauged from the fact that those who knew him subsequently are divided in their opinion as to whether or not he exhibited the traits of the 'typical Wykehamist'.

After Winchester, university. Not, however, to the college of his father and grandfather—Trinity, Cambridge—but to University College, Oxford. And, somewhat surprisingly, as the family ambition for him centred on a diplomatic career, he read law. There is no evidence that he was particularly active in Oxford political circles, but his friends were in no doubt from the outset of his deep commitment to the cause of Conservatism. One of them, Compton Mackenzie, in his second year at Magdalen and editor of a student journal *The Oxford Point of View*, regretted in retrospect that he had not asked the freshman Lloyd-Greame 'to write about the outlook for Conservatism'.[6] Lloyd-Greame's commitment to his academic studies seems to have been somewhat less. Despite a 'blissful and idle' second year he still managed to secure a place among the twenty-one awarded second-class honours of the seventy-one who graduated in law at Oxford in 1906, with a little help (for his international law examination) from an external coach. He even had a viva for a first, and conceived a permanent contempt for written examinations when the chief examiner told him that if his knowledge of property law (in which he had worked reasonably hard) had equalled his knowledge of international law (which Lloyd-Greame knew he owed merely to the question-spotting skill of the coach) he would have joined the three who got firsts that year.[7]

With an Oxford law degree Lloyd-Greame entered, not the

diplomatic service, but the law. He took articles with the Wigan solicitor Sir Thomas Ratcliffe-Ellis, who, in addition to his legal interests, was a leading figure in the coal-mining industry and principal organizer of the Mining Association of Great Britain (of which he was secretary from 1892 to 1921). Working with Ratcliffe-Ellis, Lloyd-Greame gained his first insights into the troubled industry for which he was to have ministerial responsibility in the 1920s. It was not surprising that when, through Ratcliffe-Ellis's good offices, Lloyd-Greame moved over to the Bar (being admitted at the Inner Temple in 1908 and setting up chambers in Lincoln's Inn in 1910), he should decide to find a niche for himself in a crowded profession by specializing in mining law. More surprising, but characteristic of what was to be his practical approach to the later tasks of politics and administration, was his decision to gain experience of his specialist field by working for six months in a coal-mine.[8]

It was while he was practising at the Chancery Bar in London that Lloyd-Greame got the opportunity of setting his foot on the ladder of the political career that had been in his mind when he decided to become a lawyer rather than a diplomat. In 1911 the prospective Conservative candidature for the East Riding constituency of Buckrose, which included Bridlington and Sewerby, fell vacant. The previous candidate, Mark Sykes, who had been fairly narrowly defeated by a Liberal in both the elections in 1910, had departed to the Central Hull constituency, where, in July 1911, he was successful in retaining the seat for the Conservatives after the December 1910 election there had been declared void as a result of suspected electoral malpractices by the sitting Conservative member. Lloyd-Greame was invited by the Conservative association to take Sykes's place. Although Buckrose, a constituency created in 1885, had returned a Liberal ever since 1892, the majorities (apart from 1906) had been small—in December 1910 only 232 —and it thus held out reasonable prospects for a Conservative candidate. Lloyd-Greame decided to accept the invitation.

His involvement in Conservative Party politics at this time was not confined to his new role as prospective candidate. He was secretary of the Unionist Agricultural Committee which in 1913 published, in pamphlet form, *A Unionist Agricultural Policy*, calling for radical reform of the social conditions of agricultural workers.[9] Lloyd-Greame was also involved in the Unionist Social Reform Committee which F. E. Smith (Lord Birkenhead) had founded in April 1911 to interest Conservative back-bench MPs in social policy questions. A series of sub-committees were established to examine particular topics; Lloyd-Greame participated in that studying industrial unrest (others dealt with education, housing, health, and the poor law), and its report was published in June 1914.[10]

In the meantime the most important event in his domestic life, and one which would fundamentally shape his approach to his political career, had taken place. In July 1911 he became engaged to Mary Constance Boynton, only daughter of the Revd Charles Ingram Boynton, vicar of the parish of Barmston, about seven miles down the coast from Lloyd-Greame's family home at Sewerby. The couple were married in September of the following year; Lloyd-Greame was now twenty-eight, his bride not quite twenty-two. Mary Boynton's mother, who had died when Mary was only six, was fourth of seven children of the remarkable Samuel Cunliffe-Lister (1815–1906). Cunliffe-Lister, an immensely wealthy mill-owner, industrialist, and inventor, was in 1891 created Lord Masham of Swinton, after the estate of over 20,000 acres at Masham near Ripon which he had bought in 1882. His many enterprises included the Manningham Silk Plush Mills at Bradford (where he is commemorated by a statue) and the Ackton Hall Colliery Company at Featherstone and Pontefract; the most notable of his inventions were a compressed-air brake for railways and a wool-combing machine (although the validity of his patent in the latter was bitterly contested by a one-time associate and rival manufacturer).

In 1911, when Lloyd-Greame became engaged to Mary Boynton, the eventual disposition of the enormous wealth and property of his fiancée's maternal grandfather was uncertain. Lord Masham had died in 1906, to be succeeded by his elder son. The second Lord Masham, who was 54 in 1911, was unmarried, and his heir was his brother, ten years younger and married but with no children. The other five children of the first Lord Masham were all girls, of whom only Mary Cunliffe-Lister (Mary Boynton's mother), the second daughter, had married. Matters were complicated by the fact that the first

Lord Masham had in 1894, twelve years before his death, executed a strict settlement of the Swinton estate with the intention of ensuring that its owner should always bear the surname of Cunliffe-Lister; perhaps even as early as then he realized that neither of his sons were likely to have children to succeed them and wished to seek other means of perpetuating his name.

Thus when Philip Lloyd-Greame married Mary Boynton (or 'Mollie' as she was known to family and intimate friends) there were distinct prospects of her eventual succession to an immense fortune if they were both prepared to change their joint name to Cunliffe-Lister.[11] Exactly when this might occur was highly problematic, however. Granted that both the second and third Barons Masham remained childless, there were still the four surviving unmarried daughters: any succession of the sole representative of the generation that followed them (Mary Lloyd-Greame) depended upon their death—and the last sister did not die until 1962—or their waiving their rights to the Swinton entail. It was in fact the latter act of self-denial which followed the death of the third Lord Masham in 1924 (his elder brother, the second Baron, having died in 1917) and saw the Lloyd-Greames, transmogrified by royal licence into Cunliffe-Listers, assuming the ownership of Swinton and its 20,000 acres.

If it is uncertain whether Lloyd-Greame 'married money'— since in 1912 his wife's future succession to Swinton was possible but by no means inevitable—it is also uncertain whether his political ambitions were necessarily furthered by his marriage. While financial independence (even if gained through one's wife) was obviously an asset for a rising politician, in Lloyd-Greame's case there were elements working the other way. Mollie Lloyd-Greame was by no means the archetypal politician's wife, intensely ambitious for her husband's success. She did not much care for London, although prepared to reside there if her husband's career required it, but (at least after 1924) understandably preferred the freedom of their magnificent home in the Yorkshire moors. Her husband, too, felt the pull of Yorkshire and on at least one occasion, only a few years after his wife succeeded to the Swinton estate, was seriously contemplating retirement from politics.

Whatever financial considerations there may have been in the match, the marriage of Philip Lloyd-Greame and Mollie Boynton, which ended with Lord Swinton's death a few weeks short of 60 years later, was a happy and successful one. The letters from Swinton to his wife which still remain among his private papers (there are relatively few from Mollie) indicate the closeness and easy understanding of their relationship: invariably prefaced by 'My dearest', humorous (both had an earthy, even ribald, sense of humour), and redolent of the interests they had in common—the countryside, gardening, love of good paintings (such as those which adorned Swinton, both by inheritance and subsequent purchase). They had two children, both boys: John, born in 1913, and Philip, born in 1918.

By 1914 Lloyd-Greame, making his way at the Bar in London and nursing his Yorkshire constituency, could have reasonable expectations of being launched on a parliamentary career at the general election due to be held before the end of 1915. But, as for millions of others, the outbreak of war upset all future plans. On 5 August 1914, the day after the declaration of war, he enlisted as a private soldier in the Inns of Court Officer Training Corps, and in September he was commissioned as a temporary lieutenant in 5th Battalion Prince of Wales's Own Yorkshire Regiment (Green Howards). For several months he was stationed at Scarborough, engaged in training recruits, until in October 1915 he was transferred as a temporary major to help Lord Feversham recruit and train a battalion of Yeoman Rifles at Lord Feversham's Yorkshire home at Duncombe Park (Feversham also enlisted the services of a young subaltern called Anthony Eden).[12] It was not until early May 1916 that he was able to get into action, when he accompanied the battalion—21st Battalion (Yeoman Rifles), King's Royal Rifle Corps—to the Ypres salient in Belgium. Almost immediately, however, the commander of 124th Brigade, of which the battalion formed part, selected Lloyd-Greame to be his brigade intelligence officer, in which capacity he was responsible for reports on enemy movements, observation posts, and patrols. At the end of May brigade headquarters took over Lawrence Farm, near the village of Ploegsteert, recently vacated by the battalion commanded by Winston Churchill; and although there is no evidence that the two men met at the time Churchill was fond of recalling in later years their common experience (which they shared with Eden) of the patch of Belgium the British troops referred to as 'Plug Street'.[13]

Lloyd-Greame's experience of the front line was fated to be short. He distinguished himself in the Battle of the Somme, especially the engagement on 15 September 1916 which saw the first battlefield use of tanks. As his superior officer wrote to Mollie soon afterwards: 'I wanted to drop you a line to say what invaluable assistance your husband has been to the Brigade and myself in particular since he came to us. He is a tiger for work and quite *exceptionally* clever in addition to being a very gallant gentleman. He behaved *exceptionally* well, even amongst a good crowd, in the battle of the 15th. and will shortly receive the D.S.O. which he has so thoroughly deserved.'[14] The award when it came—in the New Year's Honours List of 1917—was not, however, the DSO, but the MC. By then Lloyd-Greame had been invalided home. On 27 September he had been appointed Brigade Major, but within a few days of this signal advancement after less than five months at the front, he was struck down with crippling arthritis in both legs, no doubt brought on by the atrocious conditions of trench warfare. On 28 October he returned to Britain for several weeks of treatment at St. Thomas's Hospital. He did not return to the trenches. After a brief posting to Sheerness in January 1917 he became a Brigade Major in Northern Command at York in February. From thence, in July, he was posted to the War Office in London, to work in the department of the Director of Recruiting, Sir Auckland Geddes. It was Geddes who, only a few weeks later, gave Lloyd-Greame the chance of making what—for all the gallantry he had shown in action—was to be his outstanding contribution to the conduct of the war.

By December 1916, when Lloyd George ousted Asquith from the premiership, it was obvious that the ramshackle arrangements by which Britain had attempted to secure its battlefield and industrial manpower requirements were totally inadequate to meet the increasingly voracious demands of war. The various service and civil departments with an interest in the supply or use of manpower went their own way, virtually regardless of overall needs, while the trade unions had been able to prevent any effective scheme for the direction of industrial labour, even after the introduction of compulsory military service. Within a fortnight of Lloyd George's becoming Prime Minister a Department of National Service was established, 'charged with the task of creating machinery capable of controlling and distributing in the most economical and effective manner the whole man-power of the country'.[15]

Initially, however, the powers of the new department were ill defined, and its difficulties were compounded by the equivocal position of its first head, Neville Chamberlain, who had only reluctantly left his highly successful local government work in Birmingham. Chamberlain was a director-general, not a minister (although his department became a ministry in March 1917 when the necessary legislation had been passed); he was not, and was not expected to be, an MP; and he was not a member of the Cabinet proper, let alone of the War Cabinet, nor even—an indispensable badge of full ministerial status—a Privy Councillor. No doubt weakened by his inexperience of the ways of Whitehall and Westminster and his own errors of judgement, Chamberlain was unable to assert his department's executive authority against uncooperative fellow departments like Labour, Munitions, and the War Office (which still managed to retain control of military recruiting), or to enlist Cabinet support for direction when the voluntary system of recruiting workers for essential industries had demonstrated its inadequacy. By 8 August 1917 he had had enough and submitted his resignation to Lloyd George, pointing out that 'for the success of any scheme of recruiting, it is essential that the head of the department should have the full support of the Cabinet, especially in his dealings with other labour-using or labour-supplying departments', and that 'past experience does not encourage me to hope that I should enjoy this support'.[16] Lloyd George had no difficulty in accepting the resignation—indeed he had virtually provoked it. Chamberlain's successor proved to be a key figure in one of those labour-using departments he had found so troublesome: Lloyd-Greame's War Office chief, Auckland Geddes.

Rumours about Geddes's appointment had been circulating before the actual announcement, but it seemed to be widely believed that although he would be associated with the ministry it would be as a kind of chief of staff to a minister recruited from the ranks of the politicians rather than as minister himself. Lloyd-Greame was quite certain that to be effective, Geddes must himself be the minister. In no way abashed by his relatively lowly position on Geddes's staff, he seized the opportunity of discussing the matter with Geddes when the latter gave him a lift in his official car from the War Office late one night. The same night he put his thoughts on paper in a letter to Geddes which he posted in the morning just before leaving for a week's duty tour: 'In it I said it would be a profound misfortune if anyone else became Minister. He had the ideas. Success would depend on the right plans and the speed with which they were carried out. Far too much time had been lost already. If Geddes had to teach a politician, the latter would only learn half and probably fail to put it across. The only way was for Geddes to be able to put his plans direct to the Prime Minister and the War Cabinet. Political inexperience mattered little in war. Let him insist firmly with Lloyd George that if he was to do the job he must have full powers and not the half way house that Neville Chamberlain had been induced to take.'[17]

The conversation and letter may well have influenced Geddes. On 25 August he asked Lloyd-Greame, just returned to the War Office after his duty tour, to see him. After telling him that he had accepted appointment as Minister of National Service, with clear powers defined by Cabinet minute, he invited Lloyd-Greame to take a senior official position in the ministry. Lloyd-Greame recounted the conversation in a letter to his father the following day:

Yesterday the Minister sent for me, and showed me a memorandum setting out the constitution of the . . . Ministry. There are about nine departments. The heads of these departments are to form a Board presided over by the Minister. This Board will, subject to the directions of the War Cabinet, decide the principles by which man-power is to be allocated. The Board will have a general secretary, who is the chief permanent official of the Ministry, and three assistant secretaries, one to deal with the War Cabinet secretariat and the Prime Minister's secretariat, one to deal with the other Ministries and one with the War Office. He then told me that he had nominated me to be the first of these assistant secretaries.[18]

Lloyd-Greame accepted the invitation with alacrity. Within four days of his interview with Geddes he was in his place in the Ministry, for the first meeting on 29 August of the National Service Council—the 'Board' to which Geddes had referred—whose secretary was Lloyd-Greame himself, not, as Geddes had indicated, the permanent secretary, E. A. Sandford Fawcett. Lloyd-Greame was initially ranked as chief assistant secretary, immediately after the permanent secretary, but in less than four months he was promoted to be 'conjoint secretary', responsible for policy and executive action, leaving the permanent secretary primarily concerned with the general administration of the department.[19] This curious dichotomy of functions was undoubtedly the result of the high regard Geddes had for his youthful import from the War Office (Lloyd-Greame was still only thirty-three), and the fact that Fawcett himself was hardly the traditional type of permanent secretary, having come to the Ministry from the Local Government Board, of which he had been deputy chief engineering inspector (he ended his civil service career as chief engineer to the Ministry of Health). The indications are that Lloyd-Greame was in fact fulfilling the primary functions of a permanent secretary.

Geddes, although—unlike the hapless Chamberlain—he immediately became a MP (a convenient constituency vacancy in Hampshire being found for him), a Minister of Cabinet rank, and a Privy Councillor, was no ordinary minister in his relations with his senior officials, looking to them to complement his predominantly political role with their administrative expertise. He had come to the Ministry direct from being in charge of recruiting at the War Office and was fully conversant with the complex inter-departmental ramifications of his ministerial portfolio. Many years later Lord Swinton recalled Geddes as 'a grand chief to work for. If he had confidence in you he gave you the fullest responsibility. He was keen to have all your ideas. He never shirked a decision.'[20] It was a style Lloyd-Greame was to emulate when he embarked upon his own ministerial career.

Geddes's first task was to draft new terms of reference for the Ministry, and this he did, with the assistance of Maurice Hankey, Secretary of the War Cabinet. They were approved by a Cabinet committee consisting of Lord Milner, General Smuts, and G. N. Barnes on 10 September, and by the War Cabinet two days later.[21] While they certainly did not entirely remove areas of inter-departmental discord, they at least enabled the Ministry, under more effective ministerial and official leadership than in the brief tenure of Neville Chamberlain, to maintain its autonomy in the matters assigned to it. It was, among other duties, to advise the War Cabinet 'as to the meaning, in terms of manpower and consequential results, of all Departmental proposals put forward to the War Cabinet'; to arrange the transfer to urgent national work of men from the forces and from less important civil occupations; to obtain the men required by the forces without dislocating civilian life and industrial production; to issue lists of reserved occupations; and to provide substitutes for labour withdrawn from civilian life. The object was to create a single agency responsible both for providing the army with the fighting manpower it needed, and, at the same time, for meeting as far as was practicable the demands of vital industries.[22]

It was rarely that the War Cabinet did not have a manpower question on its agenda, and Geddes was consequently a frequent attender. On many of these occasions he was accompanied by Lloyd-Greame, who attended twenty-four War Cabinet meetings in the nine-month period between 14 December 1917 and 24 September 1918.[23] On certain issues the War Cabinet would constitute itself into a committee specifically to discuss manpower, as in the Committee on Manpower which met from 10 to 15 December 1917 (with Lloyd-Greame in attendance) to discuss—inconclusively—the balance between the demands of the forces and the needs of the economy.[24] There was also the War Priorities Committee of the War Cabinet, originally established in September 1917 to deal with aircraft production but which in the following month had its remit extended to cover questions of priority in all munitions programmes. Chaired by Smuts, it included the service ministers, the Minister of Munitions, and, from October, the Minister of National Service. Labour questions were, of course, inextricably bound up with its work and that of its official subcommittees, which handled much of the detailed co-ordination of departmental activities. It was not, however until May 1918 that the Smuts Committee set up a subcommittee with comprehensive coverage of manpower priorities. Lloyd-Greame was appointed chairman, and its other members were senior officials from the Admiralty (Sir Robert Horne), War Office (Sir William Furse), Ministry of Munitions (Sir Stephenson Kent), and Ministry of Labour (Sir David Shackleton).[25]

Lloyd-Greame's labour subcommittee first met on 28 May 1918 and then twice weekly until its final meeting on 6 November. Its terms of reference were sweeping in their scope. It was 'to secure by common administrative action' both the best use of labour in the shipbuilding and munitions industries and 'the expeditious release for military service of the numbers of men from time to time agreed, or ordered by the War Cabinet, to be released from Admiralty, War Office and Ministry of Munitions work'. It was also to monitor action taken by departments and to act as a 'Court of Reference' in cases of inter-departmental dispute about the administration of agreed policy; while acting in the latter capacity its decisions would be simply promulgated by the War Priorities Committee except where the subcommittee was unable to come to a unanimous decision, when the parent committee would itself be called on to arbitrate.[26]

To judge from the brief report Lloyd-Greame submitted to the Smuts Committee when his committee was being wound up immediately after the Armistice, his chairmanship style must have reflected his later performance as Minister: brisk, practical, and decisive. 'The chief feature of this Committee', Lloyd-Greame wrote on 21 November 1918, 'was rapid agreement on controversial subjects, complemented by the speedy executive action of the Departments concerned. Agreement was in no case the result of sterile compromise. Quick action was undoubtedly facilitated by the fact that the members, all of whom attended practically every meeting, held positions which enabled them to issue immediate instructions.' Lloyd-Greame's report went on, 'The Departments making great and mutually irreconcilable demands on manpower were brought into a close and practical relationship. The struggle for men between the Services and the Departments responsible for production was clearly appreciated and unanimous agreement on questions involving widely divergent claims was achieved.' The surprising feature was that effective machinery at the inter-departmental level was developed so late in the war. By the end of May 1918, when Lloyd-Greame's committee began its work, the major manpower crisis—precipitated by the German offensive of March 1918—had been more or less, if painfully, surmounted. Lloyd-Greame's report hinted at his regret that the committee had not begun its work earlier. The process which it had supervised, he wrote, 'would have had cumulatively greater effect had the War continued'.[27]

Public recognition of the value of Lloyd-Greame's work at the Ministry of National Service was made with the inclusion of his name among the Knights Commander of the new Order of the British Empire (KBE) in the long list of awards in the Order published at the end of March 1920; neither of the officials formally his superior at the Ministry—Sandford Fawcett and his successor as permanent secretary, W. Vaughan—were similarly honoured.[28] But, more importantly, he was now quite exceptionally well equipped for the parliamentary and ministerial career which was opening up before him as the war came to an end. Few of the hundreds of new MPs who entered the House of Commons at the election of December 1918 had Lloyd-Greame's familiarity with high-level departmental administration and the problems of inter-departmental co--ordination, or the insights into the leading politicians of the day—Lloyd George, Bonar Law, Balfour, Austen Chamberlain, Curzon, Churchill, and the rest—which frequent attendance at the War Cabinet has given him.

There was no doubt in Lloyd-Greame's mind that he intended to follow a political career. The potential candidature at Buckrose had virtually lapsed, although he told his wife while he was at the front in 1916 that if there was an election during the war and the constituency association met all the expenses he would be willing to stand.[29] In March 1918, came the offer of an even more tempting parliamentary prospect: to contest the new Hendon division of Middlesex as a Coalition Unionist.[30] Despite his temporary status as a senior civil servant, he had no hesitation in accepting the invitation. And he was also able to ensure that his election expenses would be covered.

However ambitious he may have been for a political career, Lloyd-Greame had naturally to lay plans for earning his living after his spell as a civil servant came to an end, not least because of his growing family responsibilities (his second son was born in February 1918). He could have tried to pick up the pieces of his pre-war practice at the Bar. But, according to a tantalizingly brief reference in his memoirs, 'a chance friendship deterred me from returning to the Bar after the war and diverted me into business'.[31] His papers, which contain hardly any mention of his business interests, are silent on the identity of this friend. The probability is that it was Dannie Heineman, the American engineer who built up the world-wide financial and commercial concern Sofina (Société Financière de Transports et d'Enterprises Industrielles) of Brussels; Lloyd-Greame first met him in 1919 and his memoirs pay warm tribute to Heineman's business acumen and political finesse as he had observed them as a close friend and business associate over many years.[32] Lloyd-Greame's work at the Ministry of National Service had, however, brought him into contact with a wide variety of industrialists and businessmen, and it would not be in the least surprising if offers of employment had been made to a young, obviously able, and above all temporary, civil servant. What is clearly established is that well before the end of his time at the Ministry Lloyd-Greame was an extremely active member of a body known, after the adoption of its constitution in May 1918, as the British Commonwealth Union.

The British Commonwealth Union had actually been formed in December 1916, soon after the establishment of the Federation of British Industries, with which it was closely associated in both personnel and activities. In some senses the Union could be viewed as the political arm of the FBI, many of whose large corporate members felt constrained from taking overt political action in pursuit of their commercial and industrial interests, however much they might individually favour (as most of them did) such controversial political aims as tariff reform. Those firms which joined the BCU did so explicitly to pursue political objectives, and, at least initially (for the purposes of the 1918 election), by securing parliamentary representation for business interests. Business, so these political activists believed, required above all two major political conditions: industrial protection and—perhaps even more crucially for the immediate future—the defeat of 'bolshevism/socialism', which, for BCU members (as for most industrialists and Government supporters), involved both the defeat of Labour

Party election candidates and the effective dissemination of propaganda to counter the threat of revolutionary direct action which an outbreak of strikes was believed to portend.[33]

If the British Commonwealth Union's formal existence should be dated from the adoption of its constitution in May 1918, Lloyd-Greame, still, of course, a civil servant, was a founder member. By May he was a member of the Union's general purposes committee and in July he became its vice-chairman (a post he retained until taking junior ministerial office in August 1920). His chief role at this time was as chairman of the candidates' committee, which, after considerable preliminary vetting, decided to sponsor twenty-four candidates, mainly Conservative, at the December 1918 election. Lloyd-Greame himself was among them, and so was his wartime colleague, Sir Robert Horne. Eighteen of the twenty-four, including both Lloyd-Greame and Horne, were successful, although how much (apart from financial assistance) they owed to BCU support was difficult to say: most of them were in any case official supporters of the Coalition Government, which recorded so absolute a triumph at the election.[34]

At Hendon Lloyd-Greame had a handsome victory, gaining over 73 per cent of the votes cast and a majority of 9,205 over the combined vote for his two rivals, a Labour candidate and a representative of the Women's Parliamentary League. In only one of the four subsequent elections he fought in the constituency did he capture so much of the vote (in 1931, with over 81 per cent and an overall majority of 51,000), but he never recorded less than 50 per cent. Hendon from 1918 to 1931 provided little encouraging evidence for supporters of proportional representation.

By the time of his election, or shortly after, Lloyd-Greame had joined the board of directors of several companies. One of them—the Metropolitan Carriage, Wagon and Finance Company, based in Birmingham—had as its managing director Dudley Docker, a moving spirit in both the Federation of British Industries (he was its first president) and in the British Commonwealth Union. Then there were various public utility companies in Argentina, whose boards Lloyd-Greame almost certainly joined through the agency of Dannie Heineman; the most important of them—the Anglo-Argentine Tramways

Company—was later taken over by Heineman's Brussels-based firm Sofina (of which Lloyd-Greame also eventually became a director). He was by no means a sleeping director, and his contacts as a former senior civil servant and now as a parliamentarian were used on behalf of his companies and of the corporate groups of which he and they were members. (In addition to his BCU posts Lloyd-Greame joined the executive committee of the Federation of British Industries in January 1920.) In January 1919, for example, Lloyd-Greame and Sir Vincent Caillard, the FBI president, saw Bonar Law, in charge of the Government during Lloyd George's absence in Paris, to seek representation for FBI and BCU interests at the Peace Conference; they were able to report to the BCU general purposes committee that of the five members appointed to the British delegation's advisory committee on economic questions three were associated with the FBI and BCU.[35] For much of the first half of 1919 Lloyd-Greame was occupied with other BCU officials in attempting (unsuccessfully, in the end) to persuade the Government and, in particular, the Board of Trade (of which Sir Auckland Geddes was now President), of the merits of a scheme they had devised to secure British involvement in the economic regeneration of Romania, to the great benefit, it was anticipated, of British industry and commerce.[36] Much BCU effort was expended in trying to develop trade links with countries in eastern Europe (there were elaborate schemes for Poland and Estonia as well as Romania). In part this was to save them from the contagion of 'Bolshevism' from their Russian neighbour, but it was also for hard-headed, if long-term, commercial reasons. The ambitious individual schemes foundered on the understandable unwillingness of the Treasury to provide or guarantee sufficient loan finance. But the Union can probably claim some credit for convincing the Government of the need for some measure, however modest, of government finance for the opening up of trade links, and for the early passage of the export credits scheme with which Lloyd-Greame was to be closely associated as a Board of Trade minister.

The area of world trade which the British Commonwealth Union was most concerned to expand was indicated by its title. And with the expansion of inter-imperial trade went, almost symbiotically, tariff reform and imperial preference. Lloyd-Greame had always been a convinced supporter of tariff reform (as were the other participants in F. E. Smith's pre-war Unionist Social Reform Committee); and the immense dislocation to British and world trade caused by the war had only served to increase his belief in its efficacy. He had told his Hendon constituents in August 1918 that he favoured the tariff protection of key industries along with effective preferences for Empire products,[37] and one of his earliest interventions in the House of Commons was in support of the work of the Import Restriction Council of the Board of Trade. 'If the Government came back with any mandate at all at the election,' he told the House, 'it was a mandate to see what could be done, in a thoroughly businesslike way, to secure and stimulate home production.' The Council was taking each case of proposed import restriction on its merits 'as a business proposition and as to what is the best thing to be done'.[38] That pragmatic approach was to characterize Lloyd-Greame's own attitude to protective measures when he himself assumed ministerial responsibility for trade policy.

The first post-war Parliament met for the first time on 4 February 1919 (just a month after Lloyd-Greame had been officially demobilized from the Ministry of National Service). Within a fortnight Lloyd-Greame had delivered his maiden speech, without fuss or announcement, and on a piece of what seemed fairly routine legislative business. Before 1926 (when the practice was finally ended) those appointed to certain designated ministerial offices after a general election were required to submit themselves for re-election in their constituency—a hurdle at which Winston Churchill, for one, had fallen in 1908. The Coalition Government was now proposing, by its Re-election of Ministers Bill, to remove this necessity entirely. Lloyd-Greame, not for the last time demonstrating his independence of the Government he was elected to support, joined Liberal and Labour speakers in arguing against the measure as 'a restriction both on the general power of the House of Commons, and what is even more important, upon the general power of the country outside'. He later moved an amendment to limit the abolition of re-election to the first six months of a new Parliament. On behalf of the Government

Bonar Law expressed a willingness to accept the amendment if the period were extended to nine months. Lloyd-Greame agreed to the change and the amendment was then passed without a vote.[39] The tiro back-bencher could be well satisfied with having thus checked a Government with a 250-seat majority.

Thereafter Lloyd-Greame was one of the most active of the new members, taking in such varied subjects as housing and rent restriction (where he showed no sympathy at all for grasping landlords but much for their tenants); price controls (he was a member of the Commons select committee on high prices and profits which sat from July to August 1919, as also, from April 1919 to August 1920, of the National Expenditure select committee); the Government's Overseas Trade (Credit and Insurance) Bill, on which he, with FBI and BCU colleagues, made private representations to ministers; allotments; patents and designs; restrictions on undesirable aliens (which he thought should be spelt out in legislation rather than be left to the Home Secretary's discretion); industrial courts; and women's emancipation.

Lloyd-Greame was in the van of those who felt that the government's manifesto commitment to the equality of the sexes should be fulfilled to the letter. He even went so far as to ally himself, in company with other dissident Conservatives (Lord Robert Cecil, Sir Samuel Hoare, and Edward Wood among them), with the Labour and Liberal Opposition to defeat the Government on a Labour private member's Women's Emancipation Bill designed to give women full voting equality with men. A Government motion to reject the Bill failed to pass by 100 votes to 85, with Lloyd-Greame both speaking and voting against the motion.[40] This success for the cause of equal franchise rights was, however, short-lived, for the House of Lords rejected the Bill and women had to wait another nine years for voting parity with men. Lloyd-Greame also spoke and voted in favour of the right of women to sit in the House of Lords, a proposal which similarly came to grief at the hands of the upper chamber.[41]

One of the dominant legislative concerns of the first postwar Parliament, as it had been of its pre-war predecessor, was Ireland. And it was Ireland which provided the basic but not exclusive *raison d'être* of the small informal 'Group' of

Conservative back-benchers with which Lloyd-Greame (son of an Irish mother) was associated until he joined the Government in August 1920. Its full membership is uncertain (varying with the recollections of those who considered themselves to be part of it) but the leading members were Walter Guinness, Samuel Hoare, Edward Wood, Lord Winterton, and J. W. Hills, all pre-war MPs and all prominent in the Unionist Social Reform Committee.[42] With other members of the Group, Lloyd-Greame helped to secure the passage, against fierce Conservative back-bench opposition, of the Government of Ireland Bill, which seemed to him to provide the only hope of peace in Ireland. On 1 April 1920 *The Times* carried in its letter columns a lengthy defence of the Irish Bill by Lloyd-Greame, together with some suggestions for strengthening it, which he later attempted, with little success, to get incorporated at the committee stage of the Bill in May. Some of his amendments were designed to increase the powers of the Council of Ireland —he was clearly paying more than lip-service to the ideal of a united Ireland—but his most substantial effort was directed towards attempting to ensure that Northern Ireland should consist of all nine counties of the ancient province of Ulster, not just the six which the Bill (and the subsequent Act) provided.[43]

The Group was not necessarily homogeneous in policy terms. One of the policy issues on which Lloyd-Greame was likely to have been at odds with most of his Group colleagues was his advocacy, at least for a time in 1920, of the idea of 'fusion', of a national party joining together Conservatives and Lloyd George Coalition Liberals. Hoare, for one, always rejected the limitations on separate Conservative identity involved in what he saw as merely a marriage of convenience.[44] But important voices in the leadership of the Coalition Government—Churchill, Birkenhead, Balfour, Austen Chamberlain, even Bonar Law, among them—were raised in its favour, and it was an indication of the strength of 'grass roots' opinion in the supposedly 'deferential' Conservative Party that the idea was so summarily and speedily dispatched. Lloyd-Greame, it must be said, was no uncritical or unqualified supporter of the national or centre party. He regarded it as essential, he explained in a letter to *The Times* on 9 January 1920, that a national party should be based on fundamental principles and not on compromise and expedients in which members of neither of the constituent elements could believe. Just over a fortnight later he was invited to Downing Street to put his points in person to Lloyd George, who was later joined by Bonar Law. According to the account he gave his father, Lloyd-Greame was almost brutally frank in telling the Prime Minister of the suspicions that Conservatives harboured about him. He could remove the mistrust, Lloyd-Greame told him, by 'committing yourself to a real side'. If he did that he would get support in the country, which would not only strengthen the position of the Government but, even more important, restore confidence in parliamentary institutions as against 'direct action' by the Bolshevik left.[45] Lloyd-Greame was later told by the Prime Minister that he had tried the idea on his Liberal supporters but they were unwilling to commit themselves, and thus the opportunity, such as it was, was lost.[46] In view of the attitude of the great mass of the Conservative Party it is, however, highly doubtful whether there was ever any realistic prospect of its success.

It did not take Lloyd-Greame long to make his mark in the Commons. Less than three months after the opening of the 1919 session he was being talked of in the national press as one of the five 'rising hopes of Toryism'; and the others (Hoare, Wood, Hills, and Guinness) were all well-established MPs, not, like Lloyd-Greame, new arrivals.[47] More importantly for his future political career he was catching the eye of leading members of the Government. Even before his discussion with him in Downing Street early in 1920, Lloyd George had picked him out as the most promising of all the Conservative back-benchers.[48] Walter Long, First Lord of the Admiralty and a pillar of the Conservative establishment, wrote to Lloyd-Greame in flattering terms about his national-party letter in *The Times*: 'I read your letter on the future of the coalition with much agreement and real pleasure. In tone and argument it was thoroughly of the position you have already made for yourself in the House of Commons.'[49] Towards the end of February 1920 the definite prospect of office was held out to him, and he decided, after discussion with his wife, that despite the substantial loss of earnings that office would entail (since it would mean giving up his directorships), he would accept an offer if it were made. A letter he wrote to his father on 3 March gives an insight into the considerations which weighed with him, his attitude to a political career, and his frank estimate of his own abilities:

Bonar Law sent Horne to see me the other day, and I saw the Prime Minister afterwards. The upshot of this is that when the Government is reconstructed, if the basis is efficiency as apart from long service, I shall probably be offered an under-secretaryship. I have talked the whole thing over with Mollie; and we have decided that if the P.M. definitely thinks I am needed, I cant hold back. The obligation is not much less than in 1914. It would mean that we should be poor instead of being well-off and it may even mean—probably will—drawing on capital for a few years. But the children are provided for ultimately. And if it is right for the country it has got to be done.

This of course is for your ears alone; but I wanted to tell you at once. Dont worry about it. And dont offer to make me an allowance. I dont want it.[50]

The definite offer was not long in coming. On 20 August 1920 (eighteen months after he had entered the House of Commons) it was announced that Sir Philip Lloyd-Greame had been appointed parliamentary secretary to the Board of Trade. His departmental chief was Bonar Law's emissary of the previous February, Sir Robert Horne, who was familiar with his work both at the Ministry of National Service and as a fellow-activist in the British Commonwealth Union.[51]

Lloyd-Greame seems to have assumed governmental duties even before the public announcement of his ministerial appointment. On 18 August he attended a meeting of the Cabinet Supply and Transport Committee which had Sir Eric Geddes (Auckland's brother), the Minister of Transport, as chairman and included the Home Secretary (Shortt), the Minister of Labour (Macnamara), the Food Controller (McCurdy), the Secretary of State for War and Air (Churchill), and the President of the Board of Trade (Horne). The committee discussed, among other things, what action should be taken in the light of the threat of another coal strike. Should the Government adopt a policy of immediate overt action or should it wait until the strike had been definitely declared? The committee decided that 'simple propaganda showing the immediate effect on the cost of living of a coal strike, and the ruinous effect of such a strike on employment was required, and not overt action. It was necessary to convince the people, and to form a wall of solid opinion against revolution.' Horne was able to tell the committee that Lloyd-Greame (who was familiar with this kind of work from his association with the British Commonwealth Union) was willing to undertake the duties of chairman of an inter-departmental publicity committee which the Supply and Transport Committee had decided to establish (or rather reconstitute, as there had been various precursors) at its previous meeting on 12 August. It was agreed that Lloyd-Greame should be appointed, and act under the instructions of the President of the Board of Trade, who would have general responsibility for government publicity. The first meeting of the publicity committee, composed mainly of civil servants from the interested departments, was held on 23 August, by which time its chairman had become parliamentary secretary at the Board of Trade. Lloyd-Greame continued to co-ordinate government publicity until 1921, taking in not only the coal strike of October 1920 but the even more serious strike in the industry from April to June 1921.[52] It is doubtful whether the activities which the committee sponsored—such things as press publicity and advertising, briefs for speakers (distributed through a variety of bodies, including the British Commonwealth Union), posters, and pamphlets—made a significant contribution to saving the country from revolution. But the experience of his very first ministerial assignment must surely have recurred to Lord Swinton's mind when, thirty years later, he accepted a not dissimilar role from the hands of Winston Churchill.

The Board of Trade was to be Lloyd-Greame's governmental home for the next nine years, apart from the brief interlude of the 1924 Labour Government. Although the wartime creation of separate Ministries of Labour and Transport had removed from it certain responsibilities, the functions of the Board were still multifarious. They included trade policy and commercial treaties, industrial policy, the administration of the law relating to companies, copyright, patents, and bankruptcy, shipping, and the Merchant Navy, local authority gas undertakings, and the coal-mines (taken over in February 1917 and not returned to private companies until March 1921).

Lloyd-Greame joined the largest ministerial team in the White-hall of the day (where the standard pattern of a departmental minister and one junior minister was almost universal outside the service departments). Under the President of the Board of Trade (Horne), there was a parliamentary secretary—the post to which Lloyd-Greame was initially appointed—and two other parliamentary secretaries who had designated responsibilities, one (Cecil Kellaway) in charge of the Department of Overseas Trade, which for policy matters was responsible to both the President and the Foreign Secretary but administratively was completely under the President; and the other (W. C. Bridge-man), Secretary of the Mines Department, with a high degree of administrative autonomy (the department had its own per-manent secretary and accounting officer) but answerable to the President on all important policy matters.[53] The two parlia-mentary secretaries, with their own recognizable departments, ranked among the most senior in the junior ministerial echelons of any government, and it was thus promotion for Lloyd-Greame when, after less than eight months at the Board, he was placed in charge of the Department of Overseas Trade, not as parliamentary secretary but as Director, a title (used, apparently, only in his case) which itself seemed to enhance the autonomy of his post.

He was beginning his ministerial career at a time when the brief post-war boom had exhausted itself, to be succeeded by long years of recession in the basic industries, unemployment, and underemployment. It cannot be said that he brought any particularly original insights to the attempts to cure Britain's economic ills by the Coalition Government, or its inter-war successors (of most of which Lloyd-Greame was a member). In the battle which still raged between the proponents of free trade and the advocates of protection he aligned himself with the latter, but on pragmatic, not ideological, grounds. The next few years were to give him ample scope to practise his pragmatism.

The ramparts of free trade had been breached in 1915 with the McKenna duties which imposed duties of 33⅓ per cent on imported goods then considered as luxuries and whose importation would take up scarce resources of shipping and foreign exchange: motor cars and motor cycles, clocks, watches, and musical instruments among them. In 1919 these duties were used to discriminate in favour of British Empire imports of the same commodities which, thereafter, attracted a third less tax than those from foreign countries. Other industries had been thought so vital to the war effort that dependence on imports must be avoided and domestic production fostered—hence the wartime embargoes on imports of dyes, optical glass, and scientific instruments (for all of which Germany had been a major pre-war source). All this *ad hoc* protection seemed to provide a spring-board for those who advocated its widespread extension to cope with the slump and unemployment, whatever might be the long-term effects of that on the general health of international trade on which any permanent hope of Britain's economic prosperity depended. But the new movement had learnt some of the lessons of the pre-war tariff-reform battles. The edges of conflict were softened by euphemistic changes such as the substitution of 'safeguarding' for 'protection', 'key industry' for 'home industry', and 'dumping' for price competition by foreign rivals. And the process was to be gradual and specific, not the application of a comprehensive nostrum.

Lloyd-Greame's appointment came in the parliamentary recess. It was not until 19 October that he performed his first parliamentary duty as a minister and appeared at the dispatch-box to take some of the questions addressed to the President of the Board of Trade. The first piece of legislation in which he was involved represented a significant protectionist move, albeit confined to one industry. The Dyestuffs (Import Regulation) Bill was designed to 'regulate' (in other words, restrict) the importation of foreign, chiefly German, dyestuffs, through the agency of a Dyestuffs Licensing Board. It completed all its Commons stages between 7 and 17 December, with Lloyd-Greame in close attendance on his departmental chief, Horne.

The Board's chief legislative measure in the last two years of the Coalition Government was the Safeguarding of Industries Act of 1921. At the end of 1920 Horne had proposed a draft Bill which met heavy criticism from Coalition Liberals in the Cabinet, notably, Montagu, Churchill, and H. A. L. Fisher. The result was the setting up in February 1921 of a Cabinet committee, under Horne's chairmanship, with Balfour (Lord

President of the Council), Worthington-Evans (Secretary of State for War), Mond (First Commissioner of Works), Churchill (Colonial Secretary), Hewart (Attorney-General, and Lloyd-Greame as its members, to consider the draft Bill. After four meetings the committee's amendments were reported to the Cabinet and approved by it.[54] But before it could be fitted into the legislative programme and presented to the Commons there had been a change at the head of the Board of Trade.

Bonar Law, leader of the Conservative Party and Lord Privy Seal in the Coalition Government, resigned on grounds of ill health on 17 March 1921. His successor in both his party and governmental posts was Austen Chamberlain, who was succeeded as Chancellor of the Exchequer by Sir Robert Horne. The question of Horne's own successor at the Board of Trade exercised Lloyd-Greame, although as a junior minister he could exert little influence on the appointment. Stanley Baldwin, the Financial Secretary to the Treasury, was an obvious candidate, but there could be difficulty in changing both Chancellor and Financial Secretary so near the presentation of the Budget. On 19 March Lloyd-Greame wrote to Horne to suggest the free-trader and Coalition Liberal Sir Alfred Mond as the new president:

I do not underestimate the political objections, but he is an extraordinarily able business man and he is a fairly astute parliamentarian. If the Board of Trade is to lose you, I think the business community would like to see a business man there. Stanley Baldwin fulfils this qualification in a sense, but he has been disassociated from his business for a considerable time and I think he is rather associated in the public mind with the Treasury point of view. Further, politically, it would be no small advantage to have a distinguished Liberal Free-Trader in charge of the Safeguarding of Industries Bill—and Mond is a firm believer in the Bill.[55]

Mond did indeed get promotion from the Office of Works, but to the Ministry of Health, not the Board of Trade. It was Balwin who became President and with whom Lloyd-Greame (now Director of the Department of Overseas Trade) was to work in the closest harmony in the department for the remaining eighteen months of the coalition. Together, Baldwin's intimate John Davidson later recalled, they made a powerful team: the self-confident, somewhat hectoring Oxford man and the 'Cambridge yokel' Baldwin.[56]

The combination was seen at work in the prolonged and

often acrimonious debates on the Safeguarding of Industries Bill, which dominated parliamentary time between May and August 1921.[57] Part 1 of the Bill provided for an import duty of 33⅓ per cent on certain articles deemed to be of particular importance to British industry (and for which Germany happened, in most cases, to be the principal source), including optical glass, electrical instruments, and chemicals (when the Board of Trade later worked out the details of these categories they were found to cover 6,500 items). More potentially far-reaching was Part 2 of the Bill, which sought to protect British industry from 'unfair competition'. Manufacturers who could show that their industries were suffering from imported goods 'dumped' below the cost of foreign production or sold at less than the domestic price through a depreciated currency in the country of origin (Germany, with its runaway inflation, was again the chief target here) might secure an order imposing an import duty of 33⅓ per cent on those goods. Applications for the imposition of duties on these grounds were to be referred by the Board of Trade (provided it thought there was a prima-facie case) to an independent *ad hoc* committee of inquiry appointed by the Board. If the inquiry resulted in a recommendation of a duty it could be imposed by a Board of Trade order, subject to parliamentary confirmation. It was a procedure which was to occupy a great deal of Lloyd-Greame's time when he himself became President of the Board of Trade.

The minister responsible for the Bill's progress through the Commons was, of course, Baldwin, but he had had no hand in its drafting and was thus more than ordinarily dependent on his chief parliamentary assistant, Lloyd-Greame, who had been a member of the Cabinet committee which had finalized the draft. Baldwin had to accept several amendments to the original Bill in the course of the debates, but the main structure remained unaffected. In a typical gesture of warmth and sensitivity which made Baldwin so attractive a politician, he wrote to thank his assistant on the day the third reading was successfully concluded (12 August 1921):

My dear Philip,

    Before the sun goes down I must write and thank you for the invaluable help you have given me throughout the passage of our Bill. I could not have done it without you.

You will know in due time what it means to the man in charge to have someone by his side on whom he can depend absolutely and entirely, I hope indeed that your first experience may be as happy as mine has been.

Yours ever

S. B.[58]

The tribute was both sincere and well deserved.

The Coalition Government's efforts to revive British industry and trade were not confined to negative acts of protectionism. Britain's trade obviously depended on the prosperity of other countries, and genuine steps were taken to assist Europe's economic recovery, including those ex-enemy countries whose depreciated currencies had exercised the framers of, and pressure-group influences on, Part 2 of the Safeguarding of Industries Act. There was the Overseas Trade (Credits and Insurance) Act of 1920, together with an amending Act of 1921 (piloted through the House by Lloyd-Greame), which provided up to £26m. in government grants or guarantees to finance trade with countries suffering from depreciated currencies and lack of credit. And there was the major effort by Lloyd George, almost alone among his colleagues (who in this, as in so much else, lacked his prescience and imaginative flair), to normalize relations with the Soviet Union.

Lloyd George had from the first taken a more sympathetic attitude to post-revolution Russia than the rest of his Government or the governments of the other Allied Powers. If he had had his way Russia would have been represented at the Paris Peace Conference. And although he cannot be exonerated from a charge at least of ambivalence towards Allied intervention on the side of the White Russians in the civil war, he exercised a restraining influence on anti-Bolshevik hotheads like Churchill. Perhaps rather naïvely he thought that diplomacy could divert the course of the Russian revolution into paths more palatable to Western parliamentary systems. Certainly he attached an exaggerated importance to Lenin's 1921 confessions of the regime's economic failures (of which the Volga area famine of 1921–2 provided tragic proof), not least that in November 1921 in which Lenin was reported as describing the new economic policy as 'the transition to the re-establishment of capitalism to a certain extent'. A Soviet trade delegation under Krassin came to London in May 1920 and on 16 March 1921 a limited trade agreement was concluded, under which each country extended to the other 'most favoured nation' treatment and Britain conceded *de facto* status to the Soviet government, which undertook to refrain from disseminating Communist propaganda in British territories (a promise never kept). On the other hand, nothing was said about British trade credits, nor, on the Soviet side, about the payment of debts incurred by the previous Tsarist regime or compensation to foreign individuals and firms for the seizure of their property. Lloyd-Greame played a major role in the negotiations with the trade mission and was involved, too, in measures to relieve the Russian famine, being nominated in August 1921 as British delegate on the Allied Supreme Council commission on Russian famine relief.

But Lloyd George's supreme effort to bring Russia back into the comity of nations was to be the international conference which eventually met at Genoa in April and May 1922. After much persuasion of his colleagues and resignation threats from Churchill, the Prime Minister was able on 28 March to get Cabinet authorization for the British Empire delegation to Genoa (which he was to lead) to accord the Soviet Union 'full ceremonial recognition' with the exchange of chargés d'affaires if the Soviet representatives were willing, in good faith, to accept the conditions which the Allied Supreme Council had laid down at its Cannes meeting in January.[59] The Cannes resolutions, while conceding that no country could dictate to another the 'principles on which they are to regulate their system of ownership, internal economy and government', declared that if foreign investors were to be persuaded to participate in the process of a country's economic reconstruction, they would have to 'be assured that their property and rights will be respected and the fruits of their enterprise secured for them'. This involved the acknowledgement of all public debts and obligations, the restoration of private property or satisfactory compensation in lieu, and the establishment of a legal system which would 'sanction and enforce commercial and other contracts with impartiality'. Moreover, financial and currency reforms would be necessary and the nation concerned would have to undertake to refrain from propaganda and aggressive actions against other countries.[60] The reconciliation between these Western capitalist norms of good economic behaviour and the revolutionary economic philosophy of a shunned and suspicious Communist Russia was the virtually impossible task that Lloyd George pursued at Genoa (along with that other intractable problem which stood in the way of European economic reconstruction—German reparations). One of his principal lieutenants—considerably less optimistic than he—was the young Director of the Overseas Trade Department, Sir Philip Lloyd-Greame.

The ministerial component of the British delegation to Genoa consisted of Lloyd George, Horne (the Chancellor of the Exchequer, who was present for the opening stages only), Sir Laming Worthington-Evans (Secretary of State for War), and Lloyd-Greame, the only ministerial delegate not a member of the Cabinet; Lord Birkenhead, the Lord Chancellor, who was cruising in his yacht in the Mediterranean at the time, also occasionally attended. Curzon, the Foreign Secretary, should have been a member but just before the opening of the conference he succumbed to a genuine—but, in view of his doubts about the Prime Minister's Russian policy, convenient—attack of phlebitis. No other Foreign Office minister took his place, so Lloyd-Greame, with his joint responsibility to both the Foreign Office and the Board of Trade, exercised a watching brief; all the more necessary, in the Foreign Office's view, because of the Prime Minister's propensity to use his confidant, E. F. Wise, officially a member of the Board of Trade team at the conference, for delicate foreign negotiations. Curzon's absence, and Lloyd George's regard for his young colleague's ability, meant that Lloyd-Greame joined Lloyd George and Worthington-Evans in the work of the most important of the various commissions that the conference established: the Political Commission, which dealt with Russian questions. He was a member, too, of the less important but none the less arduous economic and transport commissions. He seems also to have acted as an informal liaison officer with the representatives of the Dominions (Australia, New Zealand, and South Africa) and India in the British Empire delegation, who rarely participated in the crucial discussions.

It is not proposed to attempt to unravel here the often tortuous proceedings in the five and a half weeks of the finally abortive Genoa Conference. Thirty-four countries, including Soviet Russia and Germany but not the United States, were represented, but—as so often at large international gatherings —informal meetings between members of the more important delegations were more significant than the formal conference and committee sessions. Lloyd George was an indispensable element in the behind-the-scenes discussions, and for several of them, particularly in the opening stages, he was accompanied by Lloyd-Greame. Later the two men seemed to draw apart somewhat as Lloyd George strove to secure the great coup of a normalization of relations with the Soviet Union (so much needed by his increasingly accident-prone administration), and his younger colleague, attuned to the deep uneasiness of Conservatives on the Russian question, risked his political career in confronting his Prime Minister with the cold facts of the situation as he saw it.

Something of the flavour of the Genoa Conference can be gained from the letters Lloyd-Greame wrote to his wife as the conference developed.[61] At first the auguries seemed propitious. On 10 April, the day the conference formally opened, Lloyd-Greame told his wife: 'Genoa is off its head with enthusiasm; there is a great feeling of faith that something is going to be done.' This was due in part, he felt, to Lloyd George's 'really fine [opening] speech—sincere, clever, tactful and soothing while not ignoring any difficulties'. On the following day the First (Political) Commission, set up to consider Russian questions, held its first meeting but Lloyd George had already decided that private diplomacy was much more likely than formal sessions to induce the Russians to make concessions to the norms of private enterprise in exchange for *de jure* recognition and trade and economic assistance. In a series of meetings between 13 and 15 April at Lloyd George's private residence some six miles outside Genoa delegates from Britain (Lloyd George and Lloyd-Greame), France (Barthou and Seydoux), Italy (Schanzer), and Belgium (Theunis and Jaspar) tried to reach agreement on outstanding problems with the Russians (Chicherin, Litvinoff, and Krassin), but to no avail: the Russians flatly refused to accept any obligation for Russian war debt and, indeed, made counter-claims in respect of Allied intervention on the side of the White Russians.[62] News of the

meetings leaked out, with the result that the excluded delegations, as Lloyd-Greame wrote to his wife on 16 April, complained bitterly of 'Supreme Council Methods'. The Foreign
Office was also disturbed. One of its officials in Genoa, J. D.
Gregory, wrote to a colleague in London bemoaning the Prime
Minister's 'weakness' for 'the infamous Wise' and the tendency
for the official sessions to become merely formal, registering
'what has been done behind the scenes'. Lloyd-Greame's presence, however, provided some comfort: 'Lloyd-Greame is the
greatest ally we Foreign Office have got here, and with his help
I hope to be able to keep the Foreign Office end up. But I am
not frightfully sanguine.'[63]

On 17 April Genoa was electrified by the news that delegates
from the two countries whose affairs provided the dominant
themes of the conference—the Soviet Union and Germany—
had the previous day (a Sunday) taken matters into their own
hands and concluded a separate agreement between themselves
at Rapallo, a resort about eighteen miles from Genoa. Germany
extended *de jure* recognition to the Soviet Government and
each country granted 'most favoured nation' status to the other
and mutually renounced all claims for debts and damage. The
terms thus covered bilaterally the very matters which the
Genoa Conference had been convened to attempt to settle at
an international level. Lloyd-Greame's obviously rushed letter
to his wife on 19 April painted the scene of consternation:

Monday [17 April] I worked with the Dominions and experts through
Customs, Prohibition, Transport. Hoped to be out in an hour. Sudden call
to urgent meeting. Russo-German treaty. Fat in the fire. Meeting P.M.
and I, Barthou and Seydoux, Theunis and Jaspar and Schanzer. French
at first anxious to withdraw [from the whole conference]. A speech of
great power and insight from the P.M. on ultimate danger of German-
Russian combination. French most impressed. Agreed we should draft
Note [for] German Government that night for meeting next day. Worked
on this. Brought Lord Chancellor over from Porto Fino to breakfast
next morning [18 April]. Full meeting British and Dominion delegation.
Then P.M., Lord Chancellor and I went off to meeting at Schanzer's
villa. Facta [Italian Prime Minister] presiding. Little Entente [Czech-
oslovakia, Yugoslavia, and Romania] and Poland also present. French
delighted at our draft. Long discussion. Italians obviously very anxious
not to offend the Germans and terribly afraid of the break of the conference. Wanted to adjourn for Cabinet. Impossible.

The note of protest approved by the meeting thus described

by Lloyd-Greame was delivered to the German delegation (Wirth, the Chancellor, and Rathenau, the Foreign Minister) the same day, 18 April. It deplored 'the secret conclusion of a Treaty covering the very questions under discussion at the conference, which was 'a violation of the conditions to which Germany pledged herself on entering the Conference' and 'of the principles on which the Conference is based'.[64]

When Lloyd George, accompanied by Lloyd-Greame, met Wirth and Rathenau in informal conference at noon on 19 April, he left the Germans in no doubt of his anger at their action and of the effect it would have, if not immediately retracted, on their continued participation in the conference. Obviously shaken, Wirth and Rathenau eventually agreed to withdraw from the treaty if the Russians would agree; failing that, they would take no further part in the conference sessions on Russian questions. Rathenau undertook to speak to Chicherin, the Soviet Foreign Minister, and report back to Lloyd-Greame in the evening. At 8 p.m. he came to see Lloyd-Greame, who had with him J. D. Gregory, head of the Foreign Office Northern Department. Rathenau's mission had failed. Chicherin had refused point-blank to consider the withdrawal of the treaty, and when Rathenau had then suggested that the difficulty might be met by postponing its immediate application and making it part of the general settlement at the end of the conference, Chicherin made no answer. The German delegation must now consider its future action, Rathenau told Lloyd-Greame. Withdrawal of the treaty being ruled out as impossible, all that remained was to consider whether the German delegation should remain in Genoa and take part in the work other than that concerned with Russia, or whether it should withdraw altogether. A German note two days later confirmed that the delegation was remaining in Genoa.[65]

The importance of the Rapallo pact was probably a good deal less than was thought at the time. It changed Soviet–German relations very little in the long term, even though it was followed by a secret military agreement, providing the Germans (in defiance of the peace treaty) with certain facilities for military training and arms production in the Soviet Union. The chief significance of the Treaty of Rapallo lay rather in the evidence it gave of the re-emergence of Germany and Russia as forces to be reckoned with in European diplomacy. Genoa had been convened to settle their problems and the conference had instead witnessed the two problem nations joining forces to defy the international community.[66]

Lloyd George did not allow the Rapallo set-back to dampen his optimism that he could pull off an agreement with the Soviet delegation. At one stage, it seemed, he was even contemplating trying to buy Soviet co-operation with a unilateral British promise of trade credits. On 23 April Lloyd-Greame was reporting to his wife: 'We have had a row . . . The P.M. is so anxious to settle that it makes him lose all sense of proportion in relation to domestic politics, particularly our party . . . He is very anxious to give credits to Russia.' Horne (on the eve of his return home) and Lloyd-Greame argued strongly against the Prime Minister, insisting: '(1) that we could not buy [Soviet] recognition of debts (2) that we could not ask the House of Commons to give direct credits to Russian Government (3) that we could not do more than put Russia in the same category and under the same conditions as other countries for Trade Facilities, Export Credit etc. (4) that we should not act without other countries'. Lloyd George seems to have conceded the point to these two representative voices in the dominant Conservative element in his Coalition Government, for the following day Lloyd-Greame informed his wife that 'The breach is healed—or bridged—but the P.M. is desperately anxious to settle and the dispute may break out again at any time.'

Lloyd-Greame clashed again with the Prime Minister in a discussion on 27 April with Japanese and Italian delegates on the British draft of the memorandum to be presented to the Russians and of which Lloyd-Greame was one of the principal authors. The clause relating to the rights of former foreign property-owners in Russia provided for the resumption of their rights or, in cases where this was not possible, for compensation in the form of alternative property or bonds, as fixed by an arbitral tribunal (containing equal numbers of Soviet and foreign representatives under an independent chairman) if the claimants and the Soviet government could not agree between themselves. Lloyd George, not unreasonably, thought the clause derogated from Soviet sovereignty and could not be accepted by the Soviet delegation. Lloyd-Greame argued that the clause 'did not challenge the Soviet Government's rights in this matter, but since they were not in a position to pay practical compensation it was essential that, wherever possible, they should return the property . . . what was provided was fundamentally an agreement between Soviet Government and former owners to refer disputed points to arbitration'. With Schanzer, the Italian Foreign Minister, pointing out that the French and Belgians would almost certainly insist on the clause, it was agreed that it should stand as drafted.[67] On 29 April Lloyd-Greame reported to his wife: 'I have got my clause on property into the British draft after a long struggle. The P.M. hates it . . . [and as he] . . . has been encouraging the Soviet to refuse it . . . I have wasted no time in letting the French and Belgians know my views on this point. I hope to win through; but I have no doubt it will block my promotion.' But neither this clause nor many of the others in the British draft memorandum to the Russians were strong enough for the French and Belgians, and when the document finally went to the Soviet delegation late on 2 May it was officially sponsored by only seven of the nations represented at Genoa (Britain, Italy, Japan, Poland, Romania, Switzerland, and Sweden).

The Soviet reply, when it came nine days later, was intransigent. It placed responsibility for the lack of progress at the conference entirely on the Allied insistence on Soviet acceptance of liability for State debts and the claims of private individuals rather than allowing discussion on less controversial issues. The only chink of light—and some evidence that Russia still wanted a settlement if one could be had on its terms—was the Soviet suggestion that a 'meeting of experts' should be held the following month. Before the conference ended on 19 May it was agreed that all outstanding questions relating to debts, private property, and credits should be referred to a further conference, excluding Germany, at The Hague in June.

Lloyd-Greame was named joint leader, with Hilton Young, Financial Secretary to the Treasury, of the British delegation to the Hague Conference. Seemingly the Prime Minister harboured no resentment against him for having opposed him on a Russian settlement. Indeed, at a pre-conference meeting of ministers in Downing Street on 12 June, Lloyd-Greame was clearly being looked upon as the real leader of the delegation, although due deference had to be paid to the status of the Financial Secretary among junior ministers.[68]

The representatives of twenty-six nations met in The Hague on 15 June (the delegation from the twenty-seventh, the Soviet Union, did not arrive until ten days later). Unlike the delegations at Genoa, whose leaders were either heads of government or senior ministers, at The Hague the representatives were 'experts' rather than politicians, on the premise that they were concerned with 'technical' rather than 'political' problems. As Lloyd-Greame described it later to the House of Commons, 'We met not as politicians or plenipotentiaries but as experts dealing with purely practical questions. Politics were left in the cloakroom.'[69] This rather naïve hope could not be realized in practice, and much of Lloyd-Greame's time in The Hague was spent in telegraphing to the Foreign Office to report progress and request instructions on matters of policy.[70]

As at Genoa the main conference divided into subcommissions, this time on private property, debts, and credits. The subcommission on credits soon rejected the Soviet demand for £322,400,000 of credits over the next three years as 'impossible in the current economic and political situation of Europe'; while the subcommission on debts ran into the perennial conflict between Soviet refusal to recognize any responsibility for Tsarist debts and Western insistence on the recognition of obligations accepted by previous governments as part of 'the general law which governs relations between civilized states'.[71]

The most important of the subcommissions was that dealing with the question of private property. The 'whole history of the Hague Conference', wrote the secretary of the Soviet delegation at both Genoa and The Hague, was 'essentially the history of the negotiations on private property'.[72] The chairman of the subcommission was Philip Lloyd-Greame, who described its opening stages in a letter to his wife:

I have got my Property Commission to agree on the whole of their programme of work. They have met most difficulties by saying that they were content to leave the conduct of negotiations [with the Russians, due to arrive in The Hague in two days time] in my hands; and I have, of course, tried as much as possible to get my ideas formulated by other delegates. The French have ceased to try to block and have been very complimentary. Luckily all the Sub-Commission understand both French and English; so we speak in either language and hardly ever use an interpreter. The result is that our meetings are much more conversational and less formal as well as much more rapid than the other Sub-Commissions.[73]

The ease and informality of the subcommission's proceedings under Lloyd-Greame's chairmanship could not, however, do much to reduce the gap between what the Western countries wanted in terms of property restitution or compensation and what the Russians were prepared to offer (and then only on the assumption that Western credits were promised first). On 4 July Lloyd-Greame presented the Soviet delegation led by Litvinoff and Krassin with the total list of Western property claims. The Russians asked for time to present their own list of concessions to be offered to foreign nationals. When the Soviet proposals came to be discussed at the subcommission eight days later (12 July), Lloyd-Greame condemned them as quite inadequate, including only an insignificant part of formerly foreign-owned property and failing to indicate, for example, what compensation would be offered and how former owners, and the new investors the Soviet delegation claimed their government were prepared to involve in the country's economic recovery, would be treated if they entered the Soviet Union. The only real compensation which the Soviet Government could give, in his opinion, would be the restitution of property in all cases where that was still possible. At the Standing Orders Committee of the conference the following day it was agreed, on Lloyd-Greame's initiative, that the abortive nature of the discussions with the Russians showed that there would be no useful purpose in carrying on the work of the subcommission, and that it should be wound up. Lloyd-Greame drafted its report, which was transmitted to the Foreign Office on 15 July.[74]

The conference seemed bound to end, as had Genoa, in complete failure. But just before a plenary session with the Russians on 19 July Litvinoff and Krassin gave signs of a new flexibility. They indicated that they would be prepared at once to ask their government whether, even in advance of the granting of Western credits, it would be willing to acknowledge debts to foreign nationals incurred both by itself and its predecessors,

and to give effective compensation to foreigners whose property had been nationalized (in both cases, the terms to be
negotiated between the Soviet Government and the nationals
concerned without the arbitration provision contained in
Lloyd-Greame's property clause). Litvinoff and Krassin were
seen informally by Sir Sydney Chapman (permanent secretary
at the Board of Trade) and J. L. Urquhart (president of the
Association of British Creditors of Russia) the evening before
the plenary session, and, on the morning of the session itself,
they met in discussion with Lloyd-Greame and Hilton Young,
with Chapman and Urquhart also present. The Russians would
have preferred the statement to be elicited in the form of questions put to them, but when the difficulty of this was pointed
out they agreed to make the statement formally. Litvinoff
proceeded to do so at the plenary session. Lloyd-Greame's
colleagues in the other delegations were rather less sanguine
than he about its significance. At the Standing Orders Committee meeting which followed the plenary session (without
the Russians) Lloyd-Greame hailed the statement as 'extraordinarily important', but the committee agreed only that
'in the event of its acceptance by the Russian Government'
other governments 'should take note in whatever terms they
might consider expedient'. Then the Russians themselves began
to cool when, at a later meeting with Lloyd-Greame, Hilton
Young, Chapman, and Urquhart, they were told that the conference was not prepared to recommend to the various governments represented that the proposals be accepted as the basis
for agreement, or—something that Litvinoff had apparently
been taking for granted—that the Soviet Government be given
de jure recognition. Litvinoff now doubted whether it was
worth referring it to Moscow at all. However, at the final
session of the conference (again without the Russians) on 20
July a resolution mainly drafted by Lloyd-Greame was passed,
noting with satisfaction the Russian proposals and declaring
that, while the conference could not find the basis of an agreement within their terms, it considered that if accepted and
loyally carried out by the Soviet Government they would 'contribute to the re-establishment of the confidence which is
necessary for the co-operation of Europe in the reconstruction
of Russia'.[75] With that the conference ended.

Lloyd-Greame retained for some time his optimism that something had been achieved in the final moments of the Hague Conference. Reporting to the House of Commons on 26 July he declared that the conference represented 'a long step on the path towards a Russian settlement' and the Soviet delegation's statement was a 'very distinct, indeed a remarkable advance on their previous position'.[76] But when the reply eventually came from the Kremlin it was little more than a reiteration of that previous position: Western credits were indeed needed but they must be given without prior conditions. The five weeks of the Hague Conference, for all the work that Lloyd-Greame (and others) had put into it—Sir Sydney Chapman later described him as having done all that could be done[77]—cannot be said to have had significantly more success than the five and a half weeks of the preceding Genoa Conference.

With his return home Lloyd-Greame had some hard thinking to do about his future career. While in The Hague an American friend (the indications are that it was Otto Kahn, partner in the New York banking firm of Kuhn, Loeb and Co.) offered him a partnership in an American bank at 'a fantastic salary', to spend half the year in New York and three or four months each year in Europe, maintaining contact with national governments.[78] The offer was held over, at his request, until the autumn when he thought the political situation, and the way to his acceptance of the offer, would both be clearer. It is tempting to speculate as to what considerations might have been in his mind at this time.

He had obviously made his mark in the two years since he had accepted junior ministerial office, both in national politics and, more unusually, in international relations. Permanent secretaries are by no means always indulgent towards junior ministers in their departments, and it is significant that Sir Sydney Chapman considered that Lloyd-Greame 'built up his reputation as Minister of Overseas Trade'. Chapman recalled one occasion when Lloyd-Greame said to him 'in jest, when he had done a day's work and I had been more or less sitting back, "Why should you get £3,000 a year and I only £2,000?" I replied, not in jest, "Because you will soon be getting £5,000 [the salary of a Cabinet Minister] and I shall never get more than £3,000" '.[79] But in what government was Chapman's prophecy likely to be realized? Lloyd-Greame had, for a junior minister, been exceptionally close to the Prime Minister, but his clashes with Lloyd George over Russia at Genoa must have made him less than certain of early preferment in an administration headed by Lloyd George. A Conservative administration would, of course, be a different matter, for his defence of Conservative principles had been noted in the right quarters. On 18 May Leslie Wilson, the chief Conservative whip in the Coalition Government, had written to Lloyd-Greame in Genoa to express the relief of party members 'that no credits—in any form—have been given to the Bolos [Bolsheviks] . . . however guarded any scheme of credits might have been, I should have been faced with grave difficulties in getting the House to accept it: for which relief much thanks'.[80] But it was not until almost the end of the Coalition Government that Lloyd-Greame gave any sign of expecting, or even desiring, a separate Conservative government, perhaps because of his continuing admiration for Lloyd George, perhaps because, with many other Conservatives (although a decreasing number as 1922 wore on) he felt Lloyd George to be essential to electoral success. His letter to *The Times* in January 1920 had shown distinct 'fusionist' leanings, and even as late as February 1922 he was reported in the press as proclaiming himself an 'unrepentant Coalitionist'.[81] In April he thought it possible that an election might be held in June or July, but clearly contemplated its being fought by Coalition Liberals and Conservatives as coalition partners.[82]

The issue which seems to have tipped the scales for Lloyd-Greame was the government's handling of the problems raised by the Graeco-Turkish war and in particular the so-called Chanak crisis in the middle of September. As he wrote to Otto Kahn in America a few months later:

We were given to understand that when the House rose in August no final decision [about an election] would be taken until we had further discussions in the autumn. In spite of this the inner cabal in the Cabinet agreed to force an election. In the middle of September the [Near] Eastern crisis flared up and prevented any immediate implementation of this design. The action which was taken, the astounding S.O.S. to the Dominions and the whole policy, both in its character and still more in the manner of its conduct—made it clear to me that I could not go on once the crisis was over.[83]

In October he joined the junior ministers' 'revolt', in which
Leo Amery was the moving spirit, against the Conservative
leadership's attempt to force a coalition election on their party
before the end of October. The direct evidence of his activity
at this time is, however, slight, and it does not seem that he was
present at some of the crucial meetings which preceded the
Carlton Club meeting on 19 October.[84] On 16 October he submitted his resignation, along with other junior ministers, to
the party leader, Austen Chamberlain. As he subsequently told
Otto Kahn: 'On the Monday before the Carlton Club meeting
those of us opposed to the continuation of the Coalition had
wished to resign. Chamberlain refused to take the resignations
until after the Carlton meeting. We did not know on that
Monday . . . that any members of the Cabinet were definitely
prepared to do the same; though after we had taken our decision they were free as regards their colleagues to tell us
where they stood.'[85]

One of the only two Cabinet ministers unequivocally to
refuse to accept the election decision was Lloyd-Greame's
departmental chief, Baldwin. Both men believed that the
action they were taking meant 'going out of effective political
life' (as Baldwin put it in discussion with Lloyd-Greame on
17 October), and Lloyd-Greame had submitted his resignation
to Chamberlain 'with the full expectation that I should not
be in government again for years'.[86] They were not alone in
anticipating, in advance of the party meeting, that the decision
would go in favour of the party leaders and that those who had
opposed them would suffer politically. The 'fantastic salary'
awaiting him at the American bank must have seemed particularly attractive to Lloyd-Greame at that moment. But the
Carlton Club meeting did not go according to Chamberlain's
plans, and Lloyd-Greame voted with the more than two to
one majority in favour of the Conservative Party fighting the
election as an independent party with its own leader and its
own programme. Within hours Lloyd George had resigned
and Bonar Law—the man who, probably more than any other,
had swung the result at the party meeting—was invited to
form a government. Immediately after his election as party
leader on 23 October he proceeded to do so. With important
Conservative members of the Coalition Government like

Austen Chamberlain, Balfour, Horne, and Birkenhead standing aside in distaste at the disloyalty of their erstwhile colleagues, opportunities for advancement for more junior Conservatives were correspondingly enhanced. But nevertheless it was a singular recognition of the position he had attained after just four years in the Commons, two of them in junior office, that Lloyd-Greame, at the early age of thirty-eight, should have been offered one of the sixteen Cabinet posts as President of the Board of Trade. After tentatively mentioning to Bonar Law the American bank offer, he took little time in indicating his preference for the Cabinet room over the boardroom.[87]

CHAPTER 2

Board of Trade

AMID the jibes of disgruntled Conservative coalitionists at the composition of the Bonar Law Government—'the second eleven' and so on—Lloyd-Greame's appointment as its youngest member seemed to pass unscathed. Perhaps, for all their assumed contempt, the coalitionists realized that it was with Lloyd-Greame's generation, rather than their own, that the future of the Conservative Party lay. Austen Chamberlain, indeed, was generous enough to pick out Lloyd-Greame as the most promising member of Law's Cabinet. Hankey's view of the new Cabinet from his vantage-point as Cabinet Secretary was almost as jaundiced as that of the excluded politicians, no doubt the result of his devoted service to Lloyd George over six years, but even he saw some hope in Lloyd-Greame: 'I really do not know what will happen if Bonar's health cracks [he confided to his diary]. Except in Lord Curzon and Lord Cave I have not seen a spark of ability . . . Stanley Baldwin hardly ever speaks. The Duke of Devonshire looks like an apoplectic idol and adds little to counsel. The rest—except possibly but doubtfully Amery and Lloyd-Greame—are second rate.' Beyond the ranks of party politicians the business community, with which a President of the Board of Trade must necessarily have close contact, was pleased with Lloyd-Greame's appointment, and the chairman of the Association of British Chambers of Commerce wrote to Bonar Law to tell him so.[1]

The 'Coalition Parliament' was dissolved on 26 October and the election held on 15 November. In it Hankey's second-raters finally laid the myth of Lloyd George's electoral indispensability: the Conservatives, fighting separately on a minimalist programme (including Bonar Law's pledge not to change the country's fiscal system without another election), secured a comfortable overall majority in the Commons. In Hendon Lloyd-Greame was opposed by Asquithite Liberal and Labour candidates. He defended his change of mind about the value of the Coalition, which he had hitherto loyally supported. He told the Hendon electors that he profoundly disagreed with Lloyd George's pro-Greek policy in the Near East, and was completely opposed to the sending of reinforcements to try to bolster up the situation. In a higher than average turn-out of voters (nearly 76 per cent compared with the national average of 71.3 per cent) Lloyd-Greame won two-thirds of the vote cast and a majority over his nearest rival (the Liberal) of 11,572.

Bonar Law's premiership survived his electoral victory by only six months, and several weeks before it ended his colleagues could see that his failing health was making his continuance in office impossible. Probably few of those colleagues regretted his enforced departure more than Lloyd-Greame, who owed so much to Law for launching him on a significant political career. His relations with Law were close—almost certainly closer than those he enjoyed with any of the other prime ministers under whom he served, including Baldwin. On most Friday evenings Lloyd-Greame joined Beaverbrook and Reginald McKenna at No. 10 Downing Street for the unclubbable Prime Minister's favourite leisure pursuit of bridge. Law treated him almost 'as one of the family': 'I shall always be thankful [he later wrote] that I began my career as a Cabinet Minister under him. He taught me much, and he gave me a friendship I shall always cherish.' The closeness of the relationship between the two men was noted even by outside observers. 'Bonar is relying on Lloyd-Greame . . . [who] is sadly lacking in experience', Sir James Stevenson, an industrialist and former official in the Ministry of Munitions, wrote to Winston Churchill (his former ministerial chief) on 14 March. But this was a considerable underestimate of Bonar Law's power of independent decision, had ill health not intervened. In Lord Swinton's retrospective judgement the resignation and death of Bonar Law were 'a terrible loss to the Conservative Party; Bonar's wisdom and clarity of judgement would have provided invaluable leadership to the country throughout the harsh post-war challenge of the "twenties".[2]

Foreign affairs, and in particular Britain's relations with its two main wartime allies, France and the United States, dominated the brief Bonar Law administration. In Franco-British relations the crucial element was the varying national responses to the problem of German reparations under the peace treaty. The inevitable defaulting by Germany was staved off during 1922 by the decision of the Reparations Commission to accept German treasury bills in lieu of its huge periodic instalments, which was tantamount to a moratorium. But at a conference in London in December the French under Poincaré refused to allow any further such expedients and the Reparations Commission officially declared Germany to be in default. The French threatened to occupy the Ruhr to compel payment by main force. In an attempt to prevent this an allied conference was hastily arranged in Paris from 2 to 4 January 1923.

Bonar Law decided to lead the British delegation himself, and asked Lloyd-Greame to accompany him. Curzon, the Foreign Secretary, was engaged in Turkish peace-treaty negotitations in Lausanne, thus providing Law with a convenient excuse for taking with him to Paris a more congenial Cabinet colleague. 'We can't do anything at this meeting except agree to go our own ways for the time being,' he told Lloyd-Greame (as the latter later recalled), 'and to do that in as friendly a way as we can and with as little prejudice as possible to future relations. Curzon will be fully occupied at Lausanne; and he and Poincaré don't mix. It is all going to be very disagreeable, and I would like to have someone with me I can treat as if he were my son.'[3]

At the conference the British delegation put forward a plan for a four-year moratorium in German reparations, but Poincaré would have none of it; and a week after the conference ended the French and Belgians began to occupy the Ruhr. But all was not lost, Lloyd-Greame told his father:

The best we could hope for [from the conference] was to show to the world that we were ready to do the big thing; and to differ from the French in as friendly a manner as possible. I think we managed both. The last and much the most difficult was entirely due to the tact and simple sincerity of the P.M. The former I can take some credit for, as I have urged throughout that we should table our scheme at once and publish it to the world . . . Bonar was wonderful. Clear as crystal, firm and friendly. The result—a marked reaction in favour of wanting British friendship; the final luncheon at the Elysée, which I had rather dreaded, was one of the pleasantest parties I have ever attended.[4]

While the Prime Minister and the President of the Board of Trade were in Paris, the Chancellor of the Exchequer, Baldwin, was on his way across the Atlantic to negotiate terms for the funding of the British war debt to the United States, amounting to the dollar equivalent of £978m. It was an incredibly difficult assignment from which it was almost impossible to emerge with credit. On the one hand, Bonar Law was insisting that repayment of the British debt to the United States should be geared to what Britain received from its own war debtors, notably France; he was apparently prepared to contemplate an interest level up to 2½ per cent. On the other hand, the American Government—and even more members of Congress —understandably saw the transaction as a purely bilateral one to be settled on commercial terms. They first proposed that payments should be spread over sixty-one years at 3½ per cent, but when Baldwin cabled home for Cabinet approval it was withheld. The only concession he was able to win from the Americans was a reduction to three per cent for the first ten years; this, too, found little favour with Law, and Baldwin was recalled. But the terms were leaked in the American press, and, on landing at Southampton, Baldwin managed to offend the Americans by criticizing the narrow vision of some Congressmen representing rural constituencies and also his own Prime Minister by implying that the terms should be accepted as the best obtainable.

Although the Cabinet meeting on 30 January and what happened thereafter was crucial, there is—and can be—no finality about the details. The Cabinet conclusions are tersely unrevealing and we are left largely to the powers of recall of participants, which were no more comprehensive or reliable in a Lord Derby or a Leo Amery than they were, for a subsequent generation, in a Richard Crossman or a Barbara Castle. What seems indubitable is that Bonar Law was in a minority in the Cabinet in urging rejection of the latest American terms, and that he clearly implied that their acceptance would result in his own resignation. But the identity of those who supported the Prime Minister remains something of a mystery. Amery recorded in his diary that the division was on 'racial lines', with the two Scots—Bonar Law and Lord Novar (Secretary for Scotland)—against the English, with Derby and Lord Cave most active among them. Derby's own account makes no mention of Novar but asserts that 'With the exception of Lloyd-Greame we were absolutely unanimous in saying we ought to accept the terms.' What appears to be a much fuller but obviously unofficial version of the Cabinet conclusions among the Davidson papers confirms Novar as alone in giving real support to the Prime Minister, and records interventions by Lloyd-Greame which give no clear guidance as to his attitude towards acceptance or rejection. On the other hand, Hankey, who drafted the Cabinet conclusions, told his deputy, Tom Jones, six days after the Cabinet meeting, that Lloyd-Greame and Novar had both supported Law. Lord Swinton left no contemporary account, but in his 1948 memoirs wrote that although 'on merits' he took the same view as Bonar Law he felt 'the pitch had been hopelessly queered by the premature announcement of the terms'—implying that he did not, in the circumstances, support their rejection.[5] The mystery remains.

There is no mystery, however, about the final outcome of the Cabinet's deliberations: the terms were accepted and Law, having relieved his feelings by writing anonymously to *The Times* to criticize the debt agreement, remained Prime Minister. On the morning of 31 January members of the Cabinet met without Law in Lord Cave's room in the House of Lords, and Cave, Baldwin, and Devonshire were deputed to urge the Prime Minister to withdraw his threat of resignation. The success of their mission (supported as it apparently was by the private advice to Law of his confidants McKenna and Beaverbrook, and also Lloyd-Greame[6]) was demonstrated in a brief Cabinet meeting under Law's chairmanship that afternoon, which agreed that the Treasury should draft a telegram of acceptance for dispatch to Washington. The Cabinet crisis was over.

If Lloyd-Greame's exact stance in the Cabinet crisis of January 1923 is unclear, his role in another contentious issue, fought out mainly in Cabinet committee, was quite unequivocal. A little over a week before its fall the Coalition

Government had signed a treaty of alliance with King Feisal of Iraq, one of the League of Nations mandates carved out of the former Turkish empire which had been assigned to Britain as the mandatory power (under the category of mandates, also including Palestine and Transjordan, which were expected to receive independence at an early stage). The treaty, which was intended to remain in force for twenty years, provided for the later conclusion of a number of subsidiary agreements defining the precise nature of the obligations undertaken by the British Government. The new Conservative administration felt that it needed to review its predecessor's Iraq policy, especially as Turkey was disputing the inclusion of Mosul, with its oil wells, in the country, and British forces there (under RAF command) were currently having to cope with a Kurdish rebellion. A Cabinet committee was set up, which held nine meetings between 8 December 1922 and 26 March 1923.[7]

The committee was chaired by the Duke of Devonshire, the Colonial Secretary, and contained Lord Derby (Secretary of State for War), Amery (First Lord of the Admiralty), Edward Wood (President of the Board of Education), Hoare (Air Secretary), Lord Peel (India Secretary), Novar (Scottish Secretary), and Lloyd-Greame. Curzon, the Foreign Secretary, was also a member but for the first four meetings he was absent in Lausanne on Turkish treaty negotiations and his place was taken by his parliamentary under-secretary, Ronald McNeil. William Ormsby-Gore, colonial under-secretary, joined the committee from its second meeting.

It was at this second meeting, on 12 December, that battle was joined between those who argued that the treaty should be repudiated and British forces (now almost wholly RAF personnel) withdrawn from Iraq, and those who felt, however reluctantly, that the commitment entered into by the Government's predecessor had to be upheld, subject to the satisfactory conclusion of the subsidiary agreements for which the treaty provided. The leading protagonist of what a member of the other side (Hoare) described as 'the policy of scuttle' was Lloyd-Greame, who, according to Sir Eyre Crowe, permanent under-secretary at the Foreign Office, reporting on the meeting to Curzon, 'urges his views with almost fanatical insistence'. 'He and those who support him', Crowe continued, 'may be described as so bent on the necessity of withdrawing that they naturally minimize the binding nature of any pledge or any obligation, whether formal or moral.'[8]

Lloyd-Greame was supported by Novar and—much to the embarrassment of Sir Eyre Crowe—McNeil, who considered that as well as representing the Foreign Office (and he read out at the meeting extracts from a letter from Curzon recommending ratification of the treaty) he was entitled to express his own personal views. By four votes to three, with three abstentions, the committee formulated its view that Britain was indeed bound by the treaty. Derby seems to have been the deciding influence in the discussion, declaring his personal preference for evacuation but also his belief that 'our commitments of honour in the matter were too strong to be overlooked'.[9]

Perhaps emboldened by the narrowness of his defeat, Lloyd-Greame returned to the attack on 15 February 1923, with a memorandum to the committee submitted with the full concurrence of Novar. His objections to the treaty were partly economic and financial, and partly strategic considerations of defence and foreign policy. It was clear that the British taxpayer was not going to get any return on the heavy expenditure incurred in maintaining British forces in Iraq; nor would the presence of those forces affect the exploitation of the oil resources in the Mosul area or the ability of the British to trade with Iraq. Moreover, a country 'requiring so vast an expenditure on so small a population merely to maintain peace within its own borders cannot be regarded as a substantial barrier against outside aggression', or as 'a staunch or valuable ally' once the British forces were withdrawn, as they would eventually have to be. The British had already fully implemented their pledges by clearing the Turks out of Iraq and giving the Arabs the opportunity of governing the country. They were not bound to ratify the treaty, which in any case implied a commitment to fight Turkey if it attacked Mosul—a commitment 'which no British government could persuade the British Parliament to accept'. 'In these circumstances,' Lloyd-Greame concluded, 'I submit that the Committee should boldly face the broad issue of withdrawal.'[10]

The committee none the less reaffirmed its original conclusion which the Cabinet accepted. The one major change

in the Coalition Government's arrangements was that a protocol signed in Bagdad on 30 April 1923 provided that the treaty
would terminate when Iraq became a member of the League
of Nations. This took place in October 1932, when responsibility for Iraqi affairs passed from the Colonial Office to the
Foreign Office. A few months before this event the then
Colonial Secretary had to cope with a crisis which called for
the dispatch to Iraq of a battalion of British troops. The minister concerned must have appreciated the irony of the situation: he was Sir Philip Cunliffe-Lister.

On 20 May 1923 Bonar Law finally submitted his resignation
as Prime Minister after a holiday in Italy and France earlier in
the month failed to alleviate what proved to be his last illness.
The circumstances of the surprise selection of Baldwin to
succeed him in preference to the much more senior and experienced Curzon are familiar. Lloyd-Greame's role in the
transition is, however, unclear. He certainly at the time anticipated a Curzon premiership, along with many others, including
Neville Chamberlain (who was becoming one of his closest
colleagues).[11] One of the advantages of Curzon as Prime Minister, it was thought, might be an early reunion with the dissident Conservative coalitionists, above all Austen Chamberlain,
who would find it easier to serve under Curzon than the comparatively junior Baldwin, who, moreover, had—unlike Curzon
—been unequivocal in his opposition to the continuance of the
Coalition Government. But Lord Swinton's published recollection of the episode over forty years later was that he joined
with several other members of the Cabinet to represent strongly
to Lord Stamfordham, the King's private secretary, that Curzon
would be unsuitable since he was 'autocratic without being
strong, and intellectually arrogant and unwilling to consider
other men's views'.[12] No reference to this concerted approach
is, however, to be found in any of the other accounts, and it
seems unlikely that Lloyd-Greame would have been available
in London to join it. Bonar Law's resignation and the King's
consultations about his successor took place during the Whitsun weekend, and Baldwin's appointment was announced the
day after Whit Monday, that is, Tuesday 22 May. But on Whit
Monday Lloyd-Greame was at Sewerby House, for he wrote
to Curzon from there that day to express his regret at Law's

enforced resignation, of which he clearly had not had any advance information: 'I have just seen the papers', he told Curzon. 'I had hoped against hope; but the suddenness is a shock . . . Fortunately we are, at any rate as a party in the House of Commons (and I think generally), in a much better position to meet this shock than we should have been when Bonar first became ill again. The party has pulled itself together. It has been playing as a team, and a team increasingly confident of itself.'[13] This letter would suggest that Swinton's later recollection was inaccurate. If he had only just seen in Monday's papers that Law had resigned he would hardly have participated in the discussions on the succession on the immediately preceding Saturday and Sunday, especially as he was almost certainly at Sewerby for the whole of the Whitsun weekend. Nor, if he had been actively canvassing against Curzon, would the latter seem the most appropriate repository for his immediate reaction on hearing the news of Law's resignation. A more convincing explanation of the letter to Curzon is that Lloyd-Greame wrote it because he assumed that Curzon would be called on to succeed Law.

Whatever may have been Lloyd-Greame's contemporary views about the respective merits of Curzon and Baldwin, on purely personal grounds he must have welcomed the elevation of a man with whom he had a personal relationship—stemming from his service under him at the Board of Trade—of a warmth which would have been impossible with the aloof Curzon. Two days after writing to Curzon, and while still at Sewerby, Lloyd-Greame sent a friendly note of congratulation to Baldwin and placed his office at the new Prime Minister's disposal: 'You know without my saying it that if it helps you to put some one else at the Board of Trade, you will have my whole-hearted support, just as if I had stayed there.' His purpose in doing so (apart from obedience to the convention that an incoming Prime Minister is completely free to allocate or reallocate portfolios), he later told Austen Chamberlain, was to assist in bringing about the reunion of the Conservative Party.[14] In the event his proffered sacrifice was not required, and he continued in the same office, as did all the other members of Bonar Law's Cabinet, including Curzon as Foreign Secretary. Baldwin himself retained control of the Treasury for the time being, in the hope that he could persuade Reginald McKenna to become Chancellor.

With the continuing French and Belgian occupation of the Ruhr and violent German reactions to it, foreign affairs figured large in the eight months of the first Baldwin Government. Since they impinged crucially upon Britain's trade, Lloyd-Greame was necessarily closely involved in the resulting discussions in Cabinet, with Baldwin, and, in particular, with the leading Francophile in the Cabinet, Derby, who confided in his younger colleague without reserve.[15] The French action in the Ruhr had imperilled not only the *entente* but propects of German economic recovery, and, with it, any hope of Germany meeting a significant part of the vast reparations debt laid on it by the peace treaty; while increasing political and military control by the French in the Ruhr in response to German passive resistance and later acts of terrorism, fed fears that France was trying to Balkanize Germany. The crisis threw into stark relief the differing approaches of France and Britain to the German problem: on the French side, the overriding concern with security against any possibility of a militarily resurgent Germany, and insistence on reparations at whatever cost; on the British, the hope for reconciliation with the former enemy, the belief that German capacity to pay reparations must first of all be established by rebuilding its economy, and the attempt—vigorously resisted by the French, as the main war debtor—to link reparations with the repayment of inter-allied debts. In the light of subsequent developments French realism might seem more prescient than British humanitarianism. But the Ruhr occupation—which lasted for two and a half years, despite British and American condemnation—was hardly an impressive advertisement for realism. It cost the French far more than they were able to secure in enforced reparations in kind from passively resisting Ruhr workers, and helped to fuel the astronomic inflation and resultant social chaos which provided such fertile breeding-ground for violent nationalist movements.

The Cabinet was by no means united in its approval of the way in which Curzon (with some interventions by Baldwin) handled Anglo-French relations at this time, and Derby for one considered him gratuitously offensive to the French; he was unhappy, too, about British branding of the Ruhr occupation as illegal. Although Lloyd-Greame was the repository of many of Derby's confidences—and helped to stave off a Derby resignation threat—it does not seem that he shared Derby's criticisms of the policy, even if he, too, was critical of Curzon. He was insistent that everything possible should be done to restore the German economy as a prerequisite both for the payment of reparations and for European economic recovery. His own prescription was a conference at which the United States and Britain with its European allies would arrive at a guaranteed reparations settlement. And if this were to fail Britain should withdraw its army of occupation in Germany and also its offer (repeated by Curzon in August) to write down its inter-allied debt.[16] It is clear that Lloyd-Greame could not be numbered among the Cabinet's Francophiles, however close his relationship with Derby.

The other dominating concerns of the first Baldwin Government in a sense converged on the Imperial Economic Conference which, originally planned by Bonar Law for April, was eventually held at the beginning of October 1923, concurrently with the more conventional Imperial Conference (which had the same personnel). The development of the resources of the Empire (particularly in the self-governing Dominions), empire settlement, imperial preference, protection—all these familiar expedients, of varying merit or hope of practical realization— were again rehearsed during 1923 as British industry and trade failed to revive and the level of unemployment remained obdurately high. Lloyd-Greame was in the thick of these discussions, by virtue both of his departmental responsibilities and his own convictions about the importance of imperial development, already evinced in his membership of the British Commonwealth Union.

The Bonar Law Cabinet had concluded in February 1923 that 'the main policy of the Government lies in the development of trade and industry in all their branches, and more particularly of Empire Development and Empire Settlement'. The exploitation of imperial resources, it was believed by active imperialists like Lloyd-Greame and Amery (who, from the Admiralty, continued to take the closest interest in imperial affairs), would not only increase Britain's trade with the

Dominions but absorb significant numbers of unemployed, who would emigrate to the Dominions to take up the jobs created by new developments. Naturally enough, the Treasury was reluctant to place much reliance on these quite unsupported assumptions; while among the Dominions only Australia displayed much enthusiasm for such imperial visions, although it made no secret of its overriding interest in the clear material benefits to be gained, notably from preferential tariffs for its goods in the British market.[17]

Imperial preference was a theme to warm the cockles of many a Conservative heart, and in Baldwin's first Cabinet Lloyd-Greame hardly yielded even to Amery in the ardour with which he pursued it: if on protection in general he was a pragmatist, on imperial preference he was an unashamed enthusiast. But Bonar Law's fiscal pledge in the 1922 election always seemed to stand in the way of its introduction. In June and July he served on a Cabinet commitee, under Devonshire's chairmanship, set up to prepare the Government's policy line for the forthcoming conference. The committee recommended that imperial preference should be extended as far as the electoral pledge allowed, in order to encourage the development of empire settlement and the granting of Dominion preferences to British goods, and to alleviate unemployment. It considered that a total remission of the duty on certain empire products would not be inconsistent with the pledge and—developing a tactic to deal with the contentious issue of food taxes—that 'the imposition of any new or increased duty on food should be conditional on adjustment being made in respect of other duties on food, so as to secure that food taxation should not be increased in the aggregate'.[18]

The committee's report was given general Cabinet approval on 2 August. The same meeting of the Cabinet also considered a paper by Lloyd-Greame on the future of the Safeguarding of Industries Act of 1921, which was less easy to reconcile with Law's fiscal undertaking.[19] Part 2 of the Act—allowing for the imposition of duties where, on inquiry, unfair competition was found to stem from dumping or depreciated currencies in the exporting countries—was due to lapse in 1924, and Lloyd-Greame urged that it be replaced by the power to impose a general duty in any industry where foreign competition resulted in unemployment. The industries which he thought might immediately qualify for such a duty were silk, lace, tyres, and possibly woollens. The response from his colleagues was generally muted, but in the case of Lord Robert Cecil (Lord Privy Seal), a convinced free-trader, like his brother Lord Salisbury (Lord President of the Council), it was positively hostile. Baldwin, emolliently, suggested that nothing could be settled 'offhand in a moment' and the proposal was deferred.[20]

The Imperial Economic Conference was opened by Lloyd-Greame on 2 October, the day after the main Imperial Conference had convened. According to one interested and informed auditor (Amery), 'Philip led off by reading a carefully prepared statement which on the whole struck the right note very well.' The burden of his opening speech was that the economic problems of the various parts of the Empire had a common origin in the world war. They could all be solved by the restoration of lost markets and the development of new ones, the latter method holding out the greater prospects since many former markets had been permanently lost to new competitors as a result of the tremendous growth in production necessitated by the war. But if they co-operated with each other, member countries of the Empire could develop their own intra-imperial markets. Britain proposed to foster this development by extending imperial preference as far as practicable.[21]

The conference lasted five weeks. Its deliberations were succinctly reviewed in the memoirs of its chairman a quarter of a century later:

The broad objectives which we set ourselves at the Conference were to develop Imperial resources by an extension of preferences and by financial co-operation between different parts of the Empire and the mother country; to increase the opportunities of Empire settlement; to improve Imperial communications; and to see whether some machinery could be set up which would facilitate the carrying on of our agreed general policy between conferences. All these matters were interdependent. It was made abundantly clear by Dominion representatives that Empire settlement must depend upon markets, and that, unless they could see a market assured, it was impossible for them to encourage settlement on a large scale and to incur financial commitments entailed by intensive development programmes, even if these were assisted by the mother country. Preferences made the whole difference. They made the settlement proposals real, and they enabled the Dominions to discuss and agree with us the conditions of financial co-operation as a practical scheme.

He thus summarized its rather limited results:

The British Government agreed to propose to Parliament new preferences of three kinds. First, the stabilization in value of the sugar preference irrespective of a reduction in the rate of duty; secondly, increased preferences on a number of articles [already] subject to duty, such as tobacco, wines and dried fruits; thirdly, new duties on apples, canned fish, canned fruit and fruit juices, all of which the Empire could produce in large quantities, with complete freedom from duty for Empire products. The Conference confirmed and extended the work of the Imperial Shipping Committee, and established an Economic Committee on similar lines to deal with economic questions.[22]

Modest though these various proposals were, they were overtaken by the Government's unexpected commitment to a general tariff policy and its equally unexpected replacement by a minority Labour Government traditionally committed to free trade.

Writing over forty years after the event, Lord Swinton expressed regret that Baldwin's decision in November 1923 to hold an election on the tariff issue, and the Government's subsequent loss of office, had squandered the successful results of the Imperial Economic Conference. Baldwin's decision to dissolve Parliament 'was very much his own', Swinton wrote. 'He acted on instinct rather than reason. Indeed, it became clear that he had not thought the issue out in any detail.'[23] The careful and detailed account of the episode by Baldwin's principal biographers establishes that Baldwin did in fact come to his own decisions about the timing and programme for the election. But it also makes abundantly clear that before doing so he engaged in the widest possible consultations, among others, with Austen Chamberlain and Birkenhead about their possible entry into the Cabinet (one of the aims of the tariff programme being to secure a Conservative reunion); with Cabinet free-traders like Derby and Salisbury; and—above all—with a group of protection-minded Cabinet colleagues, most notably Neville Chamberlain (whom Baldwin had at last persuaded to take over the vacant Chancellorship of the Exchequer at the end of August 1923), Amery, Hoare, and Lloyd-Greame.[24]

Lloyd-Greame's contemporary letters to his wife give a rather different impression from his retrospective published account. 'I would not be surprised if we got into an election on the whole hog of Tariff Reform with the whole Press with us', he wrote to his wife on 8 October; and two days later: 'personally I am convinced that the only way out of our economic impasse is a full tariff and preference. I believe that this will be the general view. If so, you can expect a general election early next year. But this very secret.' For the weekend of 13-14 October he and Amery were invited to Chequers for detailed discussions with Baldwin, Davidson joining the party on the Sunday (14 October). From there he wrote to his wife: 'We are just a small Council of war . . .'; and, in a reference to the plans laid in September 1922 by Lloyd George, Churchill, and Birkenhead for a coalition election to forestall Conservative Party opposition to the continuance of the Coalition, he added: 'It is rather amusing to think of the other party here just over a year ago, plotting to spring a surprise election on an unwilling party. That will not be our tactics.'[25] The Chequers 'Council of war' concluded that Baldwin should announce at the party conference, meeting in Plymouth on 25 October, 'a whole hearted policy of protection and [imperial] preference . . . but meet the House . . . in November and give the country a chance of understanding what it is all about by postponing the election until after the middle of January'.[26] When the Cabinet came to consider the new policy at its meeting on 23 October the disquiet expressed by several members (despite the firm support for Baldwin from Chamberlain, Amery, Hoare, and Lloyd-Greame) ensured that Baldwin's statement to the party in Plymouth two days later was made in a personal capacity rather than as definitely committing the Government.[27]

On 24 October Baldwin spent much of the day with Hoare and Lloyd-Greame going through the draft of his Plymouth speech. While Lloyd-Greame would have found nothing to criticize in Baldwin's emphasis upon the protection of the home market as the only effective weapon to fight unemployment, it is likely that he regretted the absence of any reference to imperial preference and empire development in the speech. Baldwin to some extent made good the omission in his Manchester speech on 2 November, but nevertheless explicitly excluded any possibility of duties on wheat or meat, the two products in which imperial preference would have the greatest impact. As Lloyd-Greame told his wife on 4 November: 'Of course the policy is very incomplete because it limits enormously the imperial market side', but he recognized the limitations under which Baldwin had to work, not least the fact that the Cabinet was divided on the issue. And, according to Victor Cazalet, he was confident about the Government's electoral prospects.[28]

Neither at Plymouth nor at Manchester had Baldwin positively committed himself to an election, but an appeal to the country was implicit in so radical a policy departure (and statements by a Prime Minister could hardly fail to involve his government, however much he might stress their personal nature). The question was when that appeal would have to be made. Few in the Cabinet anticipated that the election would be before January 1924, while Amery and, apparently, Lloyd-Greame had even contemplated its being delayed until after the Budget in April. There was clearly much to be said for a delay, which would give the opportunity for a co-ordinated effort to mobilize party and electoral opinion in favour of the new policy; and, indeed, Baldwin, Neville Chamberlain, Amery, Lloyd-Greame, and Worthington-Evans constituted themselves as a 'sort of inner circle' to work out campaign organization and electoral tactics.[29] Weighty material for the programme was expected to emerge from the deliberations of the Tariff Advisory Committee whose establishment was announced by Lloyd-Greame on 7 November; he secured the services of Lord Milner as its chairman, and the indefatigable tariff-reform expert W. A. S. Hewins was among its members.[30]

The timing of the election came up at the Cabinet meeting on 9 November, at the instance of Curzon, who said he deprecated an immediate general election 'as savouring of trickery at the expense of the electorate and of our opponents, as fatal to the proper and resolute conduct of foreign affairs during the very serious foreign crisis through which we are passing [presumably a reference to the continuing breach in Anglo-French relations arising from the occupation of the Ruhr], and as likely to lead to electoral disaster'. Six ministers—Chamberlain, Lloyd-Greame, Hoare, Bridgeman, Sir Robert Sanders, and Worthington-Evans—nevertheless expressed themselves in favour of an immediate dissolution. Amery kept to his favoured April, now forsaken by Lloyd-Greame, but a clear majority (which included Curzon) voted for January. Baldwin himself kept his own counsel.[31]

Baldwin's moment of decision about the dissolution has been identified by Maurice Cowling as being at a meeting with Lloyd-Greame, Amery, Worthington-Evans, and Bolton Eyres-Monsell on the evening of Sunday, 11 November.[32] Since these ministers (with the absent Neville Chamberlain) constituted the protection campaign's 'inner circle', with the appropriate addition of the Chief Whip (Eyres-Monsell), it is quite conceivable that in so far as Baldwin shared the decision he should have done so with this group of colleagues. The decision, confided to the King on 12 November and announced in the House of Commons the following day, was for an immediate dissolution on 16 November and an election on 6 December. Thus, if Cowling is right (and he gives no source for the meeting of 11 November), Amery, like Lloyd-Greame at the Cabinet two days before, must have been prepared to waive his preference for a spring election and to forgo the benefits of a carefully mounted propaganda campaign. The motivations for the surprising volte-face over the timing of the election are difficult to comprehend as the decision seemed to make so little political or electoral sense. In view of its consequences for the Conservative Government, it is understandable that participants in it should, like Swinton, seek retrospectively to saddle Baldwin with the sole responsibility for it.

The Conservative Party was more or less united in fighting the election under the banner of protective tariffs (although thirteen of its candidates resisted the tide and stood as free-traders). As defined by Baldwin on 17 November the tariff programme was designed to raise revenue; to assist industries suffering from unfair foreign competition; to provide a weapon in negotiations for the reduction of foreign tariffs; and to give substantial imperial preference (but since food taxes were explicitly ruled out there was little room for manoeuvre here). The Asquith and Lloyd George wings of the Liberal Party were able to unite in defence of free trade; and the Labour Party similarly rejected protection. In so far as British elections can be said to be about specific issues rather than the performance of the government in office (and with an electoral system based upon simple majority voting in territorial constituencies this can be true only to a very limited extent) the election of December 1923—which saw the Government confronting parties united in their opposition to its main electoral plank—showed the electorate's disapproval of trariffs, or at least was so interpreted by Baldwin. The Conservatives had a net loss of eighty-seven seats compared with their 1922 total, although their share of the poll declined only from 38.2 per cent to 38.1, partly because they were contesting sixty-four more seats than in 1922. They remained the largest single party, but were far short of an overall majority over Labour and the Liberals. At Hendon Lloyd-Greame's victory was less overwhelming than it had been in 1922, but was still comfortable: 52 per cent of the votes cast, and a majority of 5,954 over the nearest of his two rivals (a Liberal).

It was inevitable that an electoral reverse for a party in an election called by its leader so suddenly and for so contentious a purpose would lead to critical post-mortems. There was in any case the question of what the proper constitutional course of action was for a Prime Minister leading a party which had lost its Commons majority while still having the most seats, especially when the next largest party was the Labour Party, whose dedication to the conventions of parliamentary government many Conservatives seriously doubted. Should he resign at once or await defeat on the floor of the House? But the criticism of Baldwin in party ranks and in the Rothermere and Beaverbrook newspapers was so great that this question was seen by many as subordinate to the prior resignation of Baldwin as party leader and his replacement by one of a variety of favoured candidates of greater or less plausibility—Balfour (aged seventy-five), Austen Chamberlain, Derby, and Horne being among those canvassed. With a leader other than Baldwin, so one argument ran, it might be possible for the Conservatives to continue in office, with the direct or tacit support of the Liberals, and thus avoid the horror of a Labour government or (perhaps even worse) a Labour-Liberal coalition. The contemporary evidence (which includes the diaries of two members of the Conservative Cabinet, Amery and Sanders) indicates that Worthington-Evans, Joynson-Hicks, and Derby—together with Austen Chamberlain and Birkenhead outside the Government—were active in the anti-Baldwin plotting, while Neville

Chamberlain, Amery, Bridgeman, and Davidson (who had lost his seat in the election) remained absolutely loyal to Baldwin.

Lloyd-Greame's attitude in this situation seems to have been equivocal. Although there is no firm evidence that he took a leading role in seeking to undermine Baldwin's position there is no evidence either that he was actively supporting him. Sanders recorded in his diary on 12 December, on the strength of what was presumably hearsay, that Worthington-Evans, Joynson-Hicks, and Lloyd-Greame wanted the Prime Minister to resign at once, hoping to get some combination under Balfour or Austen Chamberlain to keep Labour out. On the following day Amery noted in his diary that Neville Chamberlain had given him additional information about the intrigue to get rid of Baldwin and 'have a mugwump combination under Balfour or any one they might find'. Worthington-Evans, Joynson-Hicks, and Derby were identified as the main plotters, but 'Even Philip [Lloyd-Greame] seems to have been shaky over all this business; he is much too impressionable I fear.' On the other hand, Derby's diary for 17 December describes a conversation with Lloyd-Greame which made no mention of ousting Baldwin—a strange omission if Lloyd-Greame was indeed one of the anti-Baldwin cabal—but was concerned with the contents of the King's Speech when the Conservatives met Parliament. Derby considered it would be fatal if they were 'to brazen out defeat' by keeping to the protection policy; Lloyd-Greame, however, 'would go a bit further than I would in the way of sticking to our programme'. Later that day Derby saw Hoare, with whom he did in fact discuss Baldwin's future, Hoare expressing the view that it was quite impossible for Baldwin to go on as leader but that as long as he did not resign voluntarily Hoare would not do anything disloyal to him.[34]

The difficulty experienced by Hoare (and no doubt several others), and the absence of any credible successor, combined to ensure the impregnability of Baldwin's position once he had decided to remain and meet the Commons again as Prime Minister. The King's Speech on 15 January 1924 proved to be closer to Lloyd-Greame's views than Derby's, since, while recognizing that the Government (if it continued in office) would not be able to carry out its protective policy, it announced

the Government's intention of doing whatever was possible
to reduce unemployment, in particular by asking Parliament to implement the proposals of the Imperial Economic
Conference over which Lloyd-Greame had presided. Six days
later the Government, mustering all but two of its total Commons membership, was defeated by a Labour and Liberal
majority of seventy-two, and Baldwin resigned as Prime Minister next day. Little time was then lost in securing the adherence
of the Conservative coalitionists to the party under Baldwin's
leadership, and on 7 February Austen Chamberlain and Birkenhead attended a meeting of the Shadow Cabinet, thereafter
taking their places (with others in Austen Chamberlain's group)
on the Opposition front bench. On 11 February Baldwin effectively abandoned the general tariff issue for the foreseeable
future by telling a party meeting that 'I do not feel justified
in advising the Party again to submit the proposal for a general
tariff to the country, except on the clear evidence that on
this matter public opinion is disposed to reconsider its judgement of two months ago.'[35]

For the first time since he had entered the Commons five
years before Lloyd-Greame now found himself on the Opposition side of the House, albeit on the front bench. In the
nine months of the minority Labour Government of Ramsay
MacDonald he undertook his full share of parliamentary business for the Opposition, particularly, of course, in trade and
economic matters. A former Cabinet colleague, now out of
the Commons, even reported in April a feeling in the party
that 'things are run too much by a little clique, Amery, Lloyd-
Greame, Davidson and the rank and file never consulted'.[36] A
less jaundiced indication of his standing in the party at this
time can be gained from a study of current Conservative leaders
published in July 1924 by Harold Begbie, a prolific author
and journalist both sympathetic to, and well informed about,
Conservative thinking. According to Begbie:

Philip Lloyd-Greame is unquestionably one of the ablest men now in
Parliament, and one of the most eager and energetic. He has the economic facts of the British Empire at his fingers' ends, and his brain is a
series of pigeon-holes stuffed with the documents of world trade. Like
all true experts he is an enthusiast. His mind seems to rejoice in the
smoothness and decision with which it works, in the unerring deductions

it makes from the facts it has so thoroughly accumulated, and in the lucidity of the language with which he can state an unanswerable argument or conclude an appeal to the intelligence of reasonable men.

Of Lloyd-Greame's appearance, 'which helps one to understand the workings of his mind', Begbie wrote:

He is tall and powerful, but with a slight stoop of head and shoulders. He is boyish-looking, but prematurely bald over the forehead. His clean-cut and well-bronzed face is chiefly noticeable from the structural point of view for a jowl which a prize-fighter would regard as a stroke of genius; but the blue eyes are so kindly, and the mouth is so bent on smiles, that the strong jaw seems to be thrown away on him. In brief, here is the face of a man who might remove mountains, but for an occasional whim-sicality which sets him laughing at ant-heaps. He is an Edward Carson with a sense of humour.

Begbie's general assessment of Lloyd-Greame's future was 'that he is a great man in the making. . . a man of the very highest promise, and one who may yet do as much for the prosperity of the British Empire as any man now living'.[37]

After making due allowance for the somewhat gushing nature of these encomiums Lloyd-Greame's contemporaries would not have found much to quarrel with in Begbie's evaluation of him. He was clearly able, articulate, and highly skilled in preparing and mastering a brief, and with a position in the party at the age of forty which, barring unforeseen accidents, must augur even higher things. His sense of humour, although well developed, was perhaps not quite as gentle as Begbie implied: it was, and remained, ribald, and, for those who were on occasion its butts, excoriating.

An event by no means unforeseen which transformed Lloyd-Greame's way of life took place in 1924. In January the third Baron Masham died, and, through the waiving of their testamentary rights by the Misses Cunliffe-Lister, their niece Mollie Lloyd-Greame succeeded to the Swinton estate. Much of the year was occupied in moving into the great house. On the last day of October the Lloyd-Greames welcomed their first house-guest there and at the end of the year Neville and Anne Chamberlain came for the first of their normally annual Christmas–New Year visits to Swinton. In December, in obedience to the will of the first Lord Masham, Lloyd-Greame changed his name by royal licence to Cunliffe-Lister. Henceforth the magnificence of Swinton, its gardens, farms, woodlands, and grouse moors competed in his affections with the excitements of political life in London; most weekends and the beginnings of the summer recess saw him depart for Yorkshire, while Mollie increasingly spent her time there and only reluctantly took up residence when necessary in their London house in Lygon Place, Ebury Street.

Having surrendered the seals of office, Lloyd-Greame was able to resume his directorships and in the summer recess spent two months in Argentina on the business of the Anglo-Argentine Tramways Company. He returned home on 7 October, the day before the Commons debate on the so-called Campbell case, and was immediately involved in hurried Shadow Cabinet discussions on tactics. The Conservative Opposition had decided to table a motion of censure on the Government for alleged political interference in the dropping of the prosecution under the Incitement to Mutiny Act against J. R. Campbell, acting editor of the communist *Workers' Weekly*. But the Liberals had separately proposed a select committee to inquire into the matter. Some members of the Shadow Cabinet, including Edward Wood and Samuel Hoare, were convinced that it would be much better tactics to maximize the chances of the Labour Government's defeat by supporting the Liberal motion, especially as MacDonald had said that he would treat this motion, like the Conservatives', as one of no confidence: he would resign if either were passed. Lloyd-Greame threw his weight on the side of supporting the committee of inquiry, but it was not until the debate was under way that the decision to do so was finally taken. The result was the defeat of the Government by 364 votes to 198. Parliament was dissolved the next day and the third general election in three years held on 29 October. In the ensuing overwhelming Conservative victory Lloyd-Greame recorded at Hendon a result which more than regained the ground lost in 1923: over two-thirds of the votes cast and a majority of 13,565 against his Liberal rival, who just edged the Labour candidate into third place.

The formation of Baldwin's second administration was complicated by the necessity of finding appropriate Cabinet posts for leading Conservative coalitionists (and in the case of Sir Robert Horne Baldwin failed to do so). There was also the question of the possible return to Conservative ranks of Winston

Churchill, who had just regained a seat in the Commons under the label of a 'Constitutionalist' but on a platform indistinguishable from that of a traditional Conservative. Lloyd-Greame could have no firm expectation that he would be able to return to his former post or be appointed to one of equal seniority. In what appears to be a list of suggested Cabinet appointments prepared for Baldwin by the Chief Whip on 31 October, Lloyd-Greame's name appears as Colonial Secretary (a post which eventually went to Amery), and Churchill as President of the Board of Trade.[38] But at that time Baldwin was still uncertain as to whether to include Churchill at all, partly because of his unpopularity with organized labour and partly because of the number of claimants for preferment in the orthodox Conservative ranks. An important factor in the process of strengthening Baldwin's resolve seems to have been the advocacy of Churchill's inclusion by Lloyd-Greame and Hoare, both anxious that the administration should be seen to be attracting new talent such as the wayward but brilliant Churchill undoubtedly possessed. But Baldwin was not easily convinced. On 1 November, four days before the principal Cabinet appointments were announced, Lloyd-Greame wrote to Hoare:

I saw Stanley on Friday morning and put the Churchill position as strongly as I could. I did not find him very responsive. I think his unwillingness is mainly due to a feeling that Winston is anti-Labour; and he wants a side and a policy that will attract sound trade unionists. I said that on the Conservative side Winston w[oul]d be all for progressive reforms. Baldwin also remarked that you c[oul]d not get a quart in a pint pot. To which I replied that none of us felt we had any prescriptive claims. And we certainly don't want the old brew much longer. I have done my best. Do yours. Time may be short.

For Baldwin in the end the prime consideration may have been the tactical advantage of having Churchill a member of his Government rather than a formidable critic outside it, but he must have been impressed by the fact that two of the younger and most progressive members of his ministerial team should have been pressing so strongly for Churchill. As the Government's term progressed, however, they may well have come to regret their earlier advocacy.[39]

When Churchill accepted the Exchequer the Board of Trade was left free for Lloyd-Greame's return. On 5 November Baldwin wrote briefly to him: 'I hope you will continue at the Board of Trade and attend at the Palace on Friday to kiss hands. Please wire me to Palace Chambers on receipt.'[40] Informal though the invitation was it was not one Lloyd-Greame had any intention of refusing, and he entered a period of office which was to make him the longest-serving President of the Board of Trade since 1866. Among the letters he received on his reappointment was one from his Labour predecessor, Sidney Webb, to congratulate him on his appointment 'when so many others had to be dropped' and to bring him up to date on the affairs of 'a quite excellent department'.[41]

The excellence of a department from the minister's point of view depends predominantly on two officials: the permanent secretary and his own private secretary. And at the Board of Trade Cunliffe-Lister (as it is now appropriate to call him) was singularly fortunate. The permanent secretary was Sir Sydney Chapman, a distinguished economist who had joined the Board of Trade in 1917 from a professorial chair at the University of Manchester. He had been permanent secretary since 1919 (for a year jointly, thereafter as the sole head of department) and his tenure had thus covered the whole of Cunliffe-Lister's previous ministerial service at the Board. Chapman subsequently testified to the ease of his official relations with Cunliffe-Lister, but at the same time left no doubt about the latter's ability to exercise ministerial control over his wide-ranging department: 'The mass of detail he could grasp seemed unlimited . . . There could be no scamped work after it had been through Lord Swinton's cross-examination.'[42] Chapman remained permanent secretary until 1927 (when he was succeeded, from outside the Board, by Sir Horace Hamilton), but stayed on in the department for the rest of Cunliffe-Lister's tenure in the post of Chief Economic Adviser to the Government, succeeding another former permanent secretary of the Board, Sir Hubert Llewellyn Smith. Cunliffe-Lister's private secretary initially was Arnold Overton, but when in 1925 he was transferred elsewhere in the department on promotion, his successor was the assistant private secretary, William Brown, who served Cunliffe-Lister for the rest of his Presidency: to Brown, he was later to record, he owed 'more than I can say'.[43] A man of outstanding ability, Brown became permanent secretary of the Board of Trade in 1937, at the early age of forty-four, and subsequently headed several other departments until ill health deriving from war wounds in the first world war led to his retirement and early death.

The internal structure of the Board of Trade at this time exhibited one unique feature, at least for a civil department. With its extraordinarily wide range of responsibilities, covering —to name only its chief functions and excluding the quasi-autonomous departments of Overseas Trade and Mines—commercial relations and treaties, industrial policy, economic statistics, shipping, companies and bankruptcy, patents, trade marks, merchandise marks, and copyright—the Board was always liable to display the particularist tendencies of all deeply subdivided government departments. In part to meet this danger the traditional monocratic hierarchy of British departments—with all official authority concentrated in the permanent secretary, who controlled access to the minister— had been somewhat modified. Building upon the informal 'morning meetings' of ministers and senior officials which had been developed during the war, a Board of Trade Council was formally constituted in 1919 by Sir Auckland Geddes (who may well have had in mind the similar body he established at the wartime Ministry of National Service), initially meeting two or three times a week but eventually settling down to a pattern of weekly meetings. Those attending included the President, the parliamentary secretary (Sir Burton Chadwick for most of Cunliffe-Lister's 1924–9 tenure at the Board), the permanent secretary, and the heads of the more important departments of the Board, together with other officials summoned when matters concerning their departments came up for discussion. Papers were circulated in advance of meetings and minutes and decisions were recorded. 'All important questions came before the Council,' Sir Sydney Chapman later wrote. 'Each was thrashed out, and the President there and then gave his decision, if he was present, and if he was not, a recommendation was made to him.' The Council broadened both the basis of consideration of departmental matters and the outlook of senior officials. Some thought it delayed the process of decision-taking, but Chapman believed the time was well spent. Ministers varied in their attitudes to it. Most parliamentary secretaries welcomed it because it brought them automatically into the inner circle of policy-making from which they were (and perhaps still are) all too often excluded. As for the Presidents, 'Some ministers liked the Council, others put up with it. It all depended on how a minister preferred to work,' Chapman wrote. Cunliffe-Lister was happy to work through the Council; but after his tenure of the Presidency the council fell into disuse.[44]

To review all the matters with which Cunliffe-Lister was concerned at the Board of Trade would be a daunting task even if the necessary space were available in what must be a relatively brief account of a long career. Among the major pieces of legislation he had to pilot through the Commons were the Cinematograph Films Act of 1927, which established the system of minimum quotas for the cinema showing of British films; and the Companies Act of 1929, the first comprehensive company law measure for twenty years. Then there were numerous less important legislative items, which still necessarily occupied a good deal of ministerial time, like the Merchandise Marks Act (which provided for the labelling of imports with their country of origin), the Bankruptcy (Amendment) Act, the Weights and Measures (Amendment) Act, and the Sale of Food (Weights and Measures) Act, all passed in 1926. Significant developments in industrial safeguarding were mediated through a white paper prepared by the Board early in 1925; the British Dyestuffs Corporation was reorganized (before its absorption in the great ICI merger of 1926); a new export credits guarantee scheme was launched in 1926; a Food Council was established in 1925, and a National Fuel and Power Committee in 1926; international conventions were negotiated, most notably that concerning safety at sea.[45] And much more. But of all his departmental concerns those which most preoccupied Cunliffe-Lister throughout the second Baldwin Government were almost certainly the extension of industrial safeguarding and the problems of the coal industry (together with the General Strike that those problems precipitated).

With memories of his 1923 electoral discomfiture fresh in his mind, Baldwin had been careful, in his 1924 election address, to exclude any possibility of a general tariff from his party's intended programme, while maintaining its determination 'to safeguard the employment and standard of living of our people in any efficient industry in which they are imperilled by unfair foreign competition, by applying the principle of the Safeguarding of Industries Act or by analogous measures'. Imperial preference fell under the same interdict, as the formidable new recruit to the free-trade element in the Cabinet, Winston Churchill, was quick to point out to Baldwin. Not much therefore could be rescued from the proposals emanating from the Imperial Economic Conference, which Amery (now Colonial Secretary) and Cunliffe-Lister would have dearly liked to implement now that a Conservative Government was back in power. The projected new import duties on such items as apples, canned fish, canned fruit, and fruit juices (all of interest to empire producers) were, however, introduced; but the revenue raised by the new duties was, as a result of a suggestion by Cunliffe-Lister, devoted to improving facilities for marketing imperial produce through what became the Empire Marketing Board of 1926 to 1933.[46] Moreover, the Dominions benefited from new safeguarding duties since a third was remitted on empire goods.

On safeguarding, Cunliffe-Lister resumed where he had left off early in August 1923, when the Cabinet had deferred consideration of his proposal to replace Part 2 of the 1921 legislation (which had lapsed in 1924) with a power to impose a general duty in any industry where foreign competition could be shown to have resulted in unemployment. He discussed the matter several times with Baldwin and they both agreed that the safeguarding of some half-dozen industries in the course of the Parliament was a reasonable objective. Moreover, they were able to secure the important assent of Churchill to what he himself described as 'a very honest and straightforward fulfilment of our mandate and pledges'.[47]

Cunliffe-Lister set out what he considered should be the aims of the new policy in a Cabinet paper dated 14 January 1925. The Government should seek to carry out the Prime Minister's election pledge and to avoid the development of another free trade versus protection controversy. 'The simplest way to attain the second aim is to confine all discussion and debate to the actual duties we intend from time to time to impose. If this can be done, we jump no fence until we come to it; we jump no fences we need not jump; and we give no excuse to anyone to shy at a fence which is not on the course.' And he was convinced it would in no way prejudice the achievment of the first of the Government's aims. He made it clear that, of the various possible methods, he favoured the imposition of any recommended duty through the Budget or a supplementary Finance Bill rather than another Safeguarding of Industries Act. In this way 'public attention is focussed on the facts of a particular industry . . . whereas in a preliminary Bill attention is . . . diverted to a hundred and one difficulties and dangers, which will not arise in practice'.[48]

Churchill congratulated Cunliffe-Lister on his 'most admirable memorandum' which 'should carry all before it', and indeed it was approved by the Cabinet on 21 January.[49] A committee under Churchill's chairmanship was set up to consider the rules under which applications for an inquiry should be considered, and, following its two meetings, the Board of Trade issued a White Paper on 3 February.[50] It proposed that if any industry (other than those concerned with food or drink) felt that it was being subjected to excessive or unfair foreign competition it could make a complaint to the Board of Trade. If the Board was satisfied that a prima-facie case had been established it would appoint a committee of inquiry. The committee would then investigate and report on (1) whether the industry was one of 'national importance'; (2) whether the products in question were imported in abnormal quantities and sold (by reason, for example, of depressed wage rates and working conditions in the country of origin) at prices below those which would secure a reasonable profit for British manufacturers; (3) whether unemployment would result from the abnormal competition; and (4) whether the imposition of a duty would cause unemployment in any other home industry. In deciding whether to act on a favourable recommendation from a committee of inquiry the Board of Trade would have to satisfy itself that the applicant industry was efficient. Any duty decided upon would be imposed in a Finance Act.[51]

Under the White Paper procedure safeguarding duties were, after application and inquiry-committee report, imposed on imports of lace, leather, and fabric gloves, cutlery, gas mantles, packing and wrapping paper, translucent pottery tableware, buttons, and enamelled hollow-ware. By no means all this heterogeneous list got through unscathed, the fabric gloves duty, for example, provoking intense opposition from parliamentary free-traders. Nor did Cunliffe-Lister always have an easy time in Cabinet, where Churchill soon abandoned his co-operative stance. When, in September 1925, Churchill was trying to prevent applications from the cutlery and worsted trades being referred to committees of inquiry, Cunliffe-Lister complained to Neville Chamberlain that 'I am quite certain that the country as a whole wants us to act up to the limit of our pledge, but some of our colleagues are sure to take the opposite view. This seems to me very short-sighted, for it is not easy to find alternative policies for dealing with unemployment.'[52] The trouble was that however bereft of ideas for dealing with unemployment Cunliffe-Lister's free-trade colleagues may have been, the contribution of safeguarding duties to the solution of the problem was almost ludicrously small. Employment and production in the trades concerned (apart from gas mantles, fighting a losing battle against the electric light) may well have increased, but the impact on the overall employment situation was negligible. The major source of unemployment was, of course, the declining basic industries such as textiles, coal, steel, and shipbuilding, and here the safeguarding procedures proved of no avail. The test case was provided by the iron and steel industry, whose application for a committee of inquiry was considered by the Cabinet over a period of six months from June 1925. Both Baldwin and Cunliffe-Lister thought the prima-facie case for a safeguarding inquiry a strong one, but Churchill would have none of it, arguing that a protective duty for such a basic industry, with so many industrial users, would almost amount to a general tariff, and hinting at resignation if one were to be proposed. Cunliffe-Lister then suggested that the whole question be remitted to the newly established Cabinet Committee of Civil Research, and this was done. But, although after an exhaustive inquiry occupying fifteen meetings the committee was impressed with the parlous state of the industry, Churchill won the day. On 21 December 1925 Baldwin had to announce in the Commons that the Government could not grant the iron and steel inquiry since 'the safeguarding of a basic industry of this magnitude would have repercussions of a far wider character which might be held to conflict with our declaration in regard to a general tariff'. With that decision went any chance of safeguarding having anything more than a peripheral effect on unemployment.[53]

The impact of safeguarding, and other similar duties imposed in the 1920s, on Britain's pattern of trade was also small, and by the end of the decade *protective* duties (as opposed to *revenue* tariffs such as those on liquor, tobacco, tea, and sugar) affected no more than two or three per cent of Britain's imports.[54] But their importance for particular industries could be decisive. Of none was this more true than of the British film industry, which was saved from virtual extinction by Cunliffe-Lister, and by a unique expedient which still exercises its influence on the contemporary film industry.

Before the First World War British film production had supplied about a quarter of the relatively few films being shown in Britain in those early days of the cinema. During the war production practically ceased—unlike that of the already dominant American industry—and in the years after the war the British industry was fast losing the struggle for survival against American competition, the main American-linked distributors and renters in Britain being able to lease to exhibitors American films which had often already fully covered their production costs by their American showing and could thus be shown here at a cost much less than that of the limited-market British films. By 1926 less than five per cent of the vastly increased numbers of films shown in British cinemas were British made. With the predominance of American films —fully understandable in terms of their entertainment value— went various monopolistic practices by renters, including 'blind booking', by which exhibitors were asked, or even required, to accept films for exhibition in advance of the trade showing; and the 'block booking', whereby a renter would refuse to allow exhibitors to rent a film in popular demand unless they booked perhaps as many as forty or fifty other films at the same time. The result of such block booking was that many exhibitors were booked ahead for as much as a year, greatly reducing the chances of British films being accepted for showing, and, if they were, leaving their producers to wait many months for some return on their production costs.

So pervasive and compelling was the film medium that a healthy national industry seemed essential both for Britain's prestige and its trade prospects. Clearly something had to be done if British film-production was not to be completely submerged by the immense American flood. From the middle of 1925 Cunliffe-Lister consulted with the three sections of the industry—exhibitors, renters, and producers—and with other interested bodies such as the London County Council and other large local authorities, the Federation of British Industries, the British Empire League, the National Union of Teachers, the Society of Authors, and the Stage Guild. He also saw representatives of American interests, since he was anxious to try to avoid charges of anti-Americanism. At first he was hopeful that the industry could come to some voluntary agreement to increase the number of British films shown and to restrict 'blind' and 'block' booking, but as the months wore on the prospect of this receded. In February 1926 he asked for, and received, Cabinet authorization to inform the industry that, failing voluntary agreement, there would be government legislation.[55] At the beginning of August he had to announce that agreement had proved impossible to achieve: although all sections of the industry were in favour of restrictions on block booking, the body representing exhibitors had rejected by a small majority the proposal (apparently first made in an FBI memorandum in June 1925) that there should be a compulsory quota of British films exhibited in cinemas. Matters were then delayed for the Imperial Conference which assembled in October 1926 and which, among the many weighty matters it discussed, found time to resolve that 'it is of the greatest importance that a larger and increasing proportion of films exhibited throughout the Empire should be of Empire production', and that 'Any action it might be possible to take in Great Britain would undoubtedly be of the greatest assistance to the other parts of the Empire in dealing with the problem.'[56]

The necessary legislation could now be prepared, and, according to his subsequent memoirs, practically the whole of it was drafted by Cunliffe-Lister himself, for the first and last time in his ministerial career. He and his officials engaged in long and elaborate consultations with representatives of producers, renters, and exhibitors, who were all shown the draft Bill and agreed that it was framed in the most workable form. Following Cabinet approval it had its second reading in the Commons on 16 and 22 March 1927.[57] Cunliffe-Lister had earlier anticipated that the measure would have support among all parties, and even suggested that it might be first introduced in the Lords as a relatively non-contentious measure. But the second reading was opposed by both Labour Opposition and Liberals on orthodox free-trade lines, and while the majority in favour of the Bill was substantial, the Opposition was able to muster 135 votes to the Government's 243. The Bill then passed to standing committee where the Opposition was able to delay its progress until November by proposing over 250 amendments, all of which had to be debated (chairmen of standing committees not then having the power they now possess to select amendments). It finally received the Royal Assent on 22 December.

The Cinematograph Films Act of 1927, which was to run for ten years, provided that no film could be rented to an exhibitor unless it had been first shown to the trade, and restricted advance booking to a period not exceeding six months. All films had to be registered as either British or foreign, a British film being defined as one made by British nationals or by companies registered in the British Empire and British controlled, with a scenario by a British author, and produced in the British Empire by personnel predominantly British. Quotas of British films were imposed both on renters (the agents of producers in placing their films with exhibitors) and on exhibitors, with the former higher than the latter (a point to which Cunliffe-Lister attached the greatest importance, since he felt that if renters as producers' agents had more films available than exhibitors could show a premium would be placed on the production of films of good quality).[58] The renters' quota of British films began at 7½ per cent of the total length of film acquired for renting, and the exhibitors' quota at 5 per cent of the film length leased from renters, in each case rising annually by 2½ per cent to a maximum of 20 per cent by 1936-8. Administration of the Act was the responsibility of the Board of Trade—the exhibitors were most anxious that it should not be in the hands of local authorities—assisted by an advisory

Films Council composed of both independent members and representatives of the industry.

Some problems naturally arose in the working of the Act, in particular the growth of the so-called 'quota quickies'— invariably bad films made cheaply and rapidly to comply with the quota requirements—but means were found to deal with them (in the case of quota quickies, by tightening the qualifications for registration). The legislation succeeded in its essential aims. By 1936 British film production, with 418 films registered, had exceeded the minimum quota, and a small export trade had developed.[59] A departmental committee under Lord Moyne concluded in 1936 that 'The evidence has been virtually unanimous in favour of the continuance of the legislation . . . of 1927 as the most suitable method of protection. This Act has, in essence, proved to be framed on sound lines.'[60] The resultant Cinematograph Films Act of 1938 was so uncontentious, after the ten years' experience of Cunliffe-Lister's Act, that there were no divisions on either the second or third readings in the Commons. The minister who piloted it through the Lords in March 1938 was Cunliffe-Lister, now Lord Swinton and Secretary of State for Air, who could have been excused any sense of pride he may have felt at hearing Lord Moyne refer to 'the very remarkable skill with which the original Act had been drafted . . . it showed remarkable prevision on the part of the noble Lord, who is now in a different office, that he was able so far to foretell the difficulties and find a sound foundation for this system on entirely unknown and untried ground'.[61]

Safeguarding and the other protective devices with which Cunliffe-Lister was ministerially concerned as President of the Board of Trade could have no relevance to the problems of a basic industry for which he had special responsibilities—the coal industry. The semi-autonomous Mines Department which had been set up to administer the wartime control of coal remained in being, linked with the Board of Trade, despite the ending of government control in March 1921. Much of the detailed work was in the hands of the Secretary for Mines (from 1924 to the end of 1927, George Lane-Fox, thereafter H. Douglas King), but as a junior minister under a ministerial head of department he was not a member of the Cabinet, and

Cunliffe-Lister had necessarily to exercise close control over policy. And the problems of the coal industry were fast becoming the dominant issue of domestic politics. The brief respite in a grim situation which had been afforded by the increase in coal exports, largely as a result of adventitious factors like the prolonged coal strike in the United States in 1922 and the occupation of the Ruhr in 1923, had come to an end before Cunliffe-Lister returned to the Board of Trade in November 1924. Exports were slumping and the coal-owners' insistence on either a reduction in wages or an increase in working hours opened up the prospect of an imminent coal stoppage, and, beyond that, of more widespread industrial conflict, perhaps a general strike.

Any settlement of the problems of the coal industry was clearly going to be a long-drawn-out affair and this placed Cunliffe-Lister in considerable personal difficulty. Included in the property to which his wife had succeeded in the previous year was the sole ownership of the Ackton Hall Colliery Company, with coal-mines at Featherstone and Pontefract. Cunliffe-Lister himself had no direct role or share in this enterprise, but the closeness of his relationship with its nominal owner (whose functions were in fact exercised by trustees) made it impossible, he felt, for him to play any public part in negotiations with coal-owners or unions, although the same objection might not be said to apply to his participation in confidential policy discussions in Cabinet and committee. During June 1925 he submitted his resignation to Baldwin. The Prime Minister did not accept it, however—at least for the time being—but instead made arrangements for Bridgeman, First Lord of the Admiralty and a former Secretary for Mines, to take Cunliffe-Lister's place in the coal negotiations. At first this arrangement remained confidential, but in a letter to Baldwin on 1 July Cunliffe-Lister asked for it to be put on a more formal basis:

The coal-owners will I think make their offer to the men tomorrow. The men meet on Friday. The situation will therefore develop immediately. I understand too that the opposition have asked for a debate early next week. In these circumstances may I suggest that you should now inform R. MacDonald and Lloyd George that I had tendered my resignation, and that though you had not accepted my resignation, you had requested

Bridgeman to represent the Board of Trade in all mining matters at the present juncture. I think you will agree that it is both convenient to everyone and fair to me that this should now be done. I want again to repeat that of course I treat my resignation as in your hands during the whole of the discussions, and that I beg you to accept it if at any moment you feel that my position in Cabinet in any way prejudices or might even tend to prejudice a settlement.[62]

Then at the end of July came the Cabinet's decision—just in time to avert the immediate threat of a coal lock-out—to give a subsidy to coal-owners in order to maintain existing levels of wages and hours of work pending a Royal Commission inquiry. It could now be represented that Cunliffe-Lister's wife was a direct beneficiary of the Government's new policy. But beyond this specific embarrassment for him, Cunliffe-Lister was becoming convinced that the way 'this wretched coal business continues and penetrates into all the domestic issues of the day' (as he expressed it to Samuel Hoare) made the recent temporary rearrangement of ministerial responsibilities no longer adequate to meet the situation in which he was placed.[63] After prolonged consideration, and against the unanimous advice of the Cabinet colleagues he consulted,[64] he decided to write formally to Baldwin on 13 August to renew his request to be allowed to resign:

When I tendered my resignation to you last June, you asked me to carry on for the time being. The subsequent course of events has perpetuated the difficulties which I put to you then; and I am convinced after careful consideration that you ought to accept my resignation.
I appreciate most sincerely your desire to retain me as a colleague in your Ministry; and I am more than grateful to you for your unvarying help and kindness while I have served under you. But the best thing in English public life is the standard it expects; and I think you agree that I can best conform to that standard by asking you to relieve me of my office.[65]

Baldwin's response, by letter two days later, was characteristic: warm, sympathetic, and paternal, but leaving his younger colleague in no doubt that the eve of his departure for his annual holiday at Aix-les-Bains was a singularly ill-timed moment for such gestures. Before accepting Cunliffe-Lister's resignation, he felt 'bound to make one or two observations'. He was conscious of a special responsibility towards him, for they had worked together 'so closely and harmoniously' over the past few years. The desire of the Cabinet to retain him was 'strong and genuine'. Derby had just written, on the strength of rumours which had reached him (speculation about the impending resignation had already appeared in the press, including *The Times* on 12 August), 'begging me not to let you go'. And at a meeting with ministers only the day before, Tom Richards, one of the miners' leaders on behalf also of his colleagues Herbert Smith, A. J. Cook, and W. P. Richardson, had said 'that it was absurd that you should go and that none of them saw the least reason why you should'. Baldwin asked him to forget the matter for two or three weeks: 'Review it after you have had a complete rest. We are all tired men. If you are then in the same mind, I will say no more. You know I understand your position.' While he disliked mentioning his own difficulties, 'there could not be a more awkward moment for me to publish a resignation when I am leaving for my holiday tomorrow', and when other members of the Cabinet were now scattered for the recess. Baldwin concluded with words not so much from a Prime Minister to a colleague but 'as from an older man to . . . a younger brother': 'Think again after a rest. I am, I believe, the only one who understands and sympathizes with your point of view. Yet I cannot feel that you would be doing wrong in subordinating your feelings to the unanimous desire of your colleagues. If you stay with us, I shall rejoice. But whatever you decide, you will have my full support wherever it is wanted. Bless you, and a right judgement to you!'[66]

Baldwin's letter touched Cunliffe-Lister deeply. Replying from Swinton on 17 August he agreed to postpone a final decision until after the Prime Minister's return from France: 'I will indeed try to give the decision you want. You do understand better than anyone; and I hate to be the unwilling cause of so much worry to you.'[67] Meanwhile advice was coming to him from several quarters, both inside and outside the Government. The junior minister working most closely with him on the coal crisis, George Lane-Fox, the Secretary of Mines, wrote on 18 August to urge him to take no action until after he had had a good holiday, when he would be able to see things in a different light. Like Baldwin, Lane-Fox quoted a conversation he had had with Tom Richards in which the president of the Miners' Federation expressed the complete failure of himself and his colleagues to understand why the Minister should have to resign 'because his wife has interests in a coal mine': 'Everybody is interested in some way—what does it matter if the man is honest?' Lane-Fox went on to put the speculative case of a Minister of Agriculture deciding to put a subsidy on arable land: would the Cabinet members who owned such land have to resign?[68] From the Liberal ranks Walter Runciman, himself a former President of the Board of Trade, made a similar point. Under too pedantic a rule it would be possible to debar from the Cabinet 'nearly every man of property for one reason or another'. Provided he made (as he already had done) a clear public declaration of personal interests and abstained from negotiations for a coal settlement, 'all the reasonable proprieties' would, in Runciman's view, be satisfied.[69] This was the view also of Winston Churchill, who thought that to accept Cunliffe-Lister's position would be to pronounce 'a sentence of exclusion' on many who would adorn public life:

My steady opinion is that so long as you are not personally in charge of the negotiations with a great industry in wh[ich] you have a legitimate interest and so long as that interest is known and declared, there is no reason whatever why you sh[oul]d not take part in Cabinet decisions affecting it, still less in all other manifold business of Government . . .
I do hope that cool reflection will lead you to allow y[ou]r judgement and sense of delicacy to fall along the broad lines of public precedent and policy; and that you will not take exceptional views wh[ich] w[oul]d interfere with your career and deprive us all of a valued colleague and friend.[70]

In the event a fortnight sufficed for Cunliffe-Lister to reconsider his position in the way Baldwin hoped he would. The turning-point, he later told Neville Chamberlain, was the remark of Tom Richards quoted in Lane-Fox's letter of 18 August: 'What does it matter if the man is honest?' Coming from such a source the advice was even more significant than that of his Prime Minister and other Cabinet colleagues.[71] On 26 August he wrote to Baldwin at Aix-les-Bains:

I have given much anxious thought to the considerations which you urged in your all too kind letter. The line you wish me to take is advocated by many others whose judgement I respect and value. I still feel a genuine difficulty and I do hope most sincerely that the future may not give you any cause to regret the decision to which I now agree. But in all the circumstances I feel bound to subordinate my own feelings to what is today at any rate the general wish and judgement. You will I know so arrange matters that I am not called upon to take part in matters relating to coal.

On 3 September Baldwin replied from France with an almost audible sigh of relief: 'Your letter has taken a load of my mind . . . I am feeling a different man now and all my natural tendencies to idleness are having full play.'[72] Cunliffe-Lister was left in no doubt that Baldwin's sense of relief was shared by others in the Cabinet. Neville Chamberlain expressed the sentiment most clearly when he told him that it would have been a calamity if he had left the Government. 'Not only are you the right (and possibly the only right) man at the Board of Trade but I have long remarked that your gifts make you one of the most valuable of our colleagues in council. I think you see the point more clearly than most of us and your presentation of it and your views upon it have often been most helpful to me as expressing what I have been thinking but had not put into words satisfactorily to myself.'[73]

Although Cunliffe-Lister took no part in the overt negotiations with both sides in the coal dispute he continued to play a prominent role in Cabinet and Cabinet committee discussions on the situation in the industry, and, during the six-month respite (from September 1925 to March 1926) which the deliberations of the Samuel Royal Commission gave, in the Government's contingency preparations for the interruption of essential services that a general strike would bring. After the Samuel Commission report was published on 11 March he was a member of the Cabinet committee set up to examine its findings.[74] He was quite prepared to contemplate a settlement imposed by the Government if coal-owners and miners could not come to an agreement. As he wrote to Baldwin on 27 April: 'If the parties cannot negotiate or agree, it will be necessary for the Government to pronounce the terms of settlement which the Government consider the parties ought to have arrived at . . . So far certainly. I should be inclined to go even further, and to say: "We will impose such a settlement by legislation if the parties cannot settle without a strike".'[75] But on the Labour movement's threat to back the miners' position by a general strike he was quite clear: it could not be tolerated and had to be resisted. On this he was firmly with the Cabinet 'hardliners'.[76] As far as he was departmentally concerned, however, he would do nothing to exacerbate or precipitate the conflict: he resisted, for example, the requests of his officials to set up the London milk collection centre planned for Hyde Park until midnight on 3 May, when the General Strike began, in order to avoid any provocation.[77]

No minister was more closely involved in the organization of services during the nine-day General Strike than Cunliffe-Lister. In addition to his wide responsibilities as President of the Board of Trade, Baldwin had asked him to co-ordinate at Cabinet level the work of the Ministry of Transport in relation to road and rail transport and electricity supplies, since the Minister himself was not a member of the Cabinet. The Board of Trade was itself directly responsible for food supplies (ensuring unloading at the ports, and the supervision of markets, distribution, and prices), oil supplies, the importing and distribution of coal, and oversight of the elaborate regional and area organization.[78]

The system worked well under the test, and essential services were maintained. Cunliffe-Lister confessed to Lord Irwin (the former Edward Wood, then Viceroy of India) that 'The first days were an anxious time because . . . the whole organization was on a voluntary basis, but everyone played up extraordinarily well and the team work in the Government was excellent.' Although as President of the Board of Trade he had acquired emergency powers to impose price control and rationing of food and other commodities, these were exercised only in the case of coal; elsewhere voluntary agreement sufficed. He described to Irwin how the food agreement worked: 'I had arranged with five or six representative men in the great food trades that if they would agree prices with me and would enforce them through their wholesale trades by agreement and by their control of supplies upon retailers, I would not only not control, but I would stand by their prices and broadcast them as fair. The result was that we never had to do a single requisition or control arrangements over food supplies.' The trade associations proved formidable policemen. When a British-based subsidiary of the Chicago meat-packing company of Swift and Armours began selling lard at a price above that agreed between Cunliffe-Lister and the chairman of the trade association, the reaction of the rest of the trade was swift.

'Without even bothering to come to me [Cunliffe-Lister told Irwin] the Association sent for the Americans, told them that they had broken a gentleman's agreement, turned them out of the Association neck and crop, and said that I should requisition all their stocks. Within six hours a telegram came from Chicago ordering the American company to refund all the extra price they had charged, to apologize to me and to apologize to the Association and ask for re-admittance. This was typical of the whole business.'[79]

The abrupt ending of the General Strike did nothing to alleviate the coal stoppage, which had begun with the employers' lock-out on 1 May and dragged on to November. By the end of July the Government had secured the passage of two Acts, one designed to gain the employers' co-operation in an eventual settlement, the other attempting, however inadequately, to appease the miners' demand for nationalization: the Coal Mines Act (often referred to as the Eight Hours Act) and the Mining Industry Act. Cunliffe-Lister would normally have piloted both Bills through the Commons, but as a result of his withdrawal from public involvement in coal questions his legislative responsibilities were taken over by several Cabinet colleagues, including Steel-Maitland, Bridgeman, and Worthington-Evans, and he took no part in the debates. The Coal Mines Act—bitterly contested by the Labour Opposition but passed nevertheless at great speed (with the second reading on 28 and 29 June and the royal assent on 8 July)—extended by one hour the time during which miners might be below ground, thus raising the miners' permitted working day from seven hours to eight. The Mining Industry Act found no place for the nationalization of coal royalties or the municipal selling of coal recommended by the Samuel Commission, but instead made tentative steps in the direction of rationalization of the mass of independent production units in the industry, large and small, efficient and inefficient. The Act provided facilities for voluntary amalgamation of neighbouring concerns, and, in certain circumstances, for the compulsory absorption of an unwilling concern if the overwhelming majority of its neighbours desired amalgamation. Cunliffe-Lister considered that the two Acts, in combination, were on sound lines, and rather optimistically forecast that 'By means of the extension of hours, the reduction of costs, the policy of amalgamations, the concentration of production in the most fruitful areas, there would result a larger output per man and the maximum number of miners would be employed.'[80] As regards the rationilization of industry, however, he had to acknowledge later that the results of the Mining Industry Act of 1926 were negligible, dependent as they were on the initiative of the coal-owners. By 1929 he was prepared to recommend to the Cabinet a proposal for taking statutory powers to compel unwilling coal-owners to join district selling syndicates which earlier he had condemned as 'perilously near to nationalization'; but the Government left office before it could decide whether or not to act on this advice.[81]

With the miners' enforced return to work in November 1926, the Government's one outstanding piece of unfinished business arising from the General Strike was legislation aimed at preventing the unions from calling a similar stoppage in the future. Even if members of the Cabinet had not wanted it, their supporters in Parliament and the country would have demanded nothing less. It was discussed in Cabinet and Cabinet committee at the end of 1926 and early 1927, and the parliamentary debates on the resulting Bill occupied much of May and June. Cunliffe-Lister was quite convinced that the Trade Disputes and Trade Union Act was essential, and on the whole believed that it was right to confine it to a limited number of important issues such as the banning of strikes called for any purpose other than the furtherance of a trade dispute, and intimidatory picketing. But he would have been happier had it contained more positive proposals. As he later told Irwin:

Personally I would like to have added conciliation machinery on the lines of the [Canadian] Lemieux Act for the transport services and basic industries like coal . . . Neville [Chamberlain] and I drafted proposals on these lines; but the view of the Ministry of Labour was that compulsory conciliation of this kind would prevent disputes being settled within the industries themselves. I very much doubt whether this view is right. I think, when you come to a crisis, you are bound to set up a court, and I think it is so important to mobilize public opinion in support of conciliation and fair play that I would gladly have taken any such risk. However it may be that we shall come to this later on.[82]

The strain of the prolonged coal crisis, the General Strike, and their aftermath left its mark on Cunliffe-Lister. For a period he seems to have lost his zest for politics. In part this was due to overwork, coupled with indifferent health. *The Times* not infrequently chronicled bouts of ill health compelling his absence from duty, including February and March 1926, October 1928, and February 1929. Usually these were fairly minor complaints, but in December 1927 he was reporting to Baldwin that his doctor, after giving him 'a complete overhaul', had issued 'a general warning. Nothing radically wrong but most things are down and below par. Warning "Go easy for some weeks, or you may have to slow down for much longer".'[83] But there were other factors, perhaps even more important. Although an able and versatile politician, he was attracted by the positive side of politics—running a department, mastering a brief, persuading by informed and rational argument, getting things done—rather than by the often far less rational world of the hustings and the floor of the House of Commons. He made little effort to hide his impatience of irrelevance and loose thinking, and this did not always endear him to MPs, who could recognize and respect his lucidity and grasp of detail without admiring his occasional intolerance of those who lacked his own quickness of mind: one observer (a Cambridge man) later recalled his 'somewhat hectoring' Oxford manner of speech in the Commons.[84] If they are to succeed as parliamentary performers, ministers must perforce become accustomed to dealing with the frequently inane behaviour of members at times of high tension, but Cunliffe-Lister's reserves of patience with such performances were probably more limited than most. His experience at the end of an Opposition censure debate on unemployment in the coal industry in November 1927—when he was shouted down as he rose to begin the closing speech for the Government (Labour MPs were demanding a reply by Baldwin)—could not have made him anxious to remain a member of the Commons any longer than he had to.[85] As far as electoral activity was concerned, general questions of strategy and tactics engaged his interest (he was to play an important part in the general running of Conservative campaigns in several elections from 1945 onwards), but he derived little enjoyment from the rough and tumble of elections in his own Hendon constituency, despite his large majorities and good relations with the constituency association there. As another election approached—Parliament would have to be dissolved during or before 1929—his mind turned to possible alternatives to full-time politics, the more readily as he had had to contemplate them in August 1925 when he had submitted his resignation over his wife's connection with the coal industry. There was always business, for the firms with which he had been associated out of office would have been delighted to have his services on a permanent basis; or there was the management of the superb estate at Swinton, where his wife's interest chiefly lay; with the strong possibility that either or both options could be combined with a much lessened but continuing involvement in politics from the benches of the House of Lords.

Something of his attitude to his political future at this time can be gauged from the correspondence of some of his closest colleagues. In January 1927 Lord Irwin was asking Lord Robert Cecil from India whether it was likely 'that Philip Cunliffe-Lister will shortly join the House of Lords and divide his time between it and the directions of Big Business?' Sam Hoare, the Air Minister, who had recently been the Viceroy's guest after a historic air flight to India, had told him that 'this is not unlikely'. In a letter to Irwin seven months later Neville Chamberlain expressed doubts as to whether Cunliffe-Lister, who, while 'one of the ablest members of the Cabinet ... does not go down very well in the House where his manner does not please', would 'remain very long in political life': 'His wife doesn't care about it and his beautiful Yorkshire Estate keeps pulling at him, I fear.' Chamberlain repeated the point in a letter to Irwin written on Christmas Day 1927, this time describing Cunliffe-Lister as 'very quick and clever ... one of our best administrators'. In March 1928 Hoare was reporting to Irwin that there was talk of Cunliffe-Lister (and Bridgeman) not standing again, although there was, he thought, no question of anyone resigning before the election. By August 1928 Chamberlain had, however, detected a shift in Cunliffe-Lister's position: 'Philip still hankers after a peerage and high finance, and his wife loathes politics. But he has done well this year and has felt the satisfaction of it and I fancy he would have much greater difficulty in leaving political life today than he would have done a year ago. And indeed I should be sorry to see him go.' Nevertheless before 1928 was out it appears that Cunliffe-Lister received a most attractive offer from 'big business' or 'high finance' (the exact nature of which remains a mystery) which initially he was disposed to accept, informing Baldwin that he would not be available for office if the Conservatives won the forthcoming election. But discussion with Chamberlain during the latter's Christmas visit to Swinton led to a change of mind, which Chamberlain conveyed to Baldwin on his return to London. On 8 January 1929 Chamberlain wrote to Cunliffe-Lister to tell him that Baldwin 'was evidently very pleased' with his decision:

I hope that you, too, on maturer consideration, feel that you have taken the right decision. I feel no doubt of it myself, and not merely on Party or even National grounds, though both of these weighed very strongly with me. But I am sure that if you were to go out now, after such a brilliant start, and with so much of your life before you, you would soon begin to feel that you had made a mistake and sacrificed the bigger for the smaller career. I am sure Molly will appreciate this too, and she cannot but be grateful that your colleagues value your help so much.

Cunliffe-Lister seems to have succeeded in convincing those colleagues of his resolution to remain fully committed to the life of politics. In October 1928 Baldwin was confiding to Thomas Jones that he thought Cunliffe-Lister might want to go to the House of Lords; but the following March, when discussing with Jones possible post-election Cabinet changes, he was considering Cunliffe-Lister's name for the one post absolutely incompatible with membership of the Lords—that of Chancellor of the Exchequer.[86] While, however, Cunliffe-Lister may have renewed his commitment to politics, his distaste for its more populist aspects remained and played its part later in what must be accounted the most ill-advised action of his political career—the decision to accept a peerage in 1935, which permanently confined him to the second rank of politicians.

It was probably no accident that Cunliffe-Lister's agonizing reappraisal of the course his career should take occurred during the last two years or so of the first full-term government in which he had served. In addition to the exhaustion born of continuous years of onerous office, there was the failing sense of purpose which afflicts most governments nearing the end of their term. Baldwin's second Government was, in many ways, outstanding for its constructive legislative achievements. But there was no hiding the fact that from 1927 onwards its morale and that of its supporters in the House and the country was affected by internal dissensions on policy and signs of ebbing public support as revealed, for example, in a crop of by-election reverses. Unemployment inevitably remained the overriding domestic problem confronting the Government, and much of the major policy being canvassed in the closing years of Baldwin's administration was designed to deal with it. Cunliffe-Lister was centrally concerned with these measures, and, now that his moment of personal doubt was over, threw himself into their discussion.

As the limited and slow-moving nature of the new safe-guarding procedures became manifest, demands arose for an intensification of safeguarding, or, even better, in the view of convinced protectionists in the party, a full-blooded policy of protection regardless of electoral inhibitions. Within the Cabinet Amery was the leader of this movement, the more ardently after his return from an imperial tour in February 1928. But his old alliance with Cunliffe-Lister had sensibly weakened, not because the latter had lost his devotion to tariff reform and imperial development but because of his greater awareness of what was politically practicable. A curious incident in March 1928 illustrated the difference between the two men. Cunliffe-Lister had ended a speech on safeguarding at a parliamentary party meeting with a question which he clearly intended to be rhetorical, since it was established party policy as well as electorally inevitable: 'I assume we are all unanimous in rejecting the idea of any food duties?' This crime against the pure doctrine of protectionism was immediately reported by Henry Page-Croft to Amery, who wrote to Baldwin the same evening to express his serious concern 'that Philip should have deliberately tried to evoke an answer which was intended to preclude any extension of Imperial Preference. You know that I could not possibly accept that position, and should have to fight all I know how to defend it, whatever the cost to myself. I do trust you understand that I am in earnest.'[87]

Amery's annoyance was the more inexplicable since, in his quieter moments, he was quite prepared to accept the principle of no additional taxation on food. When the matter came up in Cabinet on 2 August 1928 Amery, at Baldwin's invitation, opened the discussion by arguing that a positive declaration on safeguarding was needed before the election. The formula he suggested was: 'no general tariff but a simpler and more effective safeguarding procedure and no efficient industry excluded from consideration, and the maximum Imperial preference and Empire development consistent with no addition to our existing food taxation'. Neville Chamberlain and Cunliffe-Lister spoke in support, the latter emphasizing the need for a simpler kind of safeguarding (implying that this could include iron and steel) and specifically stating that agriculture—a traditional area of Conservative support and naturally unenthusiastic about the safeguarding of manufacturing industry—should be given the opportunity of lodging a complaint under the safeguarding procedure. Even Churchill reluctantly conceded that a safeguarding inquiry would have to be extended to iron and steel, although he thought it would lose the Government a great many votes. The Cabinet eventually agreed that a declaration of policy should be made in the form of a letter from Baldwin to the Chief Whip, which balanced a renewed assurance that there would be no general tariff with the positive statement of a simplified safeguarding procedure, whereby an industry could go direct to an appointed tribunal (without the necessity of a preliminary Board of Trade inquiry to determine whether it had a prima-facie case) and from which no industry would be excluded.[88]

Cunliffe-Lister was anxious that the Government should retain its flexibility of approach by divulging as little as possible of its detailed proposals for safeguarding reform (here again there was a contrast with his old ally Amery); but, on the other hand, he thought sufficient should be said to keep the factions in the party more or less satisfied. Just before a Commons debate on the subject in November 1928 he wrote to Baldwin to give his views. He was quite prepared to agree to the test of any safeguarding being, as Churchill had recently suggested, that it would do more good than harm to general trade and employment. The important changes the Government contemplated were (1) the substitution of *substantial* competition from foreign countries for *abnormal* competition as a reason for extending safeguarding to a particular industry, if efficient; and (2) inquiry by a standing tribunal rather than by an *ad hoc* committee as at present. The first change was 'not a big pill to swallow' if at the same time it was made clear that the competition must be unfair in terms of wages or hours (or in exchange rate if that should be applicable); that employment in the applicant industry was, or was likely to be, seriously affected; and that other industries, including agriculture, would have the right of appeal to the tribunal. To present the policy with these qualifications would at the same time 'satisfy keen safeguarders' and allay the anxieties of those in the party 'who may be nervous that we are going too far'.[89]

The Commons debate of 14 November 1928 effectively marked the end of the story of industrial safeguarding begun with the legislation of 1921. When the Conservatives next had the opportunity of implementing industrial policy—in the National Government from 1931—safeguarding was submerged in the final accomplishment of a general tariff.

If Cunliffe-Lister's alliance with Amery on the imperial preference front had been somewhat eroded by the end of the second Baldwin Government, his alliance with Neville Chamberlain both on protection and on most issues of social policy—had strengthened. It was Cunliffe-Lister who on 7 December 1927 first announced in the House of Commons the new plan for reform of the Poor Law which was later to be incorporated in Chamberlain's Local Government Act; and he did much to assist Chamberlain in the extensive parliamentary discussion on the measure in 1928–9. But on one of its most important features his alliance had been with Churchill rather than Chamberlain. This was industrial derating, to which Chamberlain had been only reluctantly converted, while Cunliffe-Lister had from the first welcomed Churchill's imaginative idea. Nearly a fortnight before he sent his memorandum on the proposal to Baldwin in December 1927, Churchill had discussed it with Cunliffe-Lister and gained his support—and he and Chamberlain were sent copies of the Churchill memorandum. When the matter came before Cabinet on 20 January Cunliffe-Lister strongly backed the complete derating of industry, stressing how staple industries—and above all employment within them—would benefit from the relief, an argument to which he returned in a Cabinet paper he circulated in March.

He supported Churchill, too, in his eventually successful efforts, against Chamberlain's opposition, to include railways in the industrial derating scheme; a victory gained in part by the substitution of 75 per cent derating of industry for the complete derating they had both wanted.[90]

The Local Government Bill received the royal assent on 27 March 1929, just six weeks before the parliamentary session ended, preparatory to the general election on 30 May. Two new factors made the result of the election more than usually hazardous to predict: the addition of some five million women to the electorate as a result of the lowering of the female voting age from thirty to twenty-one in 1928, a measure which had the enthusiastic approval of Cunliffe-Lister, a life-long supporter of voting equality between the sexes; and the energetic campaign fought by the Liberals under Lloyd George's radical banner, in which they fielded more candidates than in any election since January 1910. Despite their by-election defeats and the manifest unpopularity of several of their policies, the Conservative leaders (including Cunliffe-Lister) and Conservative Central Office were optimistic that the party would win an overall majority, however reduced it might be from the triumph of 1924. Cunliffe-Lister was a member of a small committee of ministers, chaired by the Lord Chancellor, set up rather belatedly on 2 May to draft Baldwin's election address—in effect, the party manifesto—and which stayed in being during the campaign to deal with 'the flood of questionnaires that was pouring in' from Conservative candidates and others.[91] But no manifesto, even if superficially attractive (and the Conservative document, by contrast, was imprecise and dull, as befitted a campaign waged with the theme of 'Safety First') could have stemmed the running of the electoral tide against a government after four and a half years of office during which it had given its full share of hostages to fortune. While six million more electors voted than in 1924, the Conservatives succeeded in attracting only some 600,000 additional votes, compared with 2.4m. additional votes for the Liberals (only derisorily reflected in seats won) and 2.9m. additional votes for the Labour Party. The Labour Party was now the largest single party by twenty-eight seats, leaving the Conservatives with the consolation of a slim majority of the popular vote. Cunliffe-Lister's victory was assured in his Hendon stronghold (where the electorate had more than doubled to 84,000), with 52.3 per cent of the votes cast and a majority of 16,324 over his nearest rival. The chief interest lay in the fact that Labour had at last succeeded in ousting the Liberals from second place at Hendon.

Cunliffe-Lister, in common with most of the Cabinet, thought that Baldwin should not resign until defeated in the newly elected House of Commons. Baldwin went his own way and resigned five days after the election, to make way for the second minority Labour Government under Ramsay MacDonald. The resignation honours list submitted to the King by the outgoing Prime Minister included Cunliffe-Lister's name, advanced to Knight Grand Cross of the Order of the British Empire (GBE).

A member of the Baldwin Cabinet who did not stand in the 1929 election has left his contemporary impressions of his colleagues. Cunliffe-Lister, Lord Bridgeman wrote, 'has a very good brain and quick perception. At his comparatively early age he exercised considerable influence in the Cabinet. Outside, a somewhat excitable manner of speech is apt to irritate people.'[92] It was a shrewd assessment, which goes some way to explain the subsequent course of Cunliffe-Lister's political career.

CHAPTER 3

Colonial Office

In June 1929 Cunliffe-Lister began what was to be his longest period out of ministerial office since entering Parliament over ten years before. For what proved to be more than two years he was free to practise those alternatives to politics which had exerted such a powerful attraction for him a few months before the election. He resumed his directorships in the Anglo-Argentine Tramways Company and in Dannie Heineman's Brussels-based firm of Sofina, in whose interests he visited Berlin in March 1931 for talks with Brüning, the German Chancellor, and leading industrialists.[1] But there were now additional board appointments. He became a director of Consolidated Tin Smelters and in September 1929 was elected chairman of the Tin Producers Association, a pressure group for the industry, bringing together representatives from the Federated Malay States, Nigeria, Siam, Burma, Australia, and Cornwall. Then, in June 1930, came directorships in two South African gold-mining companies, through the agency of his friend Oliver Hoare (younger brother of Samuel Hoare and a frequent house guest at Swinton): Consolidated Gold Fields of South Africa and New Consolidated Gold Fields.[2] Plenty here, it might have been thought, to occupy fully a man of drive and administrative flair. Gone, however, were any doubts Cunliffe-Lister may have had about his vocation in politics: the boardroom provided an absorbing supplementary occupation for days of opposition but could not now displace his primary interest. For the next nine years he was at the centre of Conservative and national politics, in Opposition and in Government. A much younger Conservative colleague who worked closely with him in 1930 and 1931 was convinced that

Cunliffe-Lister at this period nourished an intense political ambition, which did not fall short of the highest office of all.[3] It would not be surprising if this were in fact the case. A politician who was to be a principal formulator of the party's major item of policy for the next few years, who in his mid-forties had already been a Cabinet minister for nearly six years and in August 1931 was to be one of only four Conservative members of the National Government, had every reason to look forward to even greater advancement. Many of those who were informed about the political scene in the early 1930s would have placed Cunliffe-Lister's name on their short list of potential Conservative prime ministers. And the prospect of having to find a new leader for the party did not seem a remote one in 1929–31, so shaky at times was Baldwin's control over a party riven by the old issue of protection—cross-cut and confused by the Beaverbrook-Rothermere campaign for 'Empire Free Trade'—and the newer issue of self-government for India.

Beaverbrook launched his 'Empire Crusade' on 7 July, less than a fortnight after the new Parliament met for the first time (and the day before Cunliffe-Lister moved the Conservative amendment to the King's Speech, regretting the absence of any declaration of policy by the new Government on safe-guarding and imperial preference). The proposal—essentially for complete free trade within an Empire protected from foreign competition by virtually impregnable tariff walls—was clearly impracticable. It ignored, among other things, the often competing economic interests of an industrialized Britain and fast-industrializing Dominions, and the patent absence of imperial self-sufficiency in food and raw materials. But the campaign posed embarrassing problems for the party leadership, especially when, in February 1930, the two press lords formed their own party, the United Empire Party, and began systematically sponsoring candidates at by-elections. It was not, however, an unmixed evil, since it forced the Conservative party to clarify its attitude to the further development of the policy of industrial safeguarding and imperial preference with which Cunliffe-Lister had been so closely associated since achieving ministerial office. He was now to play a major role in its extension and reformulation.

As the former President of the Board of Trade he naturally acted as the chief party spokesman on trade and industrial matters. In July 1929 he was elected chairman of the Conservative trade and industry committee and in November he replied to the debate on safeguarding and imperial preference at the annual party conference, surprising delegates by the passion which he brought to the theme.[4] Early in January 1930 he prepared a memorandum on Conservative trade policy at Baldwin's request, and this provided the basis on which the party leader could tell the Shadow Cabinet on 30 January that he was going to put forward a policy of bolder safeguarding and some sort of rationalization of industrial production within the Empire, coupled with imperial preference but with no taxes on food. Apart from Amery, who deprecated the exclusion of food duties, Baldwin seems to have gained his colleagues' consent.[5] On 3 March Cunliffe-Lister accompanied Baldwin to a meeting with Beaverbrook, from which the basis of a *rapprochement* with the official Conservative party seemed to emerge: Baldwin undertook to put the question of food taxes to a public referendum.

On 8 March one of the leading exponents of a 'forward' imperial trade policy, Neville Chamberlain, returned from a three-month visit to East Africa and immediately made his presence felt. It was apparently at his suggestion that on 12 March Baldwin formed a small Business Committee, in effect to replace the Shadow Cabinet of ex-ministers which had been meeting with decreasing frequency. The regular membership of this new body was, besides Baldwin, the two Chamberlains, Churchill, Cunliffe-Lister, Eyres-Monsell (the Chief Whip), Hailsham, Hoare, Salisbury, and Worthington-Evans.[6] Already chairman of the newly established Conservative Research Department, in June Chamberlain displaced Davidson as party chairman. By this time the fragile alliance with Beaverbrook had again been broken, and on 18 July, at a private dinner-party attended only by Chamberlain, Cunliffe-Lister, Sir Robert Horne, and Beaverbrook, another attempt—in the end unsuccessful—was made to repair it.[7]

Cunliffe-Lister and Chamberlain were now co-operating closely on trade policy. 'It is a great comfort to feel that you are always ready to help and your help is always worth having,'

Chamberlain wrote at the end of July. 'Your friendship makes me feel that politics are worth while even when things go contrariwise.'[8] From this co-operation emerged perhaps the most significant step towards a general tariff taken by the Conservatives in Opposition.

Some time in the autumn of 1930 Chamberlain, as chairman of the Conservative Research Department, decided to commission a full-scale study of the possibilities of implementing new tariff legislation as part of his general effort to ensure that the party entered the next election with a well-thought-out programme as opposed to the skimpy 'Safety First' appeal of 1929. Cunliffe-Lister was the obvious choice as chairman of this Emergency Tariff Committee, and other members who accepted Chamberlain's invitation were Amery, George Tryon, Hilton Young, and Herbert Williams—all members of the previous Conservative administration—Lord Lloyd (chairman of the Empire Economic Union, a propaganda group formed by Amery and Lord Melchett—the former Sir Alfred Mond— in July 1929), and Sir Basil Blackett, a director of the Bank of England and former Treasury official. The committee's secretary was a young member of the Research Department's staff, Henry Brooke. Twenty-five meetings were held at the Research Department in Old Queen Street, usually to discuss papers collected and circulated by Brooke under Cunliffe-Lister's direction. Outside experts (but not government departments) were consulted, including former deputy speakers of the House of Commons, to advise on ways of expediting parliamentary consideration of tariff proposals. Surprisingly, considering the experience and commitment to tariffs of the committee's members, Cunliffe-Lister soon became impatient with the lack of application—and even of knowledge—of his colleagues, and increasingly he and Brooke came to bear the main burden of the committee's work. This was by no means disagreeable to Cunliffe-Lister, as it suited his decisive, rapid style. It was he who determined the committee's priorities, which he defined as: (1) an emergency tariff as soon as possible after the party regained power; (2) legislation for a permanent tariff; (3) maximum simplicity of tariff structure. The committee's report was presented to Chamberlain on 24 June 1931. Briefly (it was a document of over 100 pages), the report proposed that an emergency tariff should be introduced by special resolution and that the later permanent tariff should be embodied in a special Tariff Act rather than in the Finance Act, to avoid the embarrassment of an annual debate on tariff rates. An independent Tariff Commission should be established to remove from the Minister (the President of the Board of Trade) the responsibility for fixing different rates for different industries, and to supervise the transition from the emergency tariff to the permanent tariff. The proposals were backed by a wealth of illustrative detail which, in Chamberlain's words expressing his thanks formally to Cunliffe-Lister, left 'No aspect of the subject . . . unexplored' and transformed 'what was merely a vague outline' into 'a definite, practical working plan, which can be put into operation without delay'.[9]

In the meantime Baldwin had met and survived a crisis of confidence in his leadership, born of doubts about his handling of the burning issues of tariffs and India, highlighted by the campaigns of Beaverbrook and Rothermere (with India the dominant issue for Rothermere, Empire Free Trade for Beaverbrook). On India Cunliffe-Lister ranged himself on the liberal side espoused by Baldwin, believing it important that the Round Table Conference of the three British parties and Indian representatives, called on the initiative of his friend Irwin, the Viceroy, and the Labour Government, should not be allowed to fail.[10] But Baldwin's attitude on India, liberal though it undoubtedly was, did not endear him to die-hards in the party (joined on this issue by Churchill) or contribute to confidence in his leadership. On the question of the party leadership Cunliffe-Lister was, with Neville and Austen Chamberlain, Hailsham, and Hoare, among the anti-Baldwin dissidents. It was he who personally took to Baldwin on 1 March 1931 the memorandum which H. R. Topping, the chief party official, had sent to Chamberlain on 25 February (expressing the view that 'it would be in the interests of the Party that the Leader should reconsider his position'). Cunliffe-Lister apparently told Baldwin that he, Neville Chamberlain, and the others thought he ought to resign as leader, although unfortunately no record of what must have been a fascinating conversation has survived. Initially Baldwin seems to have taken the advice and agreed to resign, but, with his resolution stiffened by his old friend

Bridgeman, his resignation was deferred until Duff Cooper's victory over the Beaverbrook-sponsored anti-Baldwin candidate in the St. George's, Westminster by-election served to confirm him in the leadership and effectively remove the Empire Free Trade campaign as an electoral threat. There followed an agreement—announced in a published exchange of correspondence on 30 March—between Beaverbrook and Chamberlain (in one of his last acts as party chairman), under which Beaverbrook promised to assist the Conservative Party at the next election on the assurance that the party would aim at increasing agricultural as well as industrial production. Cunliffe-Lister was prevented by illness from attending the meeting of the Business Committee on 25 March at which the Beaverbrook agreement was approved. The meeting also gave the dissidents the opportunity to impress upon Baldwin the need to show 'as much vigour in attacking the Socialists as he did in attacking recalcitrant Conservatives and the Press'. As Chamberlain described it to Cunliffe-Lister: 'S.B. had a terrible bucketing from his colleagues last night. He said he would digest what had been said but I think he certainly means to carry on. The others expressed great pleasure that such a frank and open talk had at long last been possible.'[11]

Not for the first time Cunliffe-Lister had identified himself as disenchanted with Baldwin as party leader. Baldwin seems to have borne him no ill will, partly no doubt because it would have been completely out of character for him to do so, and partly because the members of the dissident group—led by Neville Chamberlain, now almost certain, given good health, to be Baldwin's eventual successor—were too important in the party to risk their permanent alienation. But it cannot have been an episode of which Cunliffe-Lister was proud, and it is notable that in neither of his published volumes of memoirs does he as much as hint that he was ever disloyal to the party leader to whom his political career owed so much.

The dominance Chamberlain had achieved in the party was graphically illustrated in the negotiations with Ramsay Mac-Donald during the financial and political crisis in August 1931 which led to the formation of the National Government. Baldwin briefly interrupted his annual holiday at Aix-les-Bains for discussions with colleagues and with MacDonald on 13 and 14 August, but thereafter, until his final return from France

eight days later, he delegated to Chamberlain the chief responsibility for representing the Conservative Party in the rapidly
developing crisis. It was Chamberlain who, perhaps more than
any other, shaped the eventual outcome. He chose Hoare to
assist him at the inter-party discussions between 20 and 22
August. His other chief political friend, Cunliffe-Lister, was
at Swinton for the summer recess, but was kept in touch with
developments by Chamberlain and Geoffrey Lloyd, Baldwin's
private secretary.[12] On 20 August Chamberlain summoned him
to London, where he found, in addition to Chamberlain and
Hoare, Eyres-Monsell, Hailsham, Kingsley Wood, and Davidson.
On the following day he wrote to his wife: 'Neville is handling
the situation admirably . . . We are all agreed on what has been
done, is being done and will be done from our side . . . As
regards the general position everything turns on whether the
Government will cut the dole—without that you can't get the
necessary economies, and moreover the other economies hang
on it. You can't cut teachers, sailors, police, civil servants
while leaving the dole as it is. Nor can you justify taxation.
A tariff is no alternative. First and foremost you must have
drastic economy. That alone will save the situation.' Of the
various alternatives confronting MacDonald, all of them unpleasant, Cunliffe-Lister reported to his wife that the most
likely was an invitation to the Conservatives and Liberals to
join a National Government to put through the necessary public expenditure cuts. 'That could not be refused if the plan
was adequate and fair, and the co-operation was for the limited
purpose of carrying it out.'[13] That weekend—during which
Baldwin returned home—Cunliffe-Lister spent with the Hail-
shams at their Sussex home. The telephone kept them in touch
with events in London, and in the early hours of Monday
morning (24 August) they were asked to return to London as
soon as possible. That morning the final decision was taken,
although what it would be was in doubt until the last moment.
As Cunliffe-Lister told his wife, in a letter written on Monday
afternoon:

Last night MacDonald said he must resign; and that it was doubtful even
whether he would come into a Government formed by Baldwin. This
morning to everyone's surprise he said he would go on as P.M. if he could
have the support of Conservatives and Liberals in his Government. The

Government would be for the sole purpose of meeting the financial emergency; and there would be a dissolution as soon as their job had been done. This means an election in November. It would have been very difficult to refuse co-operation in the circumstances—and really impossible having regard to the need for immediate action. Also it is a tremendous thing that economies including a cut in the dole should be proposed by a Government headed by MacDonald and with Thomas and other Socialists in it. Baldwin has asked me if I will serve if I am wanted; and I felt I could not refuse, though it will be very unpleasant. As soon as I know my fate I will let you know. The changes in the situation have been kaleidoscopic.[14]

His 'fate' was to be offered, and to accept, his old post of President of the Board of Trade in the Cabinet of ten which formed the inner core of the National Government: MacDonald and three other members of the outgoing Labour Cabinet—Snowden (Chancellor of the Exchequer), Thomas (Dominions Secretary), and Sankey (Lord Chancellor); four Conservatives —Baldwin (Lord President), Chamberlain (Minister of Health), Hoare (Secretary of State for India), and Cunliffe-Lister; and two Liberals—Samuel (Home Secretary) and Reading (Foreign Secretary). The Liberals would have liked Runciman, a Liberal, to have had the post of President of the Board of Trade, but their leader, Samuel, had to acknowledge that with two Cabinet portfolios they already had 'considerably more than our due proportion of the major offices'; and since 'The Conservatives also put in a claim for the Board of Trade . . . that . . . had to be allotted to them.' Cunliffe-Lister was, however, expected to have a Liberal as his parliamentary secretary, and managed to persuade Lloyd George's son Gwilym to act in this capacity in preference to the names suggested to him by Samuel.[15]

The hectic atmosphere of the early days of this crisis-created administration is conveyed in the letters Cunliffe-Lister wrote to his wife at Swinton. On 1 September: 'Life is very hard; and I like Samuel less and less every day. Neville and Sam [Hoare] and I play very well together . . . I have had to deal with the London Traffic Bill in addition to all my other problems . . . I do nothing but work so I have not much gossip. I am dissipating as well as I can the idea that this Government will hang on after it has balanced the Budget and made the economies. No one can suggest any policy on which we could possibly agree.' A week later, following a rare weekend visit to Swinton: 'Things are in some ways very difficult. But I think there is general agreement that the election must come as early as possible. I am hopeful that a Government could be established for that election which would include MacDonald, Thomas and Simon.'[16]

The 'general agreement' on the need for an early election seems to have been confined to opinion in the Conservative Party, since neither MacDonald nor Samuel were at all anxious for an election. And it could hardly be maintained that the crisis with which the Government was created to deal was anywhere near over, with the continuing weakness of sterling and drain on the gold reserves, despite savage cuts in public-service pay (but not without a naval 'mutiny' at Invergordon) and massive loans from the United States and France. 'Our immediate difficulty', Cunliffe-Lister told his wife, 'is that do what you will, gold slips away . . . Foreigners are nervous'. So nervous, indeed, that the National Government had to do what it was designed to prevent: take Britain off the Gold Standard. Retrospectively, Cunliffe-Lister was to say that he 'had never been happy about the deflationist policy which had brought us back to the Gold Standard' in 1925, and thus, presumably, he saw merit in Britain's departure from it, blow that it clearly was to the credibility of the Government's proclaimed financial policy. He attempted, not without some success, to moderate the immediate adverse effects of the currency depreciation on domestic prices by the method he had employed to keep prices steady during the General Strike. Before the produce markets opened on the day the abandonment of the Gold Standard was announced, he met representatives of large importing companies and persuaded them to delay increasing the price on current stocks in line with the extra costs they would have to meet in replacing stocks. 'I do not think', he later wrote, 'you could find a better justification of free enterprise than the public spirit these traders showed on that occasion.'[17]

By the middle of September the Cabinet, at the insistence of its Conservative members, was considering the introduction of a tariff: and with such adamantine free-traders as Snowden and Samuel within its ranks so major a policy decision seemed to compel an election before it could be implemented. On 15 September Cunliffe-Lister wrote to his wife:

Things are moving quickly behind the scenes . . . The result is tariff or no tariff? And if tariff, a full and adequate tariff or some compromise? I think the position is Ramsay and Thomas would like the full tariff, Snowden and Samuel would have none. Beyond that the Liberals are divided—a few would be against any tariff; more, perhaps half, would be for some washy compromise. The rest would go the whole hog, and [Hore-]Belisha assures me this includes Simon. The tariff issue must be dealt with in the Cabinet or by the Cabinet within the next few days. There will remain the question of the election . . . On the whole I think the most likely course is that we would finish our business as quickly as possible; resign; S.B. form a Government and go to the country. But Ramsay may covet the premiership, and as he is erratic and emotional he may take a sudden decision as he did when he changed his mind about resignation and formed this government.[18]

By 6 October the decision for an immediate election, with MacDonald remaining as Prime Minister, had been made. Cunliffe-Lister wrote on that day:

We are really in a very strange position. We have decided definitely on the election. We have decided that Ramsay shall issue a statement of his own. It will probably be colourless and ask for a free hand. I think Samuel has decided to stay in the Government. Baldwin and, presumably, Samuel will issue statements of their own. What really happens, I presume, is that we try to beat as many Socialists as possible. But we are not in the least agreed in reality on the tariff issue, and I think this will become more apparent as the election goes on . . . it means that we shall have to do the settling up and the reshuffle when we come back.[19]

There was never any doubt that the National Government would 'come back' at the election held on 27 October, although the uniquely overwhelming size of its victory, both in terms of the popular vote (67 per cent) and in seats gained (554), may not have been so widely predicted. In what was to prove his last election at Hendon Cunliffe-Lister got over 81 per cent of the votes cast, and a majority of 51,000 over his single, Labour, opponent; and this despite an attack of influenza and his commitments to the national Conservative campaign.

After the election came the reshuffling of posts Cunliffe-Lister had envisaged—and his post was one of those affected. The Cabinet now reverted to the orthodox size, but in every other way the process of Cabinet-making was extraordinary. As leader of the dominant element in the Government, Baldwin, and perhaps even more his party supporters, would naturally expect a lion's share for the Conservatives. But MacDonald was Prime Minister, and, apparently backed by the King, was surprisingly successful in retaining the conventional patronage powers of that office, including the decisive voice in the allocation of portfolios. He was helped by the general wish, which the King shared, to project the image of a *National* Government, and this meant a position out of all proportion to their numerical strength for the handful of National Labour members and for what had virtually become the two wings of the Liberals—a free-trade wing led by Samuel, and a protectionist wing led by Simon. The work was long-drawn-out and often painful. A week after the election Baldwin was complaining that 'he'd had the most unpleasant week of his life' and matters were still not settled, made no easier by the Prime Minister's departure for his Scottish retreat to ponder his new dispositions. Cunliffe-Lister's name figured in the various permutations of both Baldwin and MacDonald. Baldwin and other Conservatives wanted him to replace the Liberal Reading as Foreign Secretary. When Baldwin mentioned this to the King, the latter expressed doubts about the wisdom of appointing as Foreign Secretary someone whose caustic wit might flutter diplomatic dovecots. In any case MacDonald had other plans for the Foreign Office, which went to Simon, whose great merit for MacDonald was that he was not a Conservative. This seemed to leave Cunliffe-Lister at the Board of Trade. At this point Snowden, fierce free-trader that he was, represented to MacDonald that, in the present delicate position regarding the Government's attitude to tariffs, the two key economic posts at the Treasury and the Board of Trade should not both be occupied by 'such pronounced protectionists' as Chamberlain and Cunliffe-Lister. Snowden subsequently made it clear that his objection to Cunliffe-Lister at the Board of Trade was on policy grounds alone: he had a high personal regard for him (a feeling which Cunliffe-Lister reciprocated) and thought that 'apart from his obsessions with tariffs he was a very efficient President of the Board of Trade'. MacDonald agreed that Cunliffe-Lister was 'so good' at the Board of Trade but nevertheless accepted Snowden's objection. He himself proposed that he be appointed Colonial Secretary instead, and this was done—but not without damaging the political career of Leo Amery, who had been half-promised by Baldwin that he would be returning to the Colonial Office and was in the end left without a post in the Government. Runciman, a supposed Liberal free-trader, went to the Board of Trade.

Cunliffe-Lister was by no means displeased with the course of events. After spending his whole ministerial career so far in the Board of Trade he felt the time had come for a change and the Colonial Office attracted him even more than the Foreign Office (Baldwin had told him of this latter possibility). Neville Chamberlain later told him that if he had not himself gone to the Treasury his preference would have been for the Colonial Office, to carry on the work of his father; but 'since I could not, there is no one I would be as glad to see in my Father's old seat as you'. Beaverbrook wrote, with characteristic hyperbole, to tell him that 'In your new office you can and will change the history of your race. I would rather have the place than any other post'.[20]

The reconstituted National Government had to turn its attention immediately to the tariff question. Overseas exporters to Britain, not surprisingly, were increasing their exports to dumping levels in anticipation of the imminent imposition of a tariff. Cunliffe-Lister had been planning for this contingency before the election, but it fell to his successor (now apparently converted to tariffs by his new responsibilities) to rush through the Abnormal Importation Bill in four days in November, giving the Board of Trade power for six months to impose duties up to 100 per cent *ad valorem* on manufactured goods entering the country in excessive quantities: the first duties came into force on 25 November, within hours of the legislation receiving the royal assent. There followed the Horticultural Products (Emergency Duties) Act, imposing duties on certain vegetables, fruit, and flowers.[21]

The story of the legislative enactment early in 1932 of a permanent system of protective tariffs and of the interconnected extension of imperial preferences, for which provision was made at the Imperial Economic Conference in Ottawa in the summer of the same year, is too complex to be recounted in any detail here.[22] Cunliffe-Lister, who at the Board of Trade in the 1920s had been involved in all the earlier developments,

was, at the Colonial Office, still intimately concerned departmentally; and, as a senior member of the Cabinet and one of
its leading protectionists, continued to be a major participant
in the wider policy discussions.

Of several Cabinet committees working on aspects of pro-
tection at the end of 1931 the most immediately important
was that on the balance of trade. It was appointed, on Chamberlain's initiative, on 11 December, and contained, in addition to
Chamberlain as chairman, the two leading Cabinet free-traders
(Snowden and Samuel), the President of the Board of Trade
(Runciman), the Dominions Secretary (Thomas), the Minister of Agriculture (Gilmour), the Minister of Health (Hilton
Young), and Cunliffe-Lister. There was genuine concern in the
Treasury about the deficit being run on the current trade
account—estimated to be in the region of £100m. for 1931—but
there seems little doubt that Chamberlain was hoping to edu-
cate his free-trade colleagues in the seriousness of the situation
and thus persuade them that a general tariff was the only solution. If so, he was unsuccessful. The committee met for the
first time on 16 December and held four further meetings in
January. The only unanimity among its members was in their
agreement to back Cunliffe-Lister's proposal to restrict Russian
imports to the amount Britain was able to export to the Soviet
Union. But to the main proposal in the committee's report
(dated 19 January)—that there should be a 10 per cent general
tariff—Snowden and Samuel both dissented. They maintained
their dissent, backed by the two other Liberal Cabinet members, Maclean and Sinclair, when the report was discussed, and
essentially approved, by the Cabinet on 21 and 22 January.
The result was the 'Agreement to Differ' suggested by Hailsham
in order to preserve the Government's national character, considered so important for international confidence and for
domestic consent to measures of financial austerity. Snowden
and the Liberals were 'allowed to speak and vote on tariffs
against the proposals of the majority' and thus to oppose their
colleagues both inside Parliament and outside.[23]

The Import Duties Bill, incorporating the 10 per cent general tariff, was now in draft. The main responsibility rested
with the Treasury and the Board of Trade, but the Colonial
Office kept a close watch on its likely impact on the colonies.

It had been decided that the tariff would not apply to Dominion imports, but that there should be a time-limit for this concession, ending in November, in order to induce concessions from the Dominions when the much-delayed Imperial Economic Conference met in Ottawa in July 1932. It was agreed that no such time-limit should be enforced against imports from the colonies, but as late as 27 January—just a week before the Bill's second reading—Chamberlain was still wanting to limit this indefinite free entry for colonial imports to products specified in the Act. Cunliffe-Lister successfully argued that if this were done there would be continual colonial negotiations and parliamentary debates on proposals to add products to the schedule because so many new colonial products were likely to emerge in coming years.[24] In addition to these Dominion and colonial exceptions the Import Duties Bill explicitly did not apply to commodities already covered by earlier 'McKenna' or safeguarding arrangements, and provided for free entry for wheat, meat, and other foodstuffs, as well as important raw materials. On other commodities (largely manufactured goods) it imposed a general tariff of 10 per cent *ad valorem*, and established an independent Import Duties Advisory Committee to suggest alterations to the general tariff for particular classes of goods, very much on the lines of the Tariff Commission proposed by Cunliffe-Lister's Research Department committee in June 1931.

The enactment of the legislation by which Britain ceased to be a predominantly free-trade nation was hailed as a triumph for Joseph Chamberlain's son, who was the principal author of the Import Duties Act and its pilot through the House of Commons. But in his moment of glory Neville Chamberlain did not forget the contribution of his fellow workers in the protectionist cause. He wrote to Mollie Cunliffe-Lister on 6 February, two days after the second-reading debate:

Philip has done more than anyone else to bring about this triumph.

All the work he did at the Board of Trade and the Research Department has borne fruit for without it I do not believe we could have got a working scheme in time. It is a constant joy for me to work with one who understands so completely and contributes so whole-heartedly.

I hope we may continue our collaboration for many more years.[25]

A major objective of the Import Duties Act was to provide

an opportunity, which a basic free-trade economy denied, for establishing a truly inter-imperial preferential trading system. The coping-stone of the protectionist edifice was to be the preferential arrangements arrived at with Britain's imperial partners at the conference in Ottawa five months later. But the reality was rather different.

Throughout the first half of 1932 the Whitehall departments most closely involved—Treasury, Board of Trade, Dominions Office, India Office, and Colonial Office—were preparing for the Ottawa Conference and liaising with Dominion governments, whose preparations were clearly much less thorough. Then on 13 July the *Express of Britain* set sail from Southampton with the large and high-level British delegation to Ottawa on board (accompanied also by the South African, New Zealand, Southern Rhodesian, and Indian delegations): Baldwin as leader, Chamberlain, Runciman, Thomas, Hailsham, Gilmour, and Cunliffe-Lister, together with their official staffs. The conference opened on 20 July, under the chairmanship of the Canadian Prime Minister, R. B. Bennett. It ended an exhausting month later in an atmosphere falling far short of imperialist euphoria. What had been hammered out was not a comprehensive inter-imperial plan but a series of bilateral agreements between Britain and the Dominions (excluding the Irish Free State) and between the Dominions themselves. In general, preferences for British exports to the Dominions were to be given by raising duties against foreign imports rather than by lowering the rate against British goods, already often impossibly high (although under the 'domestic competition' clause British traders were given the right to make representations to certain Dominion tariff boards which would decide how much protection domestic industries really needed). In exchange for these relatively unimportant concessions Britain, among other things, was to impose new or higher duties on a whole range of foodstuffs, including wheat, butter, cheese, eggs, apples, pears, oranges, bananas, and other fresh fruit, and on canned fruit: food taxes had arrived at last. The general result of the Ottawa agreements was to divert part of the trade previously conducted with non-empire countries towards the Empire, mainly the Dominions and India. In the process the trade of the overseas Empire gained considerably more than did British trade, British imports from the Empire rising nearly 13 per cent between 1931 and 1937, compared with a 7 per cent rise in British exports to the Empire (although factors other than imperial preference clearly also played a part).[26]

Tempers became frayed and personalities clashed in Ottawa, perhaps not surprisingly, as none of the British ministers or officials, coming from an erstwhile free-trade country, had ever been involved in trade negotiations of this kind. As Professor Drummond has observed: 'it is extraordinary that such neophytes should attempt to construct seven major trade agreements in thirty-one days. Depending on his mood, the historian may thus explain their particular failures by remembering their inexperience, or admire their general and administrative success in obtaining agreements at all.'[27] The particular *bête noir* of the British delegation was Bennett, the Canadian Prime Minister, although S. M. Bruce of Australia was not far behind him in British disesteem for the crudeness of his negotiating style and the paucity of what he had to offer. On 19 August, the day before the conference ended, Cunliffe-Lister wrote to his wife:

I write now in an atmosphere of comparative calm. We are now assured of agreements with everyone . . . The last few days have been hellish. Bennett has behaved like a madman. I have never been so disappointed over anyone. Someone said that he had the manners of a Chicago policeman and the temperament of a Hollywood film star; and it is exactly true. He has been at loggerheads with half his Cabinet; and Ministers have apologized to us for his behaviour in their talks, and spoken frankly of their difficulties. Neville and Douglas [Hailsham] have had to bear the brunt of insufferable treatment in their negotiations with him; and they have both been admirable. I doubt if I could have kept my temper. This kind of negotiation has been a sad disillusionment for Neville. He looked forward to the prospect of planning the culmination of a life's work with sympathetic and willing partners; and Bennett has treated him like a trickster. Even Canadian journalists are furious. In the end we demanded to meet the whole Canadian Cabinet. Rather than face this Bennett finally came to terms. The last details are being settled now.

Cunliffe-Lister's own personal relations with Bennett were, however, excellent, and at the invitation of the Canadian Prime Minister he remained in Canada for several weeks after the end of the conference, travelling to every province in a magnificent private railcar lent by the president of the Canadian Pacific Railway.[28]

Although Baldwin was its titular leader, Neville Chamberlain was the dominant member of the British delegation to Ottawa. Of the others Hailsham and, to a lesser extent, Runciman and Thomas, seem to have been the most active.[29] Cunliffe-Lister's role was a secondary one, as representative of the colonies (which had no direct representation at the conference), rather than of major British departmental interests. In any case, in several important dependencies in east, central and west Africa, and in Palestine, preferential or discriminatory tariffs were barred by international agreements or League of Nations mandate. In the rest, the British Government had the power to impose preferential tariffs, but, since British colonial policy emphasized the administrative autonomy of the dependent units, was naturally reluctant to do so without their consent. Before Ottawa only Canada and New Zealand had offered any colonial preferences. By vigorous advocacy Cunliffe-Lister was able to obtain the inclusion of colonial preferences in all seven of the agreements the British delegation concluded at Ottawa: those with Canada, New Zealand, Australia, South Africa, Newfoundland, India, and Southern Rhodesia. The commodities concerned covered a wide range of foodstuffs and primary products, including tea, coffee, cocoa, sugar, timber, tobacco, bananas, oranges, grapefruit, canned fruit, tomatoes, potatoes, sisal, maize, honey, coconut oil, groundnuts, and oilseeds. The implementation of these preferences was dependent upon the confirmation of the colonies themselves, and on 15 February Cunliffe-Lister was able to report to the Commons that of those colonies not debarred by international agreement or mandate only Malta, Ceylon, and certain Malay states had failed to approve the agreements. As regards the sugar preference, he claimed on 14 July 1933, less than a year after the Ottawa Conference, that it had saved the sugar industry in the West Indies, Mauritius, and Fiji. In December the government and people of Mauritius signified their agreement with this assessment by presenting Cunliffe-Lister with a portrait of himself painted by Oswald Birley.[30]

A senior Dominions Office official at the Ottawa Conference, describing his impressions of it to a colleague in London while returning across the Atlantic, was critical of his ministerial superiors. There were too many of them and consequently too many advisers, but 'never, in my experience, have Ministers used their advisers so little, or disregarded so wholly such advice as they did receive'. By contrast, Bennett afterwards complained to Amery that the British ministers 'were always leaning back on their officials', the only exception being Cunliffe-Lister, 'who had a complete grasp of his Colonial problems'. And the impression of one of the Colonial Office officials at the conference was that his minister 'had something like a personal triumph at the Conference; certainly the Colonial Empire, his particular child, got as much out of the pool as anyone'.[31]

A policy to which Cunliffe-Lister had devoted much of his political life had thus come to fruition. That policy was considerably less important for Britain's economic revival and its trade relations with the Commonwealth than he and its other authors believed, but it none the less brought benefits, if fairly limited ones. In face of a world trend to tariffs and inter-governmental bilateral bargaining, and other forms of pressure, a free-trade Britain was in a weak position, with little scope for bargaining. After 1932 it could offer concessions to countries which were prepared to lower their tariff barriers. Domestically, economists now seem to agree, protection provided some stimulus to the economy, helped to improve the balance of payments by reducing imports and promoting import replacements, and played a role of some significance in relation to specific industries such as iron and steel—and the British film industry.[32] But its chief benefits were more political than economic. Protection with imperial preference was a policy around which the Conservative Party and, to some extent, the electorate (apart from 1923) could be mobilized: it promised coherent action to deal with the apparently intractable problems of slump and unemployment, and it appealed both ideologically and practically to important strands of Conservative opinion and support.

The anticipated impact of the Ottawa agreements on the composition of the National Government were not long delayed. The tenuous and fraying bonds of the Agreement to Differ finally snapped, and Snowden, two Liberal members of the Cabinet (Samuel and Sinclair—Maclean having died in June), and eight Liberal under-secretaries, including

Cunliffe-Lister's under-secretary at the Colonial Office, resigned from the Government on 28 September. The 'National'
character of the Government now rested with MacDonald
and his handful of National Labour supporters, and National
Liberals like Simon and Runciman. Cunliffe-Lister regretted
Snowden's departure, but, in common with most of his Conservative colleagues, was delighted to be rid of the sanctimoni-
ous Samuel.

The resignation of Snowden and the Liberals took place
while Cunliffe-Lister was still in Canada on his post-conference
tour of the provinces, from which he returned during October.
He had now been Colonial Secretary for almost a year and
was to remain in that office for the best part of the next three
years. It was a department completely different from the Board
of Trade, where all his previous ministerial experience had
been gained, but, to judge from his memoirs (disappointingly
reticent though those are) it was one which gave him peculiar
satisfaction. And it is clear that he left his imprint on the
Colonial Office even more than on the Board of Trade, despite
his longer tenure at the latter.

In formal terms the Secretary of State for the Colonies was
the minister responsible for advising the Crown on the exercise
of its authority over British dependent and mandated territories, and for conveying the Crown's instructions to the officers administering the governments (usually called governors)
of the fifty or so separate administrative units into which those
territories—spread over five continents with a land area of two
million square miles and a population of fifty million—were
divided. Since 1925 he had ceased to be responsible for the
self-governing Dominions, whose relations with the British
Government were now dealt with by a separate department,
the Dominions Office. The Colonial Office could be described,
again in formal terms, as 'the secretariat provided to assist the
Secretary of State in carrying out his duties: to furnish him
with the necessary information on matters requiring decision
and to translate his decisions into appropriate action'.[33] In
practice as well as form, much of the work of the Colonial
Office derived from and emanated in correspondence between
governors, representing their territories, and the Colonial Secretary, representing the British Government. For a long time

the organization of the office reflected this, with internal divisions based almost exclusively on territorial areas rather than functions (apart from those functions common to all government departments, like establishments and finance); only in the 1920s was any recognition given to specialist functions, in the appointments of a chief medical adviser and an agricultural adviser. The individual relationship of each colony to Britain was emphasized, too, in the insistence that they should pay their own way from their own resources: with administrative autonomy went financial responsibility. It was seen, also, in the legal basis of the employment in colonies of expatriate officials from Britain: 'every officer of the so-called Colonial Service was in fact in the employment of one or other of the territorial governments and not in any sense in the employment or pay of the United Kingdom government, the Colonial Office, or the Secretary of State'.[34] This remained true even when, in 1930, the principle of a unified Colonial Service, with various specialist branches, was officially accepted.

A tentative step towards viewing colonial problems as a whole rather than as those of discrete and disparate territories was made in the Labour Government's Colonial Development Act of 1929, which provided, for the first time, regular if limited funds (up to £1m. annually) for agricultural, industrial, and public health developments in the colonies. But this modest measure was soon overtaken by a more potent factor in the process of formulating an overall colonial policy—the world economic depression of 1929–33. The unprecedented fall in the prices of primary products devasted the economies of all the colonies, dependent as they were on the export of food and raw materials. Several had to be rescued from complete financial collapse by Treasury grants-in-aid, but this was clearly a temporary and highly unpopular measure; others would have gone the same way had they not been able to call on accumulated reserves. From the outset of his tenure of the Colonial Secretaryship, in the middle of a world depression, and fresh from controlling an overtly economic department, Cunliffe-Lister saw the main task as the effort 'to put the Colonies economically on their feet'; and to do so by his preferred expedients of imperial preferences and international commodity control.[35]

He soon found the Colonial Office to be ill-equipped to provide the information he thought necessary to perform this task, and to prepare for the forthcoming Ottawa and world economic conferences. Immediately on taking office he called a meeting of officials to discuss the development of colonial trade. His first question was: 'What are the most important products of the Colonial Empire?' But, as an official who was present recalled a few years later, 'Nobody could tell him, because nobody knew. We had our ideas, some of them wrong; we knew that rubber, for instance, was important, and tin and cocoa, and tea and sugar, and we knew what the principal products of the individual Dependencies were, but we had no idea of their relative importance to the Colonial Empire as a whole, because it had never been anybody's business to add the figures up to find out.'[36] It was perhaps at this meeting, too, that Cunliffe-Lister asked an elderly official who numbered sugar among his responsibilities what the middle market price of sugar was. ' "The middle what?" he asked in surprised tones. "Don't bother about ordinary market terms if you have never heard of them. What is the price of sugar?" Shocked, he answered, "I would not know, Secretary of State, my wife buys the groceries." ' Cunliffe-Lister soon found, and took to lunch, a junior official who did know the middle price of sugar: he was Sydney Caine, an economics graduate who had been secretary to a departmental committee of inquiry into West Indian sugar in 1929–30. Caine was an early recruit to the economic and financial section under Gerard Clauson which Cunliffe-Lister immediately instructed to be set up within the General Department, and which became a separate department of the office in 1934.[37]

The Colonial Office in general, and the new economic section in particular, was put to work by Cunliffe-Lister on assembling the essential facts and statistics about colonial trade and production. In addition to consulting the various colonial governments, he brought in to help with the task outside experts like Sir Edward Davson, chairman of the British Empire Producers' Organization, who accompanied the British delegation to Ottawa as Adviser on Colonial Trade; and William McLean, who had just become a Conservative MP after many years in the civil services of Egypt and the Sudan (where he had planned the new city of Khartoum under the direction of Lord Kitchener). McLean was immensely impressed with the speed with which Cunliffe-Lister had taken a grip on colonial problems: not even under Kitchener had he seen 'a quicker move than you got on the Colonial Office', he wrote to him on 10 December, barely a month after Cunliffe-Lister had taken up his post.[38]

An Economic Survey of the Colonial Empire, or 'the Bible', as it was more familiarly known in the Colonial Office, was completed in 1932, in time for the Ottawa Conference. It was a monumental work of some 600 pages, the first part containing descriptions of the economic situation of each colony, the second part dealing, commodity by commodity, with the production of the whole Colonial Empire. From the point of view of the formulation of future policy the second part was the more important, for in it 'we tried to show the scale on which commodities were being, and could be, produced in the Colonial Empire as a whole. In the case of the more important export products an account was given of how the commodity was produced and prepared for the market, the recognized grades, the total annual production, the countries where it was produced, and the principal consuming countries.'[39]

Armed with information like this, Cunliffe-Lister was able to show at Ottawa that mastery of detail that Bennett reported to Amery, and to secure colonial preferences in all the agreements the British delegation concluded there. There remained the problem of certain commodities—notably tin, rubber, sugar, and tea—where huge stocks had been accumulated and for which world prices had become completely uneconomic. Cunliffe-Lister was convinced that 'the only way of getting production back on an economic basis would be by international commodity schemes . . . designed to secure the maximum use of the commodity and to stimulate efficient production'.[40] This involved negotiations with other producing countries and metropolitan powers, and in conducting them (in close consultation with the Foreign Office and Board of Trade) Cunliffe-Lister was able to draw on the experience he had gained as chairman of the Tin Producers' Association during earlier negotiations undertaken by the Labour Government for the international regulation of tin production. It was in these negotiations that he had first met Colijn, the Dutch Prime Minister, with whom he was now to be closely associated, since the Netherlands East Indies was a producer of all the commodities concerned.

In all our plans Colijn and I insisted on certain fundamental conditions [he later wrote]. The restriction must be the minimum necessary. Supplies must always be fully adequate to meet current requirements and any possible expansion. The price must not be higher than that which would give an efficient producer an economic return. Every effort must be made to stimulate improved methods of production and new uses of the product. Schemes must be elastic and flexible. The consumers must be consulted throughout and associated with the operation of the schemes.

Cunliffe-Lister believed that the schemes introduced met all these conditions, which themselves were similar to the criteria which the World Economic Conference, meeting in London in June 1933, with Cunliffe-Lister among the British delegation, had—in a rare moment of unanimity—laid down:

Basic tonnages were agreed which were fair to the producing countries. Quotas of production on these tonnages were fixed at regular intervals and on the basis of meeting all possible demands. Large buffer stocks were held in order that any unforeseen expansion of consumption could be promptly and fully met. For example, under the tin scheme large buffer stocks were always held in the United States. The consumers were not only consulted but represented on committees of management. Research both in production and use was stimulated by a levy on producers, thus providing ample funds for research.[41]

On another commercial expedient with which Cunliffe-Lister was closely associated at the Colonial Office his memoirs are less forthcoming, and indeed what little they have to say on the matter is misleading. This was the controversial decision in 1934 to impose quotas on the import of Japanese textiles into the colonies, primarily in the interests of the British textile industry, which had been hard hit by the flood of cheap Japanese goods made possible by the low wages and standard of living in Japan, and to which no tariff rate was an effective barrier. One problem was that the Anglo-Japanese Treaty of 1911 gave Japan 'most favoured nation' status, and abrogation of the treaty required a year's notice. At Cunliffe-Lister's insistence the Cabinet in March 1933 agreed that steps should be taken to withdraw West Africa and the West Indies from the treaty so that quotas could be imposed there without having to wait for treaty abrogation.[42] The idea of textile quotas against Japan was by no means universally popular in Whitehall, however. Runciman, President of the Board of Trade, while accepting their necessity, seemed to wish to proceed more circumspectly than Cunliffe-Lister, and the Foreign Office was extremely reluctant to risk offending Japan. There was opposition, too, within the Colonial Office and from some governors at what could so easily be represented as colonial exploitation.[43] In March 1934, following the break-down of talks between British and Japanese textile industri-alists designed to secure voluntary restrictions, the Cabinet established a committee of Runciman (chairman), Neville Chamberlain, Simon, Thomas, Cunliffe-Lister, and Ormsby-Gore. In April 1934 the Cabinet approved the committee's recommendation that the Colonial Secretary be authorized to arrange with various colonies the institution of a quota system; it being recognized that in East Africa international agree-ments (the Treaty of Saint-Germain) made this impossible, while in other colonies it would be necessary to devise quotas which were not discriminatory, to avoid the 'most favoured nation' obstacle.[44] According to Lord Swinton's memoirs, 'This proposal was welcomed by the Colonies.' This is difficult to believe. It could hardly be expected that inhabitants of colonies, all with low living-standards, would welcome paying more for cotton goods in order to protect the vastly more advanced living-standards of those engaged in the Lancashire textile industry. It is true that in all but one of the colonies concerned the quotas for Japanese textiles were formally agreed by the Legislative Council, but this was often because the official majority was able to outvote the unofficial, rep-resentative members; and in the Strait Settlements the legis-lation was carried in the face of unanimous opposition by the unofficial members of the Legislative Council. In Ceylon, which had an unofficial majority in the legislature, the Board of Ministers refused to introduce the necessary legislation and the Governor had to be empowered to take the requisite ac-tion himself. By May 1935 Cunliffe-Lister was able to tell the Dominion prime ministers, assembled in London for the Silver Jubilee of King George V, that the colonies were now buy-ing 64m. yards of British textiles instead of the 25m. yards they would have been buying had the quotas not been imposed.[45]

No doubt any Colonial Secretary at the time, under the political and commercial pressures exerted on Cunliffe-Lister —among them, the powerful textile interests of Lancashire, stronghold of the Conservative party, and the desire to do almost anything in the effort to preserve employment in Britain—would have done as he did. It cannot, however, be gainsaid that it was a decision taken in the interests of Britain, not of the colonies. On the other hand, Cunliffe-Lister was prepared on occasion to argue for colonial interests even when they might conflict with Britain's. In June 1934 he was arguing in Cabinet that 'though colonial manufactures might sometimes hurt British trade' colonial industrialization should not be discouraged and Britain 'should place no duties or quotas on colonial produce'. In a Cabinet paper later in the year he expatiated on the difficulties colonial producers were experiencing in trying to sell their goods in certain foreign countries. Reminding his colleagues that the colonies had accepted quotas and preferences to benefit British goods, he suggested that it should be the declared policy of the Government (1) to secure equal treatment for colonial products in all trade negotiations with foreign countries, and (2) to make it plain that Britain would be ready to use the bargaining power arising from its large volume of imports to force foreign countries to give favourable treatment to colonial goods.[46] There is no evidence that the Cabinet took any specific action on these suggestions, but the fact that they were made does something to temper the critical judgement inevitably prompted by the episode of the Japanese textile quotas.

Surveying the economic results of his incumbency at the Colonial Office in his memoirs, Lord Swinton felt able to claim that the:

combination of Imperial Preference, commodity schemes, and applied research, in fact our whole Colonial economic policy, proved of great benefit to the Colonies. Producers were given a new chance; Colonial revenues increased and social services were extended; within three years the poorest Colonies were off the dole [ceased to need Treasury grants-in-aid] and the richer Colonies were no longer drawing on their surplus balances. Health and standards of living improved, and the Colonies were able steadily to increase their imports.

This seems altogether too optimistic an assessment. Leaving aside the question of how far any improvement in economic conditions in some colonies, so far as it occurred, was due more to general factors like a gradual revival in world demand than to the specific measures with which Cunliffe-Lister was associ- ated at the Colonial Office, there remain the stark facts of con- tinuing colonial proverty and disease. For all the preferences and restriction schemes from which its staple commodity, sugar, may have benefited, the vast majority of the inhabitants of the West Indies, for example, were still sunk in conditions of appalling deprivation. The report of the Royal Commission on the West Indies, submitted to the Colonial Secretary in December 1939, revealed social conditions so deplorable that the Government considered it impolitic to publish the report at that stage (two months after the outbreak of the war) lest it cast doubts in the minds of neutral countries, above all the United States, about Britain's role as a colonial power.[47] To say this is not to devalue the worth of Cunliffe-Lister's con- tribution to colonial economic development, but rather to put it in the perspective of the overwhelming problems with which any Colonial Secretary in the 1930s had to deal.

In economic policy Cunliffe-Lister sought to view the colonies as a whole rather than the heterogeneous collection of territories with varying needs and potentialities which in fact they were. The same attitude influenced his approach to personnel questions in the Colonial Office and in the newly unified Colonial Service. He noted, as had several of his pre- decessors, 'the lack of personal contact between the men in the Colonial Office and the men in the Colonies. Not only were there Colonial Office officials who had spent twenty or thirty years without ever visiting a single Colony, but there was singularly little ordinary human contact between the men from the Colonies and the men from the office when the former were home on leave.' Some had argued, and were to continue to argue, for the actual merging of the staff of the Colonial Office with thousands of expatriate officials who provided most of the staff of, and monopolized the higher positions in, the local colonial governments. But this had been rejected in 1930 by a committee under Sir Warren Fisher, official head of the Civil Service, on the grounds that the great disparity

in size of the two sets of staff (the Colonial Office establishment in 1930 numbered only 365), and the fundamental differences in their work, made amalgamation inpracticable. Instead,
following the committee's recommendations, it was decided
that the Colonial Office should continue to be staffed by
home civil servants, while the overseas staffs should be loosely
unified in the Colonial Service, the chief characteristic of
which would be that members were under an obligation to
accept transfer to another territory if the Secretary of State
considered that the new post was 'of no less value, due regard
being had to climate and other circumstances', than the one
they currently held. In addition, it was arranged that a number
of administrative posts in the Colonial Office would be regu-
larly filled on secondment from the Colonial Service, usually
for periods of two years; that administrative recruits to the
Colonial Office would be required to accept a liability to serve
overseas as required, particularly in the early years of their
service; and that official and personal contacts between Colonial Service officers and the Colonial Office should be systematically developed at all levels.[48]

These steps were well advanced when Cunliffe-Lister arrived at the Colonial Office towards the end of 1931 (even if
their effects were not immediately apparent), and he clearly
thoroughly approved of them. Indeed, it appears that he gave
notice of carrying them further by expecting all members of
the Colonial Office staff, including the overwhelming majority
who had entered long before the change in entry procedures,
to be prepared to serve overseas if required. He later described
what happened:

I heard that a few [Blimps] were canvassing the office and pressing
members of the staff to insist on their static rights. I promptly held a
meeting. I said that as far as I was aware I had never broken a contract
in my life and I hoped I never should. If any members of the staff wished
to live out their official lives in the security of Surbiton, I should certainly not press them to waive their contractual rights; nor indeed would
a man imbued with that spirit be of much use in a Colony. I took leave
however to observe that the Secretary of State had the right to advance
those men whom he regarded as most fit and most likely to serve the
public interest.[49]

No charge of lack of overseas experience could be levelled
at the permanent head of the office when Cunliffe-Lister took

over. He was Sir Samuel Wilson, who had been successively Governor of Trinidad and of Jamaica before becoming permanent under-secretary of state in 1925. When Wilson retired in 1933 he was succeeded by Sir John Maffey, who, while he had no direct experience of colonies, had been in the Indian Civil Service and came from the governor-generalship of the Sudan. Cunliffe-Lister's relations with both men were good, although he was probably closer in sympathy to Wilson than to the rather languidly elegant Maffey. But Cunliffe-Lister, at the height of his intellectual and physical powers, was so much the master of the administrative detail that he was in a sense his own permanent secretary, especially when Maffey, who was unfamiliar with the ways of the Colonial Office, held that post. Sir Stephen Luke, who was Cunliffe-Lister's assistant private secretary during his last year as Colonial Secretary, recalls him as the most dynamic minister he served in thirty years in the public service, exuding energy and vitality combined with great personal charm (when he chose to exercise it), and a keen sense of humour. A voracious worker, he took files home with him, reading and commenting—very frankly—on every minute, however lowly the writer (it had to be suggested to him that he might be gentler with the young tiros). In general he felt officials relied too much on written communications rather than direct contact, and recommended to them the virtues of the motto, 'bumph breeds bumph'. On matters requiring his decision he insisted on speaking to the official directly concerned, however much this might offend senior officials' sense of hierarchy. His dedication to work could make him at times an uncomfortable man to serve. Shorthand-typists summoned to the Secretary of State's office to deal with his correspondence would find they were expected to take dictation as soon as they entered the vast room and while they were seeking the sanctuary of a chair.[50] On one occasion F. G. Lee, who had just become Cunliffe-Lister's assistant private secretary, returned from lunch to find the typist much distressed because she had had to bear the full weight of the Minister's fury when, on returning unexpectedly early from his own lunch, he had found neither the private secretary nor his assistant available. When Lee went in to see him he was greeted with the blackest of looks and 'Where the hell have you been?' 'Well,' answered the unabashed Lee, 'I've been for a walk in the park with a girl.' 'Oh,' said Cunliffe-Lister, 'That seems a reasonable excuse.' From then on the two men got on perfectly together (and a quarter of a century later Sir Frank Lee, whose appointment as joint permanent secretary at the Treasury had just been announced, wrote to tell Lord Swinton: 'It is a long time since I started as one of your private secretaries, but I have never forgotten the lessons of judgement, courage and sound administration which you taught me then').[51]

This trivial incident serves to illustrate a characteristic of Cunliffe-Lister to which many who worked with him have testified. Like other possessors of powerful personalities he expected people to stand up to him, rather than meekly submit to his often uncertain temper. In any case his bark was usually more formidable than his bite, for when he thought someone 'had been a bloody fool he preferred to tell them so directly, and then to let him get on with the job'.[52] When once the test had been passed all was well with the relationship thereafter. But anyone who did not measure up to the required standard was soon dismissed from serious attention, almost certainly beyond hope of rehabilitation in Cunliffe-Lister's eyes.

The Colonial Office was an ideal department for Cunliffe-Lister. His forte lay in executive action rather than (for all his long association with the policy of protection) long-term policy planning. There was plenty of scope for the former, little for the latter, in the Colonial Office of the 1930s. Impetuous, reluctant to change his mind once he had come to his own view of a matter, not too concerned about procedural niceties if they delayed action, inclined to do detailed work best left to others: all these things Cunliffe-Lister may sometimes have been, but he was always decisive, and for this quality in a minister civil servants can forgive much. He could hardly be faulted as representative of his department's interests in the Commons, where he was a more than adequate if not particularly inspiring performer, or, more importantly, as one of the two or three most effective members of the Cabinet. In dealing with the many problems arising in the territories for which he was responsible, his gift for decisive action was at a premium, but it was always exercised on the premise that once he had given him his confidence the judgement of the man on the spot must be paramount.

For Cunliffe-Lister, as for all Colonial Secretaries between 1920 and the ending of the mandate in 1948, the dominant territorial problem was presented by Palestine, to which was devoted, a senior Colonial Office official has written, 'a wholly disproportionate amount of time and effort by Ministers and senior officials'.[53] The terms of the mandate incorporated commitment to the creation of a Jewish national home undertaken in the Balfour declaration of November 1917 and thus the Colonial Secretary, on behalf of the British Government, was responsible for 'placing the country under such political, administrative and economic conditions as will secure the establishment of the Jewish national home'; for facilitating 'Jewish immigration under suitable conditions, while ensuring that the rights and position of other sections of the population are not prejudiced'; for 'the development of self-governing institutions'; and for 'safeguarding the rights of all the inhabitants of Palestine, irrespective of race and religion'.

A new High Commissioner and Commander-in-Chief had taken office in Palestine in November 1931, just a fortnight after Cunliffe-Lister became Colonial Secretary. He was Lieutenant-General Sir Arthur Wauchope (pronounced 'Warcup'), and although Cunliffe-Lister had had no hand in his appointment he developed a closer relationship with him than perhaps any other of his overseas administrators. He had the highest admiration for Wauchope's abilities: 'we are very fortunate to have on the spot a man of great character and wisdom, who may be safely trusted to steer his ship through many shoals', he told his Cabinet colleagues in a paper circulated in November 1932; and writing to his wife during a visit to Palestine in April 1933 he described Wauchope, who had financed Arab experimental farms from his own private resources, as 'a practical saint'. But the troubles of Palestine were too obdurate and deep-seated to respond even to an able and dedicated local administrator, backed by an understanding and supportive Colonial Secretary. As Cunliffe-Lister confessed to his wife during his 1933 visit: 'It is the most difficult problem I have ever seen. Much more difficult than I thought now that I have seen it on the spot.'[54]

There was above all the question of Jewish immigration and the related extension of Jewish ownership of land previously owned by Arabs. The years of Cunliffe-Lister's Colonial Secretaryship saw a sensational increase in immigration (much of it illegal), partly, but by no means wholly, caused by mounting German anti-Semitism. As against 4,075 immigrants in 1931 and 9,553 (including only 353 from Germany) in 1932, there were 30,327 (5,392 from Germany) in 1933, 42,359 in 1934, and 61,844 in 1935.[55] The guiding principle of the volume of immigration, as stated by the British Government in 1922, was that it must not exceed the economic capacity of the country to absorb new arrivals. But how was the absorptive capacity principle to be viewed in relation to the Arab unemployment caused by the expulsion of tenants and workers on previously Arab land sold to Jews? The Jews might contend that immigration increased wealth and employment, but this was not necessarily true if only Jews could be employed on Jewish land or works. The only real solution of the problem, Cunliffe-Lister told his colleagues in a Cabinet paper in March 1934, 'lies in the Jews abandoning the exclusive employment of Jews and showing in practice that Arabs benefit directly by Jewish land purchase and industrial development'. He had been impressed by a visit the previous year to one of the settlements founded many years before by Baron Edmond de Rothschild, at Rose Pinah, above the Sea of Galilee, where Arabs and Jews lived in peace together, providing a model for the rest of Palestine. But he was under no illusions about the difficulty of applying such a solution: 'Such a change of policy will be anathema to the Jewish extremists. It will be difficult for Jewish leaders who see its wisdom and necessity. . . The theme of the prospectus on which they raise money is "Jewish money for Jewish settlers" and when even the moderate leader is appealing to his constituents, I have no doubt that the picture of the Jewish National Home often expands into one of the Jewish State.'[56]

Then there was the problem of the representative institutions Britain was pledged to introduce under the mandate. Previous attempts to establish a legislative council in 1923 and 1929 had failed through local opposition. The undertaking to institute a legislature had been renewed by the Labour

Government in October 1930. In March 1932, however, Wauchope advised Cunliffe-Lister that it would be impossible to devise one acceptable to both Arabs and Jews—and to offer a council and then withdraw it if the Jews did not participate would have a deplorable effect on Arab leaders. He recommended that he should delay taking further steps on the council but in the meantime try to secure the co-operation of both Arabs and Jews on various advisory boards concerned with agriculture, commerce, and industry, and proceed with the reorganization of local authorities, making provision for elections to them. Cunliffe-Lister told the Cabinet that he felt bound to accept the advice of the High Commissioner, 'a shrewd and unprejudiced observer', even though it meant going back on the 1930 statement. A Cabinet committee under Cunliffe-Lister's chairmanship, and with Samuel (himself a former High Commissioner in Palestine), Thomas, Hailsham, Betterton, and Ormsby-Gore as members, then examined the question and confirmed Cunliffe-Lister's conclusion.[57]

By November 1932, however, it was obvious that the position could not be held, in the face of Arab withdrawal from cooperation on the advisory boards. Wauchope now advised that it was necessary to reaffirm the Government's intention of proceeding with the establishment of a legislative council, however opposed Arab and Jewish opinions on its composition might be.[58] It was not until two years later, after exhaustive discussions, that specific proposals for a twenty-eight member council, including eleven Arabs and eight Jews, were announced.[59] The council had not been established by the time Cunliffe-Lister left the Colonial Office in June 1935, and in April 1936 the eruption of the Arab revolt finally extinguished the last faint chance of institutional co-operation between Arabs and Jews. It was symbolic of the collapse of any hopes he may have entertained of solving the Palestinian problem that Cunliffe-Lister's last Cabinet paper on Palestine should be one informing the Cabinet that he had authorized the High Commissioner to permit the Palestine police force to use tear-gas against demonstrators if it was considered necessary in order to avoid police casualties.[60]

The burden of the Palestine mandate remained throughout Cunliffe-Lister's term and for thirteen years beyond. Another mandate responsibility ended with his first year of office—but not without a crisis which called for all his decisiveness and confidence in the man on the spot. The mandated territory was Iraq, which became an independent member of the League of Nations on 3 October 1932, and the crisis—three months before that event—was a mutiny in the Assyrian levies, a locally recruited force under the command of those British forces in Iraq which Cunliffe-Lister had been so anxious to remove altogether in 1922-3.[61]

The 22,000 or so Assyrians in Iraq were the survivors of the Nestorian Christian communities who before the war had largely lived in Turkish and Persian Kurdistan—in the Hakkiari mountain area near Lake Van in south-eastern Turkey and the Lake Urmia area of north-eastern Persia. Fighting on the Russian side against the Turks during the war, they had been left high and dry by the Russian withdrawal, and had fled— with incredible hardships and the decimation of their num- bers—to seek British protection in Mesopotamia (as Iraq was still known). There most of them were kept in refugee camps at British expense until the camps were closed in 1921, when it was hoped that many of the Assyrian families could return to their former homes, at least in Hakkiari, which it was thought would be included in Iraqi territory. But in 1925 most of the Hakkiari region was awarded by the League of Nations to Turkey, and Assyrian families who had returned there were ruthlessly deported back to Iraq. Although to the Iraqis, as to the Turks, they were an alien minority, a good deal was done to resettle them in government-owned villages in Iraq. In the meantime large numbers of Assyrians—who were formidable fighters—had been recruited to local military levies raised by the British to replace the British and Indian troops withdrawn on grounds of economy after Iraq became an RAF command in 1922. The levies played a major role, in support of the RAF and the inexperienced Iraqi army, in operations against Turkish incursions and various revolts among the Assyrians' old en- emies, the Kurds; but from 1926, with the approaching end of the mandate, they were progressively reduced in size and by 1928 had become wholly Assyrian, and used primarily to guard RAF installations and airfields. A relatively well-paid, disciplined body, the levies were an important element among a scattered Assyrian community, fiercely conscious of its cultural and religious separateness under its hereditary patriarch, the Mar Shimun, and both contemptuous and suspicious of the Arabs among whom it dwelt.

As the end of the mandate approached, the Assyrians became increasingly despondent about their future as an alien group in an independent Arab Iraq, and convinced that the British had betrayed them. Unsuccessful attempts were made in Geneva by the Mar Shimun to get the League of Nations either to compel Iraq to set up an autonomous Assyrian enclave within its territory or to assist a mass Assyrian emigration from Iraq. Although the Iraqi government signed a declaration of guarantees for the protection of racial and religious minorities drawn up by a League committee, this failed to calm Assyrian fears. In the early summer of 1932 resort was made to more desperate measures.

On 1 June, without any prior warning, the British officer commanding the levies was handed a manifesto, signed by all his Assyrian officers, stating that since the British Government had failed to ensure the future of the Assyrian nation all the Assyrian officers and men (there were some 1,500 of them, in four separate stations) had resolved to cease serving from 1 July. By the military law under which the levies were serving this was an act of mutiny, but it soon appeared that it was part of a larger and more hazardous plan to concentrate all Assyrians in the Amadia district in Kurdish territory in northern Iraq. The self-discharged levies would march to Amadia, taking with them the Assyrian civilians *en route*, while at the same time those serving in the Iraqi army or police would resign or desert and join the movement north. The intention, once the concentration had been effected, was unclear, but the whole plan clearly had highly dangerous possibilities, especially as the Assyrians had between them some 5,000 modern British rifles and ammunition. If trouble had broken out between the Assyrians and the Iraqi government it might have led to the postponement of Iraq's admission to the League of Nations, with serious consequences for Iraq. The plan was, moreover, hatched at a most embarrassing moment for the Iraqi authorities, for the Iraqi army and police, with the RAF, were fully engaged in operations against the Kurdish Sheikh of Barzan.

The first news of any trouble received in London was a tele-gram on 2 June to the Chief of the Air Staff from the AOC Iraq, Air Vice-Marshal Ludlow-Hewitt, who was acting as High Com-missioner during the absence on leave of Sir Francis Humphrys. Ludlow-Hewitt reported the levies' manifesto and his decision to take the initiative by disbanding the levies himself, retaining only those members who repudiated the manifesto. He thought it possible that this drastic action 'would bring a large pro-portion of the Force to their senses and the whole subversive movement might possibly fizzle out'. Humphrys hurriedly re-turned to Bagdad on 7 June and from the telegrams exchanged between there and London it seemed the situation was well in hand. Then came the information about the threatened Assyrian concentration in the north. Humphrys agreed with the AOC that the plan had to be prevented. He arranged to see the Mar Shimun and other Assyrian leaders to try to induce them at the very least to postpone their project. But contin-gency plans needed to be made to detain the levies in their cantonments and to disarm them, if necessary, by force. Secrecy was obviously essential, so arrangements continued to be made openly for the discharges. The AOC then had to face the question of whether he had sufficient forces at his disposal to disarm and detain the levies. With the Barzan oper-ation still uncompleted he decided that he had not, and on 11 June he telegraphed the Chief of the Air Staff to request minimum reinforcements of one battalion to be in Iraq by 18 June. The Air Ministry immediately contacted the General Staff at the War Office to warn that a battalion might have to be dispatched at short notice. It also contacted the Colonial Office, which had at about the same time received a telegram from Humphrys, stressing the critical nature of the position, although not specifically endorsing the AOC's request for reinforcements.

Humphrys' telegram arrived soon after ten on the morning of 11 June, which was a Saturday. Cunliffe-Lister quickly went to the office, summoned J. Hathorn Hall, head of the Middle Eastern Department, and Hall's assistant, F. J. Pedler, to his room, and proceeded to deal with the crisis.[62] The Chief of the Imperial General Staff was consulted, but given the de-pleted state of the army, he refused to take any action without definite instructions from the Cabinet. Cunliffe-Lister there-upon arranged with Baldwin, who was in charge of the Government during MacDonald's absence through ill health, for a Cabinet meeting to be held on Monday evening, 13 June.

When the Cabinet met it was clear (even from Hankey's characteristically discreet minutes) that members had profoundly differing views about how the situation should be handled. Hailsham, the Secretary of State for War, backed by the CIGS (who was called in for part of the meeting, along with the Chief of the Air Staff), stressed what he saw as 'the very grave objections' to the reinforcement proposal: the troops, necessarily unseasoned, would suffer heat-stroke in this, the hottest period of the year in Iraq, and spread over four stations many miles apart, would invite attacks from the Kurds; and then a brigade might be needed to restore British prestige. The CIGS said the reinforcements could come only from Palestine, Egypt, or India: they could not be spared from Palestine and only with difficulty from Egypt, while the Indian Government was always against withdrawing troops from India. Unidentified members of the Cabinet made much of the supposed political objections. The dispatch of a battalion would be regarded as evidence that Iraq was not fit to be a League member. The Assyrians, who had close links with the Anglican Church, were entitled to look to the British Government to protect them from their hereditary enemies, the Kurds and the Arabs, if necessary by assisting them to establish an autonomous enclave in northern Iraq. It was inconceivable that British troops should be used to prevent the levies from returning to their homes.

The hand of Cunliffe-Lister, although not identified, can clearly be seen in the summary of the contrary view, which was essentially 'trust the man on the spot'. 'It was certain that Sir Francis Humphrys would never have supported the proposal if he thought there was any real substance in the objection to it which had been raised by the Military Authorities. The suggestion that the Assyrians should be encouraged in the matter of the autonomous enclave was deprecated. This claim had been rejected by the Mandates Commission of the League after full inquiry and it was generally agreed that it would be very unwise to instruct Sir Francis Humphrys to take any action without first hearing his views.'

Nevertheless, despite Cunliffe-Lister's efforts, the Cabinet 'generally agreed that in view of the political and military objections, the reinforcement proposal was not one that could be entertained', and the Colonial Secretary was authorized to explain the decision to the High Commissioner.[63]

The Cabinet's negative response, as conveyed in Cunliffe-Lister's telegram of 13 June, seems to have provoked Humphrys into what was now unequivocal backing of the AOC's call for reinforcements, especially as his meeting with Assyrian leaders had failed to persuade them to alter their plans. He telegraphed to the Colonial Office to say that the Cabinet had misunderstood the AOC's proposal, which was not to disband the levies (although this was still proclaimed as the overt intention, to maintain secrecy) but to disarm them and retain them in uniform under military law in their stations and with their families. By this means the levies, who had no homes to return to, would continue to draw rations and pay, and would be given an excuse, which many would welcome, to serve on and be spared a life of poverty. The mere presence of British troops would preserve calm and inspire confidence. If the levies were disbanded and allowed to join the threatened concentration in Amadia in order to secure, if necessary by force, an autonomous Assyrian enclave, there would be a grave risk of (1) Assyrian desertions from the Iraqi police and army; (2) delay in Iraq's admission to the League; (3) suspicion in Iraqi minds that Assyrian subversion had the covert support of the British Government. A small temporary reinforcement was being requested in order to minimize the risk of large reinforcements being required later.

When Humphrys' telegram was received on 15 June it was decided to hold another special Cabinet meeting the following day. By contrast with the meeting three days before there was now an obvious reluctance to overrule the expert advice of Humphrys, and a feeling that the War Office had exaggerated the health and strategic hazards. Cunliffe-Lister was authorized to inform the High Commissioner that the Cabinet would suspend its final decision on his request for reinforcements (its previous 'final decision' had been to refuse it outright) until he had supplied assurances on the health, strategic, and political points which had been giving concern, the most important of which were the precise functions the British troops would perform in preventing the levies from dispersing, and the period for which their presence would be needed. Meanwhile, it was arranged to have another special Cabinet meeting on Sunday 19 June, if necessary, to make a final decision. In the event it did not take place. Cunliffe-Lister managed to persuade the ministers concerned—Hailsham, the Secretary of State for War, and Londonderry, Secretary of State for Air—to agree to orders being sent to the General Officer Commanding and the AOC Egypt for the transportation of the 500 troops by air to begin on 20 June. Telegraphing this decision to Humphrys on 18 June, Cunliffe-Lister added his assurance 'that reluctance of Cabinet to send British troops in no way implies any lack of confidence in yourself. On the contrary, it is only our great confidence in your judgement that has enabled us to adopt a course open to so many objections. Thank God you are the man on the spot.'

The High Commissioner's telegrams were now, however, indicating the possibility of a last-minute change of mind on the part of the Assyrians, in which case the troops would not be needed; and it was left to him to make arrangements direct with the GOC Egypt. Having telegraphed to Egypt on 20 June to delay the troop movement, on the following day Humphrys asked for the operation to begin on 22 June, talks with the Mar Shimun having broken down. By 27 June, in what was at the time the largest operation of its kind ever undertaken, all four companies of 1st Battalion the Northamptonshire Regiment had been conveyed the 750 or so miles from Ismailia to Bagdad in Victoria aircraft of 70 and 216 (Bomber Transport) squadrons of the RAF. On 28 June they took over guard duties from the levies at the four stations at Hinaidi, Mosul, Sulaimi, and Diana. At this point the Mar Shimun was at last induced to send a signal instructing the levies to continue serving loyally until the League of Nations had answered his latest petition about the position of the Assyrians in an independent Iraq. This was sufficient for the levies at Mosul, Sulaimi, and Diana, but those at Hinaidi insisted upon being discharged, and they were released in batches over a period of eight days. Neither they nor any of the other levies attempted to break out of camp, so the contingency which the troops were sent to meet never materialized. On 18 July the battalion began its return journey to Egypt. Both Ludlow-Hewitt and Humphrys were convinced—probably with justice—that the presence of British troops had crucially contributed to the ending of the crisis. 'Thank heaven the Cabinet under the guidance of the Secretary of State decided to grasp the nettle and—to use a mixed metaphor—to scotch the snake,' Humphrys wrote privately to Hathorn Hall at the Colonial Office on 30 June. 'I believe we have got breathing space now to carry on peacefully until Iraq is in the League . . . Please give my warmest thanks to the Secretary of State for his generous support and confidence.'[64]

Although his responsibilities for Iraq ended with the termination of the mandate in October 1932, Cunliffe-Lister included the country, together with Palestine, Transjordan, and Egypt, in the itinerary for his visit by air to the Middle East in April and May 1933. On the same trip he was also able to visit Cyprus, where serious rioting, involving the burning down of Government House and the suspension of the constitution, had occurred not long before he became Colonial Secretary. Time did not permit, however, of a visit to another and equally troubled Mediterranean island colony, Malta, where he had only recently—not without misgivings—restored the constitution suspended by the Labour Government in June 1930; in November 1933 the Italian sympathies and financial recklessness of the Maltese ministers led him once again to suspend the constitution and leave Malta in the constitutional limbo from which it did not fully emerge until after the Second World War.[65]

At the beginning of 1934 Cunliffe-Lister set out on his second and, as it proved, last series of air visits as Colonial Secretary. This time the destination was East Africa, by way of the Anglo-Egyptian Sudan. The Sudan was administered by the Foreign Office, not the Colonial Office, and Cunliffe-Lister saw this as a matter for regret. 'It is invidious that the Foreign Office should administer this country,' he wrote to his wife. 'They know nothing about it except its political relations. It is wicked that men in the service here should not have the benefit of our accumulated experience, administrative, economic, scientific, health, police . . . What a tragedy we did not take it over when Stack was killed.'[66] The Sudan was followed by a fortnight in Uganda as guest of the Governor, Sir Bernard Bourdillon, and from there he flew to Kenya. His stay in Kenya was to be considerably longer than planned. At the end of January he became ill with septicaemia. At first it appeared to be a relatively mild attack and he seemed to be making good progress, but on 31 January the Governor, Sir Joseph Byrne, telegraphed to the Colonial Office to say that the 'Secretary of State's condition has taken a sudden and unexpected turn for the worse. Infection has become more generalized with signs of lung being involved. Under circumstances now think it desirable that Lady Cunliffe-Lister should come out at once if possible catching air mail leaving Brindisi next Friday.'⁶⁷ By the time that his wife, by these uncomfortable means, had arrived in Nairobi, Cunliffe-Lister—whose life at one point had almost been despaired of—was well on the way to recovery, attended by Arthur Jex-Blake, a distinguished physician who had retired to Kenya. His convalescence was far from idle. He had brought with him an advance copy of the report of the Kenya Land Commission, which he had set up in 1932 under the chairmanship of Sir Morris Carter. He now discussed its contents with local people. The massive report examined land tenure in the exclusively white-settled Kenya Highlands (the so-called White Highlands), and its many recommendations included the reservation of certain land in the Highlands for the African population. Cunliffe-Lister left the white settlers he met in no doubt that he intended to implement the report; and his illness did not seem to affect the vigour with which he spoke. Soon after he had returned to Britain Byrne wrote to tell him that 'things have been fairly quiet politically since you left. They were all a bit sore at being told the truth but I am sure it has done a *lot* of good. The early publication of the verbatim reports of your interviews will still further clear the air and give the lie to some silly rumours about the tone adopted at these interviews.'⁶⁸ When he was fully fit to travel Cunliffe-Lister and his wife had a leisurely four-week sea-voyage, in sharp contrast with the discomforts of air travel, and were able to take in two more colonial territories, Aden and Gibraltar, *en route*. On 19 March he attended his first Cabinet for three months. Sir John Simon wrote to Lady Swinton to thank her 'for bringing Philip back from Kenya looking so well . . . You would have been proud to see how he was welcomed in the Cabinet.'[69]

Swinton's role in that Cabinet was not, of course, confined to the interests of his department, wide though those were and effectively though he represented them. Despite having been one of the 'Big Ten' in the two months of the National Government before the 1931 election, he was not among the 'Big Six'—MacDonald and Thomas for National Labour, Baldwin and Chamberlain for the Conservatives, Simon and Runciman for the National Liberals—whose joint deliberations after November 1931 contrived to provide some inter-party scaffolding for an essentially Conservative edifice. For all his fierce party allegiances, Cunliffe-Lister himself attached importance to the National Government continuing to have an appeal well beyond those who identified with the Conservative Party. He had been glad to see the free-traders go, but now that issue was out of the way there were others who might be enlisted for National Government service. There was, above all, Lloyd George, under whom Cunliffe-Lister had won his political spurs and for whom he retained considerable affection. The transatlantic example of the Roosevelt New Deal, with its injections of purchasing power and jobs into a depressed economy through massive public works, exerted its attractions, and Lloyd George had been preaching a recognizably similar programme since at least 1929. During 1934 some of the younger members of the Cabinet, including Cunliffe-Lister (who at fifty was still its fourth youngest member, after Ormsby-Gore, Elliot, and Oliver Stanley), became increasingly restive under what they saw as Chamberlain's over-rigid financial orthodoxy at the Treasury: as a well-informed junior minister put it at the time, Cunliffe-Lister shared with Stanley and Elliot a 'yearning for a smiling Conservatism to replace Chamberlain's monetary rigour'.[70] Chamberlain got to hear of the movement through Kingsley Wood, who told him that Cunliffe-Lister 'had been the leader in insisting that the financial policy of the Government was all wrong'.[71] From around early December 1934 Cunliffe-Lister seems to have made a determined effort to get Lloyd George invited to join the Government: both Margesson, the Chief Whip, in December, and Hoare, in February 1935, reported him as 'very anxious for his inclusion'.[72] It was a suggestion not wholly unpalatable to Ramsay MacDonald, who saw in it some relief for his exposed position confronting a Conservative majority; while even Margesson was not averse to it, conscious as he was of back-bench rumblings at some recent governmental mishaps (especially the confusion about the new unemployment benefit regulations), mounting impatience at Simon's continued tenure of the Foreign Office, and the demands of the more radical Conservatives like Macmillan, Cranborne, and Boothby, for what R. A. Butler described as 'a more dramatic and Rooseveltian lead'.[73] In an effort to meet the internal Cabinet discontent, MacDonald, after consultations with the Big Six, announced at the Cabinet meeting on 30 January 1935 the formation of a General Purposes Committee under his chairmanship to 'discuss matters which did not belong only to one Government Department'; its membership was to be the Big Six with one or two others added *ad hoc*, including Cunliffe-Lister (who had criticized the idea of such a committee) and Kingsley Wood. The first topic of discussion was to be 'financial policy in relation to public works', but its twenty-five meetings between February and July 1935 yielded singularly little fruit. And although a subcommittee was set up in April specifically to examine Lloyd George's programme, in the presence of its author, no move was made to secure his participation in the Government. His many enemies there, and above all Chamberlain (despite the attempted persuasions of his brother Austen), proved too powerful, and the moment passed.[74]

The incident clearly did something to shake Chamberlain's confidence in the man who had been as close to him as any of his colleagues, and whose general view of economic policy had long been so akin to his own. When Chamberlain was discussing possible Cabinet changes with Margesson in December 1934, and in particular the dispositions which might follow the removal of Simon from the Foreign Office, he jibbed at Margesson's suggestion that he himself should take Simon's place and Cunliffe-Lister succeed him as Chancellor of the Exchequer. Not only did he not want the Foreign Office, but, he told the Chief Whip, 'I very much distrust P.C-L's judgement at the Exchequer.'[75] It was, however, a translation to the Air Ministry rather than the Treasury that the main weight of Cunliffe-Lister's extra-departmental interests in Cabinet seemed now to foreshadow.

Air Ministry I

As Colonial Secretary Cunliffe-Lister was a member of the Committee of Imperial Defence (CID) and necessarily concerned with questions of colonial defence, in which the RAF had been assuming increasing importance, particularly in the Middle East. But circumstances were conspiring to lead him into a deeper involvement with air matters. The Secretary of State for Air was Lord Londonderry, a Conservative appointed in November 1931 by MacDonald's wish, not Baldwin's. Although knowledgeable and enthusiastic (he was one of the few Air Ministers to hold a pilot's certificate), he was widely regarded as a political light-weight, with little influence in Cabinet or, as a member of the House of Lords, in Parliament. The air under-secretary, Sir Philip Sassoon, another keen amateur aviator, was not capable of supplying the deficiencies of his minister (indeed, he and Londonderry were rather similar in interests and weight, and both were among the leading political hosts of the day). Baldwin, in the non-departmental office of Lord President, was evincing a special interest in air defence and disarmament, but had little confidence in the Air Minister and tended to take over major air questions himself, sometimes after scant consultation with Londonderry. Increasingly Baldwin looked to Cunliffe-Lister as his main co-adjutor in this field and they worked closely together on the CID ministerial committee which was set up in 1932 in connection with the ultimately abortive World Disarmament Conference in Geneva from February 1932 to its collapse in June 1934.

With the Japanese invasion of Manchuria and, above all, the departure of Hitler's Germany from both the League of Nations and the World Disarmament Conference in October

1933, the first halting steps were at last taken towards repairing the damage which disarmament had caused in Britain's armed forces since the end of the war. As far as the air force was concerned it is true that a modest boost had been given to its home defence strength under the 1923 programme designed to produce fifty-two squadrons by 1928; but by 1933 this programme was still some ten squadrons short and no new squadrons were planned. In November 1933 the Defence Requirements Committee was established under Hankey to prepare a programme to meet the worst deficiencies in all three services. Its air force proposals were examined by a subcommittee of the Ministerial Disarmament Committee consisting of Baldwin, Cunliffe-Lister, and Ormsby-Gore, whose report, submitted to the main committee on 11 July 1934, became the basis of the first of the thirteen RAF expansion programmes prepared (but by no means always approved) between 1934 and 1939. This was the so-called Scheme A, approved by the Cabinet on 18 July 1934, which envisaged increasing the number of home defence squadrons from forty-two to seventy-five (with a total of 884 first-line aircraft) by March 1934, with an additional eight squadrons for service with the Fleet Air Arm and overseas. By this time, in large part as a result of Winston Churchill's relentless parliamentary probing, Baldwin had committed the Government, in the debate on the 1934 air estimates, to maintaining what later came to be called 'parity' (the word was used by Sassoon in the same debate) with what was thought to be the rate of German air rearmament, taking place in flagrant but tacitly condoned breach of the peace treaty. Failing an agreement on air limitation, Baldwin told the Commons on 8 March 1934, 'this Government . . . will see to it that in air strength and air power this country will no longer be in a position inferior to any country within striking distance of our shores'; and he renewed this pledge, with specific reference to Germany, eight months later.[1]

Immediate action was required if this pledge was to have any meaning. The modest expansion envisaged in Scheme A was soon overtaken by intelligence reports of rapidly increasing German air strength, and in November steps were taken to accelerate the implementation of the scheme. In March 1935 came the public announcement, in the White Paper

on defence, of the Government's rearmament plans, closely
followed by Hitler's claim to Simon and Eden in Berlin (subsequently proved to be unfounded) that the *Luftwaffe* had
already achieved equality with the RAF in aircraft numbers,
and would in two years equal the numerical strength of the
French metropolitan and North African air force (estimated
to have 1,404 first-line aircraft). The Air Ministry submitted
proposals (Scheme B) for enhancing its expansion plans, to
provide 1,332 first-line planes by the target date of 31 March
1939, but these were not considered adequate by the Ministerial Disarmament Committee (which retained its now wholly
inappropriate title until June 1935). On 30 April the committee set up a subcommittee, consisting of Cunliffe-Lister as
chairman, Runciman, and Ormsby-Gore, to produce a programme for restoring future air parity with Germany. In the
previous month Cunliffe-Lister had accepted the chairmanship
of a new CID committee on air defence research. It is difficult
to see what greater snub could have been offered to Londonderry as the Minister responsible for the Air Ministry and the
RAF than that both these appointments should have gone to
a Cabinet colleague whose departmental responsibilities were
only marginally connected with air matters. But Londonderry
nevertheless remained at his post.

Cunliffe-Lister set about organizing his committee on air
parity with characteristic speed and decision (its secretary
privately commented on the verve and imagination he brought
to his task).[2] The first meeting was held on 1 May, the day
following its appointment, and the second on 3 May; both
meetings were attended by members of the Air Council (including Londonderry for much of the time) and other Air Ministry officials. The discussions followed closely the sequence
laid down at the outset by Cunliffe-Lister, namely, that accepting Hitler's statement that the Germans had 850 first-line aircraft and his declared intention of achieving equality with
French metropolitan and North African first-line air strength,
the committee should investigate the qualities of German aircraft and pilots and programme completion date, and come
to a decision as to the meaning to be given to parity and the
measures needed to ensure it.

The committee's first report was submitted on 8 May, a mere

week after its first meeting. The present position was that Britain had 270 fewer first-line aircraft than Germany (580 to 850), but, the committee considered, there was reason to believe that Britain was superior in aircraft reserves, training organization, and numbers of qualified pilots. Parity should mean numerical equality with the German air force, and cover all first-line aircraft (and not only bombers, as some had suggested), while on the British side all regular and non-regular squadrons stationed at home, but excluding the Fleet Air Arm, should come into the account. The report endorsed the Air Ministry's assumption that, in pursuing its aim of numerical equality with the French air force, the German air force would have a total of 1,512 first-line aircraft by 1 April 1937. If Britain were to have parity with this German expansion it would be necessary to place orders for 3,800 aircraft (1,400 more than provided for in present plans) for delivery by April 1937, two years earlier than in the Air Ministry proposals; of these 1,512 (as compared with 1,332 initially proposed by the Air Ministry) would be first-line aircraft, the rest reserves—the reserve figure being one that could not be publicly divulged. This programme was considered to be within the capacity of the aircraft industry, but the serious delays in the design and production of new types of heavy and medium bombers would have to be overcome. The reports stressed that if the full production of aircraft and equipment were to be obtained within the specified time the orders to industry must be given without delay. The programme envisaged—involving the addition of seventy-one squadrons to RAF strength—posed problems of recruitment under a voluntary system, especially of pilots (of whom some 1,400 would be needed) and technicians, and a strenuous recruiting drive, in conjunction with the Ministry of Labour, was called for. On the other hand, no difficulty was anticipated for the present with aerodromes and the provision of buildings. In broad financial terms, the proposals would increase the Air Vote by something over £9m. on the current year's estimate of £20.5m.[3]

The report came before the Ministerial Disarmament Committee on 10 May. While it agreed to recommend to the Cabinet that the Air Ministry be authorized to proceed with that part of the programme dealing with fighters and light bombers, it decided to ask Cunliffe-Lister's committee to investigate further the heavy and medium bomber programme in view of the production delays. All this was comparatively uncontentious. But when the discussion moved to the question of relative German and British pilot strength Cunliffe-Lister caused what a member of the secretariat present described (in his diary) as 'a sensation' by querying the accuracy of the Air Ministry's estimate of the total number of trained German civilian pilots. The Air Ministry had put this at 4,000, but Cunliffe-Lister, quoting a conversation he had had (after completion of the report) with an air intelligence agent, supported from various foreign intelligence sources, suggested that the figure was 8,000.[4] As the Air Ministry's estimate had been incorporated in the report, Londonderry was naturally taken aback by this revised estimate, arrived at without reference to him or the Air Ministry staff, since it clearly reflected on the quality of the Air Ministry's own intelligence sources, already under attack in Whitehall, notably from the Foreign Office. On the following day he wrote to Cunliffe-Lister (with copies to MacDonald and Baldwin), enclosing an indignant defence of the Air Ministry's figure by Sir Edward Ellington, the Chief of the Air Staff.[5] Whatever may have been the rights and wrongs, the incident provided a by no means isolated example of unnecessary tactlessness, of insensitivity to other people's feelings, on Cunliffe-Lister's part which did nothing to endear him to colleagues who might otherwise fully recognize his obvious gifts. And by this time Baldwin had already made up his mind to move him to the Air Ministry when he took over as Prime Minister from MacDonald.[6] The definite proposal may not yet have been made but Cunliffe-Lister must have had a shrewd suspicion that he was soon to become head of the department whose methods he was impugning.

The Air Parity subcommittee met for its third, reconvened, meeting on 13 May, again with Londonderry and senior members of the Air Ministry. Although their names do not appear in the minutes as being in attendance, it would appear that Admiral Sinclair, head of the Secret Service, and at least one member of his staff, were also present, and there was further discussion of the number of trained German pilots.[7] Desmond Morton, of the Industrial Intelligence Centre, was certainly present and produced alarming data on the possible future output of the German aircraft industry: if it was indeed increasing at the present suspected rate Germany would have 5,000 service aircraft by April 1937. The rest of the discussion was incorporated in the committee's second and final report, considered in draft at a fourth meeting on 16 May and circulated to the Cabinet the following day.[8]

The report did not confine itself to the medium and heavy bomber programme that the committee had been particularly charged to consider, but sought to determine the proportions of the various types of aircraft that would be needed to make up the total of 1,512 first-line aircraft of all kinds being aimed at by April 1937. It made clear that it was following the advice of the Air Staff on this question, since 'The proportion of different types of aircraft, their relative value and fighting efficiency are clearly matters on which a civilian committee are unfitted to adjudicate and on which the considered opinion of the Air Council must be accepted.' Mention was made of experimental fighter aircraft which held great promise for the future, notably two low-wing monoplanes being designed by Hawker and Supermarine respectively, with retractable undercarriages, flaps for slow landing, and an estimated speed of 300 m.p.h. Prototypes were expected in July and October 1935, but American experience had shown that there were considerable aerodynamic difficulties with advanced low-wing planes of this type, and they could not be counted on in a two-year programme such as that being recommended (the future development of the Hawker Hurricane and the Supermarine Spitfire would be occupying a good deal of Cunliffe-Lister's attention over the next three years).

Perhaps the most significant section of this second report was that containing recommendations for accelerating the aircraft production process. At present there were five stages: (1) issue of the specification by the Air Ministry; (2) production of the design and its examination by the Air Ministry; (3) production of the prototype, entailing building a 'mock-up' and carrying out trials in a wind-tunnel preparatory to the actual building of the type; (4) testing of the type by the Air Ministry to ascertain whether it met the required specification; and (5) production in quantity. It was possible to speed up this process at the third and fifth stages—that is, in the production of the prototype and by means of bulk production when the prototype had been accepted. In general, it appeared to the committee that 'the best way of achieving acceleration is by some departure from the existing system and by the immediate placing of orders in bulk before prototypes have been tested for certain types of aircraft'. Such a policy ran the risk of failure of the aircraft to come up to specification and result-ant financial loss, but the committee was satisfied that it was justified 'in the present circumstances'. It thus proposed that firm contracts should be placed for the Fairey medium bomber (the future Battle) and the Armstrong Whitworth heavy bom-ber (the Whitley) before prototypes had been built: both firms were confident that the prototypes would come up to speci-fication. The committee also recommended that a special officer, with adequate staff, should be appointed at the Air Ministry to supervise aircraft supply; and—another recommen-dation of the greatest significance for the future—that the advisory panel of industrialists working within the organiz-ation of the Committee of Imperial Defence should be invited, individually or collectively, to assist the Air Ministry with its production problems. (It soon became clear that it was the services of one particular member of the panel—Lord Weir, a former Air Minister and prominent industrialist—that were being sought. He agreed to help, and had started work before the end of May.[9])

The report concluded with a summary of the committee's proposals for numbers and types of aircraft. The 1,512 first-line aircraft envisaged by April 1937 would be made up of 420 fighters (in 35 squadrons); 240 heavy bombers (20 squadrons); 240 medium bombers (20 squadrons); 360 light bombers (30 squadrons); 90 army co-operation aircraft (6 squadrons); 126 general purpose or reconnaissance aircraft (7 squadrons); and 36 flying boats (6 squadrons).[10]

The main Ministerial Committee considered the report on 20 May, and it did not have an easy passage. Hailsham, the Secretary of State for War—who clearly saw the implications of this new emphasis on the air arm for the budget of his own service—launched a blistering attack on the attempt to achieve numerical parity with Germany. If Britain were to have true parity in terms of bombers, he maintained, it would need to have three times the German number since the main strategic targets for the German air force, operating from Belgium, were three times nearer than their German equivalents for the RAF; moreover, German bombers carried heavier bomb-loads than British bombers, many of which would be of obsolescent types. 'If this programme were to be approved merely as eyewash— well and good, but if it was to be put forward as a serious contribution to the problem of defence, then . . . the House of Commons would be deluded . . . It would lead to a blatant and obvious armaments race which . . . we were bound to lose, as Germany had the better organization and greater capacity.' Cunliffe-Lister rejected this counsel of despair. The conclusion to be drawn from Hailsham's argument seemed to be either that we must have three times the German strength or we had no defence at all. 'He did not consider the programme was suited merely to the ends of publicity, he thought it essential from the point of view of defence, and that we should not be safe unless we had made the greatest possible efforts.' At the end of a long and often penetrating debate the committee decided to recommend that the Cabinet approve the report. The Cabinet did so next day and the substance of the new expansion plan (which became Scheme C) was announced by Baldwin in the House of Commons on 22 May.[11]

The announcement came during a debate which saw Baldwin, in face of yet another attack by Churchill, confessing to having misled the House, and being misled himself, in the figures of relative British and German air strengths that he had given to the House the previous November. This quite unnecessary 'confession' (since in fact Baldwin had neither misled nor been misled) did nothing to enhance the public reputation of Londonderry, as head of the department which had supplied Baldwin with the information. Nor did an unfortunate reference by Londonderry to the value of bombers in police operations in the Middle East and India in the course of an otherwise blameless speech in the House of Lords on 22 May: a statement which was seized upon by the Labour Opposition as evidence that the Government was advocating the horrors of aerial bombardment. Londonderry had, overnight, become an electoral liability. It could have come as a surprise to few that in Baldwin's new Cabinet appointments, announced on 7 June, Cunliffe-Lister was named as Secretary of State for Air in place of Londonderry, now Lord Privy Seal and Leader of the House of Lords (until dropped from the Government altogether in November). Londonderry later recalled that Baldwin had stressed to him the need to have the minister responsible for air policy in the Commons, and had added that Cunliffe-Lister, who had the ability to 'hustle' and wider experience of business and industry in general, demonstrated by his handling of the Air Parity subcommittee, was 'better qualified to deal with expansion'.[12]

Londonderry also recalled that after being appointed to succeed him Cunliffe-Lister wrote to say that he would dearly have liked to have remained at the Colonial Office where 'I really love my people and my work'. There seems little doubt that Cunliffe-Lister did enjoy his years at the Colonial Office and that those in a position to know appreciated the value of his work there. But there can equally be no doubt that he relished the new challenge which taking over the Air Ministry and the long-delayed expansion of the air force presented. Nor would Leslie Hore-Belisha have been alone among his governmental colleagues in recognizing the appropriateness of the appointment. 'You are just the man', Hore-Belisha told him, 'for anything that requires drive'.[13]

We now come to the decisive period in the career of Philip Cunliffe-Lister. It is possible to conceive of others carrying out with comparable ability the functions which he had performed at the Board of Trade and the Colonial Office. But the tasks at the Air Ministry from 1935 were so vital, the barriers to their successful completion so formidable, and his personality, character, and skills in general so suited to the demands of the situation, that it is difficult to envisage anyone else (certainly no one likely to be called to serve in a Baldwin or Chamberlain peace-time Cabinet) performing them with equal success. The fact that he had to carry out this task in the face of constant criticism and to lay down his post in equivocal circumstances has had much to do with the subsequent failure to accord him proper recognition for the immense contribution he made as Secretary of State for Air. In recent years, however, the voluminous literature on pre-war rearmament, largely stimulated by the opening of the official records for the period, has done much to restore the balance, and he has been described by one modern writer as 'the architect of the renaissance of the Royal Air Force and the most emphatic [Cabinet] exponent of effective rearmament'.[14]

After barely five months in his new post Cunliffe-Lister underwent his third and final change of name on his creation as the first Viscount Swinton. Since the variety and complexity of the issues with which he was concerned at the Air Ministry make it difficult to keep to the mainly chronological treatment employed up to this point, the subject of this biography will henceforth be referred to as 'Swinton', irrespective of whether the reference is to the period before or after November 1935. That having been said, it would seem appropriate at this stage to examine his acceptance of the peerage which was so profoundly to affect his future political course.

As with several other important steps in Swinton's career, the exact circumstances in which this decision was taken are unclear: neither his memoirs nor his private papers shed any light on the question. It seems unlikely that Baldwin as Prime Minister would have exerted pressure on him to go to the Lords, having only five months before told Londonderry that membership of the Lords was one of the factors in his replacement as Air Minister (although, apparently unabashed by the inconsistency, he told Londonderry's son in March 1936 that he had 'found it more convenient to make Cunliffe-Lister a peer').[15] On Swinton's part, it is to be assumed that the same considerations which tempted him to take a peerage in 1928 still continued to influence him: his impatience with the time-consuming pressures of the House of Commons, his lack of enthusiasm for the electoral hustings, his 'executive' attitude to politics. The Air Ministry clearly presented an exceptional field for executive action, and he may well have convinced himself that he would be far more able to take it effectively if he were free from the distractions that membership of the Commons inevitably involved. In 1928, however, he had contemplated leaving ministerial office altogether. That was no longer his intention. But a realistic appraisal of his political future—in which the crucial element seems to have been the advice of his Yorkshire friend and neighbour, Tommy Dugdale, his highly efficient parliamentary private secretary since 1931[16] —may have led him to the conclusion that he could no longer entertain any hopes of the highest offices, whose holders had perforce to be in the Commons. If that were the case, he may have reasoned, no damage would be done by transferring to the House of Lords. He was wrong, and the decision proved singularly unwise. Far from easing his task at the Air Ministry, his exclusion from the Commons as political controversy over rearmament, and air rearmament in particular, intensified, made it significantly more difficult and was in the end to be a major factor in his enforced departure from office. Although he was later to resume his ministerial career, it was never at the level to which his ability and experience had at one time seemed likely to take him. But a personal factor, quite un-connected with expectations of office, could also have oper-ated in his mind. It did occasionally irk him that it was his wife, not he, who was the owner of Swinton and its estates: a peerage, especially one bearing the name of Swinton, went some way towards redressing the balance and consorted well with residence in property of such proportions. Mollie Cunliffe-Lister herself probably favoured his acceptance of the peerage. The ending of the connection with a busy London constitu-ency must have come as a relief to both of them.

The actual timing of the peerage was clearly determined by the approaching general election. It was on 23 October 1935— the very day Baldwin announced the election for 14 November —that Swinton saw Sir Reginald Blair, the chairman of the Hendon Conservative constituency association, to tell him of the forthcoming peerage and his consequent decision not to seek re-election.[17] The peerage was announced on 20 Novem-ber, a few days after the election had confirmed the Govern-ment in office. On 3 December he assumed the titles of Viscount Swinton of Masham and Baron Masham of Ellington.

It would not be appropriate, even if space were available, to recount in detail the story of the expansion of the Royal Air Force during Swinton's period at the Air Ministry from 1935 to 1938. The aim here is to attempt to disentangle what is specific to Swinton's performance of his role, to give some impression of his personal impact on matters in which so many individuals and bodies were critically involved—Prime Minister,

Cabinet, committees of Cabinet and the Committee of Imperial Defence, Air Ministry service and civilian staff and advisers, the aircraft industry and its designers, scientists, and many more. Swinton later succinctly summarized the general division of responsibility between the Air Ministry and the Government as a whole:

> In deciding on a programme for the R.A.F., men and material, there are two dominating factors. First, the size, and second, the character. By size I mean the number of squadrons, the number of machines in reserve, and the number of men airborne and on the ground. On this, which involves the total expenditure, the decision rests with the Cabinet. As regards the character of the Air Force, that is to say with what machines it should be equipped, and the training of the Force, within the limits of expenditure laid down by the Cabinet, the decision rests with the Air Council presided over by the Secretary of State for Air.[18]

On the internal Air Ministry responsibility for aircraft procurement, his memoirs are equally succinct: 'In the Air Ministry recommendations as to types of aircraft and armament are based on the combined views of the Operational Staff under the Chief of the Air Staff and the Technical Staff under the Air Member for Research and Development. Operations decide what are the kind of aircraft and armament they want; the Technical Staff have to advise how these can be developed and obtained.'[19] It is safe to say, however, that no step of major importance could have been taken without Swinton's involvement and encouragement; while in matters relating to the aircraft industry and the 'shadow' industry called into existence to supplement it, he played, with Weir's invaluable assistance, an executive role unusual in a minister (provoking Neville Chamberlain, as Chancellor, on one occasion to criticize to Treasury officials Swinton's 'insistence on being "his own Managing Director" '[20]). And in so far as any decision required Cabinet approval the department could hardly have had a more forceful advocate in Cabinet and Cabinet committee: certainly in the years immediately before the outbreak of war no other service department had a minister to match him.

Writing some thirty years later Swinton paid tribute to the support he had for his work at the Air Ministry from Baldwin as Prime Minister (in contrast with his successor, Chamberlain).[21] But Baldwin's powers were failing and his interest in the technical detail in which air questions abounded could not have been great: it is likely that his chief value to Swinton was as a friendly, and still influential, presence in the background. With Chamberlain as Chancellor Swinton's official relations had necessarily to be far more continuous and direct, and initially their long-standing personal and political friendship and Chamberlain's early commitment to rearmament in the air undoubtedly eased many matters on which Treasury co-operation was vital. The relationship perceptibly changed when Chamberlain became Prime Minister. But well before the change at the head of the Government a third co-ordinating minister—and one with direct responsibilities in the defence field—had been added to the Prime Minister and Chancellor as a principal colleague with whom Swinton had continuously to deal. This was the Minister for the Co-ordination of Defence, whose appointment was announced by Baldwin on 27 February 1936, following a concerted attack in the press and Parliament on the system of higher organization for defence (which had been largely fashioned by Hankey and which he fiercely defended within the Government).[22] The new minister was to be without portfolio but relieve the Prime Minister of some of his burdens by acting as deputy chairman of the Committee of Imperial Defence and preside over the Chiefs of Staff Committee. Swinton accepted that a change was necessary, arguing, however, in a letter for the Prime Minister which was circulated to the Cabinet well before it took the decision, that the minister's function 'should not be to dictate policy, but to ensure that every aspect is fully considered, and that difficulties and differences are frankly faced'. Swinton's was in fact the first name Baldwin considered to fill the new post, but the difficulty of his being in the Lords, his obvious value at the Air Ministry, and Swinton's own reluctance to exchange an executive department for a co-ordinating role made Baldwin turn to others. The choice finally, and unexpectedly, fell on the Attorney-General, Sir Thomas Inskip, and his appointment was announced on 13 March.[23] Although the autonomy of the service departments was not formally affected, Inskip's arrival created a new situation in Whitehall. His powers and his staff might be limited, but his presence at Whitehall Gardens, his close association with Hankey and the Cabinet secretariat, the fact that he deputized as necessary for the Prime Minister in the CID and its subcommittee system, his position at the Prime Minister's right hand (to the exclusion of the service ministers) when parliamentary delegations led by Austen Chamberlain, Churchill, and Salisbury came to make representations on rearmament in July and November 1936—all this inevitably affected the conduct of business and individual responsibilities within the Cabinet: Swinton and the other service ministers were no longer, so to speak, in the front line. Inskip could be enlisted as an ally in inter-departmental and internal Cabinet disputes, but he could also be an obstacle to the ambitions of departments, and Swinton was to have experience of him in both capacities.

The Cabinet of which Swinton was a member was composed of reluctant rearmers. They came to the necessity of rebuilding Britain's military strength belatedly and with the gravest misgivings. It seemed to them inconceivable that any power could risk precipitating a repetition of the holocaust of 1914-18. This did no discredit to their humane feelings even if, with all the advantages conferred by hindsight, we may deplore what we see as their lack of realism. The policy implication of this attitude was that rearmament must be for defence, and in so far as some of the weaponry involved—above all, long-range bomber aircraft—was obviously offensive in character, its purpose was to deter a would-be aggressor against Britain, not to engage in pre-emptive action. From 1933 or 1934 that would-be aggressor was seen as Germany, whose containment would absorb most of Britain's rearmament efforts, leaving little for other defensive needs, for example, against Japanese aggression in the Far East. The identification of Germany as the prime potential aggressor had a profound effect on the shape of Britain's rearmed forces. The Air Staff's firmly held but un-proven thesis about the decisive nature of a strategic bomber offensive, unacceptable though it was to the two older services, seemed to possess for reluctant political rearmers the merit of avoiding the possibility of any major commitment of land forces to the European continent. If there had to be rearma-ment, air force expansion seemed, in fact, to be the least dis-agreeable, and least expensive, way of achieving it. Moreover, the Government's commitment to air parity with Germany, although an increasing source of embarrassment, did at least provide a quantifiable (if ever-moving) target at which to aim and by which to measure achievement or—as Churchill was never tired of pointing out—failure to achieve. It was factors such as these that ensured that expenditure on the air force, which amounted to £17,607,893 (17 per cent of total defence expenditure) in 1934-5, rose to £143,499,642 (36 per cent of total defence expenditure) in 1938-9.[24]

This unexpected largesse was received by the Air Staff with mixed feelings. The mid-1930s were witnessing radical changes in the design of aircraft, engines, and equipment, such as light alloy stressed-skin construction for wood construction, monoplanes for biplanes, retractable undercarriages, variable-pitch propellers, and power-operated gun-turrets. However much corners were cut in the design, testing, and production processes it still took years for new types of aircraft to be ready for squadron service. In the rush for numbers stimulated by the politicians' desire to achieve parity with supposed German air strength, the Air Staff was anxious to make no sacrifice in quality and to avoid the easy option of stocking the RAF with the aircraft which could be most easily and speedily produced, namely existing types which by definition were either obsolete or obsolescent. It was this reluctance which caused the Air Ministry response to the March 1935 announcement of the creation of the *Luftwaffe* to be considered less than adequate to meet the needs of the situation, and led to the establishment of the Air Parity subcommittee. The subcommittee's deliberations were, indeed, viewed with the deepest suspicion inside the Air Ministry as occasioned by panic and likely to lead to impracticable programmes.[25] As Air Minister Swinton had constantly to balance the professionals' desire for quality in aircraft with his ministerial colleagues' demands for quantity.

The Air Ministry which Swinton took over in 1935 was still a young department, having been formed only in 1918. After early years of struggle against the animus of the older service departments, it was now firmly established in the Whitehall firmament, largely as a result of the formidable combination, for most of the 1920s, of Samuel Hoare as Minister and Trenchard as Chief of the Air Staff.[26] Like the other service departments it had a formal controlling body, the Air Council, which, under the presidency of the Secretary of State, united the service and civilian sides of the department. In June 1935 the four Air Members were Sir Edward Ellington, Chief of the Air Staff, Sir Frederick Bowhill, Air Member for Personnel, Sir Hugh Dowding, Air Member for Research and Development, and Sir Cyril Newall, Air Member for Supply and Organization. With the almost painfully shy and inarticulate Ellington, who owed his appointment in 1933 to the sudden death of Sir Geoffrey Salmond, Swinton's relations were never close, nor were they with the somewhat prickly Dowding. But he had a high regard for Newall, whom he first met in January 1934 when on his East African tour as Colonial Secretary. It was Newall, not the sorely disappointed Dowding (who was never really in the running), whom he selected to succeed Ellington as Chief of the Air Staff in September 1937. He got on excellently, too, with Bowhill and Sir Wilfred Freeman, who suceeded Dowding as Air Member for Research and Development in March 1936: his memoirs record warm tributes to both men.[27]

For the first two years Swinton's junior ministerial colleague as parliamentary under-secretary was Sir Philip Sassoon, who had been in the post—apart from the period of the Labour Government 1929-31—since 1924. Despite this long experience of the department and his enhanced parliamentary role through the Secretary of State from 1931 to 1935 being in the House of Lords, Sassoon does not appear to have had much influence on policy. His role was almost exclusively as parliamentary spokesman, particularly in the presentation of the air estimates each March (his speeches being carefully composed and delivered without notes). In May 1937 he at last achieved full ministerial rank as First Commissioner of Works and was succeeded at the Air Ministry by A. J. Muirhead, who, like Sassoon, was very much the traditional junior minister, apparently seldom contributing to departmental policy discussions.

The permanent head of the Air Ministry in 1935—its secretary (the title was not changed to the more usual form of permanent under-secretary of state until March 1938)—was Sir Christopher Bullock. He had been appointed to the top post in January 1931, when still only thirty-nine, but even before that, as principal private secretary to a succession of secretaries of state from 1923, he exercised influence almost indistinguishable from that of a permanent secretary.[28] There was no question of his ability or of his passionate commitment to what he saw as the interests of the Royal Air Force and the Air Ministry, but these characteristics were combined with a degree of arrogance which made him many enemies in Whitehall, not least the formidable Warren Fisher, head of the Treasury and the civil service. And it was not a quality which would appeal to Swinton, who in his previous departments had acted in some ways as his own permanent secretary and enjoyed getting to know more junior staff: he was certainly not prepared to tolerate the direct approach to Baldwin which Bullock had been in the habit of making under Londonderry's regime. The combination was not, in any case, to last long. A year after Swinton became Air Minister Bullock was dismissed from the civil service in what, in a Whitehall context, can only be described as sensational circumstances. Although he would not normally have retired on age grounds until 1951, he saw no prospect of further advance and was contemplating the possibility of making a career in business or commerce. On various occasions between 1934 and 1936 he raised with Sir Eric Geddes, chairman of Imperial Airways, or Woods Humphery, the managing director, his possible appointment to the board of Imperial Airways as one of the two government directors, with a view to his succeeding Geddes as chairman at some future date. At the same time he was involved in negotiations with Imperial Airways over a contract for the Empire Air Mail Scheme. The fact that he had been making approaches was reported to ministers in June 1936, and on 3 July Baldwin, almost certainly acting on the advice of Fisher, set up a board of inquiry consisting of three senior serving civil servants, and in the meantime suspended Bullock from his duties. The board's report, submitted some three week later, concluded that Bullock's conduct had been 'completely at variance with the tenor and spirit of the code which precludes a member of the Civil Service from interlacing public negotiations entrusted to him with the advancement of his personal or private interests'. Baldwin, after consulting Chamberlain and Swinton (and undoubtedly Fisher as well), accepted the board's findings and on 28 July directed that Bullock be dismissed, at the same time observing that 'grave as was the offence from the service point of view, no question of corruption was involved'.

There is little direct evidence about Swinton's role in this extraordinary affair, and he makes no reference to it in his published memoirs. He testified at the board of inquiry to the fact that Bullock had obtained the best possible terms in the air-mail contract and had at no time been affected by personal considerations. He was, of course, Bullock's departmental superior, but the alleged offence was so serious as inevitably to involve the ministers with responsibilities for the civil service as a whole, the Chancellor of the Exchequer and the Prime Minister. Swinton's approval for the course of action would have been sought, but it would not necessarily have been decisive. Bullock always maintained that relevant evidence in his support had been withheld from the inquiry and from Baldwin. Whether any additional evidence could have made it possible for him to retain his post as permanent head of the Air Ministry is highly doubtful. But the punishment meted out to him seemed inordinately severe: to have allowed him to resign quietly, without the loss of pension rights he incurred through his summary dismissal, might have been more appropriate. It looks as if someone in Whitehall—and Fisher seems the only candidate—wanted exemplary treatment for Bullock.[29]

Although he must have regretted the manner of it, Swinton may well not have found Bullock's departure inconvenient. So combative and controversial an official did not make for easy relations with other departments and, above all, the Treasury. Swinton was no doubt concerned in the selection of his successor, Sir Donald Banks, director-general of the Post Office, who had been deeply involved in the formulation of the Empire Air Mail Scheme. Banks's appointment was announced a few days after the publication of the Bullock inquiry report. It did not prove a success. He knew little or nothing about the air force and lacked the experience required for the administration of a large and complex department, embarked upon a major expansion of an armed service. Much of the financial administration of RAF expansion fell on the broad shoulders of A. H. Self, promoted deputy under-secretary in 1937. Towards the end of his time at the Air Ministry Swinton, perhaps recognizing the mistake over Banks's appointment, managed to secure the transfer of Arthur Street from the Ministry of Agriculture and Fisheries to the Air Ministry as first deputy under-secretary (and eventual successor to Banks in 1939). Although, like Banks, unfamiliar with the department, Street had already shown himself to be an outstanding civil servant, and this time Swinton's choice was triumphantly vindicated.[30] And his choice of the other official of vital importance to a minister, his principal private secretary, was also eventually a most happy one, F. H. Sandford, previously No. 2 in the private office, being promoted to the senior post at the beginning of 1937, in spite of his relatively junior status in the department. He was later, at Swinton's request, to go to West Africa as his chief civil service aide. In his memoirs Swinton bracketed Sandford with William Brown, his private secretary at the Board of Trade, as 'men of outstanding ability to whom I owe more than I can say'.[31]

The immediate task confronting Swinton and his department in June 1935 was the development and production of the aircraft and other equipment required to enable the air force to be expanded in accordance with the programme (Scheme C) that had emerged from his own parity subcommittee, calling for 3,800 aircraft of various kinds by April 1937. On 22 July he introduced a supplementary air estimate to cover the necessary expenditure (the only air estimates he presented in the Commons), and made it clear that, in approving it, Parliament was committing itself to a four-year programme. As foreshadowed by the Swinton subcommittee certain types of bomber were ordered at an unprecedentedly early stage in their development. The phrase often used in this context (by Swinton, among others) was 'ordering off the drawing board', but of course this was not literally the case. Two of the new heavy bombers—the Armstrong-Whitworth Whitley and the Handley Page Harrow—were both based on experimental bomber-transports of similar design which had already been built and tested by the time the new versions were ordered for the RAF in August 1935. A private-venture prototype of the Vickers Wellesley bomber, employing Barnes Wallis's revolutionary geodetic design, had flown a few months before the order was placed in September 1935, while the

Bristol Blenheim medium bomber was a military adaptation of a civil aircraft specially built by Lord Rothermere and presented by him to the Air Ministry and tested by the RAF before the order of August 1935.[32] The nearest approach to an order literally on the basis of plans only was that placed at the end of 1935 for the Fairey Battle medium bomber, the prototype of which did not fly until March 1936. But this was an unhappy precedent, for it was clear almost from the outset that it lacked both the speed and defensive fire-power demanded by modern air warfare; large-scale orders were nevertheless placed, but only because it was available for quantity production at a time when numbers were being demanded for deployment and training.[33] Of the fighters, the Gloster Gladiator ordered in July and September 1935 had the benefit of a private-venture prototype which had first flown in September 1934. But the new types by themselves would have been nowhere near adequate to achieve the numbers required under Scheme C, and thus older, often virtually obsolete, types had to be ordered because they were already in production: the Handley Page Heyford and Fairey Hendon bombers, the Hawker Hart and Hind light bombers, and the Gloster Gauntlet fighter among them.

The Air Parity subcommittee had considered that the programme it recommended, although far beyond anything the aircraft industry had experienced since the war, was, in general, within the industry's existing capacity, but had emphasized the need for the closest contact between the Government and top management of the industry to ensure timely deliveries. Once he became Air Minister, Swinton immediately set about developing relations with the industry. In this, as in all aspects of the expansion programme, he had the indispensable expert help of Lord Weir, who had started his unofficial and unpaid work as industrial adviser to the Air Ministry some two weeks before Swinton took over (although in the full knowledge that he was to do so). On 10 June he wrote to Swinton to 'confirm that my functions are advisory in character, and that I do not propose to undertake any executive duties. I will have no room at the Air Ministry, and no staff . . . I desire no official authority beyond the public announcement already made, but it is essential that I should have copies of, or access to, all relevant important papers.' On such slender formal foundations was built a partnership without which, as Swinton later told Weir, 'I could not have tackled the job'.[34]

The system of weapon procurement of the RAF and the Fleet Air Arm was radically different from that in either of the other two services. Since the closure of the RAF factory at Farnborough at the end of the First World War the Air Ministry, although it had staff for formulating operational and technical requirements and directly controlled experimental aircraft and armament testing establishments, had nothing comparable with the navy's corps of naval constructors and naval dockyards or the army's ordnance factories. It relied on the private aviation industry, which by 1935 comprised about two dozen firms making airframes and about half a dozen aero-engine firms. Fifteen of the airframe firms and four or five of the engine firms, with a total labour force of some 27,000, were included in the so-called 'family' of firms, all members of the Society of British Aircraft Constructors, with which the Air Ministry placed the bulk of its contracts—thus ensuring their survival at a time when the steep fall in demand for military aircraft after the war had threatened the whole existence of the industry. In the last resort these firms, although in private hands, depended upon Air Ministry orders since demand for civil aircraft was virtually limited to passenger aircraft for Imperial Airways and light aircraft for flying schools, clubs, and individuals. And until Scheme C and its successors, military aircraft orders, largely for the RAF's imperial policing role, were small-scale and bore little relation to the types that would be required in a European war. Some of the firms were linked with the great armaments group of Vickers Armstrong; one, Rolls-Royce, belonged also to the motor-car industry; but most were still headed by the strong personalities who had founded them—the White family at the Bristol Aeroplane Company, Fairey, Handley Page, De Havilland, and Sopwith and Sigrist of Hawker. Fortunately, too, the industry had designers of genius, such as Fedden of Bristol, Mitchell of Supermarine, Camm of Hawker, Hives of Rolls-Royce, and Wallis of Vickers. Outside the 'family' there were 'fringe' firms to which subcontracts were let, and there were a number of firms such as General Aircraft, Alvis, and Wolseley, which were anxious to become direct suppliers of airframes or engines.

From the first Swinton and Weir were determined that, for the purpose of expansion, the Air Ministry would work mainly through the approved firms, leaving them to subcontract as necessary. It was not, of course, just a matter of placing contracts and leaving the firms with the job of producing the aircraft: the closest supervision by the Air Ministry was required in the attempt—never wholly successful—to ensure that production was up to schedule. Swinton's instrument for reviewing the whole expansion programme was the series of weekly progress meetings of the Air Council (which hitherto had met as a body only infrequently), with Weir usually present and a leading contributor to discussions. The first was held on 25 June 1935 and they continued without interruption throughout Swinton's tenure of the Air Ministry.[35] By this means, he told Churchill in August 1935, the 'whole programme, machines, engines, industry, stations, recruiting, etc. are under constant review . . . We get rapid action and avoid the curse of watertight compartmenting . . . We are I hope improving all the time. But the organization, the plan, the industrial structure are right and the machine at full pressure.'[36] Nevertheless, a constant refrain of the meetings was the difficulty of keeping firms up to scratch with deliveries. On 17 September 1935, for example, Newall, the Air Member for Supply and Organization, complained that he could not rely on any production dates given by firms which, despite production delays, seemed to prefer to 'let down the Air Ministry than sub-contract to rivals'. If they failed over deliveries by such action, Swinton observed, the industry might well have to face a universal demand for direct governmental control of production. At the meeting on 8 October it was decided to send a strongly worded letter to all firms with orders for airframes or engines to fulfil under the expansion programme, emphasizing the importance of adherence to the production schedule and the need for the most careful weekly forecasts of production 'in order that any failure to keep to promised deliveries may be brought to light and investigated immediately'. At the same time Swinton wrote to six of the leading men in the industry—Fairey, Sopwith, Siddeley, McLean,

H. J. Thomas, and Handley Page—to say that the policy of relying on the approved firms as opposed to 'bringing in new units' had been decided on 'after discussion with Lord Weir' and both he and Weir were convinced that it was 'sound and wise'. But it required the full co-operation of the favoured firms and each was requested to supply a written undertaking 'confirming your realization of your responsibilities and your ability to fulfil them'. The industry leaders were invited to arrange interviews with Swinton and Weir, and considerable time was devoted in succeeding weeks to dealing with the response to this invitation.[37]

Meanwhile Scheme C was being overtaken by developments in government defence planning, in part stimulated by the imbalance that RAF expansion was causing in the defence budget as a whole, in part by the deepening external threat posed by Germany, to which was now added, with the Abyssinian crisis, the new and wholly unexpected threat from Italy. Hankey's official Defence Requirements Committee of 1933–4 was reconvened and instructed to draw up a programme (later to be known as the 'Ideal Scheme') to bring Britain's armed forces to war readiness by 1939, on the assumption that there were no financial limitations. The resultant plan was presented on 21 November 1935, just a week after the election. In its provision for the RAF the 'Ideal Scheme' was on more modest lines than for the other two services since the air force had already benefited disproportionately by the adoption of Scheme C only six months before. Nevertheless the Hankey committee urged a substantial building-up of reserves for the first-line aircraft strength, amounting to 150 per cent war reserves by 1 April 1939, together with 75 per cent initial and maintenance reserves. These 225 per cent reserves would, the committee thought, maintain the Scheme C force in full operation during the first four months of a war with Germany and thus give time for increased factory output to keep pace with war wastage. The committee also recommended the creation of a larger reserve of trained pilots, the formation of thirteen extra squadrons for overseas duties, and an expansion in both army co-operation units and the Fleet Air Arm.[38]

When the Defence Policy and Requirements Committee (as the Ministerial Committee on Disarmament was now more appropriately named) came to consider the Ideal Scheme in relation to the RAF it attached, under Swinton's guidance, greater importance than had the Hankey committee to increasing the deterrent capability of the air striking force. The Air Ministry was directed to review the 'existing programme of squadrons to be formed and stationed at home in order to see how best we can improve the offensive power of this force and constitute the most effective deterrent to German aggression'.[39] The method by which the Air Ministry proposed to do this was outlined by Swinton in a Cabinet paper in February 1936 and it was, essentially, the replacement of the thirty squadrons of obsolete light bombers (Hawker Harts and Hinds, and Fairey Gordons) by squadrons—over half of them with eighteen rather than the usual twelve aircraft—of the new medium bombers (Handley Page Hampdens, Bristol Blenheims, and Fairey Battles). The total first-line strength of medium bombers would thus be raised from twenty squadrons with 240 aircraft to fifty squadrons with 782 aircraft. There was to be no increase in fighter strength, and thus the numerical preponderance of bombers over fighters (1,022 to 420) was increased compared with Scheme C. But Swinton drew his colleagues' attention to encouraging developments with the two new fighters soon to be known as the Hawker Hurricane and the Supermarine Spitfire; the Air Council progress-meeting held four days before Swinton circulated his paper had in fact agreed to Ellington's recommendation that 600 Hurricanes and 310 Spitfires should be ordered (and the firm orders were placed in June 1936).[40] Taken with an increase in army co-operation aircraft (from 90 to 132), the overall effect of these proposals would be to equip the metropolitan air force with 1,736 first-line aircraft in 124 squadrons by April 1939 instead of 1,512 in 123 squadrons by April 1937 under Scheme C. At the same time there would be increases in overseas squadrons and the Fleet Air Arm (more than doubled from 213 aircraft to 504).[41]

Scheme F, as it was dubbed (the letters D and E had been used for other schemes examined by the Air Ministry and not proceeded with), raised metropolitan first-line air strength by only 224 aircraft compared with Scheme C and over a period two years longer. But the types of aircraft that could now be ordered in quantity were qualitatively far ahead of those available under earlier schemes. And—of no less importance—there was now to be provision, as recommended in the Ideal Scheme, for adequate reserves (two and a quarter times the number of first-line aircraft), at a cost increased from £1.2m. to £50m. In terms of numbers of aircraft the new reserves policy meant more than doubling the figure of first-line and reserves under Scheme C (3,800), to over 8,000 aircraft. Moreover, a larger reserve of trained and part-trained pilots and ground-crews was to be built up. Scheme F—the only one of the several pre-war expansions which was actually completed—was, it has been said, 'a genuine "non-window-dressing" programme, a programme designed for operational rather than political purposes'.[42]

Scheme F formed part of a report from the ministerial Defence Policy and Requirements Committee, and, as such, was approved by the Cabinet on 25 February 1936 and announced in the Commons by Baldwin on 9 March—two days after the German reoccupation of the Rhineland had served renewed notice of the looming dangers in Europe.[43] But well in advance of this approval Swinton and his Air Ministry colleagues had turned their minds to the new programme's implications for industrial production, a subject which formed a principal theme of the discussions at the expansion progress meetings from early January 1936 onwards. Whereas the completion of Scheme C may have been considered to be within the capacity of the existing aircraft industry, there was no question that the demands of Scheme F far exceeded it, in particular the large-scale production of new types required. The possibility of increasing the capacity of the professional industry was examined but rejected as inadequate by itself to provide the necessary production. It was clear that the so-called 'shadow factory' system, originally designed to be kept on a care and maintenance basis until the actual outbreak of war, would have to be brought into operation as soon as possible to help cope with the needs of RAF expansion. (It was clear, too, that the Air Ministry needed to strengthen its staff which monitored production progress in both aircraft and shadow industries, and in March 1936 a new department of aeronautical production was established under H. A. P. Disney).

The idea of supplementing the production of the armament industries on the outbreak of war by the output of factories already established, at government expense, by other technically related large-scale industries such as the motor-car industry, had been adumbrated as early as 1927, and a paper on the subject by Lord Weir was approved in principle by the Committee of Imperial Defence at the end of May 1934.[44] As formulated in the Defence Policy and Requirements Committee's report on the Ideal Scheme in February 1936, the proposed method was to 'build up in peace-time reserves sufficient for a limited period after the outbreak of war, and simultaneously plan and arrange our industrial capacity in peace-time so that in the interval assured by the reserves it is able to turn over to full war production'. The build-up was, however, to be achieved—and this was the key passage—'without interference with or reduction of production for civil and export trade'. It was recognized that 'From the production point of view this greatly complicates the matter, but any such interference would adversely affect the general prosperity of the country and so reduce our capacity to find the necessary funds for Service programmes.'[45] A system of 'shadow' armament factories, side by side with industries still engaged in peace-time production, was admirably fitted to meet the objective of no interference with normal industry and trade.

The obvious candidate to provide shadow aircraft factories was the motor vehicle industry, since, unlike the aircraft industry, it was expanding rapidly and several firms within it were leaders in large-scale production. Moreover, by 1935 the conversion of the industry to metal-fabricated bodies and structures had been completed.[46] Of the two largest motor firms, Austin, under Sir Herbert Austin, was soon to become the leading participant in the shadow manufacture of both airframes and aero-engines. But with Lord Nuffield, head of the largest motor manufacturer of all, Morris (with Wolseley), Swinton had a clash early in his tenure of the Air Ministry which, while it may not have been decisive in persuading Nuffield to have nothing to do with the Air Ministry shadow scheme, made neither man anxious to do business with the other.

Swinton's clash with Nuffield has been documented elsewhere and need not detain us long here.[47] It began before the
inception of the shadow factory scheme, with a letter from
Nuffield to Swinton on 25 July 1935 requesting an interview
with the new Air Minister on 31 July to discuss future prospects of Air Ministry orders for Wolseley aero-engines. Not
unreasonably Swinton found the date Nuffield had chosen to
be inconvenient—it was a day on which he had the Cabinet,
two Cabinet committees, two deputations, and a public dinner,
as well as parliamentary duties. But his letter to Nuffield explaining his inability to see him on the date suggested omitted
to propose an alternative date: an omission which might have
appeared as a snub even to someone less prickly than Nuffield.
It was true that Weir and the Air Ministry experts saw no
reason why Wolseley—producing engines for civil purposes too
low-powered to be of any use in military aircraft other than
trainers—should be admitted to the select family of approved
Air Ministry aero-engine firms. It was, however, unfortunate
that Swinton's response should have been so curt. When a
meeting with Nuffield eventually took place, at Swinton's
invitation, on 27 November 1935 (just after the election), it
did little to improve the situation. As Swinton reported to the
next expansion progress meeting, 'Lord Nuffield had been in
a very bad mood and the whole interview had been thoroughly
unsatisfactory.[48] There matters were left until the negotiations
with motor firms on the shadow factory scheme early in 1936.

Having taken the decision to activate the shadow industry,
Swinton's expansion progress meeting went on to formulate
the objectives which the new capacity, when available, was to
achieve. The initial tasks were seen as supplementing the aero-
engine output of the Bristol Aeroplane Company by 4,000 engines, and, on the airframe side, providing for the production of
900 Fairey Battle bombers and 600 Bristol Blenheim bombers.
For the airframes it was considered that only two firms were
necessary, and Austin (for the Battles) and Rootes (for the
Blenheims) were selected, Austin later building a shadow factory alongside its works at Longbridge and Rootes one at
Speke, near Liverpool.[49] For the production of aero-engines
more firms would be required. Swinton began a series of interviews with leaders of the motor industry by seeing Sir Herbert

Austin on 28 February. But there was also the 'family' or professional industry to mollify. On 13 March Swinton and Weir saw Sir Stanley White of Bristol, the aircraft firm most conspicuously affected by the shadow scheme.

With the Germans having reoccupied the Rhineland only a few days before, Swinton told White that the shadow factory programme was the only practical way to meet 'the very difficult and dangerous' defence situation. There was very little time to reach the very large output required. The professional industry must work at maximum capacity and the shadow industry had to be brought into being 'to supplement the deficiencies under the present emergency' and 'to learn and be prepared for output in time of war'. He wished Bristol to appreciate that 'he was not asking them to undertake a commercial proposition but a piece of national service'. White's response was co-operative but the method he proposed for integrating the shadow industry with his firm showed clearly that he had no intention of allowing any of the shadow firms to acquire the expertise which might enable them to set up in competition with Bristol. His firm's experience both during the war and since had, he told Swinton, 'pointed unmistakably to the advantage of dividing the engine among the firms required to produce it'. Time would be saved since Bristol would not have to teach each firm how to make the whole engine; the disturbance to the peace-time activities of the shadow firms would be minimized; and the possibilities of production in war would be much greater. Both Swinton and Weir expressed doubts about this—the former about possible wartime production delays if one of the firms happened to be bombed, Weir about the time it would take to set up such a complicated scheme—but agreed to raise it with the prospective shadow aero-engine firms.[50]

Swinton wrote on 24 March to seven motor firms—Austin, Daimler, Humber (controlled by Rootes), Singer, Standard, and Wolseley—and on 7 April chaired a meeting with their representatives at the Air Ministry. At the meeting he emphasized the urgency of the defence situation and described the Government's plans for activating the shadow aero-engine industry. It would provide the capital for building the new factories and would own them on completion. The firms themselves would supervise their building close to their existing works, manage them, and recruit and train the labour force needed to operate them. They would be paid a fee based upon output and efficiency. Swinton then outlined Bristol's proposal for a division of the work between several factories, with centralized assembling of the complete engines. After some discussion he asked the representatives to go away and consider their response. The firms subsequently set up a committee under Austin, and this came down firmly in favour of the Bristol scheme, with each unit manufacturing part of the engine; it laid particular stress on the difficulty and delay which would be involved in the supply of jigs, gauges, tools, and other equipment if each firm required all the sets necessary for a complete engine. Swinton's own preferred choice, and the expansion progress meeting had agreed with him, had been for the seven firms to form themselves into two groups, with each group producing a complete engine, and he had conveyed this suggestion to Austin. But he resisted any move to reject the firms' view, strongly though Ellington at the progress meeting on 12 May argued the high risk of breakdown with seven firms concerned in one engine and the lack of educative value for future war production. Swinton felt 'it was a very great achievement to have got the firms to play as a team at all, and he thought we ought to let them start, at any rate, with the scheme they preferred'.[51]

The seven units were soon reduced to five, with the dropping of the small Singer firm, apparently on the verge of bankruptcy, in August, and the withdrawal of Wolseley, and the closing down of its aero-engine division, in September. During Nuffield's absence abroad his representative at the shadow firms' discussions had been Leonard Lord, who resigned as managing director of Wolseley in August (and later joined Austin to take charge of its shadow work). When Nuffield returned it was clear that he disliked the scheme, understandably wanting his aero-engine works to produce complete engines and in fact offering to make 2,000 engines, or half the required number. As the Air Ministry had already approved the scheme of dispersed production the offer was refused, but in any case Bristol would not have co-operated with a rival aero-engine firm. Efforts to retain Wolseley in the scheme proved fruitless and at a press conference on 22 October Nuffield relieved himself of his anger at the way he considered he had been treated by the Air Ministry, its deliberate neglect of the production facilities he could provide, and the unworkability of the shadow scheme it had devised. The Government's response to this attack was to issue a White Paper, drafted in the Air Ministry under Swinton's direction, setting out the shadow scheme and reproducing some of the relevant correspondence with Nuffield and Wolseley officials; but the Air Ministry, and Swinton himself, could not escape some parliamentary criticism. In the debate in the House of Lords on 29 October Swinton expressed his sincere regret if Lord Nuffield felt he had been treated with lack of consideration. He was reasonably satisfied with the course of the debate, in which the only real criticism of Swinton's conduct which the Labour peer Lord Strabolgi (the former J. M. Kenworthy, MP) found it possible to make was his failure to grant Nuffield, as a member of Parliament, an interview when he had asked for it in July 1935. Strabolgi recalled that as a Labour MP he 'had many dealings with the noble Viscount when he was President of the Board of Trade and when I [was] . . . representing a shipping constituency and had to worry him a good deal. He was most courteous. Therefore I was surprised on this occasion at the sending of what I think he will admit was a rather unfortunate letter.' The personal aspect of the matter was also taken up in a leader in *The Times* the following morning: 'There is little reason to doubt [the leader declared] that the personal issue arose from a clash of temperaments which might never have reached the stage of public revelation if there had been a little less impetuosity on one side and a little more tact on the other.' Swinton did what he could to repair the personal breach, seeing Nuffield immediately after the debate and reporting the result in a hurried note to Baldwin, anxious about this public row with Britain's most prominent industrialist. 'It all went very well,' he told Baldwin, 'the House friendly and increasingly so. I had tea with Nuffield afterwards. He told me I did not know how to play the 10th. hole at [the name of the golf-course is indecipherable], and how well he danced a real Viennese Valse. Both statements are quite true. I am not sure that he does not think that I am nearly as great a gentleman as Tom [Inskip]. Anyhow Tom and I are off on the night train to shoot high pheasants in Scotland; and you need not worry.'[52]

Whatever part Swinton's brusqueness may have played in Nuffield's attitude to the Bristol aero-engine shadow factory scheme, the fact is that there was no way in which Nuffield's ambition to produce complete engines could have been accommodated. It was Bristol's attitude that was the decisive factor: it wanted production to be dispersed (as, indeed, did the participating motor firms) and on no account would it have made its plans available to a firm manufacturing complete engines. Nevertheless, justly or unjustly, the reputation of having prevented the Government from taking full advantage of Nuffield's services stuck to Swinton; and it was significant that just three days after he had succeeded him as Air Minister Kingsley Wood saw Nuffield and arranged for him to build the largest of all the shadow factories at Castle Bromwich to produce, not aero-engines, but Spitfire airframes.[53]

In the early summer of 1936 another conflict had arisen in the negotiations over the shadow factory scheme which did not erupt, like the Nuffield affair, in public view. The two motor firms involved in airframe production (Austin and Rootes), and the five in the aero-engine scheme, had agreed to undertake the work subject to negotiation of the appropriate management fee with the Government. Each firm was expected to negotiate separately, but the first to do so—Austin, in respect of the 900 Battle airframes contract—was thought likely to set the pattern for the others, whether managing airframe or aero-engine 'shadows'. But the negotiations with Sir Herbert Austin went anything but smoothly. The Air Ministry, which kept in close touch with the Treasury, offered a yearly management fee, a fixed payment for each airframe, and a percentage bonus on whatever savings were made in costs as production became more efficient. The initial offer was for a management fee of £17,500 and a fixed payment of £150 for each of the 900 airframes, making £152,500 in all, apart from bonuses. Austen countered with the suggestion of a fee of £75,000 and £400 for each airframe, making a total (without bonuses) of £435,000, or £282,500 more than the Air Ministry offer. In the course of hard bargaining the difference was whittled down until stalemate was reached at £90,000, Austin asking for £275,000 and the Air Ministry refusing to go beyond £185,000.[54]

This was the stage which had been reached when Swinton raised the matter at an expansion progress meeting on 12 May 1936. Austin had written to him to reject the proposed financial terms and Swinton had asked the Chancellor if he would take a hand in the negotiations. Chamberlain had been averse to this and Swinton had told him that the Treasury must either come right in or stay out altogether. 'For his part (Swinton told the meeting) he was perfectly prepared to assume the whole responsibility for them and, with Lord Weir's help, to drive the best bargain possible with the Austin Company. It would, however, be an impossible position if, while the negotiations were taking place, we had to go backwards and forwards to the Treasury for authority to offer better terms in one respect or another.' The Chancellor had replied, Swinton said, 'that we obviously had to have these airframes and engines, that we must drive the best bargain possible with the shadow industry and that he was perfectly prepared to give us a free hand'. But Swinton had no intention of giving in to extortionate demands, even if the result was the withdrawal of Austin from the scheme and the jeopardizing of Battle production. He 'did not see how the government or the Air Ministry could defend giving the company terms which could not be justified on their merits'. In the long discussion that followed Swinton's opening statement only Weir, who believed that the terms offered were not good enough, failing to take account of the problems confronting shadow firms, expressed any sympathy with Austin's position.[55]

The progress meeting returned to the question on 22 May, after another refusal to agree the terms had been received from Austin. The alternatives discussed ranged from accepting Austin's terms to direct control through nationalization. But Swinton's summing-up now indicated the *via media*. There was no alternative to Austin setting up a shadow factory as this was the only conceivable way in which the number of Battles required, in addition to Fairey's own production, could be obtained under peace-time conditions in the time available. Consequently the Air Ministry must be ready to go to the limit it felt able to justify politically. If Austin was still not prepared to accept, the Cabinet must be asked to meet the Austin board of directors to bring the full force of the Government to bear. As part of the process of enlisting general governmental support a special meeting of the Defence Policy and Requirements Committee was convened on 25 May. It authorized Swinton to go as high as £250,000 to close the deal, but if Austin still proved recalcitrant it was ready to confront the Austin board with 'a body representing the full authority of the Government'.[56] No doubt suitably awed by this display of governmental majesty, Austin settled final terms the following day, but only after the Air Ministry had agreed to split the difference exactly at £230,000, or £45,000 more than its sticking-point; Austin apparently still felt aggrieved but was consoled a few months later by advancement to the peerage. A similar settlement was subsequently made with Rootes for the 600 Blenheim airframes and with Bristol and the five motor firms for the 4,000 Bristol aero-engines. The Treasury disliked the arrangements, but it had delegated responsibility for them to the Air Ministry and perforce had to recognize that if the airframes and engines were to be obtained in this way the firms' price, within limits, had to be paid.[57]

Shadow industry production was not without its difficulties, sometimes resulting from failure of communications between professional firm and shadow (for example, delays in sending plans), sometimes from production delays in the shadow factories. But it undoubtedly made an indispensable contribution to the build-up of air strength immediately before and during the Second World War. While its output of airframes accounted for only 12 per cent of total war output its contribution to the supply of particular types was much larger than this, amounting, for example, to 45 per cent of the total output of heavy bombers and two-thirds of Blenheim bomber output. Shadow factories produced 97,000 of the 250,000 aero-engines, including 67,000 Bristol engines (more than double that of the parent firm). Other shadow factories approved in 1937 supplemented the production of propellers, guns, carburettors, and bombs.[58] There is no doubt either that Swinton made a significant personal contribution to the implementation of the scheme in 1936 and its subsequent development. The minutes of the expansion progress meetings and other Air Ministry files provide abundant evidence of the intensity of his interest and his formidable grasp of complex detail. Others at the Air Ministry played their part, of course, notably Lord Weir, but the scheme could hardly have had the success it achieved without the unwavering support of the Secretary of State under whom it was launched.[59]

The Battles and Blenheims allocated to the shadow factories of Austin and Rootes represented together a substantial proportion of the medium bomber requirement of Scheme F; orders for both machines were also naturally placed with the parent firms. Among other bomber orders placed under Scheme F were those for the Vickers Wellington and the Handley Page Hampden, both in August 1936. Two months before had come the first production orders for the two advanced eight-gun fighters: the Hawker Hurricane, the prototype of which had first flown seven months before, and the Supermarine Spitfire, just three months after the first prototype flight. The RAF of the Battle of Britain was taking shape.[60]

In all this expansion, qualitatively and quantitatively worlds apart from anything which had preceded it, the key role continued to be played by the professional aircraft industry. Shadow factories might provide essential additional output; they could not supply the expertise, the designing flair. But the professional industry, both as individual firms and as collectively represented in the Society of British Aircraft Constructors (SBAC), required careful handling, calling on all the industrial insight and man-management skills of Swinton and Weir. The drive for expansion had come for the aircraft industry after years of struggling to survive in almost complete dependence on small Air Ministry contracts. The firms viewed the sudden change in their fortunes with caution, fearful that the expansion might peter out once the political motivation slackened, leaving them with little but redundant factory space and equipment. Having combined together in the SBAC during the hard times they were even more resolved to keep united in order to maintain and exploit the new conditions.[61] Both Swinton and Weir had a poor opinion of the SBAC and its officials, as they revealed in a progress meeting discussion on an SBAC document commenting on Air Ministry proposals for accelerating the design and development of new types. 'Generally speaking,' Swinton told the meeting, 'he was against discussing questions of policy such as this with that body, and would far rather rely on the advice of two or three members of the industry, like Mr. Sopwith and Mr. Fairey, who did know what they were talking about'. Lord Weir had agreed, saying that he thought 'we should have as little to do with the S.B.A.C. as possible until they were organized on a sound basis of technical criticism and had given proof of their capacity to give such criticism usefully'.[62] But this Olympian attitude could not be maintained when it came to the terms on which the aircraft industry would provide the machines and engines which the Government now required in such quantity. The firms, conscious of the strength of their position, were determined to drive a hard bargain, despite the undertakings Government spokesmen (including Swinton, when introducing the supplementary air estimate in July 1935) had given, under Labour parliamentary pressure, to prevent profiteering in arms.

The launching of Scheme F, with its intensification of the expansion, brought matters to a head. On 18 March 1936 the SBAC sent the Air Ministry a rather querulous memorandum calling for 'a full and frank statement' of the position on 'contract conditions, arrangements for fixing prices and other matters'. It could hardly complain of the speed of Swinton's response since he saw SBAC representatives the following day.[63] For many months thereafter he was deeply involved in negotiations with the Society, and, from May 1936, with Sir William McLintock, the distinguished accountant whom the SBAC appointed to represent it. The main lines of an agreement had been worked out by September 1936 and guided individual contracts after that date. But the Treasury, in pursuit of its general responsibility for the principles rather than the detailed administration of government contracts, wanted changes made, and negotiations for the agreement dragged on throughout 1937, the final document not being signed until the spring of 1938.

The McLintock Agreement contained provisions for 'fair and reasonable compensation' to firms for any redundant plant capacity after completion of the expansion programme—

the so-called 'Capital Clause'[64]—but its nub was the procedure for settling the price firms would be paid for their advance contracts. The negotiation of an agreed price at the outset was envisaged as the preferred method; but the problem was that for many of the new aircraft types being ordered it was virtually impossible to estimate costs in advance of actual production. Swinton himself, he later claimed, devised the method for dealing with this situation. It involved the firm completing two preliminary production runs or batches, on which it would be paid an agreed fixed rate of profit. From the experience gained, the firm and the Air Ministry would try again to agree on a fixed price or, if this proved impossible, on a maximum price. Where a firm thereafter opted to work on the basis of a maximum price and the production costs, plus the agreed rate of profit, on subsequent production runs were found to be less than the maximum price, the firm and the Government would split the savings (the firm's proportion depending upon the amount of the savings—the greater the savings, the greater the firm's share). But where the cost plus the rate of profit exceeded the maximum price, the Government would pay the maximum price only, leaving the firm to bear the loss. In the event of a firm failing to agree either a fixed or a maximum price with the Air Ministry there was provision for arbitration by a committee of three under the chairmanship of Sir Hardman Lever, a former Financial Secretary to the Treasury. In theory, the agreement should have resulted in firms having a continuing inducement to reduce costs, in a progressive reduction of the total bill to the Government, and in quicker deliveries.[65]

The practice, however, was somewhat different. Firms spun out the negotiations on fixing prices, with the result that in the interim they were in effect being paid costs plus an element of profit, without risk or much incentive to reduce costs or speed production.[66] And the agreement itself gave no guidance on what was a suitable rate of profit. The industry thought the 10 per cent it had been paid on pre-expansion contracts should continue to apply, while the Air Ministry considered 7½ per cent was more appropriate to the new situation of large orders with consequent economies of scale and diminishing production costs. Beyond that was the question of the basis on which the profit should be assessed: whether it should be calculated as a yearly percentage of the capital invested in contracts by the firm, as the Treasury wished, or as a simple percentage of the cost of each contract—the firm's turnover —as Swinton and Weir insisted was inevitable. Victory on that point went mainly to the Air Ministry, but it led to several firms making what were excessive profits on any computation, and to a consequent renegotiation of the McLintock Agreement in 1939.[67] In justice to Swinton it has to be said that the situation was a novel one in which there was no sure guide in past practice. The vital thing was to get the necessary production, and, in default of statutory powers to direct industry (something against which the Government set its face for the whole of Swinton's time at the Air Ministry), this depended on the willing co-operation of the industry, in which the assurance of good profits was not the least important element.

Some impression may already have been given of the enormous pressure of work on Swinton at the Air Ministry, pressure which was to lead in March 1937 to a month's enforced sick-leave. If we take the summer of 1936 to illustrate the point, Swinton was then deeply involved in the implementation of Scheme F, in often difficult negotiations with both the professional and 'shadow' aircraft industries, in a major reorganization of the RAF home command structure, and with the totally unexpected situation confronting the department as a result of the Bullock case: and these in addition, of course, to the inescapable round of departmental, Cabinet, Cabinet committee, and House of Lords business. But there were at least two other major policy issues demanding his particular attention at this time. One was in the field of scientific research for air defence, which in June 1936 saw an open breach between the distinguished scientists F. A. Lindemann (backed by Churchill) and Sir Henry Tizard. The other (which will be dealt with in the next chapter) was the formal reopening in July 1936 of the controversy between the Admiralty and the Air Ministry over the control of naval aviation.

The major premise of Britain's air rearmament in the 1930s, as also of the concomitant efforts to secure international agreement on restricting the use of the air arm in war, was essentially what Baldwin had expressed in November 1932 in his

famous sentence, 'the bomber will always get through'.[68] It
was the supposed supremacy of the bomber which confirmed
the Air Staff in its belief in the overriding strategic role of the
air offensive in deterring or defeating an enemy and accounted
for the relative position of bomber and fighter production in
air force expansion plans. In general, Swinton agreed with this
emphasis on the bomber, as he was to demonstrate in a conflict with Inskip over air strategy at the end of 1937. But it
could be argued that the most significant contribution of his
time at the Air Ministry consisted in the efforts to disprove
the thesis that the bomber always gets through, for it was on
these that success in the Battle of Britain in 1940 ultimately
depended. There were, of course, the high performance Spitfire and Hurricane fighter, which were ordered in bulk under
Swinton, and whose production progress formed one of the
main themes of the weekly Air Council progress meetings over
which he presided. No less important was the revolutionary
change in the operational efficiency of the fighter against the
bomber brought about by the development of the aircraft
detection system later to be known as radar. Swinton saw radar
as 'a vital part of the whole defence system'[69] and was crucially
concerned in its development both as Air Minister and a chairman of the Committee of Imperial Defence subcommittee on
Air Defence Research.

The establishment of the Air Defence Research subcommittee in March 1935 almost certainly owed something to
political expediency. Since the summer of 1934 Churchill and,
in particular, his friend and scientific confidant, Lindemann,
had been actively canvassing with Baldwin and others the constitution of a high-powered sub-committee of the Committee
of Imperial Defence under the chairmanship of someone of
the standing of Lord Weir 'with two or three service representatives and two or three scientists whose definite instructions
would be to find some method of defence against air bomb-
ing'.[70] Simultaneously a 'Committee for the Scientific Study
of Air Defence' was in the process of formation in the Air
Ministry, on the initative of H. E. Wimperis, the Director of
Scientific Research, and in December H. T. Tizard agreed to
become the new committee's chairman, with two other distinguished outside scientists, A. V. Hill and P. M. S. Blackett,

as members. When on 3 December Lindemann wrote to
Londonderry with his idea of a CID subcommittee, the Air
Minister's reply of 20 December informed him of the existence
of the Tizard Committee and suggested that he get in touch
with its chairman; Lindemann was subsequently invited to
become a member of the committee.[71] But Lindemann viewed
the Tizard Committee as an entirely inadequate response to his
demand for a politically influential inter-departmental body,
and, through his friends Churchill and Austen Chamberlain,
even got the Prime Minister, Ramsay MacDonald, to agree
with him. At a meeting with Churchill, Austen Chamberlain,
and Lindemann on 14 February, MacDonald was thought by
Churchill to have 'promised to get the Tizard Committee to
present a report at an early date and then wind it up and form
a sort of Committee under the C.I.D. which had been demanded . . . before the Air Estimates were introduced'.[72] It
was left to Hankey, on his return from a visit to Australia, to
propose a way out of the organizational muddle in which the
Prime Minister, under pressure, seemed about to land the
Government and the Air Ministry. In a minute to MacDonald
on 18 March he proposed the formation of a CID subcommittee under a Cabinet minister 'to coordinate and inspire
research and experiment' in air defence by the service departments, with the Tizard Committee continuing to exist as the
'technical' committee to the new 'policy' committee. The
creation of this committee was announced by MacDonald in
reply to a parliamentary question from Austen Chamberlain
on 19 March. Three days later Cunliffe-Lister (as he still was)
agreed to become its chairman.[73]

The Air Defence Research subcommittee—usually referred
to as the Swinton Committee although it continued in existence for a year or so after Swinton himself had resigned—held
sixteen meetings under Swinton's chairmanship, from the first
on 11 April 1935 to the sixteenth on 13 May 1938.[74] During
this period its membership fluctuated considerably. Weir,
Warren Fisher, Sir Frank Smith (Secretary of the Department
of Scientific and Industrial Research), and Tizard were members throughout. Before March 1936 Swinton had a Cabinet
colleague present in the person of Ormsby-Gore, and later, of
Lord Eustace Percy; but with his appointment as Minister for

the Co-ordination of Defence Inskip became the second permanent Cabinet member of the committee. Senior service representatives always attended, as did the Air Ministry Director of Scientific Research (Wimperis, later D. R. Pye). But the committee's most surprising member joined it at its fourth meeting on 25 July 1935, as the result of Swinton's initiative. He proposed to Baldwin, as soon as he took over as Air Minister from Londonderry, that Churchill be invited to become a member, and, according to Churchill's account, Baldwin issued the invitation in the smoking room of the House of Commons early in July. 'He sat down next to me and said at once [Churchill wrote]: "I have a proposal to make to you. Philip is very anxious that you should join the newly-formed Committee . . . on Air Defence Research, and I hope you will." I said I was a critic of our air preparations and must reserve my freedom of action. He said "That is quite understood. Of course you will be perfectly free except upon the secret matters you learn only at the Committee".'[75] Churchill made it a condition of his acceptance that Lindemann should at least be a member of the Tizard Committee. After consulting Tizard Swinton renewed the invitation already made to Lindemann and this time it was accepted.[76]

Swinton was later to say that he wanted Churchill on his committee partly because of his undoubted experience and imaginative genius and partly because he considered that if Churchill were to remain a public critic of the Government's rearmament efforts it would better for him to be a properly informed one; and he felt, retrospectively, that the committee owed much to Churchill's 'stimulating inspiration'.[77] But at the time the association was not without difficulty. About a year after Churchill had become a member Swinton was complaining in Cabinet that Churchill's attitude on the committee 'had throughout been unhelpful'. Instead of confining himself to research matters he was constantly bringing up wider issues such as the relative air strengths of Britain and Germany; and Swinton even raised with Hankey the question of whether, in view of the public activities of Churchill and Lindemann, Churchill should continue to see secret defence papers.[78] For his part Churchill, immediately after Swinton's resignation as Air Minister, expressed himself as profoundly dissatisfied with progress on the committee under his chairmanship, and looked to his successor, Kingsley Wood, to provide the driving power which, Churchill alleged, had been completely lacking under Swinton.[79]

If Churchill's presence on the Swinton Committee was not an unmixed blessing, Lindemann's membership of the Tizard Committee was little short of disastrous. The clash between Lindemann and his erstwhile colleague Tizard has often been recounted and will not be examined in any detail here. The objectives each had and the methods they adopted for pursuing them were so totally opposed that it was soon clear that they could not both remain on the committee if it were to continue to produce useful results. It fell to Swinton to deal with the Lindemann–Tizard conflict and he did so, in the words of Stephen Roskill, with 'masterly patience and political acumen'.[80]

The seeds of the most outstanding single fruit of the Tizard and Swinton committees had been sown well before Churchill and Lindemann joined them. It was at the first meeting of the Tizard Committee on 28 January 1935 that Robert Watson-Watt, of the National Physical Laboratory's Radio Research Station at Slough, who had been invited to attend the committee by Wimperis, discussed with members the role that the reflection of radio waves might play in aircraft detection. On 12 February he submitted to the Air Ministry his seminal paper on 'Detection and Location of Aircraft by Radio Methods', which provided the essential link between scientific possibilities and operational needs. On 26 February a vital experiment in the new method was successfully carried out at Weedon, following which the Air Ministry (with Dowding's enthusiastic support as the Air Council member responsible) made available £10,000 for further tests; and on 1 March, Orfordness, on the Suffolk coast, was chosen as the site for the 'Radio Direction Finding' research team under Watson-Watt, still nominally on the staff of the Department of Scientific and Industrial Research. When, on 11 April, the Swinton Committee met for the first time, it heard a report on the work of the Tizard Committee in general and on RDF (or radar, as it will be convenient, if anachronistic, to call it) in particular, and thereafter kept a close watch on radar's progress. The

Orfordness site was opened in mid-May and at the meeting of the Swinton Committee on 25 July (the first attended by Churchill) it was decided that the experiments there were sufficiently promising to justify the formulation of plans by the service departments. At its next meeting, on 16 September, the committee agreed that the Orfordness work should be expanded and moved to larger accommodation at Bawdsey Manor, on the coast a few miles south of Orfordness; and, more importantly, that Treasury approval should be sought for the building of a chain of radar warning-stations along the southern and eastern coasts. Treasury approval for the building of the first five stations in this chain was given on 19 December 1935, largely as a result of the good offices of one of the members of the committee, Warren Fisher, the permanent secretary of the Treasury.[81] By the middle of March 1936 Watson-Watt and his team had solved the most important remaining problem in detecting a daylight attack, that of determining bearing as well as distance and altitude. Soon afterwards the Bawdsey enterprise was formally transferred from the Department of Scientific and Industrial Research to the Air Ministry, and thus came fully within Swinton's departmental charge. Watson-Watt himself had been reluctant to make the change, being deeply suspicious of what he saw as Air Ministry bureaucracy —he would have responsibilities to three different directors— but was persuaded to do so by a direct request from Swinton, whom he trusted, whatever his opinions of the department he headed.[82]

While Churchill and Lindemann were both undoubtedly prepared to recognize the potential importance of radar, they were for some time considerably more sceptical about its development than the other members of their respective committees. And, in particular, they disliked the priority that work on radar was being given in the allocation of limited resources. On the Tizard Committee Lindemann was putting forward one project after another—for example, infra-red rays and aerial mines—for which he demanded separate high-priority investigation. On behalf of Churchill and Lindemann it could be said that they were from the start intent on methods of hitting and bringing down hostile aircraft—and radar was a method of detecting aircraft, not of destroying them; moreover, there was always the possibility, never openly discussed, of enemy counter-measures (such as jamming) being employed against radar. Swinton, however, never wavered in the support he gave Tizard and Watson-Watt or in his conviction that nothing should be allowed to interfere with the urgent priority given to the development of the radar chain and subsequently to the work at Biggin Hill on the revision of fighter operations to take advantage of the benefits radar brought. There could be no doubt how he would react when the almost inevitable rupture between Lindemann and Tizard (and the rest of his committee) finally took place in the middle of 1936.

On 25 May 1936 Churchill was complaining to Inskip about the 'pitiful' progress in the Tizard Committee, with the solitary exception of the aircraft-location research. Lindemann had, he said, been 'struggling vainly for eight months for certain not very costly experiments to be made' and it was only with the greatest difficulty that he had been prevented from resigning.[83] A week or so later Churchill circulated a memorandum of Lindemann's complaints to members of the Swinton Committee, which provoked Tizard to write to Swinton on 12 June to say that he had come to the conclusion 'that I must ask you either to remove Lindemann from the committee or accept my resignation': Lindemann's 'querulousness when anybody differs from him, his inability to accept the views of the committee as a whole, and his consequent insistence on talking about matters which we think are relatively unimportant, and hence preventing us from getting on with more important matters, make him an impossible colleague'. Swinton, whose sympathies were entirely with Tizard (he told Inskip), was sure that his resignation would inevitably mean the departure from the committee of Hill and Blackett.[84] The meeting of the Swinton Committee which followed on 15 June was, Wimperis noted in his diary, 'vehement . . . controversy between Churchill on one side and Swinton and Tizard on the other'.[85] Swinton's backing of Tizard at the meeting did not, however, prevent Churchill from suggesting to him next day that he (Swinton) or, if he was too busy, some other 'impartial person' like Inskip, Hankey, or Fisher, should adjudicate between Tizard and Lindemann. After consulting Inskip Swinton courteously rejected this suggestion, prompting Churchill to express his surprise and grief that Swinton was 'apparently content with the way the work is going'.[86] A tart exchange of letters between Lindemann and Tizard did nothing to improve matters, nor did the announcement that Lindemann was to contest the impending election for one of the university seats at Oxford, with the state of the country's air defences as the main plank in his platform. A meeting of the Tizard Committee on 15 July, to discuss the draft of a progress report on the investigations recommended by the committee, marked the final break. All efforts to accommodate Lindemann's views in the draft proved unavailing and Lindemann insisted on submitting his own minority report. That day Blackett and Hill each wrote to Swinton to say that they would have to resign from the committee if Lindemann remained a member of it. Swinton saw both men a week later and told them he had no intention of accepting their resignations and fully understood that their refusal to serve with Lindemann was quite definite. He read out the resignation letters at the meeting of the Swinton Committee on 24 July, at which, according to Wimperis's diary entry, 'Winston [was] in a chastened mood'; it was generally agreed that the only practicable course was to reconstitute the scientific committee with members who could work together effectively.[87] This was the course Swinton adopted. On 3 September he officially informed Lindemann of the resignations of Hill, Blackett, and Tizard (for he, too, had now formally resigned), and the consequent need to dissolve the committee. The committee was thereupon reconstituted—the only change being the substitution of E. V. Appleton for Lindemann.

Churchill later asserted to Swinton's successor, Kingsley Wood (whom he persuaded to appoint Lindemann to the erstwhile 'Swinton' Committee), that Lindemann had been removed from the Tizard Committee because he had pressed for 'more vigorous action'. On this palpable misrepresentation the comment of Robert Rhodes James seems unanswerable: 'Lindemann had to be removed because the proceedings of the Tizard Committee had degenerated into a series of extremely rancorous discussions which were in danger of wrecking its usefulness. No dispassionate observer, reading the papers of the Committee, can seriously challenge the correctness of Swinton's decision.'[88]

Swinton was to claim as one of his achievements at the Air Ministry that he had made scientists like Tizard, Hill, and Blackett 'an integral part of the Air Staff'.[89] While this could hardly be literally true it does serve to emphasize the importance he attached to forging a direct association between scientific research and its operational use by the RAF. It was in his skill in achieving this association that Tizard's most significant contribution to Britain's defences lay, and there is no doubt that his success in doing so owed much to the fact that the Air Staff and RAF commanders were conscious that he—a scientific adviser with no executive powers—had the full backing of the Secretary of State. Without this backing Tizard might not have secured service co-operation in the Biggin Hill experiments. It was these which led in the summer of 1937 to CID and Treasury approval for the construction of the full chain of twenty radar stations at a capital cost of £1m.; and to the organization of that elaborate co-ordinated reporting and ground-control system which enabled operation rooms at Fighter Command and Fighter Group headquarters to direct the Battle of Britain.[90] Tizard noted the contrast after Swinton had resigned. His committee, he told Sir Wilfred Freeman in 1940, 'suffered a serious loss when Swinton went. He was the only Air Minister that I have had to deal with who could understand the recommendations and take action on them. I have had no help from the others; indeed, obstruction rather than help.'[91]

CHAPTER 5

Air Ministry II

ONE of the most important events during Swinton's tenure of the Air Ministry represented, both personally and departmentally, a partial defeat, but one which, in terms of Britain's defence interests, was far preferable to what could only have been a temporary victory. This was the resolution of the bitter conflict between the Royal Navy and the RAF over the control of naval aviation (covering the shipborne units of the Fleet Air Arm and the coastal units of the RAF) which had bedevilled inter-service co-operation in the 1920s and 1930s. So obdurate was the navy on the issue and so damaging the prospect of continuing inter-service strife as war loomed that settlement became imperative.[1]

An uneasy truce had subsisted since Lord Salisbury's arbitration of 1928. That had, in effect, confirmed the dual control arrangement laid down in 1923 by the Balfour subcommittee (on which Weir had been the most active member), whereby the Air Ministry exercised administrative control of the Fleet Air Arm on land (as well as undivided control of the maritime aircraft of what in June 1936 became Coastal Command), while the Admiralty had operational control of Fleet Air Arm units afloat. But the Admiralty had never really accepted the Air Ministry's continued responsibility for the Fleet Air Arm and was constantly seeking opportunities to reopen the controversy. An approach by the First Lord to the Prime Minister in May 1935 led to Baldwin's statement of 25 July that he was 'wholly opposed' to a reopening of the constitutional question, a position of which he had already assured Weir when he saw him on 23 May, in order to secure his services as industrial adviser to the Air Ministry.[2] However,

Baldwin also indicated in his July statement that he was anxious that some way of improving co-operation between the two departments should be found; and in October and November 1935 Swinton and Monsell (the First Lord), together with their service advisers, met to discuss certain Fleet Air Arm personnel problems, but without result. The appointment in March 1936 of a Minister for the Co-ordination of Defence prompted Monsell to request Inskip (the new Minister) to carry out an inquiry into a question which 'shrieks for co-ordination', in a letter which Swinton, sent a copy by Inskip, described as 'a really amazing document' in view of the Prime Minister's ruling of the previous July.[3] Nevertheless, in July Inskip held four meetings with members of the naval and air staffs to examine Fleet Air Arm personnel problems. Since the subject-matter was to be detail, not policy, ministers (other than Inskip) were not expected to be present, and Hoare, who had just succeeded Monsell as First Lord, no doubt found this convenient since as Air Minister in the 1920s he had been the politician most responsible for the continued maintenance of RAF control of the Fleet Air Arm.[4] But Swinton was sufficiently concerned about what he had heard of the drift of the discussions to make him attend the third meeting himself. A disquisition from the Second Sea Lord proved too much for him. He insisted that the Admiral was going outside the terms of reference and assuming a change in control of the Fleet Air Arm. 'I have come here with complete good will to discuss how we can make the existing system work,' he told Inskip in the chair. 'I cannot take part in any inquiry which goes to challenge that system.' Soon afterwards he intervened again to make the same point: 'the fundamental thing is the Fleet Air Arm is an integral part and branch of the Air Force . . . and I cannot sit here and listen to a discussion of a proposal . . . to make the Fleet Air Arm something quite different. I am forbidden by the Prime Minister to do it and I should not do it without the direct orders of the Cabinet.'[5]

Inskip sent his report to Baldwin on 5 November. It contained recommendations clearly designed to meet the navy's complaints, including the extension to four years of the period of attachment of RAF officers to the Fleet Air Arm, and the provision of pilot training for naval ratings. More significant, however, was Inskip's somewhat ambivalent covering letter to Baldwin. On one hand, he said that at a time when the expansion programme needed all the energies of the services and when the strategical conception of air power was in a state of rapid development he would be 'most reluctant to see a change now'. On the other, while expressing the hope that his recommendations would eliminate some of the difficulties, he admitted that they were 'only a first step': 'the real heart of the controversy . . . the constitutional question of control . . . is as acute as ever'. The absence of common ground between the two services was 'very disquieting' and the 'unhealthy' controversy continued, but some form of further inquiry would be necessary before any decision could be taken to alter the system. Swinton, to whom Inskip sent a copy of his letter to Baldwin, immediately saw the dangerous implications of this reference to another inquiry. As he told Inskip, 'I cannot help feeling, whatever your intention, that your letter must lead to more agitation, whereas a plain re-statement of the Prime Minister's decision would stop it.' Nevertheless, he assured Inskip that the Air Ministry was determined to make his proposals work.[6]

Swinton's fear about a renewed agitation was borne out almost immediately, although he did not know it at the time. In a memorandum to the First Lord on 16 November, which Hoare sent to Baldwin and Inskip, Admiral Chatfield (the First Sea Lord) declared that Inskip's report offered 'no adequate solution to the problems confronting the Admiralty', and that in the interests of the navy it was essential that 'this disastrous experiment' of dual control of the Fleet Air Arm 'should be terminated and the system changed'. An element of duplicity then entered this rather unedifying story. Swinton was eventually sent a copy of Chatfield's memorandum by Inskip on 9 December, but he was not told (at the explicit request of Hoare and Chatfield) that Inskip had already, with Hankey's help, drafted and sent a letter to Baldwin proposing a wider inquiry into naval aviation. It was not until 16 February 1937—over two months later—that Baldwin, fortified in his resolve by a resignation threat by Chatfield made at a meeting with him on 11 February, wrote to Swinton (in a letter drafted by Inskip) to convey his decision that an inquiry into 'the control of and responsibility for the Fleet Air Arm and naval air operations generally' had become 'politically necessary'; and that it would be conducted by Inskip, Halifax (Lord Privy Seal), and Oliver Stanley (President of the Board of Education).[7]

Not having been privy to the correspondence and discussions between Inskip's and Hankey's offices, No. 10, and the Admiralty, Swinton was clearly taken aback by this reversal of Baldwin's previously declared position. He immediately sent a copy of Baldwin's letter to Weir and the two men met for dinner at Swinton's house in Lygon Place that evening (16 February). On the following day, after consulting with Weir again on the telephone, Swinton replied to the Prime Minister. 'As you may imagine, I received your letter of 16 February with great surprise and concern,' he wrote. 'You are proposing that an inquiry should be held not only into the whole constitution and control of the Fleet Air Arm but indeed covering a much larger field'. He reminded Baldwin that he had earlier refused to reopen the question 'on the ground that any such inquiry would divert the attention and work of staffs from the essential job of carrying out the great defence programme'. The Air Ministry would submit to the decision but it would be an additional burden for a department 'already seriously overworked by the Expansion problems'. And, even more serious, Lord Weir was likely to resign, 'as hard a blow as we could sustain' since it was impossible to exaggerate what the Air Ministry owed to his 'unique experience and constant help'.[8]

Persuaded by Neville Chamberlain, Weir delayed actually submitting his resignation for a fortnight. On 2 March he wrote to Baldwin to resign as Air Ministry industrial adviser as it had been decided, apparently for 'political considerations', to acquiesce in 'the agitation and propaganda which have been conducted' to get the Fleet Air Arm question reopened.[9] For Swinton, although it came as no surprise, Weir's resignation—and the prospect of the exhausting inquiry which had caused it—exacerbated a situation which had already led to a serious breakdown in his health. A tired heart had been diagnosed and he was ordered by his medical advisers to take a month's complete rest. On 10 March he left for Swinton and he did not return to the Air Ministry until 12 April.[10] But before his departure Weir, who saw Baldwin on 5 March and again on 10 March (when Chamberlain and Inskip were present), had been persuaded to withdraw his resignation. The *modus vivendi* arrived at proved to be a highly ambiguous one. It was that Inskip alone, assisted by the Chiefs of Staff Committee, should first investigate the general strategic questions: as Inskip expressed it in a letter to Halifax and Stanley on 12 March, he would 'work out with the Chiefs of Staff Committee a statement on the fundamental questions of air-power and the strategic use of aircraft'.[11] The ambiguity lay— and it was to prove fatal to the Air Ministry position—in what was to happen next: was there to be a further inquiry specifically on the current operation and control of the Fleet Air Arm, and, if so, when and by whom? Chatfield, who had only with the greatest reluctance accepted the change in procedure, had no doubt on the matter: Inskip would 'thrash out the problem in all its aspects with the Chiefs of Staff' and then at the appropriate moment he would bring in Halifax and Stanley 'to help him come to conclusions'.[12] In his letter to Halifax and Stanley Inskip seemed to be envisaging going straight from the broad strategic review with the Chiefs of Staff to a detailed examination of the Fleet Air Arm in committee with Halifax and Stanley. For the moment Swinton was more than content to rest and recuperate in his beloved Yorkshire, but after his return to London he attempted to act on a rather different interpretation of what Inskip had been commissioned to do.

The Chiefs of Staff had three meetings with Inskip—on 9 April and 6 and 18 May—at which voluminous evidence from the naval and air staffs on their respective strategic positions was considered.[13] Nothing new emerged and the meetings were clearly inconclusive: the Air Staff emphasized its familiar contention about the indivisibility of air power and the homogeneity of flying skills and tactics, whether over sea or land; and the Naval Staff, *per contra*, the specialized nature of air work over the sea, particularly from carriers. Although it was not relevant to this stage of the inquiry, the Admiralty also submitted to Inskip a detailed memorandum on the defects as it saw them in the current administration of the Fleet Air

Arm. Ellington minuted Swinton on 29 April with a clause by clause analysis and refutation of the Admiralty document. But despite Swinton's advice to let Inskip have the Air Ministry comments privately ('I am a little afraid of him accepting Admiralty statements about the working of the F.A.A. at their face value') Ellington failed to do so, no doubt resting on the fact that it was not yet appropriate to submit matters of detailed administration. He did, however, tell Inskip that if as a result of the present investigation it was decided to carry out a further investigation into the Fleet Air Arm itself he would want 'an opportunity of dealing with the many highly controversial statements made in the Admiralty paper'.[14]

After much prodding by Chatfield of Hoare and Duff Cooper (who succeeded Hoare as First Lord on 28 May), and by them of Inskip, the latter decided to convene the committee of Halifax, Stanley, and himself for meetings on 2, 6, and 13 July, and so informed Duff Cooper and Swinton on 23 June. Inskip was by now fully conversant with the Admiralty Fleet Air Arm memorandum, for, in writing to Ellington on 23 June to tell him of the forthcoming committee meetings, he observed: 'I have tried to summarize the defects which the Admiralty allege in the existing system and I have asked the Admiralty to be prepared with evidence of facts to support their statements . . . I have said that, speaking for myself, I should like to hear some statements from serving officers.' He left it to the Air Ministry to judge what evidence to give, but what was wanted, as far as possible, was statements of fact and personal experience.[15]

The confusion as to what was intended to be the procedure to be followed by Inskip now became salient. Swinton believed that Inskip was failing to act in conformity with what had been agreed since he was proposing to go into detailed questions of organization before deciding the main strategic principles. He immediately saw Inskip (with Hankey), and, as he later told Chamberlain, 'Inskip assured me that there was no intention to depart from the general line laid down. He asked me for my personal opinion as to whether he should continue the enquiry on his own or with colleagues [that is, with Halifax and Stanley] and I expressed the view that as Minister for Co-ordination it was reasonable that he should proceed on his own.' Inskip agreed: he would complete his paper giving his conclusions on the strategic issues and present it to the Prime Minister and Cabinet for Cabinet decision and instructions to the services. Only then would he 'take up with the Services points of difficulty in administration and organization, and . . . solve those in the light of the general decisions'. Armed with this assurance Swinton felt able to tell Ellington that Inskip's letter to him of 23 June was withdrawn (and it is so marked in Inskip's official files) and that the Admiralty Fleet Air Arm memorandum was of no immediate significance: 'the detailed points in dispute would come up for consideration in due course when the second stage of the enquiry was reached'.[16]

But Swinton reckoned without the obduracy of Chatfield. The Admiralty was informed by telephone on 25 June that Inskip's letter of 23 June, giving the dates of meetings of his committee, was withdrawn, but no reason was given. For Chatfield, this apparent further delay after two years of intense activity to achieve an inquiry which he was convinced would recommend the transfer of the Fleet Air Arm to the navy was the last straw. On 28 June he wrote to Duff Cooper to say that whereas he and the Admiralty had shown exemplary patience the Air Ministry had 'continually worked against an Enquiry'. He could no longer endure the position in which he was placed and thus, he informed his minister, 'unless this Enquiry can be immediately held and completed . . . it is no longer justifiable for me to continue as First Sea Lord'. Shortly after this, the second resignation threat by Chatfield in less than six months, it appears that Swinton and Duff Cooper saw the Prime Minister (Chamberlain, who had just taken over from Baldwin), together with Inskip, and confirmed what Swinton had already agreed with Inskip: that Inskip should produce a report for the Cabinet by himself. What remains obscure is what the main participants thought the report would cover. Swinton contined to rely on Inskip's earlier assurance that it would deal with strategic principles only. But Duff Cooper must have told Chatfield that all substantive matters relating to the Fleet Air Arm (and the shore-based maritime air units of Coastal Command which the navy also coveted) would be included, since Chatfield promptly withdrew his threat of resignation, clearly believing that his making it had forced the issue.[17]

In the light of subsequent developments it is impossible to escape the conclusion that Inskip (and, presumably, Chamberlain), no doubt disturbed by Chatfield's resignation threat, deliberately misled Swinton as to the nature of the report he was to make. When, on 21 July, after taking no evidence of any kind (although with the benefit of a detailed Admiralty memorandum which he knew the Air Ministry wished to have the opportunity of answering point by point, and a missive from Churchill, wholly pro-navy), Inskip submitted his report to Chamberlain, it contained a firm proposal for a change in the control of the Fleet Air Arm. Inskip had concluded that 'when so much that concerns the air units depends upon the Naval element in the ship in the Fleet, the Admiralty should be responsible for selecting and training the personnel, and generally for the organization of the Fleet Air Arm' but that 'the Admiralty's claim with regard to shore-based aircraft ought not to be admitted'.[18]

As soon as he became aware of what the report contained, Swinton wrote to both Chamberlain and Inskip to protest at this breach of the assurances he and the Chief of the Air Staff had been given and had acted upon in the course of the inquiry. As a result of this protest Inskip was at last sent the Air Ministry riposte to the Admiralty memorandum, and on 26 July he and Hankey met Swinton, Ellington, and two other Air Council members. At this meeting it was decided to inform the Prime Minister that the Air Ministry was anxious that no final decision should be made to approve the transfer of the Fleet Air Arm to the Admiralty, nor any announcement of a decision in principle to that effect, until the Admiralty had formulated a concrete scheme for giving effect to their demand (no such scheme yet existed, even in outline, and the Air Ministry reasonably maintained that it was therefore impossible to examine its administrative aspects). Inskip did this in a supplementary report on the same day, but coupled it with the personal statement that 'I see no reason for altering my recommendation.' The Cabinet discussed the report on 29 July and it was soon clear that it was overwhelmingly in favour of Inskip's proposals. Swinton deployed detailed Air

Ministry objections and called on his colleagues 'not to agree in principle to a scheme that no one had seen and which, therefore, no one could appraise', but, in the end, he felt constrained to say that 'though he did not think the decision a right one he was not one of those who favoured the formal recording of dissent'. According to Chamberlain, who gave Weir an account of the meeting, Swinton 'put his case admirably, without any heat but without omitting any relevant point', and 'took the decision with dignity and sportsmanship', his attitude being 'much appreciated by his colleagues'. The Cabinet agreed that Chamberlain should make a formal statement in the Commons the next day, and this he did, from a draft prepared by Inskip and Hankey.[19]

Swinton continued to regret the decision, believing that by the Fleet Air Arm transfer 'the Admiralty will cut themselves off from the varied technical and operational experience of the Air Force and Air Staff', but perforce had to accept it.[20] Weir, too, was surprisingly docile in his reaction. He told Inskip on 12 August that he was glad he had conducted the investigation himself, an experience which 'will vastly help you in the more important problems which are developing for settlement in the next six months: and, as usual, I am available if you want me'.[21] Newall, the incoming Chief of the Air Staff, on the other hand, confided to Trenchard that 'I can't help feeling that lack of guts was the prime cause of the decision which sacrifices a considerable measure of national and imperial security as a political expedient in order to meet the clamour of vested interests.'[22] But no charge of lack of guts can lie against Swinton, who, despite the onerous burdens of his office, a serious breakdown in health at a crucial time, and the equivocation of Baldwin, Chamberlain, and Inskip, fought what was clearly going to be a losing battle with skill and persistence. Under no circumstances was the navy prepared to cease to agitate for the transfer of the Fleet Air Arm and in Chatfield it had its most capable leader since Beatty. If the Fleet Air Arm were to develop properly it was essential that the inter-service and inter-departmental bickering should end—and this could be effected only by conceding the Admiralty case on carrier-borne aircraft.[23]

The Admiralty had been so absorbed in agitating for the

transfer that it had no plans ready for when it had achieved it. The result was that this essentially marginal concern continued to demand a good deal of Swinton's attention for the rest of his time as Air Minister (the process was not in fact completed until May 1939). It was an unnecessary and unwelcome diversion of his effort from the main political imperative confronting him at the Air Ministry.

Whether Swinton, the Air Ministry, and the Air Staff liked it or not, they had constantly to try to ensure some correspondence between their plans for RAF expansion and what was currently believed to be the actual and potential state of German air strength. And if they were tempted to forget it there was always Churchill to remind them, as he did in the Commons on 12 November 1936, that the British people 'were promised most solemnly by the Government that air parity with Germany would be maintained by the home defence forces'.[24] About this time intelligence sources were indicating yet another acceleration of Luftwaffe strength: to 2,500 first-line aircraft, including 1,700 bombers, by April 1939, figures considerably in excess of Scheme F's objective by the same date of 1,736 first-line aircraft, including 1,022 bombers. The Air Staff immediately prepared new proposals, which were sent by Swinton to Inskip and Chamberlain (but not to Baldwin or any other member of the Government) at the end of November and were later circulated by him to the Cabinet as Scheme H on 14 January 1937. In his covering memorandum Swinton said that the revised German figures had made it imperative for Britain to create a more effective air striking force by April 1939, quite apart from the Government's parity pledges. And on those pledges Swinton considered it unreasonable to regard them as 'compelling us to equip our Metropolitan Force with equal numbers to the Germans irrespective of circumstances': to ignore, for example, the fact 'that a great German army requires more Army co-operation aircraft than we' or 'to take no account of the Fleet Air Arm as against German aircraft intended for Fleet co-operation'. He suggested, rather, that the aim should be to have '(a) A striking bomber force not inferior to that of Germany. (b) A fighter force of a strength requisite to meet the probable scale of attack'. But he pointed out that the effectiveness of the bomber force depended not merely on numbers but also on range, performance, and load; and if these characteristics could not be guaranteed—and at the moment no such absolute guarantee could be given—a return to the aim of an equal number of first-line aircraft, with adequate reserves, was inevitable. Swinton devoted another Cabinet paper, circulated just over a week later, to the question of parity pledges, and repeated, in slightly different words, the reformulation he had suggested in his Scheme H paper. When the Cabinet came to discuss it, on 27 January, it did not reject Swinton's views, although some members expressed apprehension about the impact on public opinion of any overt rejection of the idea of numerical equality in aircraft with Germany.[25]

Scheme H had a rather makeshift air, deriving from the fact that it was impossible, in Swinton's view, to expand the current Scheme F by its completion date of April 1939 'without a complete dislocation of industry'. Thus to achieve the vital aim of a larger deterrent force by the earliest possible date the Air Staff was proposing to use reserves in first-line units and to retain at home ten of the twelve squadrons previously intended for overseas. By these expedients the first-line strength of the RAF could be raised to approximately 2,500 aircraft, including 1,630 bombers, by April 1939, rising to 1,700 bombers as soon as possible thereafter; the completion of war reserves for this enlarged first-line strength would be deferred two years, until 1941. It was clear that neither Swinton nor the Air Staff were happy with a scheme which, while it would enable the RAF to put a larger strike force into the air if war were to begin in 1939, would involve a markedly-reduced capacity to sustain operations as the war continued. In the circumstances it was not surprising that the Cabinet, in any case concerned about the additional expenditure involved, showed no disposition to approve Scheme H.

But before the Cabinet had come to any final decision Scheme H was withdrawn by the Air Ministry, on the basis of new information about the *Luftwaffe* derived, not from intelligence sources, but direct from the German authorities, in the person of General Milch, state secretary of the German Ministry of Aviation. The link with Milch, and with other

Luftwaffe generals, had been forged at least as early as June 1936, when Swinton reported to the Foreign Secretary, Anthony Eden, on a long conversation he had had with Milch at the Air Ministry. Early in 1937 Courtney, the deputy Chief of the Air Staff, led an RAF mission to Germany, in the course of which Milch vouchsafed confidentially the information that the German air force would have only 1,755 first-line aircraft by the autumn of 1938 (Milch later maintained that Courtney had misunderstood him and that he had said the spring, not the autumn of 1938).[26] If this statement were true it 'destroyed completely the hypothesis upon which Scheme H rested as it clearly implied that Scheme F itself would afford parity with only some six months difference in the dates of completion of the scheme'.[27] At this stage Milch was still felt to be a credible witness, and his testimony sufficient to warrant the withdrawal for the time being of a scheme which the Air Staff had put forward with such conspicuous lack of enthusiasm. But it was not thought prudent, in the light of clear evidence that Germany could at short notice increase its programme in personnel, aircraft, and manufacturing capacity, to leave matters exactly as they were, since it was to meet precisely this kind of rapid expansion that Scheme H had been formulated. Swinton thus sought Cabinet approval to make certain preliminary arrangements which would facilitate a rapid acceleration of Scheme H should it be decided to adopt it at a later date because of an intensification of the German programme. He proposed the recruitment of additional pilots and skilled tradesmen, the purchase of land for thirteen new operational stations, and the creation of temporary buildings to accommodate personnel trained in excess of Scheme F requirements, 'as providing in the most economical way the best additional insurance for air defence in relation to the means at our disposal'. The Cabinet agreed to the proposals on 24 February.[28]

On 28 May 1937 came the long-awaited replacement of Baldwin by Chamberlain. As Chancellor Chamberlain had been the single most important minister in Cabinet decisions on defence and the scope of his influence was obviously going to increase now that he was Prime Minister. From Swinton's point of view the change could be expected to ease his task as Air Minister, through his close political and personal relations with a Prime Minister who, unlike his ageing predecessor, had the drive and administrative ability to ensure that things got done. Chamberlain had, moreover, shown a marked tendency, on economic grounds, to favour the RAF over the other services and admired Swinton's performance at the Air Ministry. 'You are doing a great work my dear Philip [he wrote to him at Christmas 1936] and I am truly thankful that it is in your hands.'[29] But despite these apparent advantages, the year Swinton spent at the Air Ministry under Chamberlain was probably the most difficult of his whole career.

During his last months at the Treasury Chamberlain had become increasingly concerned over the mounting cost of defence expenditure, warning his Cabinet colleagues on 3 February, for example, of 'the dangers of overloading the [defence] programmes beyond the material capacity of the country'.[30] He set in train at the Treasury a long-term review of their cost in relation to total national resources which, still incomplete in May 1937, was taken over by the new Chancellor, Sir John Simon. Simon reported on the exercise to the Cabinet on 30 June, and from then on, under the energetic lead of the Prime Minister, discussions were dominated by considerations of 'what the country could afford' without putting in jeopardy its economic stability and thus its capacity to survive a protracted war. Defence programmes had to be fitted into the financial limits determined by the Treasury, with the loyal assistance of Inskip, who, in Professor Gibbs's words, 'became not so much a minister for defence matters as a minister with special responsibility for defence expenditure and for the shaping of strategy to conform to financial limitations'.[31] At the Cabinet meeting of 30 June the service departments were asked, in consultation with the Minister for the Co-ordination of Defence, to submit to the Chancellor information on the period required for the completion of their already approved programmes, together with estimates for each year of the programme and for the years following its completion. The results were considered by the Cabinet on 27 October, when Inskip was asked to carry out a review of the whole problem of long-term defence programmes and their cost.

In the meantime the Air Ministry had received alarming new information about the rate of German air expansion, which was confirmed by the impression Swinton gained from the visit in October of a German air mission headed by General Milch and General Stumpff, the Chief of the German Air Staff.[32] The Germans now planned to have 3,240 first-line aircraft, including 1,458 bombers capable of reaching Britain, by the end of 1939. On 27 October Swinton forwarded new Air Staff proposals—Scheme J—to Inskip. The Air Staff calculated that Britain's security now required as a minimum a total metropolitan first-line air strength of 2,331 aircraft, including an air striking force of 1,442 bombers. Although a significant increase in fighter strength was also recommended (112 aircraft additional to the 420 provided for in Scheme F), bombers were more than ever, in the Air Staff's view, to be the linchpin of the metropolitan air force: the essence of the concept of parity lay in 'the number and offensive power of the bomber types which constitute the respective air striking forces'. Not only were bombers to be increased by 420, or 41 per cent, over Scheme F, but they were increasingly to be of the heavier types, with correspondingly heavier bomb-loads: Whitleys, Hampdens, and Wellingtons, with plans for the even larger Handley Page Halifax (ordered in September 1937), Short Stirling, and Avro Manchester. Scheme J also had provision for an increase in overseas squadrons (from 470 to 644 aircraft), but only after the completion of metropolitan requirements. In his covering memorandum Swinton pointed out that the plan was based on the assumption that it would remain Government policy 'to avoid the control of industry and interference with normal production to meet civilian requirements' (the Air Staff had recommended that this policy should be reconsidered, but Swinton clearly felt that this was not the time to propose it); and that consequently the conflicting claims of armament programmes and civilian industry on labour and materials made it extremely difficult to forecast production with any certainty. Recruitment was the main problem, because even if the Government were prepared to compel the large-scale diversion of civil factories to armaments work in order to speed up production, the system of voluntary recruitment would not be able to keep pace with it. Thus completion of part of the metropolitan programme on the personnel side, as well as the overseas proposals, had to be postponed until the summer of 1941, involving a time-lag of eighteen months compared with the German programme.[33]

Inskip's immediate reaction to Scheme J was to dispute the Air Staff's position on the air striking force. 'You will probably agree that you are not quite in the same position as the Navy in asking for parity in striking force,' Inskip wrote to Swinton on 4 November. 'If our Fleet were defeated or unable to keep our communications open, we could not long survive. If, on the other hand, our air striking force were inferior, we should suffer more than the enemy at home . . . but the result might not at once be critical . . . My point is that we may be forced [on grounds of economy] to consider a smaller striking force.' Swinton replied the same day with a spirited defence of the role of the strategic air offensive and the concept of the 'knock-out blow' which Inskip was now questioning: 'leaving aside all pledges, is not the vital question "What is it that wins a war?" It is not the mere fact that the enemy's fleet is sunk, or his army defeated, it is that the entire country and its resources are laid open to attack. The air fleets do not meet as in naval warfare, but the whole resources of the country are none the less laid open to attack from the immediate outset. From this it follows that success will go to the nation which can most quickly overcome the will of his opponent to continue the fight.' The Government had just stated in Parliament 'that we must have a force which will be an effective deterrent and will enable us to meet the enemy on equal terms. It is surely impossible to contend that either of these conditions is fulfilled unless our striking force is equal to that of the enemy.' Inferiority in air striking power, Swinton argued, could be accepted only if Britain's defences were stronger than Germany's or if the targets for British bombers were more accessible and vulnerable than those for German bombers. Since in both cases the advantage was, and would remain, with Germany, 'I feel most strongly that we must aim at parity in striking forces.'[34]

Swinton returned to the charge three weeks later, when he sent the Air Staff's response to questions which Inskip had raised about Scheme J. The first few weeks of a war, the Air Staff maintained in its memorandum, might decide the issue one way or another, and 'unless we are ready to hit back at an aggressor immediately he has shown his hand, we may never get on equal terms with him again'. Scheme J had been worked out as a balanced whole and represented the absolute minimum requirements for security. If it were to be modified on financial grounds alone 'the dangers and weaknesses which will inevitably accrue should be fully appreciated'. Swinton reinforced the Air Staff's arguments by pointing out to Inskip that if Britain were to deter an enemy from attacking, its offensive threat must be seen by the enemy to be as effective as his own. If Britain relaxed that offensive threat the enemy would relax his defensive preparations and concentrate on attack. Although there had been recent improvements in defensive techniques—in anti-aircraft guns, balloon-barrages, and the unexpectedly good progress of radar—'it would be an illusion to suggest that we have a sure means of defence. Counter-attack still remains our chief deterrent and defence.' To accept an inferiority in the bomber striking force would be to abandon the Government's public promises. Such a change of policy would have to be announced in Parliament, and the effect of the announcement on the German Government would be disastrous for Britain's hopes of concluding an air pact with Germany: 'I believe that nothing is so important as to come to an arrangement with Germany, and I believe it would be possible. But I am convinced that we with our great resources would accept no position of inferiority.'[35]

Inskip was not moved by these arguments, either in his considered reply to Swinton on 9 December, his interim report on the cost of the defence programmes circulated on 15 December, or in the Cabinet meeting which considered his report on 22 December.[36] He told the Cabinet that, in his view, 'parity with Germany was more important in fighter aircraft, resisting aggression, than in the offensive role of bombers'; and he thus recommended that while the full increase in fighters provided for in Scheme J should be approved, there should be only a modest increase in first-line bomber strength, with the emphasis shifting to the creation of industrial capacity to produce bombers once war had begun and away from the expensive peace-time provision of bomber reserves for use when war came. Swinton agreed that if there had to be a choice it was better to reduce the piling up of reserves and increase the war potential, for example, by extending the shadow factories, which were themselves a strong deterrent to war. But, in the light of Germany's estimated air strength and the Government's parity pledges, he did not think that anything less than Scheme J could be accepted 'without a complete reversal of policy'. The aim should be to build up aircraft strength, to recruit the necessary personnel, and to prepare plans for a greatly increased war potential. Swinton was strongly supported in Cabinet by Hoare (speaking as a former Air Minister), Eden, and Halifax, but it was Inskip's views, backed by Chamberlain and Simon, which prevailed, in large part on grounds of the dangers that increasing defence expenditure held for economic stability, and consequently for the country's ability to wage the long war that the Germans (on what evidence is not clear) were thought to dread. The financial ceiling for total defence expenditure on this premise had been set at £1,500m. over a five-year period and an air force scheme costing, as did Scheme J, an estimated £650m. over five years could not possibly be accommodated within it. The result was Scheme K, sent to Inskip on 21 January 1938, and appended to his final report on defence costs, circulated to the Cabinet on 8 February.[37] In effect the new scheme represented the abandonment of the effort to keep pace with German rearmament and, equally unpalatable to the Air Staff, an unmistakable shift away from the deterrent to the defensive aspect of air power. While the fighter numbers of Scheme J (532 aircraft) were retained, with full reserves, the striking force was reduced from ninety squadrons (1,442 bombers) to seventy-seven squadrons (1,360 bombers); moreover, bomber reserves were now to be the equivalent of nine weeks war wastage instead of the previous sixteen weeks.

But Scheme K, too, fell foul of the financial limits. In the Cabinet discussion of Inskip's final report on 16 February it was decided to accept Inskip's recommendation that the financial limit be increased to £1,570m. (with an additional £80m. for air-raid precautions); but within this grand total the RAF was to be allocated £507m.—and Scheme K was estimated to cost £567m. over the five-year period. Despite Swinton's warning that the scheme was 'not what the Air Staff think

ought to be done, but what they think would be the best
value for money', Inskip undertook to negotiate with the Air
Ministry further reductions of about £60m. Of almost greater
concern to Swinton, however, was the effect this delay in
coming to a decision on the future air programme was having
on the prospects for aircraft production after Scheme F had
been completed in 1939, and on the Air Ministry's relations
with the aircraft industry. It was essential for the Air Ministry
to have a four- or five-year forward programme, he told the
Cabinet. Contracts were already committed to 1939. Unless
orders could be given extending beyond 1939 there would be
a gap in production, as some eighteen months had to be allowed
for rejigging and retooling for new aircraft types. He urged
that the Air Ministry be given authority to place orders for a
longer period, and argued that the break-clauses in aircraft
contracts would mean little wasted expenditure if contracts
had later to be altered or cancelled should the international
situation improve.[38]

Brutal evidence that the international situation was far from
improving was provided by the German occupation of Austria
on 12 March. At a special meeting that day (a Saturday) the
Cabinet decided to review defence plans, and the same afternoon Swinton and his advisers prepared and circulated a
Cabinet paper containing revised proposals for air expansion.
These were considered by the Cabinet on 14 March, but once
again no firm decision was reached—concern was expressed
not only over the financial implications but also about the
availability of the additional skilled labour needed—and Inskip
was asked to investigate the proposals further with Swinton
and the Minister of Labour (Ernest Brown). It was, however,
recognized that defence preparations had to be speeded up,
and on 22 March the Cabinet agreed that the assumption that
normal trade should not be interfered with no longer applied.
On 24 March Chamberlain announced in the Commons the
Government's intention to accelerate the completion of the
rearmament programme, with some increases in the air force
and in anti-aircraft defences, even though it involved some
interference with normal trade, on which he proposed to have
consultations with the representatives of organized labour.[39]
He did not, however, reveal the existence of fixed financial

limits on that programme, limits which he and Simon were still fiercely defending in Cabinet. Swinton's powerful and persistent advocacy no doubt played its part in overcoming the objections of the Prime Minister and Chancellor, but the decisive element seems to have been the conversion of Inskip to the need for an expanded air programme even if it meant increasing the financial limits.[40] After consultations with Swinton and others Inskip circulated to the Cabinet on 1 April proposals for accelerating the air programme, together with a memorandum by Swinton. The new plan—Scheme L—was in most· respects Scheme K revived, with its completion date moved forward from March 1941 to March 1940. It provided for a first-line bomber strength of 1,352, and, in deference to those who, like Inskip, advocated defensive rather than offensive air strength, fighters were increased from 532 to 608. The total metropolitan first-line strength was to be 2,373 aircraft by March 1940, backed by 100 per cent reserves (rather than the desired 225 per cent) by March 1941. In all, total aircraft production would have to be increased to about 12,000 over the next two years, as compared with about 7,500 under Scheme F. The cost was estimated to be roughly the same as for Scheme K—£567m. over five years—and completion was dependent upon the necessary additional labour being available, the number ultimately required being estimated by Swinton as 100,000. At this stage Inskip refrained from recommending acceptance of the Air Ministry's proposals outright, but the drift of his observations was clear. The choice, he wrote, lay between a plan which, if accepted, would greatly increase the difficulty of keeping to agreed expenditure limits and, if rejected, would mean acting against the considered views of the Air Staff on the necessary minimum of air rearmament to provide reasonable safety (an argument which conspicuously had failed to weigh with him when, before the *Anschluss*, he had recommended the rejection of both Schemes J and K). He would regret very much any decision which threw into the melting-pot the whole question of defence expenditure and thought that the provisional allocations to the service departments would 'still have to be settled on the basis of the sum already approved together with any addition involved in the approval of the present proposals of the Secretary of State for Air'. The Chancellor of the Exchequer, however, had no intention of going so far. In a paper circulated to the Cabinet on 4 April Simon expressed himself as extremely doubtful whether the right course was for the Air Ministry to 'be authorized to place orders and incur commitments in respect of a scheme foreshadowing so large an expansion of our first line strength, rather than concentrating our main endeavours on improving the readiness for war of the force already authorized and building up reserves behind the first line'. Recent events in Europe, 'serious as they are, have done nothing to increase the financial resources of the country'. He recognized that something more than Scheme F was necessary, but submitted that the Cabinet should not approve Scheme L.[41]

When the Cabinet considered Scheme L on 6 April Swinton came under great pressure to justify it on both manpower and financial grounds. Fortunately Inskip now came out unequivocally for the programme, having satisfied himself that it could be achieved without compulsory direction of labour. The risks to the nation of not maintaining sufficient air strength to deter Germany were, in Inskip's view, greater than those involved in increasing defence expenditure by £60m. beyond the previously agreed limit. Chamberlain, obviously unhappy about this breach of the limit, asked Swinton what the effect of a Cabinet rejection of Scheme L would be. Swinton replied that even Scheme L would not produce a 'safe air defence against Germany', for, as the Air Staff had repeatedly pointed out, 'they had taken as their basis minimum *known* German intentions', and these would be realized this year, nearly two years before the projected completion of Scheme L. Moreover, the Air Staff had 'deliberately put forward a scale of reserves below what they considered a proper insurance' in order to meet 'the financial stringency'. The scheme was 'a minimum dictated not by what the Air Staff considered would give safety from a strategical point of view, but by political considerations of what was possible without control [of industry] and National Service'. Anything less would be 'a confession of complete and permanent inferiority to Germany'. And once again Swinton urged the necessity of immediate approval. The Cabinet had been reviewing and rejecting Air Ministry plans for more than a year: 'We should be deceiving ourselves and others if we pretended that we could speed up or act later if we postponed action now.' To reject the Air Ministry's proposals would be to reject the country's last hope of peace, and, if the peace efforts should fail, its only hope of success in war. This display of passion left Simon unmoved. The Chancellor reiterated his belief that 'the essential principle was to preserve the financial strength of the country' and that it would 'be better to adopt the sound business method of not expanding the business until we were in a position to do so'. Faced with such an entrenched position the Cabinet referred the question to a small group, consisting of Chamberlain, Inskip, Simon, and Swinton, charged with investigating, in consultation with the aircraft industry, the maximum productive capacity of the industry over the two years until March 1940 (the period during which, Inskip had argued in his final report, rearmament should be concentrated to enable Britain to reach an accommodation with Germany from a position of relative strength). The group reported back on 27 April, when the Cabinet at last gave the decision Swinton and the Air Ministry had been seeking for at least the six months since the first presentation of Scheme J.[42] In the mean time Swinton's personal position had become fatally weakened, in part as a result of the animus directed at him by the aircraft industry, impatient at the delays imposed by Government indecision. There were other factors as well, but to assess the events leading to his resignation it is necessary to return to the last months of 1937.

As Secretary of State for Air, Swinton, like all his predecessors and successors down to 1944 (when he himself was appointed the first Minister of Civil Aviation) had responsibilities in respect of civil aviation as well as for the RAF. Understandably, the major part of his considerable energies had been directed towards the expansion of the air force and it would not be unfair to say that for him, as for the Air Ministry as a whole, apart from the department of civil aviation (physically separate from the rest of the Ministry), aviation for civil purposes came a poor second to military aviation. A single company, Imperial Airways, had been the original 'chosen instrument' and sole recipient of a government subsidy for the development of European and imperial air routes. In 1936, following parliamentary criticism of the company's apparent ineffectiveness in the face of competition from the German Lufthansa airline, and the recommendation of a standing inter-departmental committee chaired by Warren Fisher, a subsidy was also given to a second company, British Airways, formed by a merger of several smaller companies, backed by the Pearson group, in the previous year. The new company was allocated northern European services, including a night airmail service to Germany, and was later selected to develop services to West Africa and South America. Imperial Airways' operations were considerably augmented with the implementation of the Empire Air Mail Scheme in June 1937. In the same month Sir Eric Geddes, who had been chairman of Imperial Airways since its formation in 1924, died and was succeeded by a part-time chairman, Sir George Beharrel. One of the problems for both companies was the acquisition of suitable aircraft, with a British industry almost wholly devoted to the production of military types or even, as with the Blenheim, converting what had originated as a civil machine into a medium bomber. Orders had to be placed in the United States, reinforcing that American dominance in the field of civil aviation with which Swinton would have to grapple when he became Minister of Civil Aviation in 1944.

The affairs of Imperial Airways attracted critical parliamentary attention in 1937, mainly through the agency of Harold Balfour, a First-World-War pilot, and Robert Perkins, another Conservative MP, who was a founder and officer of the British Air Line Pilots' Association and a long-standing critic of the company. Perkins had voiced some of these criticisms in the air estimates debate in March, but on 28 October initiated an adjournment debate in which he accused Imperial Airways of dismissing pilots unfairly, refusing pilots' requests for de-icing equipment, and operating obsolete aircraft on its European services. His demand for an official inquiry, supported by Labour MPs, was refused on behalf of the Government by Muirhead, Swinton's parliamentary under-secretary.[43] Perkins returned to the attack of 17 November and this time included the Air Ministry in his criticisms, for neglecting to produce a medium-sized airliner of British design to compete with American civil aircraft, and for refusing to release some

Blenheims for civil use. Imperial Airways was condemned for not having a full-time chairman, for cutting pilots' salaries, and for various other sins of commission and omission. The debate that followed was an uncomfortable one for the Government, and Muirhead had to promise an inquiry. Swinton then deliberated on its composition and the members were announced on 24 November: they were to be Lord Cadman, chairman of the Anglo-Persian Oil Company, with the assistance of two senior civil servants, Warren Fisher and William Brown (Swinton's former private secretary at the Board of Trade and now its permanent secretary). The choice of civil servants was singularly maladroit since it was immediately criticized as calling into question the standing and independence of the inquiry; and the day after the announcement Swinton had to invite a second businessman, Sir Frederick Marquis, and two leading trade-unionists (T. Harrison Hughes and J. W. Bowen) to take their place. Chamberlain himself announced the new composition of the inquiry on 30 November, but not until after the unfortunate Muirhead had committed himself in a written parliamentary answer to the view that no alteration in the original membership was required.[44]

Swinton was now reaping the full consequences of his ill-fated decision to take a peerage in 1935. The fumbling over the civil aviation inquiry was widely thought to illustrate the need for the Air Minister to be in the Commons. That particular issue was brought to a head on 6 December in an adjournment debate initiated by a Labour MP, Lieutenant-Commander Reginald Fletcher. Fletcher had raised the matter with Baldwin in March 1937 and been told that the pressure of work on the Secretary of State for Air made it desirable for him to be relieved of some of his parliamentary burdens, a reply which had been endorsed by Chamberlain in July, in response to a further question from Fletcher.[45] Opening the debate by disclaiming any intention of descending to personalities—the issue was, he said, purely one of whether the Air Minister should continue to be in the Lords—Fletcher went on to list the matters which, he implied, had been exacerbated by Swinton's absence from the Commons: Lord Weir's reported resignation over the Fleet Air Arm inquiry; Swinton's sick-leave in March; the Nuffield affair; the low reputation of the

Air Ministry in Whitehall; the handling of the Cadman inquiry; and anxieties about the defence of London. The Government reply was given by Chamberlain. After observing that no amendment requiring certain ministers to be members of the Commons had been proposed in the recently passed Ministers of the Crown Act, and that the Secretary of State for Air had invariably been a peer in the Labour Governments, he responded to Fletcher with a vigorous defence of Swinton:

As regards the attack on my noble Friend, some day, perhaps, justice will be done to him. It is not possible for the public to know everything that has gone on in the Air Ministry since my noble Friend took charge, but when it is realized, as it will be some day, with what speed and rapidity, and with what efficiency, he has built up a magnificent Air Force in this short space of time, unequalled in the world in the keenness and spirit of the men, and equipped with machines of a power and fighting force undreamed of before my noble Friend came into office, he will earn, and will receive, the gratitude of the country rather, than the carping criticism of the honourable and gallant Gentleman.[46]

This was a remarkable tribute from a speaker not given to hyperbole, but the fact that Chamberlain thought it necessary to make it indicated the strength of the opposition building up to Swinton's continued tenure of the Air Ministry. Swinton himself recognized this when he wrote to Chamberlain the same day to thank him for 'his most generous speech'. 'You know [Swinton assured him] that if at any time you think my work is done, or my usefulness accomplished, or if for any reason your task would be easier without me, I would go at once . . . very readily, for I have no desire but to do a job of work that wants doing, and to help you.'[47] Chamberlain did not then take up this tacit offer to resign, but from now on few air debates went by without some MPs demanding that Swinton make way for a successor in the House of Commons.

An opportunity of dealing with the question of Air Ministry representation in the Commons without patently bowing to this back-bench pressure came with the report of the Cadman Committee. This was submitted to Swinton on 8 February, and published on 9 March, together with a Government White Paper, the composition of which had occupied much of the time of Swinton, his private secretary Sandford, and a Cabinet committee under Inskip, in the intervening month.[48] The committee said it viewed 'with extreme disquiet' the position disclosed by its inquiry. It had harsh criticisms to make of Imperial Airways, and particularly its managing director, Woods Humphery (whose role had been enhanced with the appointment of a part-time chairman). The company had 'not only . . . failed to co-operate with the Air Ministry, but it had been intolerant of suggestion and unyielding in negotiation', and 'its attitude in staff matters has left much to be desired'. Woods Humphery was criticized for having taken too narrow a view of his commercial responsibilities and for having failed 'to give the Government Departments with which he has been concerned the co-operation we would have expected from a Company heavily subsidized and having such important international and Imperial contacts'. But the Air Ministry itself did not escape the committee's strictures. There was a need, the Committee felt, for more vigorous and far-sighted planning, more co-ordination of civil and military aircraft production, and more research. It recommended that the higher control of the department of civil aviation should be strengthened by placing it under the direct supervision of the permanent secretary, and also—in an implicit commentary on the existing level of ministerial interest in the subject—that an additional parliamentary under-secretary should be appointed · with exclusive responsibility for civil aviation. It was ostensibly in response to this last recommendation that Chamberlain announced, soon after the publication of the Cadman Report, that he was promoting the Chancellor of the Duchy of Lancaster, the Irish peer Lord Winterton, to the Cabinet to act as deputy to Swinton and his representative in the Commons, leaving the parliamentary under-secretary, Muirhead, free to devote most of his time to civil aviation.[49]

Lord Cadman himself, with remarkable obtuseness (or naiveté), seemed to feel that there was nothing in his committee's report to reflect on Swinton as the responsible minister: indeed, he wrote to Swinton to assure him that 'your stock is better, if that were possible, as the result of the report of my Committee's work'. Few agreed with him, as was clear when the report was debated in Parliament.[50] Chamberlain tacitly confirmed that all was not well by remarking that 'If the development of civil aviation has lent itself to criticism

for its lagging behind or its slowness, that is largely due to the
. . . fact that . . . the Secretary of State and his staff, and the
aircraft industry itself, have been devoted to pushing forward
[the] enormously accelerated Air Force programme.'[51] And
for the second time in three months the Prime Minister felt it
necessary to make a public defence of Swinton. 'I am bound
to say [Chamberlain told the Commons on 16 March] that I
have not, in my experience, known any Minister who has devoted himself more completely and with a more single mind
to the duties placed upon him in a great office than has my
noble Friend. Far from censuring him, I feel that we ought to
pay him a tribute for the very remarkable results that have
been achieved during his administration.' Swinton was in the
chamber to hear Chamberlain's tribute, as he had been on 6
December. 'I have listened to 2 speeches both too generous in
their praise of what I have done,' he wrote to Chamberlain
that evening. 'I can only say I will do my best to make them
true.' And he added, 'I wish you had not to make so many.'[52]

The criticism of the Air Ministry, and, directly or indirectly,
of its ministerial head, came from several quarters, in Parliament and the press.[53] In the Commons there was Churchill,
with only a small band of personal supporters but briefed by
a number of contacts within the services, and members of the
Conservative back-bench air committee, most of them ex-
pilots, who jealously watched over what they conceived to be
the interests of the air force and the aircraft industry (they
included Balfour, J. T. C. Moore-Brabazon, Perkins, and Oliver
Simmonds). There was also the Labour Opposition which,
having for long opposed rearmament in favour of a nebulous
'collective security under the League', had recently changed
its tactics to one of belabouring the Government for not
pursuing air defence vigorously enough. Attlee, the Labour
leader, combined with Churchill in calling for an inquiry into
the Air Ministry and the air rearmament programme during
the air estimates debate on 15 March. Chamberlain rejected
this demand, but he was privately expressing concern over
'the growing body of criticism, ignorant and sound, malicious
and well-intentioned' which the Air Ministry was attracting.[54]

A good deal of the material for the press and parliamentary
campaign against the Air Ministry emanated from the aircraft

industry, through its forum, the Society of British Aircraft Constructors. The industry's basic complaint was what it saw as official arbitrariness, no doubt bred of the Air Ministry's knowledge that the industry depended upon government contracts for its livelihood. The speed with which the expansion programme had been initiated since 1935 had inevitably led to friction between the Ministry and firms from the delays occurred as an essentially small-scale industry endeavoured, with varying success, to cope with the demands placed upon it. The industry blamed the Air Ministry for failing to give it information about future orders to enable it to avoid gaps in production from order to order, unaware that this was primarily the result of Cabinet indecision about the future air force programme and Treasury reluctance to authorize contracts more than twelve months in advance. There was also a long-standing grievance in the industry about the tendency of the Air Ministry's technical staff to interfere with production by requesting modifications in the design, a tendency which the attempt to approach as nearly as possible to 'ordering from the drawing board' increased, since any problems diagnosed in first deliveries of a new aircraft could be eliminated only in subsequent production runs. The Air Ministry's demand for new aircraft was a constant problem for the industry. Firms were naturally unwilling to discontinue work on aircraft which had become obsolete, but which were easy and profitable to produce, in order to retool for the production of more modern types.[55]

In an effort to remove some of the difficulties in aircraft production Swinton, with the help of Weir and Chamberlain, induced the Society of British Aircraft Constructors to appoint an executive chairman, independent of any of the member companies, 'to expedite the production of military aircraft and to interpret to the Industry and to the Air Ministry the views and wishes of one and the other'. The man appointed— Charles Bruce-Gardner, the industrial adviser to the Bank of England—was very much *persona grata* to the Government and was at least as much a spokesman for the Air Ministry to the industry as for the industry to the ministry. Taking up his post in January, Bruce-Gardner was soon playing a key role in investigating the viability of the volume of aircraft production demanded by Scheme L, and in the general industrial discussions on the voluntary diversion of labour from civilian industry. While his main governmental point of contact was Swinton, he also had close relations with Weir and, mainly through Sir Horace Wilson, with Chamberlain.[56]

On 12 April Swinton sent Chamberlain a progress report on his efforts to organize the industry for the new expanded aircraft programme:

I had a very long discussion with Bruce-Gardner on the ways and means of obtaining the maximum acceleration of deliveries during the next two years, and I have begun my discussions with individual firms to ensure that they are doing everything possible in the way of getting labour. I know from what you said that you will endorse every measure which is practicable to secure maximum output in these two years and I hope I shall be in a position to show that with good will and the best efforts all round by employers and employed it should be possible to get the deliveries of aircraft to give the programme in machines which I have proposed we ought to achieve by April 1940. I am sure it would indeed be a grave misfortune if we cannot achieve this, but I think it is reasonable that I should defer asking for formal decision until I can give you the result of my discussions with the firms.[57]

But Swinton seems to have had only limited success in his interviews with leaders of the aircraft industry. His manner, never conciliatory at the best of times, may have offended some of them, but he could not have been helped in pressing for accelerated production by being hamstrung by the continuing lack of any firm Cabinet decision. He could hector without being able to promise. And the industry leaders, knowing how much the Government needed their co-operation for political reasons, could afford a show of intransigence. Moreover, an Air Ministry decision taken at this time (and approved by the Cabinet on 13 April) to send a mission to the United States under Lord Weir's brother, J. G. Weir, to explore the possibilities of purchasing a number of general reconnaissance and advanced training aircraft to fill existing gaps in the air programme aroused a furore in the British industry. On 20 April Bruce-Gardner sent Swinton a long statement of the SBAC's grievances. It pointed out that 'six weeks after the absorption of Austria, important sections of the Industry consider that they are without sufficient knowledge as to the Air Ministry's future requirements, so as to allow them to plan their future production to give maximum results'. Until decisions were given in many cases still outstanding, the output that might reasonably be expected from the industry over the next two years—the very thing the current exercise was designed to establish—'cannot be accurately assessed'. The statement went on:

The Industry's sense of bewilderment has been aggravated by statements that the Government is investigating the possibility of purchasing American military aircraft. Apart from the serious blow which such purchases strike at British aircraft export trade—on the theory that the Government could not permit export of British military aircraft when it was at the same time buying from America—the members of the Industry do not understand why foreign resources should be explored when they maintain that the industry as a whole has not been and is not working to full capacity.

The fact that the argument here was wholly fallacious—since the US purchases would be of machines not currently being produced by the British industry and would have no effect whatever on British aircraft exports—did nothing to assuage the industry's wounded pride.[58]

Bruce-Gardner sent a copy of the SBAC statement to Horace Wilson, who dutifully passed it and other related material on to Chamberlain as evidence that 'the uneasiness is widespread and may come to a head quite soon'. Wilson told the Prime Minister of a 'stormy' meeting of the SBAC on 20 April, at which proposals to attack Swinton publicly had been headed off only by Bruce-Gardner reading out the text of the letter and statement he was just about to send the Air Minister. For good measure Wilson added the information that 'Cadman, Kenneth Lee and others I have met during the week have spoken to me about aircraft production in terms which make me think that talk is becoming more general and that a wave of dissatisfaction with the Air Ministry is developing fast.'[59]

Another senior Whitehall official had already made his contribution towards undermining the Prime Minister's confidence in the Air Ministry and its ministerial head. On 2 April Warren Fisher sent Chamberlain a table of comparative air strengths of Germany and Britain, 'compiled from reliable sources', which suggested that Britain had currently only

1,634 first-line aircraft (many of them obsolete) against Germany's 5,000 to 5,200, and an estimated output of only 2,100 to 2,250 in 1938 compared with Germany's 6,100, and of 5,000 'assuming effective acceleration' in 1939, compared with Germany's 7,250. Although there could be no doubt about Germany's current numerical superiority, the figures Fisher quoted were misleading, even at the time (no account being taken, for example, of the numbers of obsolete, unserviceable, or converted civil aircraft in the German total) and have been proved to be incorrect by subsequent research. More important was the interpretation he chose to put on them. 'For some years', he told Chamberlain, 'we have had from the Air Ministry soothing syrup and incompetence in equal measure. For the first time in centuries our country is (and must continue to be) at the mercy of a foreign power.'[60] Hankey, to whom Fisher sent a copy of his diatribe, would have none of this. He told Fisher that he always reserved judgement on such matters until he had received 'the views of the responsible Department', but in any case he 'quite definitely' rejected Fisher's accusation about Air Ministry 'soothing syrup and incompetence': 'I have not observed either [and] I have felt bound, in fairness to the Air Ministry, to mention my view to the Prime Minister and Sir Thomas Inskip.'[61]

Despite the aircraft industry's proclaimed difficulty in assessing future production without a firm Government commitment, Bruce-Gardner was able to send production estimates to Swinton on 23 April, while pointing out that 'every week that passes before the accelerated programme is put into operation means a loss of 80 machines a week towards the end of next year'.[62] When the Cabinet met four days later Swinton informed his colleagues that the industry should be able to produce 4,000 aircraft by 31 March 1939, and a further 8,000 by 31 March 1940, provided the necessary additional premises and plant were available (which he anticipated would present no problem) and that there was labour reinforcement—which Swinton thought should be possible 'given good will'. The Prime Minister and the Chancellor had authorized the Air Ministry to proceed on the basis of this estimate and (an unprecedented break with the normal conventions of Treasury control) a Treasury official would be based in the Air Ministry with full authority to give immediate sanction to the necessary items of expenditure. The official would be a member, along with Bruce-Gardner, of a special committee of the Air Council under Winterton, charged with formulating plans for the accelerated programme and giving executive effect to them. Recent difficulties with the industry, which Swinton maintained were caused, not by design alterations by Air Ministry staff (as the industry had frequently alleged) but by 'the fact that it had been impossible for the Air Ministry to give decisions during recent months', could be expected to recede now that its tasks were clear. The Cabinet ratified the action of the Prime Minister and Chancellor and agreed to the ordering of up to 12,000 aircraft—or roughly the numbers which had been envisaged in Scheme L—over the next two years. The financial limits were still formally to apply, somewhat battered though they were, for the Cabinet noted that the accelerated air programme 'would involve expenditure in the next two years that would exceed the figures contemplated for those years, but not the total of £1,650 million provided for the Defence Services during the next five years, and that the Cabinet were not committed to that rate of expenditure beyond 1940'.[63]

An essential concomitant of the acceptance of Scheme L which Swinton did not mention to the Cabinet but had already raised with Chamberlain was the provision of trained crews for the aircraft which the industry was being asked to produce. During Swinton's time at the Air Ministry the annual average intake into the RAF had risen from 1,900 (including 300 pilots) in 1935 to 14,500 (including 1,500 pilots) in 1938, and the total regular establishment from some 30,000 to 83,000.[64] But the increased regular manpower requirement had seriously affected the reserves of trained crews which would be needed if war came, when each aircraft loss meant the loss also of an air-crew. 'Before expansion got underway in 1935', Swinton explained to Chamberlain, there had been 'a constant stream of Air Force pilots and men' passing into the RAF Reserve. Virtually trebling the regular RAF 'has necessarily meant keeping officers and men in the Service and using them in squadrons and training establishments'.[65] An innovation under Swinton was the creation of the RAF Volunteer

Reserve, designed to give spare-time and summer-camp training to young men, particularly those from urban and industrial centres, as airmen, pilots, and observers. Entry to the
new reserve began in April 1937 and by 1938 thirty-three
training centres had been established, while by 1939 the pilot
strength of the RAFVR totalled more than 2,500.[66] But
imaginative though this measure was, it could not make much
impression on the immediate problem, and it was necessary
for Swinton's successor to tell the Cabinet in October 1938
that the most serious limiting factor on the number of mobiliz-
able squadrons by the beginning of 1940 would not be aircraft
but trained crews to man them, particularly in the Reserve.[67]

As Swinton had indicated to the Cabinet on 27 April, Air
Ministry oversight of the implementation of Scheme L, involving the review of proposals for increasing production put
forward by the aircraft manufacturers, was to be in the hands
of a subcommittee of the Air Council with Winterton as chairman. The wider-ranging expansion progress meetings under
Swinton's chairmanship continued as before. The new arrangement had been decided on by Swinton as the responsible
minister and was calculated both to relieve himself of some
of his day-to-day burdens and to make effective use of the
second Cabinet minister in the department. It is difficult,
however, not to believe that his recent problems with the aircraft industry also played their part, making it expedient for
him to withdraw from some of the detailed contact with
them. But whatever may have motivated his decision about
its initial chairmanship, Swinton's creation of what soon
became known as the Air Council Committee on Supply was
not the least of his achievements at the Air Ministry. It was
a first step, the official historians of war production administration have recorded, 'in a reorganization of the production
side of the Air Ministry which, in the course of two years,
was to change it from a single directorate concerned with the
distribution of orders to the major part of a large Department
of State. The Supply Committee during the first month of its
existence had already begun to foreshadow the activities of
the MAP [Ministry of Aircraft Production].'[68]

The first meeting of the new Air Council Committee on
Supply took place on 29 April. A fortnight later its originator

had resigned his office. The parliamentary campaign by
Churchill and other Conservatives, now joined by Labour and
Liberal oppositions, against the alleged slowness of air rearmament came to a head in both Houses on 12 May, with critical
motions by a Liberal, Sir Hugh Seely, in the Commons, and
by Lord Snell, from the Labour front bench, in the Lords.[69]
In the calmer atmosphere of the Lords Swinton more than
held his own, but in the Commons Winterton had a disastrous
time, speaking for over ninety minutes and being interrupted
so frequently that it is often difficult to distinguish speaker
from critics in the written record. Winterton described his
speech, with disarming frankness, many years later: 'I under-
estimated the extent of the feeling against the [Air] Ministry
in the Commons. I thought I could easily dispel the hostility
which was obvious when I rose to speak. But I was too "long-
winded", too parenthetical, and too ready to reply to inter-
ruptions. [The critics] were wrong in their facts and I right in
mine, but my presentation of them had a very bad reception
in the House and the Press alike.'[70] One of the problems was
that not all the 'facts' about the Air Ministry's real achievements under Swinton could be revealed, nor was it possible
for Swinton or Winterton, loyally supporting the Cabinet of
which they were members, to indicate how the air programme
advocated by the Air Ministry had been influenced by general
governmental policy, at least until the *Anschluss* had led to
some relaxation of the financial limits (although Swinton
would have recognized that there were other constraints on
the rate of expansion, such as industrial capacity and industrial and service manpower). The Commons motion was easily
defeated by the Government's overwhelming majority, but
with only 360 votes actually recorded (229 to 131) it was
clear that there were many abstentions on the Government
side. It nevertheless made Swinton's departure virtually inevitable, since no more convincing evidence could be adduced for
the necessity in the current political situation for the Air
Minister to be in the House of Commons.

   Swinton saw Chamberlain on 13 May—according to
Churchill he was summoned to No. 10 while chairing a meeting of the Air Defence Research Committee that morning—
and agreed to resign.[71] What passed between them is uncertain,

as neither appears to have kept a record. The only extant contemporary account seems to be a letter Chamberlain wrote to his sister Hilda four days later. He had had, he said, 'a beastly weekend': 'It's a cruel job to tell one's friend that he would do well to give up his job and that is what I had to do on Friday. I felt very unhappy about it afterwards, for although I never doubted that what I had done was necessary, I knew how Philip must be feeling about it . . . the tone of the press and what I hear of conversations bears out what I said to him, that he would never have a fair chance while he remained at the Ministry but the moment he left people would begin to recognize the worth of what he had done.'[72] From this it is clear that the initiative came from Chamberlain rather than, as in December, from Swinton. And this is consistent with the account Swinton gave in his memoirs ten years later. Chamberlain told him (he wrote): 'that he was more than satisfied with everything that I had done, and that everything must continue to go forward on the lines I had laid down, and that he was convinced that month by month results would increasingly justify our plans and action, but . . . he felt he must have a Secretary of State in the House of Commons who could pacify the House. He said he was anxious that I should remain in the Cabinet, and offered me a choice of several posts; but I did not wish to accept another office, and I think I was right.'[73]

Swinton's resignation and his replacement by Kingsley Wood were announced on 16 May, along with other Government changes, including the transfer of both Winterton and Muirhead to other duties. The customary exchange of letters between Prime Minister and resigning minister was also published. Swinton's, to judge from the number of amendments and erasures on the draft among his papers, must have cost him considerable effort. The final version, a dignified and effective apologia, ran:

My dear Neville,

I have always realized the political difficulty of the Minister in charge of a great spending department being in the House of Lords and unable to speak for his department in the House of Commons; and this difficulty is enhanced when he cannot reply when important questions of policy and administration are debated there. I have more than once asked you whether in these circumstances you felt you ought to make a change. You however expressed a strong wish that my work at the Air Ministry should not be interrupted. But a stage has now been reached where the disadvantages of the interruption you wished to avoid are greatly reduced. When the earlier programme on which we have been working was undertaken, the Air Ministry planned the extension of factories and the creation of new factories on a scale which would not only discharge that programme but would also cope with a largely increased programme if that were required. In the same way the training facilities within the Service have been increased to deal with the great number of pilots and airmen entered up to the present time and additional schools are being provided. It was therefore possible as soon as the Government took the decision to accelerate and increase the existing programme to give immediate effect to that decision. Practically the whole of the orders for the new expansion have been placed. The personnel requirements of the R.A.F. over the next two years have been fully worked out as have the training arrangements for this large intake of pilots and airmen and boys.

My resignation at this time need cause no interruption or delay in the new programme either on the Service side or the industrial side, and it would enable you to meet what I have always realized was a reasonable wish of the House of Commons that a Secretary of State for Air, so long as he is responsible for heavy expenditure, should be a member of that House. As to the rest, I have never felt, as you know, that the inevitable criticism of myself on matters in regard to which public anxiety is necessarily aroused, mattered in comparison with carrying the work through. I am quite content to leave the work I have tried to do at the Air Ministry to be judged at the right time in the light of fuller knowledge than can obviously now be made available.

But what does matter is the execution of our programme and the maintenance of public confidence; and I cannot help feeling that in the actual circumstances of the moment I can help these ends, and help you, best by putting you in a position where any personal criticism of myself may no longer prejudice the full achievement of what we have tried to do together. I would therefore ask you to accept my resignation.

I shall always be deeply grateful to you for all your help.

Yours ever,
Swinton[74]

Chamberlain's reply confirmed that Swinton had 'on more than one occasion offered to make way for a member of the House of Commons if that course would make things easier for me. I have always pressed you to continue, because I was deeply impressed by the prodigious expansion of the Royal Air Force and of the country's capacity to produce aircraft, engines, equipment and trained personnel which you had created by your business ability and your complete devotion of your time and thought to the task on which you were engaged.' The accelerated air programme which the Cabinet had recently approved 'could not have started as it has done if you had not prepared in advance the plans necessary to carry it out, and this applies to all branches of your work'. But Chamberlain felt bound to recognize the truth of what Swinton had said about the head of a great spending department being in the House of Commons and had therefore decided, after careful consideration, that he must accept his resignation. He wished he had at his disposal 'another office which would have retained you in the Cabinet and given further scope for your energy and ability. But you have asked me to release you altogether and I feel I cannot press you further.' Chamberlain concluded by saying how painful it was to him to think that their 'long and I believe fruitful association in political work has come to an end', and expressed the hope that 'from time to time you may be willing to undertake further public service if the opportunity should present itself'.[75]

In a private letter from Yorkshire four days later Swinton assured Chamberlain that what had happened would not affect their friendship or Swinton's political support for him. But he hoped 'it may not be my fate to come back into political life'. If it were his plain duty he would have to do it, but most reluctantly, 'for what has hurt most was saying goodbye to men who have not only been so loyal, but who loved working with me. It is that, not outside criticism or attack, that really hurts.'[76] And abundant testimony of the regard in which he was held at the Air Ministry and in the RAF was provided in the flood of letters which descended on him immediately after his resignation became known.[77] Among them, the man who knew most intimately Swinton's work on the production side, Air Marshal Sir Wilfrid Freeman, the Air Member for Research and Development, wrote to say that he had felt too depressed when meeting Swinton on the latter's farewell visit to the Air Ministry on 16 May 'to express adequately or even intelligently my sorrow at your going and my disgust at the way it was brought about':

There can be few if any in the R.A.F. who do not realize what a lot you have done for the Service and that no one could have worked harder or better for it . . . I should like to say that I have never served a better or more considerate master than yourself—I dont throw that off as an idle thought with the object of pleasing—it just happens to be the truth . . . If we win through in the end it will only be because of the foundations you have laid, and all those who worked alongside you these last few years can have no other opinion.

At a less exalted level but with no less sincerity a RAF pilot expressed his personal regret at the country's loss of 'the most capable, sincere, foresighted and hardworking Air Minister it ever had', an opinion that 'is unanimous everywhere one goes'. Inskip, whose functions as co-ordinating minister had brought him into close contact with all the service departments, but particularly the Air Ministry, told Swinton that 'your people at the Air Ministry all worship you', and went on to pay his own tribute:

[Y]ou have had a terribly rough deal. Some day you will get the credit for all your courage in taking very difficult and critical decisions—very few people at present realize what the country owes to you . . . I . . . want to thank you with all my heart for all you have done to help me when I knew and understood nothing in comparison with you. I have had to do one or two things I know which have distressed you but I shall not forget how you accepted it all. And in other ways you have given me just the encouragement and support that I have sorely needed sometimes. You won't be able to realize how much I have appreciated more than once some word of approval from you.

Inskip wondered what the Air Defence Research Committee was 'going to do' without Swinton, while the Air Ministry's Director of Scientific Research, D. R. Pye, expressed his astonishment 'that in the midst of your preoccupation with production and supply problems you have been able to maintain so much interest [in] the research side of the Department'. Swinton's chief colleague in the area of research, Sir Henry Tizard, told him that 'when you came into office there was practically no defence against air attack and now there is a strong defence which is growing stronger every day thanks to you. I have been proud to help you in a small way—and so has everyone on the scientific side.' And from those who knew of Swinton's work in the industrial field William Rootes, whose motor firm was engaged in the production of both air-frames and aero-engines, testified that 'had it not been for the great vision and energy you displayed the Shadow Scheme would never have come into being'. Neither the Weir papers nor the Swinton papers contain any letter at this time from his indispensable industrial adviser, Lord Weir, but Weir signified his view of the resignation in the clearest possible way— by resigning himself.

Weir's resignation from his unpaid and theoretically unofficial post was the only obvious public protest about the manner of Swinton's departure. But privately there were reservations. The King was clearly unhappy about having to receive back the seals of office from a Secretary of State for Air who 'has done so well at the Air Ministry . . . and [who] will be a great loss to the country at this time'—and pointedly wrote to Chamberlain immediately afterwards to tell him so.[78] Among at least some Conservative back-benchers there was a feeling that Chamberlain had 'lost a lot of caste' over Swinton's resignation.[79] But Swinton was not a widely popular political figure— he had not attempted to make himself one—and in any case he would have given no countenance to a campaign to exploit his summary removal, had there been one. If Chamberlain had been considering his friend's feelings he might have delayed making the change until after the dust of the debate of 12 May had settled, and thus perhaps have made it possible for Swinton to consider transfer to another post without the immediate stigma of apparent failure. Chamberlain's problem was that the Government's opponents had no intention of allowing the dust to settle—there was another critical debate initiated by the Labour Opposition on 25 May (which would have been even earlier had it not been delayed because of the Prime Minister's indisposition)—and 'when a Department is under such continuous bombardment as the Air Ministry has been it is impossible to maintain its position with the head in "another place" '.[80] Churchill, who was as responsible as anyone for the attacks which led to Swinton's downfall, would have agreed. In the months following the resignation he came to realize something of the nature of Swinton's achievement at the Air Ministry and wrote to tell him so. But that achievement could not be adequately projected from the House of Lords, even had there been a more impressive Cabinet assistant in the Commons than Winterton proved to be. Churchill was surely on firm ground in telling Swinton, 'If only you had been in the House of Commons you could, I am sure, have fought your way through.'[81]

The final justification of Swinton's term at the Air Ministry came with the Battle of Britain, fought by Spitfires and Hurricanes ordered in quantity under his authority and controlled by an operational system in Fighter Command which would not have been ready in time without his enthusiastic and effective support. The connection was immediately perceived by King George VI, who noted in his diary on 4 October 1940, when the battle had been virtually won, 'men like Lord Swinton will be remembered'.[82] Surveying Swinton's record in a wider perspective, an Air Ministry official who first entered the department in 1929 and finally left it, as permanent under-secretary, in 1963, concluded that 'Swinton's name towers above those of all other Ministers who have served the R.A.F.'[83]

In May 1938, and for several months thereafter, Swinton remained hopeful that the air force he had done so much to build up would not have to be used in battle. The object of air rearmament for him, as for the rest of the Cabinet, had been to deter German aggression or induce Germany to conclude some sort of agreement on the limitation of air weapons, not to wage war. He had promised Chamberlain at the time of his resignation that he would continue to support the Government. This presented few difficulties for him. While he had not been a major influence in the formulation of the Government's foreign policy (he was not, for example, a member of the Foreign Policy Committee), he was a wholehearted supporter of the policy of appeasement in Europe, into which his view of the purpose of air rearmament fitted naturally. In so far as Eden, as Foreign Secretary, had clashed with Chamberlain on policy—and it was more on technical than substantive issues—Swinton backed Chamberlain. Indeed, some of Eden's supporters numbered Swinton among the Cabinet group (also including Hoare and Kingsley Wood) most inimical to Eden and largely responsible, with Chamberlain, for precipitating his resignation in February 1938.[84] On the ostensible cause of Eden's resignation, the timing of negotiations with Mussolini on the withdrawal of Italian troops from Spain and recognition of the Italian occupation of Abyssinia, Swinton was in full accord with the Prime Minister. A month after Eden had resigned Swinton wrote to Chamberlain, 'I felt more than ever in Cabinet this morning how wise your Italian policy has been and how important agreement there is.'[85]

Swinton, now out of the Government, naturally played no part in ministerial discussions on the Czechoslovak crisis in the autumn of 1938 or in the Munich agreement which tem- porarily resolved it at the expense of Czechoslovak territorial integrity. But, significantly, his first speech in the Lords since his resignation five months before came during the debate on the Munich agreement early in October, and he made it abun- dantly clear in the course of the speech that he considered the policy which had been pursued 'entirely and wholly right' and rejoiced that in the Prime Minister the country had a statesman of 'such courage, such pertinacity and such faith'. Munich was only a first step, and the policy of peace had to be actively pursued. Swinton did not agree with those who maintained that it was impossible to come to understandings with dictators: to argue in that way was a counsel of despair and made war inevitable. He stressed, however, the vital im- portance of completing the rearmament programmes and 'all those plans which are necessary for a nation when it goes to war'. Such military preparedness was 'in no way inconsistent with working for peace and with building up a new world, or with the full confidence that such a world can be built and such a peace can come'.[86] In another Lords debate the follow- ing month he developed the point about preparing the nation as a whole by advocating the preparation of a national register as a basis for conscription if war should come, and the crea- tion of a Ministry of Supply.[87]

Swinton continued for some time to support Chamberlain's appeasement efforts, declaring as late as 27 January 1939 that they had 'immeasurably strengthened the will to peace in men of good will in all lands'.[88] The German invasion of what remained of Czechoslovakia two months later put paid to such hopes. Thereafter Swinton's thoughts turned to obtain- ing a post which would allow him to play a full part in the coming struggle.

CHAPTER 6

War Service

RELEASE from ministerial office had enabled Swinton to pick up once again the threads of his business interests. Directorships in Sofina and other companies associated with Heineman's vast public-utilities empire followed; and since they were largely based in the Iberian peninsula and South America they were relatively little affected by the war, at least in its early stages. He also became a director of Broadcast Relay Service Ltd., which, in addition to running broadcast relay services in Britain and overseas Commonwealth countries, manufactured electronic equipment, including flight-simulators. His absorption in these activities was reflected in the infrequency of his contributions to the deliberations of the House of Lords, although he was more active behind the scenes, becoming in March 1940 a founder member of Lord Salisbury's parliamentary 'Watching Committee' formed from members of both Houses to keep a constructively critical and experienced non-ministerial eye on the administration of the war.[1] One of the committee's most consistent themes was the need for reforms in the higher organization of defence; and as late as May 1942 Swinton was calling in the Lords for a 'Great General Staff' (which, in practice, seemed to be little more than the institution of a permanent chairman of the Chiefs of Staff Committee).[2]

Even before the Watching Committee had started its work Swinton had accepted the first of two Government appointments he was to hold up to June 1942, when he resumed his ministerial career as Resident Minister in West Africa. Both of these appointments involved him in direct contact with ministers, officials, and government departments, but neither was officially a ministerial post, nor, apart from the necessity of observing official secrecy, did they limit him in his parliamentary activities (including the Watching Committee) nor compel him to vacate his directorships. A Ministry of Economic Warfare had been set up immediately war started, on the lines of the Ministry of Blockade in the First World War, with the prime objective of denying to Germany supplies from neutral countries essential to its war effort. Even if a full naval blockade could have been mounted—and the British navy was fully extended in convoy and anti-submarine work—it would not have been sufficient by itself, since a large proportion of German supplies came overland. In these circumstances it was essential to supplement blockade by the pre-emptive purchase of strategic supplies sought by the Germans—oilseed, petroleum, chrome, wolfram, and many more—inevitably at prices above the strict commercial value of the commodities. The main initial effort was concentrated on the Balkans and south-east Europe, in order to try to find some means of countering German economic penetration of the area. At first, progress was slow, hindered by the reluctance of the Treasury to finance any substantial expenditure for purely pre-emptive purposes and by the absence of a separate purchasing organization able to deploy greater freedom of action and commercial skill in highly unusual circumstances than could the officials of the various departments engaged in purchasing, such as the ministries of Food and Supply. In December 1939 and January 1940 the outlines of a new organization were hammered out by the Treasury, Ministry of Economic Warfare, Foreign Office, and other departments concerned. It was to be as close as possible to an ordinary commercial company, with its own board of directors, and able to take its own trading decisions, although subject to governmental policy control (exercised for the most part by the Ministry of Economic Warfare), with the Treasury as sole shareholder but not exercising normal Treasury financial control. The decision to create such a company was communicated to British diplomatic representatives in the Balkans, Greece, and Turkey on 26 January. Shortly afterwards Swinton accepted an invitation to become its chairman.[3]

Swinton immediately threw himself into the highly congenial

task of working out the detailed *modus operandi* of the new organisation and selecting his fellow directors and key staff. The more he studied the problem, he later recalled,

the more sure I felt that, if we were to succeed, we must do more than merely conduct a pre-emptive campaign. We must secure the goodwill of the Governments and the business communities in the countries where we should be operating . . . These countries would not only wish to sell all they could export, but they would want to be sure of receiving the imports necessary to maintain the economic life of their people. If we were to succeed, we must compete with Germany not merely as a buyer but as a seller, and must be able to assure these countries that they would receive a reasonable proportion of imports through our agency.

He therefore proposed that the company should not only be a purchasing organization but also a source of supply, and the proposal was accepted. But, this decided, there was a need to make an organizational distinction between the two functions. On the one hand, there was 'pure economic warfare', involving pre-emptive buying at almost any price: the more the Germans wanted a particular commodity the more they were prepared to pay for it (and in the case of wolfram this became fifty times the commercial price). In this field there would inevitably be heavy losses, and all that could be attempted by prudent management was to keep them as low as possible. On the other hand, following Swinton's extension of the organization's terms of reference, there would be 'a wide range of activities which were necessary to implement our policy, and which were more nearly commercial, though ordinary commercial firms would not undertake them either because of war conditions or because the risk was greater than a commercial firm could be expected to shoulder'. It was therefore decided to form two companies, under the same board of directors, but with separate accounts. On 11 April 1940 the United Kingdom Commercial Corporation (UKCC) was formed, with an initial capital of £500,000 provided by the Treasury, to handle the transactions which could reasonably be considered as commercial: and this was followed, on 24 April, by the formation of a subsidiary company known as the English and Scottish Commercial Corporation (ESCC), with an initial Treasury-provided capital of £250,000, to engage in economic warfare operations.[4]

Swinton's wide governmental and business experience enabled him to tap varied talents for his fellow directors on the UKCC (and ESCC) board. For joint managing directors he obtained F. H. Nixon, head of the Export Credits Guarantee Department and familiar to Swinton from his Board of Trade days, and J. H. Hambro, a managing director of Hambros Bank. The other directors included the American A. Chester Beatty, chairman of several African mining enterprises; G. A. McEwen, a managing director of the Co-operative Wholesale Society; and C. P. Lister, head of an engineering firm.[5] Others, of equal standing, joined as the UKCC's activities expanded, both in geographical scope—for example, to include the Iberian peninsula and much of the Middle East—and in scale. By the end of the first year of operations the capital of the UKCC had been increased threefold to £1,500,000, while that of the ESCC had risen from £250,000 to £4m. Thereafter, in a remarkable expression of confidence by the Treasury in the UKCC's managerial acumen, it was agreed that no further increases of capital would be authorized, further requirements of the two companies being provided against notes issued by them. At the peak of their operations the capital employed reached £95m. and the annual turnover £152m. The final account showed a profit of £20m. for the 'commercial' UKCC and a loss of £32m. for the pre-emptive ESCC—a state of affairs which that normally austere body, the Public Accounts Committee of the House of Commons, considered eminently satisfactory when it came to review the operations of UKCC and ESCC. Those operations, as Swinton later summed them up, had 'hardly any limit': 'We were to make every kind of purchase; minerals, raw materials of many kinds, foodstuffs, and a variety of finished goods. We were called upon to supply every range of imports, to engage in shipping and other transport on a vast scale, to conduct complicated financial transactions all over the world, and to maintain the closest relations with a host of Government Departments and Foreign Missions, and later to work in close and happy partnership with the United States.'[6]

Swinton's own contribution to the UKCC's work, as he himself described it, 'consisted mainly in the selection of my colleagues, in the conception of the scope and general lines on which the Corporation should work, in captaining a first-class team, and in agreeing general lines of policy with Ministers'. The launching and general supervision of so unusual a government agency, operating in a field so vital to the war effort, was an important-enough task in itself. But less than six weeks after the UKCC had officially begun operations Swinton accepted an even more demanding additional assignment from the new Prime Minister which meant his devolving much of his UKCC work on to his managing directors, particularly Nixon, although he continued to be consulted on important questions.[7]

Swinton's new task was the direct result of the atmosphere of near-panic, suspicion, and rumour engendered in Britain from May 1940 by the success of the German 'blitzkrieg', which, having compelled the withdrawal of British forces from Norway—and, indirectly, the replacement of Chamberlain by Churchill's Coalition Government on 11 May—had engulfed the Low Countries and northern France. The Dutch formally surrendered on 15 May, five days after being invaded, and the Belgians followed suit on 27 May, the day the evacuation of British troops from Dunkirk began. On 10 June Mussolini decided it was safe to bring Italy into the war on Germany's side. Less than a fortnight later France had surrendered.

The British people could be forgiven feelings of bewilderment and alarm at these cataclysmic events, which seemed clearly to presage a German invasion of Britain. Their political leaders, less ignorant of the realities of the situation, were even more alarmed as they studied assessments of the German victories, starting with the report of Sir Nevile Bland, British Minister to the Netherlands. On the basis of his Dutch experiences Bland expatiated on the dangers of 'the enemy in our midst', the 'fifth column' of native Germans and Austrians resident in the country who, 'when the signal is given . . . will at once embark on widespread sabotage and attacks on civilians and the military indiscriminately', in close co-operation with parachutists dropped from German aircraft. To avoid this danger Bland urged that all Germans and Austrians be interned immediately. Halifax, the Foreign Secretary, in presenting Bland's report to the War Cabinet on 15 May, asked that it be 'brought to the attention of those responsible

for Britain's defences'.[8] On the following day Swinton was
charged by Churchill to 'find out whether there is a fifth
column in this country and if so to eliminate it'.[9] Churchill
explained to the Commons two months later the circumstances of his invitation to Swinton:

> After the dark, vile conspiracy which in a few days laid the trustful
> Dutch people at the mercy of Nazi aggression, a wave of alarm passed
> over this country, and especially in responsible circles, lest the same
> kind of undermining tactics and treacherous agents of the enemy were
> at work in our Island . . . Several branches of State Departments are, of
> course, always charged with the duty of frustrating such designs. But
> they were not working smoothly. There were overlaps and underlaps,
> and I felt in that hour of anxiety that this side of the business of National
> Defence wanted pulling together. I therefore asked Lord Swinton to
> undertake this task.[10]

A number of departments and agencies were already concerned in one way or another with countering enemy subversion and disseminating information and intelligence essential
for its discovery. There was the Home Office, particularly its
police, immigration, and aliens departments, and its powers,
under defence regulation 18B, to secure the detention of suspected persons (including British subjects) without trial; the
service departments' intelligence directorates; the Foreign
and Colonial Offices, concerned with British interests overseas;
the Ministry of War Transport; the Post Office; postal censor-
ship (a fertile source of intelligence); customs and excise: the
Ministry of Information; the BBC, the Metropolitan Police
Special Branch; and the specialized security and secret intelligence services such as M.I.5 (the internal and imperial security
service), M.I.6 or SIS (secret intelligence service), and the
Government Code and Cypher School (under the head of
M.I.6 but separate from it).

Swinton's assignment—well suited to his qualities of drive
and executive flair—was to co-ordinate the activities of these
bodies in the battle against enemy subversion and sabotage,
whether in Britain itself or 'anywhere and everywhere British
ships and supplies could be affected'.[11] The chosen instrument
of co-ordination was officially designated the Home Defence
(Security) Executive, or, simply, the Security Executive, but
when its existence became known it almost inevitably came
to be dubbed 'the Swinton Committee'. Formally constituted

by the War Cabinet on 28 May 1940, it had its first meeting
(in its modest headquarters on one floor of Kinnaird House
in Pall Mall) on the same day, although it had been informally
in being since 17 May.[12] The Prime Minister had ultimate responsibility for its operation, but the Lord President of the
Council (Chamberlain until October 1940, then Sir John
Anderson) acted for him in the field of internal security.
Both were represented on the Security Executive (Churchill
by Desmond Morton, Anderson by Norman Brook), which
included representatives from the relevant departments and
agencies. It also had one, later two, independent non-departmental members, primarily to inspire public confidence that
in the internment of suspects the needs of security were
fairly balanced against the infringement of individual rights
involved. Alfred Wall, a leading trade-unionist as general
secretary of the London Society of Compositors, was a member from the beginning; but it was not until after rumours
about the work of 'the Swinton Committee' had appeared in
the press and were raised in the House of Commons in July
and August 1940 that the prominent Liberal MP Isaac Foot
joined the Executive.[13] Initially the staff consisted only of
a young civil servant, William Armstrong, who acted as secretary to the Executive (and its *ad hoc* committees) as well as
private secretary to Swinton throughout Swinton's term as
chairman. Later on, Armstrong was joined by a more senior
colleague from the Home Office, Ronald Wells. Swinton himself brought in Joseph Ball, from Conservative Central Office
(and formerly of M.I.5), as deputy chairman, a role in which
he was succeeded in early 1942 by Sir Herbert Creedy, a
former permanent head of the War Office. Two other Swinton
appointments to the Executive staff were Reginald Duthy, a
business associate of Swinton, and Kenneth Diplock, a rising
young lawyer whom Swinton had met as a legal adviser to
Heineman's Sofina.[14]

The Security Executive was a curious phenomenon, even
among the mass of *ad hoc* organizations spawned by the
exigencies of war. In form it was an inter-departmental committee, but its chairman was neither a minister nor a civil
servant. Swinton's role was, however, virtually indistinguishable from that of a minister, for while he was not officially

a member of the Government he had 'more or less the same powers as a Cabinet Minister'. Forty years on Lord Armstrong recalled his service under Swinton at the Security Executive as his first—and most educative—experience of a minister at close hand. It is thus understandable that a distinguished official war-historian who recorded this period should have assumed, incorrectly, that Swinton was in fact a minister.[15] The word 'Executive' in the organization's title was a misnomer, since, although the Executive had an originating and co-ordinating role, responsibility for executive action rested with the department or agency concerned. But Swinton's personality, status, wide governmental experience, and ability to claim the backing of the Prime Minister were sufficient to ensure that the Executive's recommendations were implemented.[16]

In one important security sphere, however, Swinton was soon to have direct executive responsibility in addition to his general co-ordinating functions. Since December 1939 the operations of M.I.5, the chief internal security agency, had—along with those of M.I.6—been under scrutiny by Lord Hankey, a member of Chamberlain's War Cabinet.[17] Hankey's work had not been completed by the time Chamberlain gave way to Churchill (and Hankey himself was removed from the War Cabinet to less exalted ministerial office), but it was no doubt on the evidence he had adduced that Churchill concluded that counter-espionage was 'not working smoothly' and required urgent remedial measures. At the end of May Sir Vernon Kell, who had been director of M.I.5 since 1909 and was then in his sixty-eighth year, was removed from his post. On 22 July Swinton was formally entrusted by the War Cabinet with personal responsibility for M.I.5, but he had probably in practice taken over control in May, and could well have played the major role in Kell's removal, as he certainly did in the selection of Kell's eventual successor, Sir David Petrie, from the Indian police.[18] This is an aspect of Swinton's work which is even more impenetrably shrouded in official secrecy than the general activities of the Security Executive (on which he was at least able to write a discreet but not uninformative chapter in his memoirs). It is clear that he took a hand in the appointment of M.I.5 headquarters staff, bringing in, for example, an expert from Burroughs Business Machines to reorganize Kell's vast card index of potential subversives and enemy sympathizers, which was inevitably frequently out of date or inaccurate.[19] He also developed a close personal interest in the work of the Radio Security Service, under Brigadier R. Gambier-Parry, which intercepted enemy intelligence traffic and maintained radio communication with British secret service officers and agents in the field; and in the M.I.5 section under J. C. Masterman which supervised the highly successful double-agent operation. With Masterman, one of the many university importations into the wartime secret services, he formed a firm friendship which lasted until Swinton's death.[20] There are indications that by the time he left the Security Executive Swinton regarded himself as having assumed certain responsibilities for M.I.6 as well as M.I.5, and that he may have been contemplating carrying out a review of the organization of M.I.6 (to which the Radio Security Service was transferred in May 1941).[21] While much, unfortunately, has to be speculative, sufficient can be gleaned to warrant the conclusion that Swinton's involvement with the secret services considerably strengthened his position as non-executive chairman of the co-ordinating Security Executive, to the activities of which we now turn.

The immediate problem which Swinton and Security Executive were expected by the War Cabinet to confront was the elimination of the risk of a Fifth Column operating in Britain, and this, as Chamberlain told the War Cabinet on 27 May, necessitated measures to control enemy aliens and alien refugees. The procedure for classifying aliens had been worked out by the Home Office early in the war and was being applied by 120 tribunals from October 1939. There were those in Category A—Germans and Austrians (and, after Italy's declaration of war on 10 June 1940, Italians) who might be expected, given the opportunity, 'to help their own countrymen or hinder the war efforts of this country'—who were to be interned; those in Category B, who were to be subject to certain restrictions short of internment; and Category C aliens—refugees who had left their countries as a result of Nazi oppression on racial, religious, or political grounds and thus 'hostile to the Nazi regime and ready to assist this country rather than to assist the enemy'—who could remain at liberty.[22] With the invasion of the Low Countries and the disasters which followed in quick succession, the process was applied more rigorously: for example, the Home Office informed chief constables on 30 May that they could now intern any Germans or Austrians in Category C 'where there are grounds for doubting the reliability of any individual'. There can be little doubt that the Security Executive had an important role in all this. While M.I.5 could in theory only advise on who constituted a security risk and it was for the Home Secretary alone to authorize internment or detention by the police Special Branch at his discretion, in practice the creation of the Security Executive had changed the relationship. As was noted in the Foreign Office some months later, 'the constitution in the spring of 1940 of the Swinton Committee, with direct access to the Cabinet independently of the Home Secretary, had the consequence of raising M.I.5 from their former advisory position to what is now in effect an executive function, so that it is in fact their view rather than that of the Home Office which over matters of internment and detention in the long run prevails'.[23] And action against aliens, many of whom were undoubtedly unjustly suspected of disloyalty, went beyond internment and detention. On 3 June 1940 Swinton, speaking for the Security Executive, represented to Chamberlain 'the danger of retaining alien internees in this country' in view of the help they might give to invading forces—a sentiment which Churchill had already expressed in the War Cabinet—and soon after this deportations to Canada began.[24] One of the deportation ships, the *Arandora Star*, which sailed from Southampton on 1 July with 712 Italians and 478 Germans on board, was torpedoed by a German U-boat and went down with the loss of many lives. This was the most tragic event in a miserable business which could no doubt have been handled with greater humanity and prescience than was displayed at the time—as two recent studies of British wartime treatment of aliens (by the Gillmans and Ronald Stent) have passionately maintained. But an embattled country, faced by imminent invasion by a well-armed and ruthless foe, is perhaps not the best place to seek for human compassion and calm deliberation. And the danger which the blunt and often inhuman instrument of internment was designed, however imperfectly, to meet—infiltration by enemy agents—certainly existed and continued to require vigilance even after the invasion threat had receded. A simple cover for such agents was provided by the mass influx of refugees from the countries overrun by the German armies, and Swinton early decided that every arrival on British shores had to be monitored. He arranged for the compulsory acquisition of the Royal Victoria Patriotic School in Wandsworth and had it converted into a British-style Ellis Island, through which all refugees and other aliens who arrived by sea or air had to pass, unless vouched for by one of the military or secret services or covered by a diplomatic passport.[25] Internment policy, Swinton was at pains to point out in the account of the Security Executive in his 1948 memoirs, 'was only a fraction of its work'. But it was the aspect which most attracted contemporary criticism, as in the House of Commons in the summer of 1940, and he must have been relieved on both humanitarian and political grounds when the removal of the threat of invasion made possible a progressive alleviation of the draconian measures which had been thought necessary.[26]

A constant preoccupation of Swinton and his Executive was the port security of British ships, their cargo, and their crews, both in Britain and, even more important, in overseas ports, especially those in neutral countries where enemy agents had so much greater freedom of action. Seamen were valuable sources of information about ships and their voyages, and (Swinton wrote) 'the Germans were fully alive to their opportunities and had a vast organization in foreign ports, well camouflaged, for trying to get hold of seamen who might talk unguardedly, if suitably entertained, and who might with luck be made to miss their ship'. Swinton saw the problem not only as one of security but also of the availability of good port welfare facilities. Well before the United States had entered the war he sent a mission under Sir Connop Guthrie, who had been Ministry of Shipping representative in America in the First World War, to develop, with generous American help, welfare organizations at US ports where British ships docked. This was, however, only Guthrie's overt role. His covert task was to run the Security Division of British Security

Co-ordination which, under the formidable Canadian, William Stephenson, supervised all British secret service work in America, in close collaboration—both before and after US entry into the war in December 1941—with the FBI and the Office of Strategic Services. On Guthrie's advice, men with wide experience of merchant shipping as well as knowledge of local conditions were recruited as consular security officers in all the main US ports to supervise anti-sabotage precautions and the suppression of information about ships' cargoes, movements, and convoys. Similar security arrangements were later extended, as a result of another of Swinton's initiatives, to the principal ports in South America.[27]

Cloaked in secrecy though Swinton's activities at the Security Executive from 1940 to 1942 were—and are—their value was placed highly by those best able to judge. When news of his impending departure for West Africa became known, two senior members of M.I.5 wrote to him to express their regret, one of them, Dick White (later to have the unique distinction of becoming head, successively, of both M.I.5 and M.I.6), remarking on the extent to which Swinton had 'raised the prestige of our department and as it were put us on the map'. But the most impressive testimony of all came from Sir John Anderson, the War Cabinet member with overall responsibility under the Prime Minister for internal security. Anderson wrote to Swinton on 4 June: 'This is a sad business for me but since the change is presumably to your liking I can only try and rejoice with you. I am certainly glad you resume your rightful station as a Minister but I wish I could think that all the security arrangements which you have built up would go on unimpeded. I have always thought it a most remarkable piece of work and if I may say so without impertinence I do not know anyone else who could have done it.' It says much for the firmness of the foundations laid by Swinton at the Security Executive that its work continued seemingly unaffected by the advent of a new chairman, Duff Cooper, of markedly inferior administrative ability and powers of application.[28]

The role of West Africa in the war effort had been transformed by the fall of France. With the closing of the Mediterranean to British shipping, the sea-route to Egypt, India,

South-East Asia, and Australia lay down the coast of Africa and round the Cape. The great natural harbour of Freetown in Sierra Leone became an important assembly port for convoys and independently routed ships, both on the route to and from the Cape and across the Atlantic; while from West African air bases general reconnaissance aircraft operated against enemy submarines. No less important was West Africa's place in air communications to the Middle East, which now lay across West and Central Africa through Khartoum to Egypt. And when the Japanese overran Malaya and the East Indies early in 1941 West Africa became as significant economically as it had already become strategically, as a substitute supplier of the raw materials, such as tin, rubber, palm oil, and oilseeds, lost as a result of the Japanese victories, and as a source of other strategic minerals, including manganese, chrome, and bauxite.

The four British colonies—Gambia, Sierra Leone, the Gold Coast, and Nigeria—were separated from each other by hundreds of miles of French colonial territories. The French colonies, constituting French West Africa, had (with the North African colonies) remained loyal to the French Government after it had moved to Vichy, and had successfully resisted the operations of the British and Free French to capture Dakar; their continuing hostility meant that at any time West Africa might become a theatre of war. The French Equatorial colonies, starting with Chad in August 1940, had, however, rallied to the Free French cause, a development of great importance in establishing the air reinforcement route across Africa. The Belgian Congo, with its rich resources of minerals and foodstuffs, had remained loyal to the Belgian Government in Exile. British naval headquarters, followed later by air headquarters, were established at Freetown, and army headquarters at Achimota, just north of Accra in the Gold Coast. American entry into the war led to the build-up of United States forces in the area in the early months of 1942.

For most aspects of the war-effort West Africa had necessarily to be regarded as a single entity, geographically scattered though the British colonies were. But their civilian administration remained in the hands of the four governors, who early in the war had established a governors' conference under the chairmanship of the Governor of Nigeria, with a secretariat and a supply-centre based in Lagos. At first the conference was restricted to making recommendations for the consideration of the individual governments, but in February 1942 the Governor of Nigeria was given overriding powers to act in certain supply and manpower matters, propaganda, and questions relating to occupied enemy territory, together with any other matters if necessitated by 'extreme urgency'.[29]

But the acquisition of these new powers by the Governor of Nigeria did not prevent the British Chiefs of Staff, briefed by General Giffard, the army General Officer Commanding in West Africa, from expressing dissatisfaction with the machinery for co-ordinating the civil administrations and the military authorities in West Africa. In April 1942 they proposed the appointment of a military governor-general for the whole area. Rather surprisingly, the proposal met with the approval of the Colonial Office, although it recognized that, for the *amour propre* of the governors and to avoid arousing controversy about the post-war development of the West African colonies, the title of 'governor-general' should be replaced by that of 'commander-in-chief' or 'supreme commander'.[30] On 13 May Cranborne, the Colonial Secretary, circulated a paper on the proposal to the War Cabinet, which discussed it on 18 May. It accepted that there was a need for new co-ordinating machinery, but, with greater prescience than Cranborne, following the Chiefs of Staff, had displayed, decided that the situation—involving quasi-diplomatic and supply functions as well as the administrative co-ordination of civil and defence services—called, not for a service officer, but for a civilian minister, on the lines of the already established resident Minister of State in the Middle East.[31]

Several names were considered for the new post before Swinton was approached, and it was first offered to H. F. C. Crookshank, the Financial Secretary to the Treasury, who declined on health grounds. [32] It was on 29 May that Cranborne minuted Churchill with the suggestion of Swinton, who, he said, would have 'immense advantages' as a former Colonial Secretary and 'with his great drive . . . would immediately take a grip on the situation'. Cranborne appreciated that 'it may be impossible to spare him from here', since Anderson, the Lord President, 'has often told me what valuable work he is doing'. There seems no doubt that it was indeed the importance attached to Swinton's work at the Security Executive which accounted for the delay in considering him for a post for which he had such obvious qualifications. But once his name had come forward Churchill lost no time in issuing the invitation.[33] Nor does it look as if Swinton took long to make up his mind to accept it. Less than a week later the Prime Minister was being informed that the details of Swinton's appointment had been worked out in discussions with Sir Horace Wilson at the Treasury and with other departments. His salary was to be the full ministerial salary of £5,000, with allowances of £3,000. It was agreed informally that the appointment was to run for six months in the first instance, 'with the possibility of extension if this is necessary to get the job well started'. The temporary nature of the assignment was underlined by the fact that Swinton, while he naturally had to give up the chairmanship of the Security Executive, still formally retained his chairmanship of the United Kingdom Commercial Corporation, his functions being taken over by an acting chairman. With typical insight into the practical needs of the job in a region with few telephones and poor road and rail communications Swinton had requested an aeroplane for his personal use in West Africa, and this, too, was being arranged by the Air Ministry.[34]

Swinton's general function, as defined by the Prime Minister's directive to him (approved by the War Cabinet on 8 June), was to ensure 'the effective co-operation in the prosecution of the war' of the civil and military services in West Africa. On the civil side he was to work through the governors, presiding over the governors' conference when he thought fit. In the political field he was to give broad political guidance to the service commanders; maintain good relations with the Free French and Belgian authorities; and deal with problems arising out of the ever-increasing interests of the United States in the region. His special task was to see that West African resources were used most effectively for the war-effort, paying particular attention to transportation questions. Where necessary, he was to co-ordinate the activities of representatives of British government departments in West Africa, including the

Ministries of War Transport, Production, Economic Warfare, and Information. The directive was, however, careful to point out that Swinton's functions were not to impair the existing responsibilities of service commanders, governors, or other British representatives in the area, all of whom would continue to correspond direct with their respective departments. Swinton himself was to be responsible to the War Cabinet through its secretary (Bridges), with the right of direct access to the Prime Minister on defence matters, though the usual channel of communication with the home Government was to be through the Colonial Office.[35]

The few weeks before flying out to West Africa on 10 July to take up his post as Resident Minister were hectic ones for Swinton, with consultations and briefing sessions in service and civil departments and the various medical precautions which necessarily precede a prolonged visit to an inhospitable tropical clime. He had also to choose his staff and the site for his headquarters. For the latter he settled on vacant buildings at Achimota College, near Accra in the Gold Coast, where General Giffard had already established his army headquarters, and it was arranged that the governors' conference secretariat and West African supply-centre should be transferred there from Lagos. As his senior official adviser—his *chef de cabinet* or chief of staff as he variously described him—Swinton obtained his highly efficient former private secretary at the Air Ministry, Folliott Sandford, who had just returned from work in Montreal, and his small staff also included representatives from the Foreign Office, the Colonial Office, and the Ministry of Information, with a young naval officer as ADC.[36]

Achimota, where Swinton and his party arrived on 12 July, was an ideal locale for his activities. Set in a spacious park, planted with many kinds of flowering trees, and surrounded by woods, the buildings and playing-fields of the college (where a boys' school still operated) provided as attractive a working environment as could be found anywhere in West Africa. Under Swinton's presiding influence the atmosphere in the office and mess of 'Resmin' (the contraction habitually used for both Minister and his establishment) was friendly and entirely free from protocol.[37] The work was absorbing and Swinton entered into it with almost boyish enthusiasm.

As early as 22 July he was writing to his wife from Freetown, Sierra Leone, where he had just presided over the first meeting of his War Council of governors and service commanders: 'This is a grand job and terribly interesting. It combines strategic problems of the three Services, every kind of supply, transport, docks and labour questions. American, French and Belgian relations. Native affairs. Health.' But it was soon obvious to him that the period of six months provisionally set for his tour would be insufficient to accomplish his task, for on 9 October he was telling his wife, 'There is so much to do here that I am afraid I shan't get home to report for some time.'[38]

The arrival in their midst of an ennobled British Minister with powers apparently even greater than those wielded by that embodiment of British authority, the Governor, was the source of some wonder to ordinary Africans. Swinton inevitably came to be referred to as 'the Lord', a practice not without potential for mild confusion, as he recounts in his memoirs. Invited to lunch in the Achimota mess soon after Swinton's arrival, the American air-force commander, General Fitzgerald (whose headquarters were in Accra and with whom Swinton developed excellent relations), apologized for arriving late. 'I had the hell of a time finding your headquarters,' the General told his host. 'No one could direct me. I asked for the Resident Minister or the Minister of State, but I drew a blank every time. At last an African said to me "Master want the House of the Lord?" I did not think I did, but I thought I had better give it a try, and here I am.' On another occasion a schoolmistress at the Achimota boys' school readily allowed one of the Resmin servant boys to take his pick of the flowers in her luxuriant and lovingly tended garden when he asked, 'Missie, may I gather flowers for the Lord's table?' Her sense of humour was put to the test when she later discovered that the floral decoration was for use, not on the church altar, but on the Minister's dinner-table, where distinguished visitors were being entertained.[39]

Limitations of space preclude a full examination of the challenging and diverse responsibilities which Swinton successfully discharged in West Africa, in a context unlike anything he had encountered in his previous governmental experience.

It is a period for which his private papers (elsewhere often disappointingly skimpy) are particularly rich. From the moment of his arrival he maintained a continuous correspondence with the two successive secretaries of state, first Cranborne and then, from November 1942, Oliver Stanley; while his letters to his wife contain abundant comment on his work. Written with the authority and knowledge of one who had himself been Colonial Secretary, Swinton's West African letters represent, for the student of British colonial policy, a unique record of developments during a period of rapid change, both social and economic.[40] It was an assignment, moreover, from which he clearly derived both pleasure and satisfaction. His contemporary, succinct, summary of his two years in West Africa was: 'I have loved my work here and I have had a grand team.'[41] His enjoyment comes through his otherwise rather unrevealing memoirs, written four years later. Whereas his lengthy period as President of the Board of Trade is covered in thirty-eight pages, his years as Colonial Secretary in forty, and the vital years at the Air Ministry in forty-seven, his account of his much briefer West African experience occupies sixty-one pages.[42]

Swinton's time in West Africa may be seen as falling roughly into two periods, with the point of division around the early part of 1943. In the first period the problems were primarily political, military, and supply, with a considerable overlap between all three. The Vichy authorities in French West Africa were for much of the period a potentially dangerous factor, and there was a risk of the air-route to the Middle East being disrupted from the north, so the construction of a second route had to be put in hand. But the British victory at El Alamein in October 1942, the joint American-British 'Operation Torch' in North Africa in November, and the subsequent complete defeat of the enemy in North Africa led to a détente with French West Africa (in which Swinton's discussions with Pierre Boisson, the Vichy Governor-General, played an important part),[43] and the dispatch of a British consul-general and economic mission to Dakar. West Africa was still a vital link in communications with the major war-zones (if less so with the opening of the Mediterranean to Allied shipping) but it had virtually ceased to be a potential war-zone itself. In

the second period, from early 1943 to Swinton's final departure from West Africa in October 1944, the external political
problems subsided, the problems of sea convoy protection
continued, but as a joint operation with the French, and the
military problem took on a different aspect when two divisions
of West African troops were formed to take part in the Burma
campaign. The supply problem remained, with the need for
West African products as great as ever, but, in addition, both
Whitehall and colonial governments were becoming preoccupied with post-war developments, and the emphasis of
Swinton's role changed.

The formal machinery established by Swinton for the co-
ordination of the war-effort in British West Africa was the
West African War Council, made up of the four governors
and the three service commanders. Much of the detailed work
took place in the Council's committees, also under Swinton's
chairmanship: the Service Members Committee, set up at the
first Council meeting in July 1942; the Civil Members Committee, consisting of the four governors, established in January
1943; and the Supply and Production Committee, which had
its first meeting in May 1943 (and which later worked closely
with the Americans in the Anglo-American Supply Committee). The strategic task of increasing West African production,
both for export and to reduce the demand for imports (and
the shipping needed to bring them), had obvious value for the
future, even without being consciously planned to do so. Improved agricultural production and marketing, the development of economic local industries, improved communications,
water supplies, the anti-malaria measures undertaken by the
services, the trade training of locally-recruited service personnel, harnessing the interest and activity of chiefs and local
administrations—all these and much else that was accomplished
contributed at least as much to the long-term development of
the region as to the effective prosecution of the war. Swinton
was soon giving thought to the task of 'marrying war experience to the future' (as he expressed it to President Roosevelt
when he met him in The Gambia, at Churchill's request, on
the President's journey home from the Casablanca Conference
in January 1943).[44] At an early meeting of the Civil Members
Committee he directed the governors' attention to future

economic policy with a paper which envisaged colonial governments pursuing actively interventionist policies for an indefinite period. His proposals were based on two political
premises. The first was that the 'parent state' (France and
Belgium as well as Britain) would remain responsible for the
administration of its colonial territories. 'It would be the duty
of the parent state to guide and develop the social, economic,
and political institutions of the colonial peoples until they
can safely assume the responsibilities of government themselves,' while their natural resources 'should be organised and
marketed not for the promotion of merely commercial ends,
but for the service of the people concerned and the world as
a whole'. Swinton's second assumption was that there would
be international regional co-operation through regional commissions comprising the parent states and other states 'which
have a major strategic or economic interest' in the region. On
these assumptions the objectives of economic policy, Swinton
believed, should be to assist the primary producer, who must
be the main centre of interest; to control more effectively
but not try to eliminate the activities of the great European
firms; and to develop local industries, free from government
management.[45]

When received at the Colonial Office, Swinton's paper met
with general approval, one official minuting that it was 'entirely in line with our own way of thinking'. The Office was
already engaged in hammering out a West African policy and
thus the paper could not have been more timely.[46] Officials
were no more capable than Swinton—or most of those giving
serious thought to colonial problems—of foreseeing the rapidity of West African political development as soon as the war
ended: that within fifteen years the complete independence
of the Gold Coast and Nigeria would be achieved, transforming
the whole colonial empire. What was being envisaged early in
1943 was 'a broadening of the basis of local institutions', the
object of which 'should be to train Africans towards taking
a greater part in the management of their own affairs', coupled
with 'a forward policy in industrial development and social
welfare'. It was recognized that there would be 'vocal elements
in Africa who will want to quicken the tempo . . . but in West
Africa the "political" elements so far are a small portion of

the population . . . It may, therefore, be possible to look forward to the application of a sound progressive policy without having too many hand-to-mouth expedients forced on us by ephemeral agitation.' In similar vein, Swinton was arguing that, by contrast to French colonial policy which he was observing at first hand, British policy sought to train Africans in order to equip them to accept real responsibility for their own affairs. But this did not necessarily mean the full paraphernalia of parliamentary government on the Westminster model: he was 'much keener on pressing on with the things that matter to the common man, agriculture and industrial development, co-operative farming and marketing, health, education; staffing the services concerned with Africans as quickly as they can be trained; assigning to African local administrations more and more responsibility for these services'. The more Africans were playing their part in the things that really mattered the less they would bother about constitutional form. 'This requires the qualification that the intelligentsia will still harp on the constitution, but the bulk of West Africans would never willingly accept the rule of that small oligarchy; and it would be a breach of our trust to vest that rule in them.'[47]

Economic and constitutional developments were among the many matters discussed by Swinton with the Colonial Office when he returned to Britain in July 1943 for his first home-leave. After a full year away—double the period initially envisaged—he needed an opportunity to consult directly with governmental colleagues in London, even if it was clear that his mission was not yet completed. But there were also reasons of a more personal nature for Swinton's being anxious to return home to be with his wife. Both their sons were on active service when Swinton left Britain in July 1942: John, the elder, with the Eighth Army in North Africa; Philip, a pilot with the RAF meteorological service. While on an official visit to Cairo early in April 1943 Swinton had heard glowing reports from the army authorities of John's gallantry and skill as a tank-squadron commander. Then, at the end of April, came the news that he had died of wounds received in action at Enfidaville in Tunisia on 14 April. To grief for the elder son was shortly added anxiety over the twenty-five-year old

Philip, who had just won the DSO for his meteorological reconnaissance flights. No sooner had Swinton (still suffering from the effects of a serious bout of malaria) arrived in London on 24 July for the start of his leave, than he was informed that Philip was missing, believed to have come down somewhere in the North Sea. It was not until Swinton had returned to West Africa that news came through that Philip had made a forced landing on enemy territory and was now a prisoner of war, but safe and unwounded.[48] Both sons were married, with children, and the Swintons were naturally intimately concerned with the welfare of the two young families.

Swinton spent only a fortnight of his six-week leave in Yorkshire. The rest was spent in London, largely in an exhausting but necessary round of discussions with ministers and officials, both in the Colonial Office and in those economic and service departments whose work in West Africa he was helping to co-ordinate. A meeting of a different character took place at Buckingham Palace on 11 August, when the King (on Churchill's recommendation) invested him with the insignia of membership of the order of Companions of Honour, in recognition of his services in West Africa.[49]

Swinton's return from his first home-leave seems to have marked something of a watershed in his relations with the British colonial governments in West Africa. From that time on there was an increasing note of asperity in his references to them in his correspondence home; and he was particularly exercised by what he saw as the Gold Coast government's 'deplorable' record in cocoa production through its failure to tackle adequately the endemic problem of cocoa disease.[50] It was rather as if, now that the war danger was removed and minds were turning to Britain's post-war role in the area, the tensions always implicit in the relationship between a resident British minister with wide co-ordinating powers, in some senses cutting across the governors' territorial responsibilities and direct link with the Colonial Office, had come to the surface. A less high-powered, dynamic, and forceful minister might well have avoided conflict altogether, but then he could hardly have measured up to the situation which had confronted Swinton in July 1942. Some indication of the governors' reactions is provided by the unanimity they displayed in recommending that the Resmin organization should be wound up as soon as the war ended. Indeed Sir Bernard Bourdillon, who had recently retired as Governor of Nigeria, expressed in public his regret that it had been found necessary to replace Swinton in October 1944, when, in his view, the need for such a post had already disappeared.[51]

Swinton's personal relations with the governors were mixed, although he had known them all in some capacity as Colonial Secretary and had appointed some of them to governorships (but not those they currently held). Sir Alan Burns, of the Gold Coast, was perhaps in the most difficult position as he had the Minister, so to speak, on his doorstep and thus experienced the greatest threat to his gubernatorial authority. On the whole relations between the two were amicable—and Burn's later published references to Swinton at this period were flattering[52]—but Swinton made no secret of his low estimation of the quality of some Gold Coast officials, and this could hardly fail to irk the Governor. Bourdillon, Governor of Nigeria until late 1943, was the most likely to resent Swinton's position, as head of the largest West African colony and chairman of the governors' conference, now superseded by the West African War Council under Swinton. Swinton was considerably more impressed by the Nigerian administration than that of the Gold Coast, and particularly appreciated the airfield construction work of the Nigerian public-works department under H. E. Walker, who was a man after his own heart: 'efficient, tireless, devoted to the public service, with a genius for getting the best out of his team, an abhorrer of red tape'. (Walker reciprocated the regard and some years later wrote to Swinton to tell him that 'So far as I was concerned, your arrival in West Africa saved me from the asylum, or at least a breakdown, for there was so much to do and so little support. You certainly put new heart into us all . . . Extensive use is being made of the aerodromes you did so much to develop and improve.')[53] But relations with Bourdillon were not easy, and when Sir Arthur Richards took over the Nigerian governorship at the beginning of 1944 Swinton did not conceal his delight. Richards, he told Stanley, would be 'a blessed change after Bourdillon and we shall enjoy working together'. Swinton had unbounded esteem for Richards, which ten months of working with him in West Africa did nothing to diminish: he was quite simply the best governor he had ever known. For his part, Richards wrote effusively to Swinton on hearing the news of his impending final departure, assuring him that 'It has been a pleasure and an honour to work under your guidance'; and six years later, speaking in the House of Lords (as Lord Milverton), he referred to Swinton in West Africa as a 'travelling dynamo' who 'split the atom of West African governmental complacency'.[54] Of the governors of the two smaller colonies, Swinton had a poor opinion of Sir Hubert Stevenson of Sierra Leone, perhaps partly because of his frequent dissatisfaction with the rate of progress in developing the facilities at the vital port of Freetown. H. R. R. Blood, of The Gambia, on the other hand, he thought well of, and expressed regret to Stanley that he was not at Sierra Leone.[55]

Whatever doubts Swinton may have had about the calibre of the local colonial officials he had none about that of his own small staff, now augmented at the senior level by the appointment of a development adviser (N. F. Hall) and a town-planning adviser (Maxwell Fry). Sandford had to return to his Air Ministry work in February 1944. He had been, in Swinton's words, 'a tower of strength: I shd. have been sunk without him'.[56] Swinton was able to delegate detailed work to his staff and rely on them for 'the accurate facts', thus giving himself time 'to think out the big stuff', as he described it to his wife.[57] He could rely on them, too, to take care of things when his contemplation of 'the big stuff' involved lengthy trips away, as when he visited South Africa at Smuts's invitation in February 1944 and Kenya in May; the journeys, which together occupied some six weeks, also took in Southern and Northern Rhodesia, Portuguese Angola, and the Belgian Congo.[58]

From the middle of July to early September Swinton was in Britain again for his second home-leave and ministerial and departmental discussions. Although, with the German war obviously in its last stages, he anticipated that his final tour of duty after his return to Achimota would be a short one, he was given no firm indication in London as to precise dates or possible alternative employment. The telegram which he

received from Churchill on 6 October—less than a month
after returning to West Africa—inviting him to accept the
new post of Minister of Civil Aviation and represent Britain
at an international conference in Chicago almost immediately
thus came as a surprise. But the invitation was couched so
persuasively ('Winston has been terribly nice about my work
here and about his keenness for me to take the new job wh.
he says he thinks I can do better than anyone', he told his
wife), and the post was so appropriate to his qualifications and
experience, that he had no hesitation in accepting.[59] After a
round of farewell visits, in the intervals of which he attempted
to master the mass of material on civil aviation sent from
Britain by RAF Mosquito, he set out for home, arriving in
London on 20 October.

The Coalition Government had been pondering the post-
war future of British civil aviation for well over a year before
Swinton's appointment as Minister of Civil Aviation. The
revolutionary developments in aeronautics stimulated by the
war had made it clear that civil air transport would burgeon
after the war in a way almost unrecognizable from the infant
pre-war industry. But Britain was entering the race under a
heavy handicap compared with its major competitor, the
United States. Roosevelt and Churchill had agreed as a war
measure that the United States should develop and manufacture transport aircraft while Britain concentrated its energies
on combat aircraft. With US domestic airlines operating almost
as usual, and the unprecedented amount of experience of
trans-ocean flying being gained from the exigencies of war,
American civil aviation was clearly going to emerge from the
war in a strong position to dominate international air-routes.
In Britain, by contrast, civil flying was heavily restricted, the
British Overseas Airways Corporation (BOAC, in which
Imperial Airways and British Airways had been merged in
1939) was placed at the disposal of the RAF and operated
alongside RAF Transport Command, and no suitable aircraft
were being developed for peace-time use. On the other hand,
with British bases around the world, the long-term prospect
looked promising.

For understandable reasons American policy sought to
secure the greatest possible degree of competition, the fullest

'freedom of the air': in effect, the freedom of any airline to fly any number of aircraft anywhere. But however dominant it might be in the aviation field the United States could fully exploit its position only with the co-operation of other countries, since under international law each state had sovereign rights over its own airspace. The Americans—for whom Adolf Berle, assistant undersecretary of state and long-time associate of Roosevelt, was the chief protagonist—wanted to achieve their aims by bilateral negotiations. The British Government, anxious to nourish its frail industry, wanted international regulation, or 'orderly development', in order to moderate the fierce winds of American competition. In 1943 and 1944 it engaged in a series of discussions with the Americans and with Commonwealth governments (in which Beaverbrook, Lord Privy Seal and chairman of the War Cabinet's civil aviation committee, took a leading part) to secure agreement on an international conference to prepare a suitable scheme. Eventually, a reluctant US Government was induced to convene an international conference at Chicago in November 1944.[60]

A subsidiary problem for the Coalition Government was the allocation of departmental responsibility for civil aviation. It had always resided with the Air Ministry, but—as Swinton knew to his cost—this was not altogether a happy arrangement and it had been difficult, even in peace-time, to meet the argument that the interests of civil flying were being subordinated to the overriding service interests of the Air Ministry. But in wartime, and with the future of civil aviation figuring prominently in international discussions, the suitability of its assignment to the Air Ministry came increasingly to be questioned. To a parliamentary questioner in May 1944 Churchill had specifically reaffirmed that the Secretary of State for Air remained responsible, although, somewhat unusually, he revealed the existence of Beaverbrook's co-ordinating committee.[61] Another War Cabinet committee—that on the machinery of government, under Sir John Anderson—then recommended that after the war civil aviation should be transferred to the peace-time successor of the Ministry of War Transport, a recommendation approved by the War Cabinet on 1 September. In the interim period Churchill suggested that a third parliamentary under-secretary in the Air Ministry

should be appointed to deal exclusively with civil aviation.
But this proposal failed to satisfy Conservative back-benchers
and on 5 October Churchill told the War Cabinet that he had
decided to set up a separate department under a minister of
Cabinet rank and to ask Lord Swinton whether he would
accept the post. Despite an attempt by Sinclair, the Air
Minister, to preserve his department's role, the War Cabinet
ratified Churchill's decision and the invitation was cabled to
Swinton.[62]

As he contemplated his new responsibilities during the fortnight in which he wound up his affairs in West Africa and flew
home, Swinton could have been under no illusions about the
difficulties of the task. There was the awkward overlap with
the Air Ministry which, while the war lasted, would continue
to have first call on British air-transport facilities and whose
minister—until existing legislation could be amended—remained statutorily responsible for BOAC. The physical separation
of the department of civil aviation from the rest of the Air
Ministry helped here, since it was comparatively easy for the
staff to work direct to the new Minister; and whatever the Air
Minister's residual responsibilities might be, Swinton was
clearly expected by the War Cabinet to take the lead in planning for civil aviation at home and overseas, including long-
term decisions about future organization and the role of
government, and—most immediately, with the Chicago
Conference looming—the conduct of complex international
negotiations. The five days between taking up his duties on
23 October and departing from North America witnessed
activity of extraordinary intensity, even by Swinton's standards. On the very first day he circulated to the War Cabinet
a paper on the future organization of civil aviation which
opened in typical Swinton fashion with the declaration, 'I
want as early as possible to put to my colleagues some general
ideas . . . They are not just first impressions. I have read all
the papers. I have also, during the last two years, had the
opportunity of seeing British and American air transport at
work in Africa. I have talked with Field Marshal Smuts and
his Ministers and we have prepared in West Africa comprehensive plans for the trunk and subsidiary services to meet the
post-war needs of the area.' He then outlined what was later

to be expanded into the 'Swinton plan', as it was almost universally known.[63]

Discussion of Swinton's ideas on organization had to wait the outcome of Chicago, preparation for which naturally occupied the bulk of Swinton's attention in these hectic few days. The Government's policy had already been enshrined in a White Paper, and Swinton did not cavil at it: all were agreed that the aim must be to secure an international multilateral convention regulating all aspects of international airline operations, commercial as well as technical, including nomination of routes, designation of airlines, control of capacity provided by each state's airlines, determination of frequencies of service, and so on. Importance was attached to securing Dominion agreement, and the official members of the Commonwealth delegations to Chicago were meeting in Montreal from 23 to 28 October with this end in view. Swinton indicated how he proposed to conduct the British side of the Chicago negotiations in a minute to Churchill on 24 October and verbally to the War Cabinet on 26 October. He would press the White Paper policy, but if this failed in the face of the expected American insistence on a period of unrestricted competition, followed by a distribution of national services based on experience during it (calculated to rebound to American advantage), he would resist any attempt to line up with other countries against the United States. Rather he would try to secure a convention on technical matters and face the possibility of a series of bilateral negotiations—all the time working for combined British Commonwealth action. This approach gained the general support of the War Cabinet, which expressed 'the greatest confidence' in Swinton's ability to conduct 'the difficult negotiations which lay before him'.[64]

Flying direct to Montreal on 28 October, Swinton was able to meet the Commonwealth delegations for two days before they all went on to Chicago for the opening of the conference on 1 November. Close Commonwealth consultation was indeed a feature of the conference, and the Dominion Office representative felt that seldom could the British delegation to an international conference have held so many meetings with other Commonwealth delegations: usually once a day, and, towards the end, twice a day.[65] Canada was, however, the odd man out, favouring as it did the American proposal for a period of unrestricted competition. Another feature of the conference from the British point of view was the care Swinton took to consult with his Government colleagues at home. At his request a special War Cabinet committee was set up under Beaverbrook to keep a watching brief over developments at the conference.[66]

Even if Swinton had been the model of diplomatic tact and persuasiveness he could hardly have achieved an international agreement on the commercial aspects of civil aviation at Chicago: the positions of the two main powers, Britain and America (the Soviet Union was invited but failed to attend) were so opposed as to be irreconcilable. It was clear that the key to the conference lay with these two countries and that the other fifty represented at Chicago hardly counted, aligning themselves with one or other of the two main contenders as their interests seemed to dictate. The conference thus turned into a confrontation between Britain and America and something of a gladiatorial contest between Swinton and Berle, the latter combining the roles of president of the conference and leader of the US delegation. The two men took a dislike to each other almost from the start, Swinton telling his wife on 23 November that Berle 'is easily the most disagreeable person with whom I have ever negotiated', while Berle confided to his diary on 26 November that Swinton tended to be 'arrogant and inflexible, not having quite appreciated the difference between the atmosphere of the coast of the Gulf of Guinea and that of the shores of Lake Michigan'.[67]

The issues were highly complex and the arguments detailed, but very roughly the discussions turned on the applicability of the so-called 'Five Freedoms' of civil air transport. The first two—freedom to fly over a country without landing ('innocent passage') and to land for non-traffic purposes such as refuelling, repair, and emergency—were largely technical and presented few difficulties (although the War Cabinet was reluctant for Swinton to concede them except as part of a general agreement).The crucial freedoms were the 'commercial' ones: freedom three (to set down traffic from the country of origin of the aircraft in a foreign country), four (to pick up traffic in that foreign country for the country of origin of the aircraft), and five (to carry traffic between two foreign countries). Freedom five was far and away the most contentious of these commercial freedoms, for if it were freely granted it would make it possible, for example, for a US airline operating a service from New York to Australia via London, Egypt, and India to pick up traffic at intermediate points in direct competition with the national airlines *en route*. In the American view all these freedoms should be universally applied and, moreover, be subject to the 'escalator clause', under which airline operators could run additional planes on services on which the existing aircraft were substantially (at least 65 per cent) full. While the British delegation was willing to have an international agreement, administered by an international civil aviation body, which incorporated all five freedoms, with the escalator clause operating for third and fourth freedom traffic (that to and from two countries), it baulked at an unrestricted fifth freedom. For fifth freedom traffic, it maintained, the escalator clause should not apply and fares charged by foreign operators should be higher than those for any parallel services operated by the countries concerned. At one stage it seemed as if this package, which contained significant concessions by Britain (especially on the escalator clause, which Beaverbrook's committee had not wanted Swinton to concede), had been agreed by the American delegation. But then Berle made further demands: first asking for the application of the escalator clause to fifth freedom traffic, and later for the unconditional grant of all the freedoms, with any airline operator free to fly anywhere with any number of aircraft. These demands Swinton rejected as involving that 'wasteful cut-throat competition' which it was the British delegation's primary aim to avoid.[68]

The crisis provoked the exchange of several telegrams between Roosevelt and Churchill and there was even an implied threat that what the Americans saw as, and represented to be, British intransigence might lead to a reduction in American lend-lease aid to Britain.[69] Swinton attempted to break the deadlock by proposing a scheme (hammered out in telegraphic consultation with Beaverbrook's committee) for determining the allocation of fifth freedom traffic between the air services of the countries concerned. It involved, among other things, splitting long international air-routes into separate divisions (for example, the US-Australia route, into US-Europe, Europe-Egypt, Egypt-India, and India-Australia), with the capacity of the services which each country should be entitled to operate in each division being fixed by the international organization it had been generally agreed should be set up, in accordance with certain agreed principles (such as the state of development of local air services).[70] The Americans then made a counter-proposal: that there should be no restriction on fifth freedom traffic but that any country sustaining 'injury or prejudice' should have a right of appeal to the international organization. This hardly met the British objection to unrestricted competition, but before the conference ended on 6 December the Americans had managed to persuade twenty-one other delegations to subscribe to a 'five freedoms' agreement under which each country's airline operators were given the right to enter all the other countries to discharge, and take on, passengers and freight; they included all the Latin American countries but no significant aviation powers apart from the Netherlands and Sweden. The conference as a whole, following Britain's lead, adopted only a 'two freedoms' agreement, granting its signatories 'innocent passage' and the right to land at designated public airports for the purpose of refuelling, repair, or overhaul.[71] Modest though this was, it represented a significant voluntary modification to the concept of a country's sovereign rights over its airspace. There was also agreement on the need to standardize safety, navigational, meteorological, and communications procedures, and on the establishment of the international body which shortly became the International Civil Aviation Organization, based in Montreal and with W. P. Hildred, former British director-general of civil aviation, at its head.

For Swinton, as a long-standing protectionist, the task of arguing at Chicago for restriction and 'orderly development' as against the traditional virtues of free competition being projected by the Americans was perhaps less embarrassing than it might have been for others. It was unquestionably in the interests of British civil aviation that he should do so. It is true that during the remainder of his time as Minister of Civil Aviation he was increasingly concerned at the way the United

States—even before the war ended—was taking advantage of its dominant position around the world to conclude highly favourable bilateral agreements with a variety of countries.[72] But not long after leaving office he had the satisfaction of noting that the bilateral agreement which the United States concluded with Britain at Bermuda in February 1946 represented a substantial shift in the American attitude and specifically acknowledged the general principle of 'orderly development'. The Bermuda Agreement, it has been said, 'proved to be one of the most important events in international aviation history', producing compromises 'to resolve the deadlock at Chicago' and providing 'not merely a bilateral agreement between the two major air transport nations, but a general philosophy on the way in which the economic regulation of the industry should be achieved'.[73]

Any immediate disappointment Swinton may have felt at the apparent failure of the Chicago Conference was moderated by the close understanding he had developed with the Dominion delegations. Capitalizing on this, he attended an informal conference of the delegations in Montreal before flying home on 15 December; a conference which continued in London, where the delegates reassembled on 22 December. At these meetings, Swinton later recorded, was 'evolved a complete plan for Commonwealth air routes and full arrangements for Commonwealth co-operation'. Agreement was reached on, among other things, the formation of a Commonwealth Air Transport Council to review the development of Commonwealth air communications, to act as a forum for the exchange of views and information, and to consider and advise on matters referred to it by member governments; and on the principal Commonwealth routes—the transatlantic, those linking Britain with South Africa, India, Australia, and New Zealand, and the route across the Pacific between Canada, New Zealand, and Australia. In March 1945 Swinton flew to Pretoria for a conference which saw the conclusion of an agreement with the Smuts Government which it was hoped would provide a pattern for other Commonwealth agreements. Arrangements were made for the sharing of revenue and expenses between the airline companies of the two countries on the UK–South Africa air-route, for the use of similar types of aircraft, for repair and maintenance, and for the operation of airfields and meteorological and radio services. Early in July Swinton presided over the first formal meeting of the Commonwealth Air Transport Council in London, which, following the UK–South African agreement, worked out detailed arrangements for the other main Commonwealth routes, and dealt with a number of technical questions.[74]

One major piece of unfinished business awaiting Swinton on his return from Chicago and Montreal was to establish his ministerial responsibilities on a proper formal basis. At the end of January he instructed Hildred, his departmental head, to proceed quickly with a Bill to transfer the Air Ministry's civil aviation functions to him and give authority to appoint a parliamentary secretary. The Bill, giving the Minister of Civil Aviation 'the general duty of organizing, carrying out and encouraging measures for the development of civil aviation, for the designing, development and production of civil aircraft, for the promotion of safety and efficiency in the use thereof, and for research into questions relating to air navigation', had its second reading in the Commons on 11 April and in the Lords on 24 April, receiving the royal assent the following day.[75] The provision for appointing a parliamentary secretary had, however, been anticipated a month earlier. The choice fell, by strange irony, on that same Robert Perkins whose indefatigable Commons probing had led to the setting-up of the Cadman inquiry on civil aviation which had done so much to erode Swinton's position as Air Minister before the war. Swinton clearly bore Perkins no ill will and the brief period of their ministerial co-operation seems to have been entirely amicable.

The achievement during his nine months as Minister of Civil Aviation of which Swinton was proudest was the Swinton plan for the post-war organization of civil aviation. Although fated in the end to come to nothing, it represented at the time a considerable personal triumph. The plan was an interesting attempt to find a compromise between unrestricted private enterprise and complete public monopoly. Swinton was early convinced that BOAC would be inadequate by itself to cope with the great expansion of civil flying anticipated after the war. He was impressed by the fact that many interests were concerned in civil aviation in one way or another. In addition to BOAC for the government-subsidized exploitation of overseas routes there were the railway companies, which by 1939 had acquired a controlling interest in most of the private companies operating domestic air services; while some of the shipping companies had expressed a wish to enter the air transport field. Then there were the travel agencies, which were large customers of air travel.

It appeared to me [Swinton wrote many years later] that in this cumbrous and chaotic mixture there were elements of order, economy and efficiency. The essential but hitherto not obvious truth was that aviation was a transport business. The airmen were expert in aviation but not in transport business. The shipping lines, the railways and the travel agencies were experts in the transport business; and they had world-wide offices and agencies. Was not the sensible thing to do to combine all these interests with their assets and experience in three or four groups, which would enable all to participate and operate to the best advantage? I found they were all attracted by this conception.[76]

In the paper which Swinton circulated to the War Cabinet on 20 January he proposed that Britain's civil air-routes should, for the most part, be in the hands of several organizations, rather than the existing 'single chosen instrument'. BOAC would continue to run the Commonwealth services, in partnership with the Commonwealth governments concerned. But other overseas routes—for example, those to the United States and South America—would be run by BOAC jointly with shipping companies in varying proportions, with the latter having a preponderant share in the new South American services. For British domestic and continental services there would be a single company made up of interested railway companies, shipping lines, the pre-war private air companies, BOAC, and travel agencies. The Government would have strict control over the formation of companies, allocation of routes, and matters of broad policy, but would not interfere with detailed operation and management.[77]

Swinton's paper was discussed at the War Cabinet on 24 January. The only uniformly critical voice was Beaverbrook's: he maintained that the only effective way of securing civil aviation development was to give the freest scope to private enterprise and that operating units made up of BOAC and private companies would not work satisfactorily or be able to stand up to the formidable American competition. Elsewhere there was general approval, with Leathers (Minister of War Transport) and Cranborne (Dominions Secretary) enthusiastic in its favour, and even Sinclair expressing the view that the plan provided a basis on which agreement could be reached. But the crucial intervention was Bevin's, on behalf of the Labour element in the Coalition Government. He and his Labour colleagues, he said, recognized that this was a matter on which there was a divergence of political views, but they thought it important that the main lines should be laid down during the lifetime of the Government and were prepared to accept the proposals. Anderson, the Chancellor, had one or two financial matters to discuss with Swinton but, apart from this, the Cabinet battle was over.[78] He was understandably elated when he wrote to his wife at Swinton: 'I have won through all along the line . . . it was very difficult for my Labour colleagues to swallow it vis-à-vis their party . . . But, thank God, they trust me; and I persuaded them to forget all politics, as I was doing, and try to get the best plan on merits, irrespective of whether it was private enterprise or state ownership . . . The result is that we have a complete plan . . . which we can put forward as a National Government.'[79]

The War Cabinet reaffirmed its acceptance of the plan on 8 March (the Chancellor's points had been satisfactorily met) and authorized Swinton to publish it as a White Paper, which was debated in the Lords on 15 March.[80]

Although Swinton remained Minister of Civil Aviation for another four months (latterly in Churchill's caretaker Conservative Government), this was really as far as his ambitious plan ever got. With the end of the Coalition on the departure of its Labour and Liberal members on 23 May came the end also of the inter-party consensus on post-war civil aviation. The Labour Government which took office after the July election introduced the nationalization of civil aviation as one of the first of its nationalizing measures, and the legislation came into effect on 1 August 1946. In a sense the Civil Aviation Act of 1946 was far less radical than the Swinton plan, since it merely carried on the process begun with the creation of BOAC as a public corporation immediately before the war. Swinton regretted in retrospect the lost opportunity 'for having a sensible and commercially realistic policy for civil aviation linked with all the major transport services, a novel experiment in merging public and private enterprise in the national interest'.[81] However, although the Swinton plan was never debated substantively in the House of Commons, there was sufficient critical comment from the Conservative back-benchers to suggest that, even if the Conservatives had won the 1945 election, it would not have emerged unscathed from the attacks of those on his own side less willing than he to 'forget politics' in planning the development of civil aviation.[82]

CHAPTER 7

Elder Statesman

By 1945 Swinton, now aged sixty-one, had rehabilitated himself in governmental and party terms after the nadir of 1938. He had not, of course, recovered the position he held before his acceptance of the peerage in 1935 and clearly could never do so: the peerage itself, and the advance of many younger men since 1935, had seen to that, even if the aura of apparent failure in his most important pre-war ministerial office had not still persisted. His wartime ministerial assignments were not, it is true, at the level which his previous experience would have justified, but then most ministers were, like Swinton, outside the War Cabinet (which still had only eight members when the Coalition ended in May 1945); and while, as Minister of Civil Aviation, he was not even a member of Churchill's caretaker Cabinet, he shared this exclusion with eighteen other ministerial heads of department. However, his party role in Opposition, following the 1945 Labour victory, belied the relatively junior status of the ministerial appointments which preceded it.

The party role began even before the ministerial one had ended. When, on 23 May, Churchill submitted the resignation of the Coalition Government and was asked to form a caretaker administration (necessarily almost wholly Conservative) he was also granted a dissolution of Parliament. From then until polling on 5 July the Conservative Party had to prepare for and fight an election campaign with the minimum of policy preparation and an organization rusty after being virtually laid up for the duration of the wartime electoral truce between the parties. In these circumstances more than usual importance was attached to the joint ministerial–central-office committee which was set up by Churchill to provide policy guidance to Conservative candidates, a high proportion of whom were inexperienced, many, indeed, being hurriedly nominated by constituency associations taken unawares by the speed of events. Swinton was designated chairman of this Emergency Business Committee and was the most active of its ministerial members, the others usually being away on speaking engagements. His main coadjutors were David Clarke, of the Conservative Research Department, and the civil service secretary of the committee, W. S. Murie of the Cabinet Office, who proved himself, despite his official position, 'unusually adept' at giving 'a political edge' to the factual drafts on current government activities prepared by departments which had largely to do service for a party electoral programme.[1] But while the committee rendered useful service in briefing candidates its best efforts could hardly do much to turn what proved to be an irresistible Labour tide. With the declaration of the election results on 26 July Swinton began only his fourth year in Opposition (and his first since 1931) in a parliamentary career already spanning a quarter of a century.

The period 1945-51 provided incomparably Swinton's busiest experience of Opposition. Not only was he again—as he had been in 1924 and 1929-31—a member of the Shadow Cabinet, but he was now also deputy leader of the Conservative Opposition in the Lords, under the leadership of Cranborne (who had entered the Lords in his own right in 1941 before succeeding his father as Marquess of Salisbury in 1947). Theirs was an easy and intimate co-operation, which continued into Government in 1951 and only ended with Swinton's resignation in 1955. 'It was a perfect partnership,' Swinton testified in his Lords' tribute to Salisbury on the latter's death in February 1972. 'I do not think that we ever disagreed on policy or on the handling of policy.'[2] Salisbury's frequent absences through illness, however, meant that on many occasions Swinton had to shoulder the full burdens of Opposition leadership. Evidence of the range and intensity of his activities is provided by the numerous entries under his name in the sessional indexes of the House of Lords Hansard volumes of the period. It is perhaps significant that, despite being formally free to do so, he did not feel able to resume his Sofina directorship until late in 1946, and for three years thereafter this was his only directorship.[3] Moreover, although Spencer Curtis Brown, the literary agent, and the publisher Walter Hutchinson persuaded him to write his memoirs shortly after the war, pressure of other work delayed until September 1947 the completion of the manuscript, which was almost immediately serialized in the *Sunday Times*; the book was published at the end of the following year.[4]

The Labour Government's nationalization programme presented obvious problems for the Conservative Opposition in the Lords. With its overwhelming majority it could have thrown out the legislation and invited a clash with the similarly overwhelming Labour majority in the Commons. But that way lay disaster for the Lords as a legislative chamber, and in any case it would have been difficult to reconcile with the Government's decisive electoral mandate. Salisbury and Swinton had to steer a difficult course between outright confrontation with the Government and the expectations of their own followers. They were helped in this task by the development of a good understanding with the Labour leadership of the aged Addison, the Leader of the House, and Jowitt, the Lord Chancellor. For all of them it was, as an expert witness of their proceedings has said, 'an awkward and unreal situation, made tolerable by the Parliamentary skill and good manners of those mainly concerned'.[5]

Swinton's many contributions to debates showed no diminution either in combativeness or mastery of subject-matter, one of his Labour opponents recalling him as 'a hard-hitting Parliamentarian especially dangerous in riposte'.[6] He made no secret of his total opposition to nationalization, even that of the Bank of England, which many on his own side were prepared to accept as inevitable. 'The real gravamen of the charge against this Government', he declared in the second reading debate on the Bank of England Bill in January 1946,

is not that they are planners—I am a planner and I believe everybody wants to be a planner—but that they are entirely failing to plan . . . You do not do any planning by buying out the Bank of England. It is how you manage the Bank of England which is planning. You do not plan by buying out the mines, the railways, civil aviation, or any other industry. It is how you are going to run an industry. And I cannot see the least evidence that the Government are planning industry in the sense of trying to see how industry can be made more efficient, how you can get a greater output per man hour, a larger production of the things we need at home, and how we can build up our export trade. For those things you do not want this kind of measure. You want the closest co-operation and the greatest confidence between the Government of the day, who must have their part in planning, and the industry and commerce of the country.[7]

The haphazard nature of the Government's organizational plans for the various industries which were being nationalized lent some weight to Swinton's critique, as perhaps also did the subsequent performance of some of them. But it was naturally the nationalization of civil aviation which caused him the greatest personal concern, as he saw the destruction, for what he considered merely doctrinal motives, of his carefully worked-out scheme which had been approved by the Coalition Government.[8]

In large part as a result of the discretion and moderation with which Salisbury and Swinton marshalled their Conservative majority, the Labour Government was able to get its initial flurry of nationalization measures virtually unscathed through the Lords, even if it was often by virtue of the House's agreement not to press amendments in the face of Commons objections. The nationalization of iron and steel was, however, more contentious (and not exclusively within Conservative ranks), and the Government felt it necessary to make contingent plans for a reduction in the period of the Lords' veto power in case of total Lords opposition to its last major nationalizing measure. With Eden, Sir David Maxwell-Fyfe, and Salisbury, Swinton was a member of the four-man Conservative delegation to the inter-party talks on House of Lords reform between February and April 1948.[9] The failure of the talks and the immediate unilateral introduction of the Government's Parliament Bill simply to reduce the Lords' veto from two years to one did nothing to ease the task of Salisbury and Swinton in maintaining a responsible Conservative stance in the Upper House. Clearly anticipating that the numerous and damaging Lords amendments to the Iron and Steel Bill would not, as in previous nationalizing Bills, be dropped if unacceptable to the Commons, Addison and Jowitt sought a compromise. On 1 November 1949 they saw Salisbury and Swinton to propose that the vesting date for iron and steel nationalization be postponed until 1 January 1951—well after the next general election, which had to be held by July 1950, had given the Conservatives, if returned, the opportunity of repealing the measure—and that in the meantime no steps be taken to appoint members of the Iron and Steel Corporation before 1 October 1950. On the following day Salisbury and Swinton discussed the Labour proposal with five of their Shadow Cabinet colleagues—Churchill, Eden, Oliver Stanley, Lyttelton, and Woolton. They were all agreed, according to Swinton's contemporary account, that 'the only reason why the Government were prepared to climb down in this way was to dispose of the matter this session, and leave them free to go to the country early in the New Year'. Both the leader and chairman of the party welcomed the prospect of an early election.

Winston said that an early election was so clearly in the interests of the country that we could not possibly oppose it, indeed we had all been insisting on this. Woolton said the Party machine was all geared up for an election, and that from the point of view of the operation of the Party machine, the sooner the election came the better as, if it was delayed, the machine might run down. A quick election also gave the Liberals less time to make mischief. He thought in a January election we should get a majority of 80.[10]

On these optimistic electoral assumptions Salisbury and Swinton were able to signify to Addison and Jowitt the Shadow Cabinet's agreement to the Government's proposals.

On another issue the Shadow Cabinet was less united, at least initially. This was the question of India's position in the Commonwealth with the country's adoption of a republican constitution in 1949. On the face of it a Commonwealth all of whose members acknowledged allegiance to the Crown could hardly accommodate a republic within its ranks. But India's importance clearly merited every effort to find a formula which might make it possible for it to retain its membership. The matter was to be discussed at the London meeting of Commonwealth Prime Ministers convened for 21 April 1949. On 31 March the Shadow Cabinet met, under Eden's chairmanship (in Churchill's absence), to consider the Conservative attitude. Salisbury was also absent (not, in fact, returning to London until 3 May), and Swinton wrote to him to keep him informed of the progress of events. Eden seemed to favour India's continued membership, being impressed 'by the apparent desire of Nehru and others to remain within the Commonwealth and by their obvious anxiety about Communism', which was likely to take them 'further on the road of co-operation than Nehru's neutrality speeches indicated'. Churchill's first reaction—surprisingly in view of his past record of opposition to Indian political advance—'had been that it would be unfortunate if it should appear that the Crown, which had been the symbol and focus of unity, should become the cause of India leaving the Commonwealth', and he had told Attlee of this view, so Eden reported to the Shadow Cabinet. The feeling of the majority of his colleagues, however, 'was that it would be wrong to sacrifice the reality of the Commonwealth partnership in order to keep India in', for 'the Crown and the personal attachment to the Sovereign is a vital reality to some of the Dominions, as it is to us.'[11] A fortnight later Swinton reported to Salisbury on a meeting which Conservative leaders (including himself) had had with Attlee, who had told them that there was a general feeling among Commonwealth members that India should be retained, possibly by including some such non-monarchical phrase as 'Head of the Commonwealth' in the royal title. But Churchill's attitude had changed, much influenced, Swinton thought, by the anticipated effect on Conservative Party opinion of the hostile declaration on India's position recently made by Smuts in South Africa, where he was now Leader of the Opposition. Churchill told Attlee that it was unlikely that the Conservative Party would agree to India's membership as a republic and asked for the matter to be postponed; but, with the Commonwealth conference due to assemble in a week's time, this was obviously impossible.[12] However, when that conference decided on the formula which made it possible for republican India (and any other future Commonwealth republics) to acknowledge the King simply as Head of the Commonwealth, Churchill welcomed it in the Commons as enhancing the 'significance and value of the monarchy'. Salisbury was furious, telling Swinton that he was 'more and more out of sympathy with Winston', despite his deep personal respect and affection for him. 'He seems to take an extreme view when he ought to be moderate, and yet, on an occasion like this he swings right round and abandons all those fundamental principles for which I believe the Conservative Party stands; and, willy nilly, he drags the Party in his wake.'[13]

Swinton and his wife had already made a signal contribution to the discussion and inculcation of 'those fundamental principles' of Conservatism by donating a large part of Swinton (which had housed Harrogate College during the war) to form a Conservative College in 1947. Since the war the party had been without a residential educational centre such as the Bonar Law Memorial College at Ashridge provided for ten years before the war. The origins of the Swintons' offer are obscure, but it seems that two of the prime movers in the development of post-war Conservative policy, R. A. Butler and Harold Macmillan, both played their part. Butler, according to Swinton's later account, had said that the party needed 'a place that is the size of a small Cambridge college and is really run intensively, and we want the right place for it'. Macmillan, apparently, was emphatic about its siting. 'We have got to have a college and it has got to be in the North. The people from the South, apart from having a very agreeable place to go to, should recognize that it's a jolly good thing for them to go to the North.' The offer of Swinton seemed to meet these desiderata and was accepted gratefully.[14] The Swintons continued to live in the house and to entertain their own guests, notably with the opening of the grouse season in August, when their visitors frequently included Tommy Dugdale (Lord Crathorne), Butler, Christopher Soames, and, from 1957 onwards, Macmillan. But in addition the college gave Swinton an exceptional opportunity, of which he took full advantage, to keep in touch with a wide range of Conservative opinion, from party leaders to constituency activists. He was immediately appointed a life governor of the college and in 1958 became its chairman, but his involvement with its work went far beyond these official positions: he was a regular lecturer (often extempore) or chairman of sessions and mixed informally with lecturers and students when in residence. Indeed, Swinton Conservative College owed much more than its splendid locale to Swinton, and it did not long survive the deaths of its donors.[15]

The establishment of the Conservative College in his York-shire home enabled Swinton immeasurably to strengthen his informal links with the party. Meanwhile his role in the party's policy-making machinery was growing. During the February 1950 election he was again, as in 1945, chairman of the candidates' advisory committee, now called the Questions of Policy Committee. It met almost daily in the Research Department in Old Queen Street and was able to circulate eighty-three rulings to Conservative candidates on policy matters which were not covered in the election manifesto or other official party publications.[16] The victory the Conserva-tives had confidently expected did not materialize, but the narrowness of Labour's post-election majority in the Commons encouraged hopes that the former's return to power would not be long delayed and intensified policy preparations for it. In March 1950 Swinton became deputy chairman of the party's Advisory Committee on Policy, at the invitation of its chairman, Butler, and with the blessing of Churchill.[17] A major policy concern, and one in which much Conservative ideological fervour had been invested, was to explore the scope for reversing some at least of the Labour Government's nationalization measures. Iron and steel nationalization, which was to come into operation as late as the beginning of 1951, might lend itself to reversal provided the arrival of a Conser-vative Government was not too long deferred, but the older-established nationalized industries presented greater problems for reconciling realism with ideology. Swinton's particular task was to examine the possibilities in relation to electricity, as chairman of a committee containing Sir Arnold Gridley, MP, and two other former leading members of the electricity-supply industry. But the problem defied even Swinton's ingenuity and in its manifesto for the October 1951 election the party was careful to commit itself specifically only to the denationalization of iron and steel and road haulage.[18] During the election campaign Swinton again presided over the Questions of Policy Committee, which met nineteen times and gave 103 policy rulings to candidates.[19] This time the committee had the satisfaction of feeling that it had contributed to a Conservative victory, albeit a narrow one.

The Conservative return to power in October 1951 found Swinton in his sixty-eighth year, an age at which political ambition might understandably have dimmed. Nevertheless, although there is no firm evidence on his attitude at the time, it would appear that he was eager to resume his ministerial career. It was clearly not unreasonable for him to entertain hopes of office in view of his leading role in the Conservative Opposition in the Lords over the past six years—and his age seemed of less account when the new Conservative Prime Minister was nearly ten years older than himself. But when the fifteen members of the Cabinet, besides Churchill, were announced in two batches on 27 and 29 October, Swinton was not among them, although they contained six peers, three of them (Woolton, Simonds, and Leathers) older than Swinton. The most extraordinary appointment of all was that of Churchill's wartime chief of staff, Lord Ismay, almost totally without parliamentary experience, as Secretary of State for Commonwealth Relations and, in effect, deputy to Churchill in the Prime Minister's capacity as Minister of Defence until the equally extraordinary appointment of another non-political general could be made, with Lord Alexander's return from the Governor-Generalship of Canada in 1952. Had Swinton been a wartime intimate of Churchill, and had no question-mark still hung over his pre-war tenure of the Air Ministry, Churchill's choice as Minister of Defence could well—and much more appropriately—have fallen on him. But with the announcement of 29 October the most he could now hope for was a ministerial post outside the Cabinet.

It is uncertain whether Churchill, unprompted, would have included Swinton in his administration. There is, however, evidence that he was advised to do so by several colleagues. Churchill had hoped to persuade Lord Waverley (the former Sir John Anderson) to become one of the co-ordinating ministers—the 'overlords'—which were an initial feature of his peace-time Cabinet. As Chancellor of the Duchy of Lancaster Waverley would have been an economic overlord, co-ordinating the Treasury, Board of Trade, and Ministry of Supply. When Waverley refused Churchill's invitation Crookshank, who was to be Leader of the House of Commons, James Stuart, and Patrick Buchan-Hepburn (Stuart's successor as Chief Whip) recommended Swinton as a replacement in what would inevitably have been a Cabinet appointment had it in the end been made. Swinton's two main friends in the new leadership of the party both urged his appointment to the Government, though in comparatively lowly positions. Macmillan, the new Minister of Housing and Local Government, suggested he be approached to see whether he could be persuaded to be Minister of Works, although he recognized that 'after so long an experience in the Cabinet it would not be easy'; while Butler, in accepting appointment as Chancellor of the Exchequer, asked Churchill to let Swinton help him with the economy 'on the materials side', a subject which Swinton had investigated for the Advisory Committee on Policy.[20] Churchill seems to have combined Butler's suggestion with the need to fill the office left vacant by Waverley's refusal to serve. In the list of ministerial appointments announced on 31 October Swinton's name appeared in the dual capacity of Chancellor of the Duchy of Lancaster and Minister of Materials, but outside the Cabinet.[21] In addition he was to be deputy leader of the House of Lords, continuing his successful partnership with Salisbury, the Leader of the House, in the management of Government business there.

The Ministry of Materials, established only three months before the Conservatives assumed office, had been an organizational response by the Labour Government to the international raw-material shortage created by the outbreak of the Korean War in June 1950. Its responsibilities covered the procurement of a wide range of raw materials and their allocation to users, both in the public and private sectors. These were not functions likely to appeal to a Conservative administration and party anxious to restore the maximum degree of private enterprise possible after six years of what they saw as socialist-imposed austerity, and Swinton was expected to close the department as soon as it was practicable to do so. However, pragmatic and undoctrinaire as ever, he formed a favourable view of its value, telling the House of Lords a fortnight after taking office that, as far as he could see at that time, 'the general set up is logical and convenient and is working smoothly, both with the Departments and with industry'; and even as late as May 1953 his successor as Minister, Sir Arthur

Salter, was explaining that 'the Government in present circumstances must continue to concern itself with problems, both long-term as well as short-term, which arise in the supply, distribution, and use of the materials needed by industry and for the strategic stockpile'.[22]

The most pressing difficulty was steel, supplies of which were desperately short, imperilling, among many other things, Macmillan's ambitious house-building programme. In his brief tenure Swinton's Labour predecessor, Richard Stokes, had been able to make little headway with the multiplicity of competing demands for steel from departments, the nationalized industries, and the private sector. The speed and decision with which Swinton, by contrast, dealt with the situation has been thus described by his civil-service private secretary at the time:

On the day after his appointment Lord Swinton said to me that Steel was clearly his most immediate problem and that he wanted to see all the papers. I produced the pile—almost 2 ft. high—for him to study and he ordered that he was not to be disturbed for an hour except for calls from the P.M. or the Chancellor. After an hour's private study he sent for the senior Treasury economists and grilled them for about an hour, displaying an astonishing mastery of the files. He then released them and dictated a lengthy minute to the Chancellor [R. A. Butler] which allocated the available steel to the whole country. His minute required no amendment at all when it came off the typewriter. He initialled it and it went to the Chancellor and was approved—all in one afternoon! Considering the size, importance and complexity of the subject this was the most impressive piece of speedy and successful administration I have myself enountered and contrasted acutely with the dither of the preceding months.[23]

Exercising the functions he did as Minister of Materials (those of Chancellor of the Duchy of Lancaster were then, as now, hardly onerous) Swinton had dealings with many of his ministerial colleagues and their departments. Indeed, so wide-ranging was the impact of his department that he frequently attended meetings of the Cabinet, although not formally a member. His closest relations were with Butler who, as we have seen, had asked for Swinton's appointment to a post which would enable him as Chancellor to draw on his advice, a process facilitated by Swinton occupying an office in the Treasury in his capacity as Minister of Materials. Lord Butler has since testified to the value he attached to Swinton's views, drawn from his great experience, particularly of international trade. It was, for example, Swinton's cautionary advice in February 1952, rather than the intransigent opposition of the majority of the Cabinet, which seems to have most influenced Butler in abandoning his plan to end the fixed exchange rate for sterling.[24] Macmillan, too, has recorded the 'invaluable help', among other things as a member of the Cabinet Building Committee established in November 1951, which Swinton gave him as Minister of Housing.[25]

Another Cabinet committee of which Swinton was a member was that set up to supervise the preparation by the Minister of Supply, Duncan Sandys, of the legislation to denationalize iron and steel. According to Sir Harold Kent, the Bill's parliamentary draftsman, the committee was a good one, with Lyttelton, the Colonial Secretary, and Swinton as its most active members. But since it had to be consulted at every stage and its approval was necessary before the final draft could go to the Cabinet, the progress of drafting was inevitably delayed and the Iron and Steel Bill, which seemed virtually ready for introduction in February 1952, was not in fact introduced until November that year. Swinton was amused to find that Kent had also drafted the Labour Government's nationalization measure, and would, presumably, draft any new legislation when and if Labour returned to power; 'rather a Penelope-like occupation', Swinton commented.[26] In more serious vein, Swinton was concerned to try to assure would-be shareholders in the newly privatized industry that they would not suffer loss if nationalization were to be reintroduced, and Kent was asked to draft a guarantee clause. Precious time was wasted, Kent tartly observes, before this futile attempt was abandoned.[27]

Swinton was in a special position in Churchill's peace-time Government. Apart from the Prime Minister he was the most ministerially experienced and, as such, was one of the few capable of talking to Churchill on more or less equal terms.[28] Although very status-conscious, and anxious to become a full Cabinet member once again, he had no major political ambitions left. He was in no sense a rival to Churchill, nor did he desire—as did others—the aged statesman's departure from office: at least as much from loyalty to Churchill himself as to dislike of his putative successor, Eden. Such men are often employed in roles well beyond their formal responsibilities, and Swinton was no exception. Without interfering with the constitutional responsibilities of the Home and Foreign Secretaries, he advised the Prime Minister on certain secret-service matters, for which his wartime work at the Security Executive uniquely qualified him.[29] But his special contribution was in the projection of the Government to the party and to the public.

Not since the First World War had the Conservatives been so long out of office as during the period of the Labour Government of 1945-51. In the intense process of party reorganization and policy formulation which had alleviated— indeed exploited—this interregnum, close links had been re-forged between the extra-parliamentary organization and the parliamentary leadership, with the permanent officials of Central Office and the Research Department acting, so to speak, as the Opposition's civil service. But now that the Conservatives were once again in office there was a danger of loss of contact between the various sections of the party. Anticipating this, John Wyndham, of the Research Department, proposed in a memorandum to his director, Michael Fraser, just three weeks after the election victory, that there should be a 'clearing house' or liaison committee explicitly to be a channel of policy information between Government and party. No doubt with his success as chairman of the Questions of Policy Committee in mind, Wyndham suggested that Swinton should be chairman of the new committee. Fraser discussed the idea with Butler, chairman of the Research Department, and it was agreed that Fraser should approach Swinton. But when he did so, on 26 November, Swinton, while appreciating the value of the committee, felt he was too busy to take on another assignment and proposed Salisbury as an alternative. Salisbury also declined, however, and Swinton was eventually prevailed on by Fraser to change his mind. He chaired the first meeting of the Liaison Committee, in his room in the Treasury, on 21 December 1951. The original membership, in addition to Swinton, included a fellow minister as deputy chairman (D. Heathcoat Amory, Minister of Pensions); a vice-chairman of the party organization; the directors of the Conservative

Political Centre and the Research Department; the chief publicity officer at Central Office; the personal assistant to the party chairman; and a representative of the Whips' Office (Edward Heath).Wyndham was the committee's first secretary.

The committee's function was 'To give guidance on the interpretation of Government policy and to take such action as, in their opinion, is necessary to sustain public confidence in the Conservative Administration'. It clearly could not perform it without the co-operation of ministers,and on 2 January Swinton wrote to his colleagues to call their attention to the existence of the committee and to request policy background information from them to enable the party organization to combat 'Socialist distortion'.[30]

So yet another 'Swinton Committee' had been created. It outlived the term of its first chairman by some nine years, continuing until the 1964 election defeat. Its effectiveness, it has been pointed out, 'depended very much on the influence and publicity-consciousness of its Chairman, and the degree of Ministerial co-operation'. There is reason to believe that both were at their optimum under Swinton and that subsequently there was some falling-off, for the secretary at one stage found it necessary to urge Heathcoat Amory, Swinton's successor as chairman, to write to ministers to remind them of the purpose of the committee's establishment.[31]

The Liaison Committee was explicitly a party organ, even though it existed only during a Conservative Government, was chaired by a minister, and looked to government departments for information from which to distil material for dissemination through party channels. It was organizationally separate from the machinery of government public relations, although in practice it was not always easy to distinguish between the two. Government information services had existed in fairly limited form in the inter-war period, were greatly expanded during the war, and, while reduced after it, were maintained by the Labour Government in a much more integrated and comprehensive form than ever before in peace-time. The central information department was retained (although demoted from the 'Ministry' to the 'Central Office' of Information); all departments had information staffs; the Prime Minister himself had the services of an accomplished journalist,

Francis Williams, as public-relations adviser; and a minister was designated with responsibilities for co-ordinating government information services (until 1951, Herbert Morrison as Lord President of the Council, and then, from May to October 1951, Patrick Gordon Walker, the Commonwealth Secretary).[32]

All these developments were anathema to Churchill, who nursed the old-fashioned (and not unattractive) belief that governments did not need public relations, only good policies and articulate ministers. On his return to peace-time office he refused to countenance either a minister to co-ordinate government information or a press spokesman at No. 10, and set in train a reduction in the staff of the Central Office of Information (including the disbandment of the Crown Film Unit). No organized link with newspaper parliamentary correspondents ('the Lobby') was deemed necessary: the press could rely on departmental hand-outs and its own coverage of prime-ministerial and ministerial speeches. It was not long before the inadequacy of these simple methods seemed to be demonstrated. Even Churchill was disturbed when, on one occasion, fourteen White Papers were issued on the same day, and, on another, when the Ministry of Food announced the ending of cheese rationing without notifying him (or apparently anyone else) in advance.[33] Moreover, Conservative back-benchers became restless at what they saw as the Government's incompetent presentation of its policies. In March 1952 the 1922 Committee sent Churchill a memorandum calling for more coherent government publicity in face of 'Socialist attacks' on Conservative policies. It proposed, among other things, a ministerial committee to act as a link between Government, press, and public, under the chairmanship of a senior minister and served by 'an official of the calibre of Francis Williams, but an anti-Socialist or non-Socialist'. Although Churchill sought Swinton's advice on this memorandum he was clearly reluctant to make any changes, and as late as 7 April he was telling a parliamentary questioner that no special ministerial co-ordination of government publicity was necessary, since 'Each Departmental Minister is responsible, subject to Cabinet guidance, for the proper presentation of the policy and administration of his Department.'[34] This did not satisfy the members of the 1922 Committee, however, and on 1 May

Swinton (presumably in his capacity as chairman of the Liaison Committee) had to appear before them to try to calm their fears that the Government was losing the propaganda battle to the Labour Opposition. In the meantime he, Butler, and, on the official side, Sir Edward Bridges, Head of the Home Civil Service, and Thomas Fife Clark, a former lobby correspondent and now a senior official in the Central Office of Information were hammering out an organization designed to provide the necessary co-ordination of government publicity while taking account of Churchill's adamant opposition to having a press spokesman. The solution adopted—and approved by Churchill—was for Swinton to assume the ministerial responsiblity for co-ordinating home information services, with Fife Clark as his chief officer and as Public Relations Adviser to the Government rather than, as Francis Williams had been, to the Prime Minister. Swinton's additional appointment was announced on 12 May and Fife Clark's the following month.[35]

Once Churchill's objections to the ministerial appointment were overcome—and it meant his going back on his parliamentary statement of only a month before—Swinton was the obvious man to fill it. On the face of it, however, the combination of his new role with his chairmanship of the Liaison Committee might seem to increase the ever-present danger of confusing party propaganda with government information. Swinton was aware of the danger and tried to ensure that the party also appreciated the distinction. The job of the official information services, he told the 1953 Conservative annual conference, was 'to give prompt and accurate information and to give it objectively day by day about Government action and Government policy. It is quite definitely not the job of the Government Information Services to try and boost the Government or to try to persuade the press to do so.'[36] The balance was a delicate one, as the curious affair of 'the Socialist mess' illustrated. Like many governments which take over after years of Opposition, the new Conservative administration professed to being horrified by 'the skeletons in departmental cupboards' left by its Labour predecessor. Butler and Cherwell (the former F. A. Lindemann) set in hand an official inquiry into the governmental situation at the

Conservative take-over, but, as Swinton later told Churchill, this was not altogether successful since 'though voluminous' the material assembled 'was of varying value and not always convincing as there was a good deal of disparity between what was found in the various Departments'. Nevertheless, stimulated by letters from a back-bench MP and from a group of 'working men Tories', Churchill asked Swinton to expedite matters soon after he had taken over his co-ordinating duties. After Swinton had conferred with Butler, Fife Clark was deputed to 'get out the facts', on the basis of which Fraser of the Research Department and Chapman-Walker of Central Office were to 'have a shot' at preparing a party booklet. Two or three weeks later Fife Clark sent the resultant papers, under the rubric 'State of the Nation: November 1951', for clearance by Brook, the Cabinet Secretary. Swinton had agreed, Fife Clark minuted, that no further official action was required: the material should be made available to the Research Department without further reference to the Prime Minister, who would doubtless see the draft of any party booklet.[37] It is difficult not to harbour the suspicion that, after the expenditure of a great deal of official time, the departmental cupboard had disgorged, not skeletons, but mares' nests; and that the boundary line between propaganda and information may have been transgressed in the process.

One decision in which Swinton was centrally involved during this period was strictly speaking peripheral to his information functions, although its public impact could hardly have been greater. This was the decision to televise the whole of the Coronation ceremony in June 1953. Arrangements for the Coronation were largely in the hands of a committee presided over by the Earl Marshal, the Duke of Norfolk. On 20 October 1952 the Earl Marshal, it was thought with the unqualified approval of the Prime Minister's representative on his committee, announced that television cameras would not be allowed west of the choir-screen in Westminster Abbey, with the consequence that by far the largest audience in the history of television up to that time would have been prevented from seeing the actual ceremony of coronation, including the Recognition, Crowning, and Homage. The committee's proposals had been formally approved by the Cabinet, but this was done as part of a very full agenda, and it was not until he had been alerted by Fife Clark that Swinton became aware of the implications of the decision and began, with others, the effort to get it reversed, which occupied much of his and Fife Clark's time in the autumn of 1952. The effort involved assessment of technical evidence relating to camera-placing, the effects of floodlighting on the participants, and so on, as well as the more intractable subjective issue of the appropriateness of the intrusion of television cameras on such a ceremony ('it would be unfitting that the whole ceremony, not only in its secular but also in its religious and spiritual aspects, should be presented as if it were a theatrical perfor-mance', Churchill told the Commons on 28 October). Eventu-ally, on 8 December, the Earl Marshal announced the removal of the ban.[38]

Swinton's particular contribution as ministerial co-ordinator of government information lay in repairing the broken links with the Lobby, which he met weekly and with whose mem-bers he developed cordial relations which continued long after he left office: the Lobby found in him, in the words to Swinton of two of its representatives, 'a most notable friend' and a 'powerful and informed advocate' of the Government's policies.[39] Among his ministerial colleagues, Butler was the greatest help, often meeting Lobby-correspondents himself. But Swinton's indispensable aide was the Government's Public Relations Adviser: any success he had been able to achieve with press relations, Swinton told the Institute of Public Relations in February 1955, was '80 per cent due to a little man called Fife Clark'. So successful was Fife Clark, indeed, that he became in fact if not in name also press officer to Churchill, with easy access to No. 10 while formally outside it.[40]

Six months after assuming the additional task of informa-tion co-ordination Swinton regained the full Cabinet member-ship he had last enjoyed fourteen years before. The choice of portfolio, while an entirely appropriate one, seems to have been largely fortuitous. Churchill's eccentric appointment of Ismay as Secretary of State for Commonwealth Relations lasted less than five months, when Ismay departed to be Secretary-General of NATO. His replacement, Salisbury, remained in office for less than nine months before returning to a non-departmental appointment as Lord President (he had previously been Lord Privy Seal). On 24 November 1952 Swinton became the third Commonwealth Secretary within a year, while retaining his deputy leadership of the Lords and his information co-ordination functions. He was to hold the Commonwealth portfolio for double the combined period of his two immediate predecessors. It was to prove his last ministerial office, but he entered it, in his sixty-ninth year, with undiminished energy and enthusiasm, and it probably gave him as much satisfaction as any of the offices he had held in a ministerial career which had begun thirty-two years before.

The Commonwealth Relations Office had been formed in 1947 by a merger of the Dominions Office, which had been responsible for handling Britain's relations with the other founder members of the Commonwealth—Canada, Australia, New Zealand, South Africa, and Eire (together with the self-governing colony of Southern Rhodesia)—and the India Office, whose original functions had come to an end with the independence of India and Pakistan in 1947 (shortly followed by Ceylon, previously the responsibility of the Colonial Office). Swinton's interests and sympathies, it is quite clear, lay much more with the former 'Dominions Office' side of the Commonwealth Relations Office than with the new members in the Indian subcontinent. He had known well over many years some of the leading political figures of the 'old Dominions', men like Menzies of Australia, Pearson of Canada, and Havenga of South Africa (where his old friend Smuts had ceased to be Prime Minister in 1948 and died in 1950). He had no such personal links with India and Pakistan, and while he made genuine efforts to develop them it cannot be said that he was completely successful. Ahead lay the prospect of independence for several colonial territories, not least those he had known so well in West Africa eight years before and about whose potential for 'Westminster type' government he had expressed considerable doubt. He was confronted with the problems of a potential new Commonwealth member immediately on taking office: the ill-fated and, as it proved, ill-conceived federation of the three British territories in Central Africa.

The possibility of some form of closer association between the self-governing colony of Southern Rhodesia and the colonial protectorates of Northern Rhodesia and Nyasaland had been under review at least since 1939, when the Bledisloe Commission reported in favour of federation, but advised against any immediate steps to bring it about, because of the extent of African opposition to what was seen as a measure designed to perpetuate the domination of the European set- lers. Instead, in 1945 a purely advisory Central African Council was set up to foster co-operation in economic, social, medical, and scientific matters. The movement towards federation—exclusively European-inspired—gained impetus from a meeting of representatives of the European commun- ities convened by Sir Godfrey Huggins, Prime Minister of Southern Rhodesia, at Victoria Falls in February 1949; and in November 1950 the Labour Colonial Secretary, James Griffiths, announced that the question of closer association in Central Africa would be examined by a conference of senior officials from the Colonial Office, Commonwealth Relations Office, and the three territories. This conference was held in London in March 1951 and was followed by another at ministerial level (with both Griffiths and Gordon Walker, the Commonwealth Secretary, in attendance) at Victoria Falls in September 1951. To calm African apprehensions, the Victoria Falls conference confirmed the continuance (in any form of federation which might be adopted) of the protectorate status of, and existing African land rights in, Northern Rhodesia and Nyasaland, the political development of which would remain, subject to the ultimate authority of the British Government, with the territorial governments rather than the federal authority. The Conservative Government which took office in October was decidedly more enthusiastic for federation than its Labour predecessor (whose members in Oppositon were stressing the vital need of securing prior African consent). As early as 17 November the new Government issued a state- ment recording its belief that federation would be in the best interests of the African as well as the other inhabitants of the territories, and its hope that, in view of the assurances agreed upon at Victoria Falls and of the economic and other advan- tages, Africans would be prepared to accept it. A further conference in London in April and May 1952 drew up a draft federal constitution and in July 1952 a White Paper was issued; reports by special commissions on federal finance, justice, and the public service followed. A final conference was planned, probably at Victoria Falls, for October 1952, but had to be postponed because of the Commonwealth Economic Conference being held in London at the end of November. No method had been devised for sounding African opinion, let alone securing the backing of Africans for the scheme. The hope was that once the federation was in being it would begin to elicit at least tacit African support.

It was at this point that Swinton became ministerially responsible, with Lyttelton, the Colonial Secretary, for the establishment of the Federation of Rhodesia and Nyasaland in October 1953. He was already on record as a warm supporter, having initiated a Lords debate on the report of the March 1951 conference of officials on 1 August 1951.[41] Within three weeks of the ending of the Commonwealth Economic Conference, which he naturally also had to attend, he was acting as joint chairman with Lyttelton of the intergovernmental conference to work out the final details of the federation, and this occupied the whole of January 1953. The recriminations which inevitably accompanied the British Government's decision, ten years later, to dissolve the Federation in order to allow Northern Rhodesia and Nyasaland to go their separate ways towards independence, retrospectively threw into sharp relief Swinton's role at the 1953 conference. Sir Roy Welensky, the second and last Federal Prime Minister, maintained that both British ministers at the time had given firm pledges that there would be no secession from, or dissolution of, the Federation, without the consent of all the governments concerned (although neither eventuality was alluded to in the Federal Constitution itself). Extracts from the verbatim proceedings of the conference which were published as a White Paper in February 1963, especially the discussions of 19 January 1953, make it clear that such a pledge was given. Lyttelton was quite categoric that 'Nothing can liquidate the Constitution unless all four [governments] are agreed on it.' Swinton was a little more circumspect, but his meaning was almost as plain. A claim to secession was the precursor to dissolution and had to be ruled out if the federal government were to be able to raise loans on its assets and securities: these would not be forthcoming if it were not known whether the federation was going to continue. But he did hint at something less than absolute permanence by declaring that it was inappropriate to be thinking of divorce when preparing for a marriage; and that 'You cannot legislate against the United Kingdom Parliament going off its head' and repealing the federal legislation.[42] Nevertheless, Welensky's accusation of bad faith amounted to little more than political rhetoric. No British minister could in 1953 have guaranteed the permanence of a federation in which neither the federal authority nor the constituent units were independent of the supremacy of the British Parliament; and which specifically reserved the political advancement of Northern Rhodesia and Nyasaland to the final authority of the British Government. The Federation could have been preserved only by denying the two northern territories the option of independent nationhood.[43]

But all this was in the future. The federal structure emerged in more or less complete form at the January 1953 conference and was subsequently ratified by a referendum of the European electorate in Southern Rhodesia and (without any African participation) by the legislative councils of Northern Rhodesia and Nyasaland. On 1 August 1953 the Federation of Rhodesia and Nyasaland (Constitution) Order in Council was promulgated—actually while Swinton was on a short visit to Southern Rhodesia to attend celebrations for the centenary of the birth of Cecil Rhodes—and at the beginning of September Lord Llewellin (whom Swinton had persuaded to accept the office) arrived in Salisbury as the first Governor-General and installed Sir Godfrey Huggins as the first Federal Prime Minister. On 23 October the Federation came fully into operation. Other Federal institutions followed, not the least important being the multiracial University College in Salisbury, in which Swinton took a particular interest and which received its royal charter in February 1955, just two months before he left office; the first of its halls of residence was subsequently named after him.[44]

For all its faults, which, with the benefit of hindsight, now seem obvious, the Federation of Rhodesia and Nyasaland represented a conscious effort to deal with the problems of political stability and economic viability in a plural society as a means to the achievement of the full self-government (it was hoped, within the Commonwealth) which was the aim of British colonial policy. At the time it seemed a *via media* between the contemporaneous horrors of Mau Mau in colonial Kenya on the one hand and the harsh rigidities of apartheid in independent South Africa on the other; and its collapse in 1963 presented British policy, in Southern Rhodesia, with one of the last and most intractable problems it had to confront.[45] For much of the rest of the British colonial empire the problems were relatively more straightforward, once the necessary mental adjustment had been made to the almost totally unexpected rapidity of political advance. No new Commonwealth members joined the existing eight (Britain, Canada, Australia, New Zealand, South Africa, India, Pakistan, and Ceylon) during Swinton's period as Commonwealth Secretary—the first was to be Ghana (the former Gold Coast) in 1957. But he was at the centre of policy planning for this eventuality. On 14 April 1953 the Cabinet set up a committee, with Swinton as chairman, to consider what status should be accorded to former colonies as they attained independence and wished to remain in the Commonwealth. Its deliberations continued over eighteen months, occasionally diverted to other related topics (as when, in September 1953, it was asked by the Cabinet to advise on the wording of the proposed government declaration on the eventual granting of full self-government to the Gold Coast), and its unanimous final report was submitted to the Cabinet in October 1954. Anticipating that some of the future members might well not have the resources to handle their own external relations and defence, the committee had considered the practicability of a two-tier Commonwealth membership, with the upper tier restricted to those countries in full control of their external relations and able to make a significant contribution to their own defence. But it came to the conclusion that this would probably lead to the secession from the Commonwealth of newly independent countries which might otherwise have been anxious to remain within it. The committee thus recommended that full

Commonwealth membership be granted to all applicant countries, although it felt that, wherever practicable— and it instanced the West Indian and East African colonies—they should be encouraged to enter as part of a wider grouping or federation. It did not follow, however, that all members would have equal influence in Commonwealth councils, and the committee pointed out that Britain and the other older Commonwealth members exchanged information and ideas (particularly in defence and foreign policy) which were not so fully shared with the Asian members. At its meeting on 7 December 1954 the Cabinet approved the report in principle—with some members expressing regret at the pace of colonial advance—and agreed that the Prime Ministers of Canada, Australia, and New Zealand should be sounded privately at the meeting of Commonwealth prime ministers opening at the end of the following month; subsequently Swinton prepared a paper for the three prime ministers, based on his committee's report.[46]

In common with most of his Cabinet colleagues Swinton regarded the older Commonwealth countries in quite a different light from the Asian (and potential African) members. This did not, of course, make for easy relations with Nehru, the leader of the largest Commonwealth country and one of the most influential figures in the non-communist 'uncommitted' world. And Swinton made them no easier by an understandable but highly impolitic clash with the Indian Prime Minister within a few months of taking over as Commonwealth Secretary. In a speech in Delhi on 13 April 1953, when the Mau Mau campaign in Kenya was still at its height, Nehru criticized the British Government for its policy in Kenya and assured the people of Kenya of India's sympathy. When Swinton saw the press reports of the speech he immediately summoned B. G. Kher, the Indian High Commissioner in London, to express his anger at what he considered to be an Interference in Britain's domestic affairs: 'how would it strike you [Kher reported him to Nehru as saying] if we criticized your policy in regard to say the separation of Andhra state or untouchability?' Further acrimonious exchanges followed, mainly conducted through Kher, who exchanged telegrams with Nehru, but which included an official British note of protest. To this Nehru replied (through Kher) on 25 April: 'Our Government is not used to being addressed in this way by any Government and I can only conclude that [Swinton] has for the moment forgotten that he is addressing the independent Republic of India . . . It has been our constant endeavour not to embarrass the British Government and we have tried to co-operate with them to the largest extent possible subject to adhering to our own principles and policies. We shall continue to do so, but we are not prepared to change these principles and policies because of any pressure exercised on us by an outside authority.'[47] The implication in Nehru's public criticism, that Britain was suppressing a legitimate struggle for freedom in Kenya, was not one which could be entertained by the British Government. Nevertheless this would seem to have been an occasion when Swinton's preference for plain speaking was at odds with the tact and sensitivity required of the head of a department handling a unique set of diplomatic relationships, rather than the predominantly executive responsibilities which had characterized Swinton's previous ministerial posts.

Swinton was fully alive to the importance of personal contact in fostering Commonwealth relationships, and in his two and a quarter years at the Commonwealth Relations Office he probably travelled to the overseas Commonwealth more intensively than any other Commonwealth Secretary. As we have seen, he visited Southern Rhodesia at the end of July 1953. In October of the following year he and Lady Swinton visited Canada at the invitation of St. Laurent, the Canadian Prime Minister, who placed his official plane at his guests' disposal.[48] Swinton's principal Commonwealth tour began on 23 September 1953, when he left London for a ten-week trip, mainly to Australia and New Zealand, but also taking in India, Pakistan, and Ceylon for a few days each on the homeward journey. In Australasia his visit coincided with that of the US Vice-President, Richard Nixon, and his wife, but Swinton does not seem to have been in any way eclipsed. He regretted that their respective schedules made it possible to meet the Nixons only once, in Wellington, before he left New Zealand for Australia. 'I liked him and he talked sense after dinner [Swinton wrote to his wife]. He has got a perfectly beautiful wife and a Secretary who is almost as beautiful. Alas they come to Canberra the day I leave.'[49] Although his talks with ministers and others in Australia (where he visited every state) and New Zealand were detailed and cordial it was probably his much briefer visits to the Asian Commonwealth countries which were more important in terms of Commonwealth relations. From India the British High Commissioner, Sir Alexander Clutterbuck, reported to Crookshank (who was in charge of the Commonwealth Relations Office during Swinton's absence) that 'Indian opinion was highly gratified that [the Secretary of State] decided to break his journey in this country notwithstanding the tiring effects of his exacting tour in Australia[,] and his keen interest and obvious desire to see and do as much as possible in his short stay, and to learn what he could of Indian conditions and the Indian point of view, made a deep impression.' Swinton, too, felt that the Indian visit, which he had told his wife he 'was rather funking' (partly, no doubt, because of any lingering ill will there may have been from his passage of arms with Nehru over Kenya), had been 'a real success', beginning 'with a two hour talk with Nehru of great frankness'. In Pakistan, also, according to the High Commissioner, Sir Gilbert Laithwaite, 'There was general satisfaction that the Minister responsible for Commonwealth affairs should have visited this country . . . the Secretary of State's alertness, his refusal to evade difficult or embarrassing questions, and his wide and detailed grasp of commercial and economic as well as political issues produced a marked impression on all who met or listened to him.'[50]

Swinton returned to the Commonwealth Relations Office at the beginning of December 1953 with greatly enhanced knowledge of both the 'old' and 'new' Commonwealth, and the insights gained would have had a general influence on his actions and outlook thereafter. But the overt result of his 1953 Commonwealth tour was both specific and controversial. During it he had observed the work of the locally based staff of the British Council, the government-financed non-departmental organization formed in 1934 primarily to develop cultural relations with overseas countries and spread knowledge of the English language, and whose operations in independent overseas Commonwealth countries came within the ministerial responsibility of the Commonwealth Secretary. Apart from the British Council offices in India and Pakistan, which he thought were doing admirable work, Swinton was not impressed with what he saw. He came to the conclusion that the Council's offices in Australia, New Zealand, and Ceylon were unnecessary and should be closed, leaving what cultural-relations work was needed in Australia and New Zealand to be done—better and more economically—by the British High Commission, and the English educational work in Ceylon by an education officer on the High Commission staff. On his return, apparently against the advice of his departmental officials, and certainly without any prior consultation with either the British Council or the governments of the countries concerned, he ordered the closure of the three offices. The decision was announced by Swinton's parliamentary under-secretary, John Foster, in a Commons written answer on 11 March 1954; Swinton himself made a statement in the Lords on 7 April.[51] The draconian nature of Swinton's decision seems somewhat less extreme when it is remembered that the British Council had never been represented in the most senior of the overseas Commonwealth members, Canada. Moreover, the transfer of the work of the British Council office in Australia and New Zealand to the respective British High Commissions had been recommended by a committee, under Lord Drogheda, which had been investigating the overseas information service, including the British Council; the committee reported to the Government in July 1953, well before Swinton departed on his Commonwealth tour (although the report was not published until July 1954, and then only in summary form). The Drogheda Committee had, however, envisaged an expansion of British Council work in the Asian Commonwealth, and it was the closure of the Ceylon office which attracted the most criticism, for example in the Commons debate on the Drogheda Report on 6 July 1954. While keeping to the essentials of his decision, Swinton, in face of the criticism, eventually allowed himself to be persuaded to sanction a modification of it, whereby a British Council liaison officer, paid for by the Council, was attached to the High Commission staff in both Australia and Ceylon (but not

New Zealand, where the Council ceased to have direct representation). The results of the 'prolonged negotiations' between
the Commonwealth Relations Office and the British Council
were announced in the course of the Lords debate on the
Drogheda Report on 8 December.[52] The whole episode
demonstrated that the years had not diminished Swinton's
confidence in his own judgement and his power of rapid decision. But in this case it was a judgement based on slender
personal observation (especially in Ceylon), and the decisiveness, in view of the negotiations which followed, could easily
be represented as impetuosity. Nothing, it seems, would have
been lost had he consulted the British Council before, rather
than after, making his decision.

With the 'Cold War' still very much in evidence in the early
1950s, defence formed one of the major themes in Swinton's
various inter-Commonwealth ministerial consultations, particularly with the older members. It was a congenial field for
him and one in which his unique ministerial experience came
into play. His 1953 talks in Australasia, for example, led to
an increase in the Australian and New Zealand military commitment to the defence of Malaya.[53] In the following year,
with Alexander, the Minister of Defence, he negotiated with
Erasmus, the South African Minister of Defence, the so-called
'Simonstown Agreement', which was converted into a formal
treaty soon after he left office. The agreement covered 'the
whole strategic and tactical command in case of war, from
Gibraltar to East Africa; and most important of all, it gave to
Great Britain and her Allies the use of South African ports,
including Cape Town and Durban, in any war against a Communist power'. Britain, for its part, undertook to sell a considerable quantity of major arms to South Africa, and it was
this commitment, in changed political circumstances and
under a Labour Government, that led to the virtual abrogation
of the agreement thirteen years later.[54]

In the 1951-5 Conservative Government Swinton, as well
as being, after its leader, the most experienced member, must
have run close to being its most versatile and heavily worked.
Deputy leader of the House of Lords, and as such, among
other things, piloting such complex Bills as those denationa-
lizing road transport and iron and steel; departmental Minister,

first at Materials and then at the Commonwealth Relations Office; co-ordinator of Government information services; security adviser to the Prime Minister; chairman of Cabinet committees (one of the last being that set up in January 1955 to oversee colonial security and intelligence);[55] main governmental link with the party organization as chairman of the Liaison Committee—in all these activities those who worked with him observed no diminution in his characteristic drive, decisiveness, and enthusiasm, despite his advancing years (he was, at seventy-one, the third-oldest member of the Cabinet after Churchill and Woolton). He had good reason to believe that his services deserved to be retained when Churchill—with whom he had probably been closer in these last few years than at any time in their long careers—at last laid down office in April 1955. But it was not to be. Eden dropped only two full ministers from the team he inherited from Churchill, and they happened to be the only surviving members of the Chamberlain Cabinet from which Eden had resigned in February 1938: Swinton and, outside the Churchill Cabinet, Lord De La Warr, the Postmaster-General. It has been suggested that in this way Eden was paying off old scores for their failure to support him seventeen years before, and it would seem to be in keeping with Eden's character that he should do so.[56] But the antipathy between Eden and Swinton was mutual, and however much Swinton might have wanted to remain in office, he could hardly have worked happily in an Eden Cabinet. Some ten years later he told the journalist James Margach of a conversation he had had with Churchill a few weeks before the latter resigned. Churchill asked him whether he thought Butler would make a better Prime Minister than Eden. Swinton replied that 'anybody would be better than Anthony . . . [who] would be the worst Prime Minister since Lord North. But you can't think like that now—it's too late. You announced him as your successor more than ten years ago.' To which Churchill, according to Swinton, replied, 'I think it was a great mistake.'[57]

The customary exchange of letters between Prime Minister and resigning Minister received less than the usual publicity because of the national press strike, appearing only in provincial papers. The letters conformed to convention in being couched in the form of an offer to resign and the Prime Minister's grateful acceptance of the offer. Swinton's, dated 7 April, ran:

My dear Anthony,
When you form your government, I hope you will not consider that your old colleagues, least of all the oldest, have any special claim. I came to office as a young man, so I have a special regard for the claims of the younger generation. Experience has much value but men can only get experience if they have responsibility. And the experience of age and long service is always at hand and at call, when we can help. If, as I sincerely hope, you have a long innings, there is a lot to be said for starting with a team you know will stay the course.
We are such old friends from the First World War onwards that I want to tell you how I feel.

Eden, predictably, wrote to say that 'I feel I must take advantage of your unselfish attitude and invite a younger man to take over the Commonwealth duties which you have discharged with so much ability.'[58]

As some compensation, however, Eden recommended to the Queen that Swinton be advanced to an Earldom, a signal honour for a retiring minister who had not been Prime Minister.[59] This undoubtedly gave Swinton great pleasure, as did Eden's invitation, conveyed by Butler, to extend his service to party and Government by once again chairing the Questions of Policy Committee for the general election which Eden had called for 26 May; and thus Swinton played his part in the substantial increase in the Government's majority which resulted from the election.[60]

Swinton's departure from the Government did not pass unregretted. Churchill wrote to him as soon as he heard the news:

My dear Philip,
I was indeed sorry to learn last night that you had ceased to hold your very important office. I was always well aware of the immense volume of business you conducted with so much skill and experience and of the distinguished services which you rendered to my Government. It was the only part of the List with which I did not agree.
We also have our enduring memories of Plug Street. You have all my good wishes for the future.[61]

At least two ministerial colleagues in the Churchill Government, one in the Cabinet, the other outside it, have since recorded their criticism of Eden's action in dispensing with Swinton's services. Harold Macmillan deeply regretted the loss of Swinton from the Cabinet and considered that Eden 'Would have been wise to have included him, at least in a sinecure post, for he was one of the ablest, most versatile and most loyal of colleagues'. John Boyd-Carpenter, Minister of Pensions and National Insurance outside the Cabinet at the time, also deplored the dropping of Swinton, which he regarded as 'unjustifiable' since he 'had been for many years one of the strongest and most efficient Ministers' who 'with his clear mind and outspoken tongue [had been] a major figure in the second Churchill Government'. Had Swinton still been a minister at the time of Suez, Boyd-Carpenter believed, 'his experience, judgement and courage would have been a source of strength to the Government'.[62]

Swinton hardly had time to meditate on the abrupt and unwelcome ending of his long ministerial career when he found himself the object of a public attack on his personal integrity. As soon as his resignation became known Swinton was approached by his old colleagues in Broadcast Relay Service Ltd., on whose board of directors he had sat between 1939 and 1942 (but which he had not rejoined during the 1945–51 period of Opposition, although he remained a shareholder), to become a director once again. He accepted the invitation, but since he was over seventy it was necessary for the directors to propose a special resolution for the approval of shareholders at the annual general meeting in July, and the fact that they intended to do so was reported in the press on 25 April. All this seemed harmless enough, except that Broadcast Relay Service happened to have a 25 per cent interest in Associated Rediffusion, one of the commercial programme companies formed to seek franchises from the Independent Television Authority set up under the Independent Television Act of 1954. Swinton had, naturally, played his part as deputy leader in piloting the Bill through the Lords, especially at the committee and report stages (he did not participate in the second reading debate). On 4 May the matter was raised during Commons questions by Ness Edwards, a former Labour Postmaster-General, who initially merely asked about the regulations covering the holding of directorships by ministers, but whose supplementaries contained accusations against an unnamed 'Cabinet Minister' (obviously Swinton, although he had ceased to be a Cabinet Minister a month before) for accepting a directorship in a company with an interest in commercial television and for failing to declare a shareholder's interest during the debates on the Independent Television Bill. Crookshank, Leader of the House, contented himself with referring to the guidelines on ministers' private interests which Churchill had announced in February 1952, and refused to be drawn on the 'wild accusations' in the supplementaries, which the Speaker had intervened to deplore as an infringement of parliamentary conventions. That evening Swinton issued a full statement of his position. He found, he said, some difficulty in understanding what the allegation was about. It had never been suggested that a minister on retirement should not go back to a business with which he had been associated before accepting office. He took it that what was being alleged was that the television company had some special relationship with the Government. But the Independent Television Authority set up under the 1954 Act, he pointed out, was an independent body (although its members were appointed by the Postmaster-General), with absolute discretion in the awarding of programme contracts. Associated Rediffusion had been formed after the legislation had been enacted and he had no knowledge of the terms of its contract with the ITA. As deputy leader of the Lords he had assisted in piloting the Bill through the House but his possession of shares in Broadcast Relay Service had no relevance whatever to that function. The offer of a directorship—which still had to be ratified by the shareholders—had come only after he had left office. A week later, in an election speech in his constituency (Caerphilly), Edwards shifted his ground to the charge that Swinton, as a member of the Cabinet, might have exerted improper influence in the allocation of commercial television wavelengths. On this Swinton sought reassurance from Brook, the Cabinet Secretary, who wrote on 12 May: 'I have verified that the decision to allocate particular wavelengths for commercial television was taken by the Post Office, without reference to the Cabinet. Thus, there is nothing in the specific point made by Ness Edwards . . . As

I said in our telephone conversation, however, the substantial decision, which benefited companies in commercial television, was the Cabinet's original decision to have commercial television at all; for that implied that, when the time came, wavelengths would be allocated for that purpose.' On the whole, Eden's description of the affair as a 'tiresome little Election trick' seems just.[63] But with his integrity impugned in this way Swinton may well have reflected wryly on the episode thirty years before when he had had to be dissuaded, with great difficulty, from resigning as President of the Board of Trade because of his wife's interest in a colliery company.

Swinton had finally left office, but for the remaining seventeen years of his long life he continued in politics: a sage, disinterested elder statesman frequently consulted by Conservative leaders from Macmillan and Butler to Heath and Whitelaw, and in intimate contact with politicians both at Westminster and at Swinton. No doubt more time could now be spent in Yorkshire, but he still made heavy use of the flat in Kingston House, Hyde Park, which he and Lady Swinton had taken when they sold their Lygon Place house at the end of 1944. His business interests provided agreeable occupation, including overseas travel—he retained until 1969 his directorship in Rediffusion, which replaced that in its subsidiary company Broadcast Relay Service—and there were numerous other organizations and activities in which he was involved. Among these were Anglo-Belgian relations, his connection with which having been developed through his association with Heineman and Sofina: he was for twenty years (1950-70) president of the British section of the Anglo-Belgian Union and in February 1963 was invested by King Baudouin with the rank of Grand Officier of the Order of Leopold in recognition of his services.[64]

Politics was, however, his abiding interest, and its institutional centre, for Swinton, the House of Lords. The House of Lords Hansards reflect the assiduity of his attendance and the frequency of his participation in debates. As time went on his set speeches on the many subjects on which he could speak with authority—economic and trade questions, defence, Rhodesia, and so on—became fewer and he restricted himself to briefer but no less telling interventions. In a relatively short biography primarily focussed, as this has been, on Swinton's years in office, justice cannot, unfortunately, be done to the range of his political interests and activities in retirement. But some mention must be made of his part in the modest but not unimportant measures of Lords reform during the period, since his principal long-term contribution to the House may well be seen to be the procedural change resulting from the recommendations of a Lords select committee which he chaired in the latter half of 1955. This committee—yet another to be dubbed the 'Swinton Committee'—reported in favour of a method of addressing the problem of absentee peers (or 'backwoodsmen'), whose occasional attendance *en masse* had sometimes swayed crucial votes and thereby contributed to undermining the credibility of the House. It recommended that a procedure be instituted by which peers who did not wish to attend applied for leave of absence, either for the duration of a Parliament or for a shorter period, during which they were expected not to attend the House. There was some delay before detailed consideration was given to the proposals, but when the new procedure was eventually introduced, in June 1958, it followed closely the recommendations of the Swinton Committee.[65] Its introduction coincided with the creation of the first life peers under the Life Peerages Act, another reform Swinton had strongly supported. He was also crucially involved in the 1963 discussions of the Peerage Bill, both as a member of the joint select committee of both Houses which preceded its introduction, and, even more important, as one of the leaders of a revolt of Conservative peers which ensured that the right to surrender a peerage which the legislation (among other things) provided came into effect immediately on the royal assent rather than, as the Conservative Government had wanted, following the next general election.[66] Swinton and his fellow rebels could thus claim—although they were not aware of it as they voted on 16 July 1963—that they had significantly widened the field of candidates for Prime Minister when Macmillan unexpectedly resigned three months later, a year before the election.[67] On the other hand, he was resolutely opposed to his party's cooperation with the Labour Government over the radical reform of the Lords' composition and powers contained in its 1968

White Paper: not because he was against comprehensive reform (although he disliked these particular proposals) but because the Lords would lose any ability to force a general election on the 'dishonest' Wilson Government. Had the resulting Bill not been later abandoned in the Commons, Swinton, it is clear, would have spoken and voted against it in the Lords.[68]

Swinton's eightieth birthday on 1 May 1964 was marked by a congratulatory telegram from the Queen and a dinner in his honour at the Savoy Hotel, attended by a large group of friends, with Harold Macmillan proposing the toast. By dint of temperament, continued activity (including the hard physical exercise afforded by the Swinton grouse moors), and particular pleasure in the company of people younger than himself, Swinton had retained a remarkably youthful outlook on life. 'You will never grow old,' his American friend, Lew Douglas, once told him, 'for you live in the future, not the past—except as it serves to provide a guide and a warning what not to do.'[69] But temperament could not defy the more disagreeable concomitants of old age, and Swinton had perhaps more than his full share of illness and accident—including osteo-arthritis, cataract in both eyes, and a broken hip—which put him out of action at various times even if they could not quench his spirit. Lady Swinton, too, suffered bouts of serious ill health. And there were other shadows on their life. Their only surviving son, Philip, had experienced great difficulty in adjusting to peace-time life ever since his return from the two years in a German prisoner of war camp which had followed his gallant RAF service. Dogged by ill health, with two unhappy marriages, no job which engaged his interest, and an acute sense of having failed his family, in June 1956, at the age of thirty-eight, he took his own life. Grievous blow that this was, the Swintons could find consolation in the development of their eldest son's two sons, David (after his father's death in 1943, the heir to the Swinton peerage) and Nicholas, to whom they had acted more in the capacity of parents than of grandparents. David, since 1955 Lord Masham, gained an agricultural qualification and began to give invaluable assistance in the management of the Swinton estate. In 1959 he married Susan Sinclair, who, sadly, had been paralysed as a result of a hunting accident the year before. When, in 1970, in recognition of her work for the disabled, Lady Masham was created a Life Baroness, Swinton could enjoy the pleasure of having his grand-daughter-in-law as a fellow member of the House of Lords. The younger brother, Nicholas, who had qualified as a solicitor, in 1966 married Susan, daughter of William Whitelaw, then Conservative Chief Whip; Susan Whitelaw met her future hus-band while she was working as Swinton's secretary when he was writing his reminiscences of prime ministers from Balfour to Douglas-Home, published under the title of *Sixty Years of Power.*[70]

If there is a hierarchy of elder statesmen, Swinton had by now attained its highest rank: since the death of Churchill in 1965 no other British political figure could rival the length and range of his political experience. On 13 December 1971 this pre-eminence was marked by a dinner given at No. 10 Downing Street by the Conservative Prime Minister, Edward Heath, in honour of Swinton in what was the fiftieth year of his membership of the Privy Council (he was by several years the most senior Privy Councillor). The actual anniversary fell on 25 October 1972, but he was not destined to live to see it. On 23 February he made his last recorded intervention in the House of Lords, a tribute to his old friend and colleague Salisbury, who had just died.[71] On 1 May he celebrated his eighty-eighth birthday, and early in July he performed what was to be his last act as chairman of the governors of Swinton Conservative College when he signed the letter of appointment of a new principal, Esmond Wright. It was at Swinton on 27 July, while his wife was reading a newspaper aloud to him (his eyesight was the one faculty that had shown any obvious signs of failing), that he had a sudden heart attack and died almost immediately, peacefully and without pain. Four days later he was buried in Masham churchyard, alongside his son Philip. On the same day the House of Lords began its proceed-ings with tributes to its late distinguished member from the leaders of the three parties and two peers who had intimate knowledge of aspects of his career: Lord Sherfield (the former Sir Roger Makins) and Lord Balfour of Inchrye (formerly Harold Balfour).[72] The national tribute was given at a memorial service in St. Margaret's, Westminster, on 18 October, attended by the Queen's representative (Lord Lothian) and a large congregation of family, friends, colleagues, and representatives from many of the organizations with which Swinton had been associated. Lord Butler delivered the memorial address, the lesson was read by the Prime Minister, and the Archbishop of Canterbury gave the blessing; the Last Post, appropriately, was sounded by trumpeters of the Royal Air Force.[73]

Considering that it included some twenty years in high office and ended as comparatively recently as 1955, Swinton's ministerial career has made curiously little impact on the public consciousness: indeed, if the head of the first Cabinet in which he served can be dubbed 'The Unknown Prime Minister' Swinton could well be a candidate for the title of 'The Unknown Cabinet Minister'.[74] Partly, no doubt, this arises from the triple name-change, although it was as Lord Swinton that he spent the greater part of his public career.[75] Partly, too, it may be a question of personality. While to those who knew or worked with him Swinton was a most forceful character—some thought too forceful, with at times almost brutal lack of regard for the feelings of others—little of this was projected to the public at large. He was no more than an adequate public speaker, without much skill in establishing rapport with a large audience, or even in the smaller ambit of the House of Commons (he was more successful in the more intimate atmosphere of the Lords). He had little public persona and no desire to cultivate one, or to ingratiate himself to secure applause. Then there were the ministerial portfolios, all of them important but none, apart from the Air Ministry in the particular circumstances of the 1930s, having much impact on the public mind. In many ways his service during the Second World War was the most colourful part of his long career, but this was necessarily submerged in the much greater events of that period.

But, as Lord Home has pointed out with particular reference to Swinton, 'The popular politician is not invariably the most useful.'[76] Swinton was, in a sense, a politician's politician, with a public reputation which bore little relation to that accorded him by those who worked with him in politics and government. His two greatest political friends after 1945, R. A. Butler and Harold Macmillan, have both recorded their high estimation of his abilities. To Lord Butler, he was of prime-ministerial calibre. 'Of all the men who have not been Prime Minister in England I always regarded Philip Swinton as having the endowments most suitable to an occupant of No. 10—prodigious memory, driving energy, whimsical resource, a certain asperity attractive to those who knew how to answer back, and very great experience.'[77] According to Macmillan, whose regret that Eden did not retain him in 1955 has already been noted, Swinton 'possessed the ablest and most versatile brain in the Conservative Party', whose 'value to the Government and the Party behind the scenes can hardly be over-estimated'.[78] An official who worked 'behind the scenes' at party headquarters for nearly thirty years, becoming deputy chairman of the party, saw Swinton as, with the one exception of Butler, the most able man he had known in politics who did not become prime minister.[79]

Swinton's conservatism owed little to ideology. While naturally believing profoundly in such civic virtues as patriotism and, above all, the ideal of public service, he found the main attraction of politics in 'getting things done',[80] and his career amply demonstrates that it was in executive action that his chief political gifts lay. He rarely allowed dogma to interfere with his perception of the realities of a situation. We have seen how he expected his Labour Coalition colleagues, and his own party, to 'forget politics' in their approach to his highly original plan for the post-war development of British civil aviation; and he clearly genuinely believed that such matters were capable of rational, non-partisan decision, on their merits. An equally apt illustration of his constructive and level-headed attitude to problems was provided by an earlier issue, outside his own departmental responsibilities: that of Indian self-government, which, with a vociferous and ill-informed Churchill at the head of the die-hard opposition, so deeply divided the Conservative party in the early 1930s.[81] The MacDonald Labour Government had called a round-table conference with Indian representatives in November 1930. What should be the Conservative attitude? Should the party call for the imposition of 'firm government', as urged by Churchill and his kind, regardless of its practicability or the movement of Indian opinion? It was not a subject on which Swinton (then still Cunliffe-Lister) was in any sense an expert, but his advice to Baldwin was clear and shrewd. It had been argued, he observed, that the Indian delegates 'do not represent the real forces in India; that they will be swept aside when they get back; that any concession made to them will be merely so much ground gained by the extremists, who will make further demands, using the concessions as a new jumping off ground'. But did not that argument imply that the only people who could carry Indian opinion were the extremists? And to concede that 'gives away most of the case that the extremists only represent a small but vocal minority, which can be easily crushed by firm Government'. He had been deeply impressed by the fact that none of the interests represented at the round-table conference was prepared to support the form of government for India which Conservatives would probably prefer to see. 'If this be so,' Swinton concluded, to face the fact as a fact is not defeatism but realism.'[82] India's progress to independence might well have been less sanguinary had the realism Swinton advocated been more widespread among his party.

If Swinton was primarily a political pragmatist there was no question of his merely following, as a minister, the advice of his departmental officials. He was indubitably the head (in practice as well as constitutional theory) of each department in which he served. For some this could be a bruising experience, since he had little patience with what he perceived as obtuseness or slackness; and it has been said that the private office at the Commonwealth Relations office received messages of condolence from some officials who had served under Swinton before the war when it was announced that he was to be the new Secretary of State.[83] But for those who worked closely with him and secured his trust and confidence the experience was quite otherwise. The comments of two of his private secretaries at the Colonial Office in the 1930s have been quoted in Chapter 3. These can be matched by those who worked in Swinton's private office in the 1951–5 Government. His principal private secretary at the Commonwealth Relations Office from 1953 to 1954 described his year with Swinton as the most exciting and enjoyable of his whole career, while his principal private secretary at the Ministry of Materials has written: 'When I joined Lord Swinton I was warned by senior civil servants who had worked with him before the war that he was intolerant and an intellectual bully. Whether he had mellowed I do not know, but I found neither accusation true. He was brilliantly quick, he was impatient with slow people and he had no time for fools, but my experience was that he sought advice and weighed it carefully and was always ready to modify his view if convinced.'[84] It is tempting to think that if all departmental ministers were as able as Swinton there would be less political and academic debate about what has in recent years been represented to be a dangerously unbalanced relationship between temporary ministers and their permanent officials.

The climacteric of Swinton's career was clearly his tenure of the Air Ministry from 1935 to 1938. His enforced resignation seemed to provide proof of his failure, and he never quite recovered the position he had enjoyed in the mid-1930s, even granted that his acceptance of a peerage had affected his political prospects. Since the war, however, the nature of his achievement at the Air Ministry has increasingly come to be appreciated. The pre-war rearmament of the RAF was, of course, a co-operative effort in which many participated, industrialists, designers, airmen, scientists, administrators, and others. But it is hardly possible to over-estimate Swinton's role as the responsible minister for three crucial years, most notably, in developing the capacity of the professional aircraft industry and in activating the shadow industry; in determining the urgent priority to be given to the production of the advanced eight-gun fighters and the new generation of heavy bombers; in encouraging radar development and the subsequent reorganization of fighter tactics; and, not least, in fighting for the air programme in face, particularly from 1937, of the marked reluctance of the Prime Minister and other senior members of the Cabinet. During the Second World War Swinton was able to make a number of important contributions in diverse fields but it is rather as Air Minister before the war began that he can safely claim to have been one of the architects of eventual victory.

It would, none the less, be difficult to maintain that Swinton was a politician of the very first rank, although there were those who, at various stages, would have confidently predicted the highest offices for him. But study of the careers of second-rank politicians can reveal more of the practical detail of the governing process than the examination of the more wide-ranging and generalized concerns of those who preside over governments. It is in government departments that the rhetoric of politics has most directly to confront the realities of policy-implementation, that politicians have to show what they are made of. Swinton, a highly effective minister in a variety of departments over three decades, triumphantly passed the test. The skill this demands is by no means universally possessed by those who achieve ministerial office, but it is vital to the proper functioning of the British political system.

Notes

CHAPTER 1. CAREER FOUNDATIONS

1 For a history and description of the house (now called Sewerby Hall) and park see Frank Johnson, *Sewerby Hall and Park* (n.d.), published by the Tourism and Recreation Committee of the Borough of North Wolds. The estate was sold by Lord Swinton's elder brother, Yarburgh Lloyd-Greame, to Bridlington Corporation in 1934, and the house is now a museum.

2 Lord Swinton, *I Remember* (Hutchinson, London, 1948), pp. 11 f.

3 Churchill College, Cambridge, Swinton Papers (hereafter Swin. P.), 270/1/1: Mrs Lloyd-Greame to Philip Lloyd-Greame, 11 July 1911.

4 Information from the Curator of Wiccamica, April 1978.

5 Swinton, *I Remember*, p. 12.

6 Compton Mackenzie, *My Life and Times*, Octave Three, '1900–1907' (Chatto & Windus, London, 1964), p. 99. Mackenzie and Lloyd-Greame were clearly firm friends at Oxford and for some years afterwards. It would seem that Lloyd-Greame played an important role in bringing together Mackenzie and his future wife, Faith Stone. Ibid, p. 250; Faith C. Mackenzie, *As Much as I Dare* (Collins, London, 1938), p. 175.

7 Swinton, *I Remember*, pp. 12 f.; *Oxford University Calendar* for 1906.

8 Swinton, *I Remember*, p. 151.

9 Published by John Murray, London, 1913. See also A Gentleman with a Duster [E. H. Begbie], *The Conservative Mind* (Mills & Boon, London, 1924), pp. 98 f.

10 J. W. Hills, W. J. Ashley, and Maurice Woods, *Industrial Unrest: A Practical Solution* (John Murray, London, 1914).

11 It would appear that it was not until 1920 that the Lloyd-Greames were confidently anticipating the Swinton succession, which came to them four years later. A letter from Lloyd-Greame to his wife, dated 15 Sept. 1920, contains the paragraph: 'Of course I am delighted about Swinton. I have told Monkate to make a note of the will. But I think it is as I say.' Swin. P., 313/1/1.

12 Anthony Eden (Earl of Avon), *Another World 1897–1917* (Allen Lane, London, 1976), p. 63. Eden and Lloyd-Greame briefly served in the same brigade in Belgium in 1916. Both later became president of the Yeoman Rifles' Association: Eden in 1946, Swinton in 1954. Swin. P., 313/7/12.

13 Martin Gilbert, *Winston S. Churchill, Companion to Vol. V* (Heinemann, London, 1979), p. 326; Lord Swinton, *Sixty Years of Power* (Hutchinson, London, 1966), pp. 136 f.

14 Swin. P., 270/1/2: Major North to Mrs Lloyd-Greame, 27 Sept. 1916.

15 Iain Macleod, *Neville Chamberlain* (Muller, London, 1961), pp. 56 f.; D. Lloyd George, *War Memoirs* (Odhams, London, 1938), p. 806.

16 Keith Feiling, *The Life of Neville Chamberlain* (Macmillan, London, 1946), p. 72. For accounts of Chamberlain as Director-General of National Service see ibid., pp. 63-75; Macleod, *Chamberlain*, pp. 55-69; Lloyd George, *War Memoirs*, pp. 801-16.

17 Swinton, *I Remember*, p. 153.

18 P. Lloyd-Greame to Colonel Lloyd-Greame, 26 Aug. 1917, quoted in Alan Earl, 'The Political Life of Viscount Swinton 1918-1938' (MA thesis, University of Manchester, 1961), pp. 6 f. Cf. Swinton, *I Remember*, p. 153.

19 PRO, NatS 1/56: meetings of the National Service Council, 26 Aug. and 6 Dec. 1917. In his memoirs Geddes referred to Lloyd-Greame as his Political Secretary and Fawcett as his Administrative Secretary. Lord Geddes, *The Forging of a Family* (Faber, London, 1952), p. 313.

20 Swinton, *I Remember*, p. 153 f.

21 A. M. Gollin, *Proconsul in Politics* (Blond, London, 1964), pp. 408-10; PRO, NatS 1/56: meeting of National Service Council, 12 Sept. 1917.

22 *War Cabinet Report for 1917* (Cd. 9005, HMSO, London, 1918), pp. 85-7; Geddes, *Forging of a Family*, p. 415 f.; Lloyd George, *War Memoirs*, p. 813; *History of the Ministry of Munitions*, vol. vi, pt. 2 (London, 1922), pp. 17-20.

23 PRO, Cab 23/4-7.

24 PRO, Cab 27/14.

25 PRO, Cab 21/118, pt. 1; Cab 15/16/1, pt. 1. Swinton, *I Remember*, p. 154, gives the impression that the subcommittee had been set up by the War Cabinet itself rather than by the War Priorities Committee, while id., *Sixty Years of Power*, p. 44, incorrectly describes the 'Service Chiefs' as members of the subcommittee.

26 PRO, Cab 15/16/2, pts. 1 and 2.

27 PRO, Cab 21/118, pt. 1.

28 *The Times*, 31 Mar. 1920.

29 Swin. P., 174/1/1: Lloyd-Greame to his wife, 5 Aug. 1916.

30 Earl, 'Viscount Swinton', p. 7.

31 *I Remember*, p. 152. (His name continued to appear in the annual *Law List* until 1921.)

32 Ibid., pp. 160-3.

33 J. A. Turner, 'The British Commonwealth Union and the general election of 1918', *English Historical Review*, xciii (1978), 528-59.

34 Ibid.; House of Lords Record Office, Hannon Papers, H/12/3: Summary of activities 1 July-31 Oct. 1918. Patrick Hannon, later an MP, was appointed BCU political organizer in August 1918 and remained with it until its absorption in the Empire Industries Association in 1926.

35 Swin. P., 270/2/7, ff. 93, 100; Hannon Papers H/13/5.

36 The originator of the scheme, Captain Harold Duncan, later maintained that the BCU had not fulfilled its obligations to him and in 1925 brought an unsuccessful court action in which Lloyd-Greame (now Cunliffe-Lister, and President of the Board of Trade) was named as one of the defendants. There is voluminous material on the Duncan case in Swin. P., 270/2/6-10, and the Hannon Papers, H/13/5, H/14/1-6, and H/15/1-6.

37 Earl, 'Viscount Swinton', p. 16.

38 114 House of Commons Debates, 5th Series (hereafter referred to as H.C.Deb.), col. 717 (27 Mar. 1919).

39 112 H.C.Deb., cols. 639-42 and 793-6 (17 and 18 Feb. 1919).

40 117 H.C.Deb., col. 1326 (4 July 1919).

41 120 H.C.Deb., col. 349 (27 Oct. 1919). The proposal came as an amendment to the Government's Sex Disqualification Bill, passed by 171 to 84.

42 J. A. Cross, *Sir Samuel Hoare* (Cape, London, 1977), p. 62.

43 *The Times*, 1 Apr. 1920; 129 H.C.Deb., cols. 1305–10 (18 May 1920).

44 Cross, *Hoare*, p. 65.

45 *The Times* letter and the letter (dated 26 Jan. 1920) to his father are reproduced in his *I Remember*, pp. 154–7.

46 Ibid., p. 157.

47 *Daily News*, 28 Apr. 1919.

48 Lord Riddell, *Intimate Diary of the Peace Conference and After 1918–1923* (Gollancz, London, 1933), p. 149.

49 Quoted in Swinton, *I Remember*, p. 157.

50 Swin. P., 313/1/1: Lloyd-Greame to Colonel Lloyd-Greame, 3 Mar. 1920.

51 Lord Swinton's later recollection was that he was offered an under-secretaryship on several occasions in 1920 but refused because of the loss of income involved, and that he was eventually persuaded to accept by Bonar Law. *I Remember*, p. 15. His account there is rather similar to his later description of his initial reluctance to accept Cabinet office from Bonar Law in 1922 in *Sixty Years of Power*, pp. 66 f. It seems likely that he confused the two occasions and that Bonar Law's persuasion was exercised in 1922 rather than 1920.

52 PRO, Cab 27/73 and 83; Thomas Jones, *Whitehall Diary*, i (Oxford University Press, 1969), 139, 143, 151.

53 For an excellent account of the allocation of responsibilities involving the Board of Trade at this period see D. N. Chester and F. M. G. Willson, *The Organization of British Central Government, 1914–1964* (Allen & Unwin, London, 1968), pp. 67–85.

54 PRO, Cab 27/140.

55 Quoted in Earl, 'Viscount Swinton', pp. 21 f.

56 Robert Rhodes James, *Memoirs of a Conservative* (Weidenfeld & Nicolson, London, 1969), p. 107.

57 See the account in Keith Middlemas and John Barnes, *Baldwin* (Macmillan, London, 1969), pp. 80–4.

58 Swinton, *I Remember*, p. 15.

59 PRO, Cab 23/29: Cabinet meeting of 28 Mar. 1922.

60 Stephen White, *Britain and the Bolshevik Revolution* (Macmillan, London, 1979), p. 62. White's book gives an excellent brief survey of the Genoa and Hague conferences at pp. 68–78.

61 They are in Swin. P., 270/2/3. See also Earl, 'Viscount Swinton', pp. 36–48.

62 PRO, Cab 29/95; *Documents on British Foreign Policy*, 1st Series, vol. xix, *The Conferences of Cannes, Genoa and The Hague 1922* (HMSO, London, 1974), pp. 371 ff. (hereafter referred to as DBFP).

63 *DBFP*, pp. 392 f.

64 Swinton, *I Remember*, p. 22.

65 *DBFP*, p. 464n. When he came to write of Rapallo in his autobiography twenty-five years later, Lord Swinton's memory seems to have played him false. He describes (*I Remember*, pp. 21 f.) a meeting with Rathenau, purporting to have taken place on the evening of the signing of the Russo-German treaty (which he wrongly dates as 17 April rather than 16 April, the correct date), at which, with the help of Ralph Wigram of the Foreign Office, he argued for hours with a 'distraught and distressed' Rathenau to try to convince him that the only possible course was to repudiate the treaty. Wigram, a very junior member of the Foreign Office at the time, is not listed in any of the official records of the Genoa Conference and Swinton may have been confusing him with J. D. Gregory, a much more senior official, who was with him when he saw Rathenau (as he indubitably did) on the evening of 19 April to hear the

results of the discussion with Chicherin on possible treaty repudiation. From the evidence available it would seem that it was the 19 April meeting Swinton had in mind when writing his memoirs so long after the event. He was also in error in stating that after Rapallo the Germans left Genoa: both Wirth and Rathenau made speeches at the final plenary session on 19 May.

66 James Joll, *Intellectuals in Politics* (Weidenfeld & Nicolson, London, 1960), pp. 122 f.; W. N. Medlicott, *Contemporary England 1914–1964* (Longman, London, 1967), p. 169; Kenneth O. Morgan, *Consensus and Disunity* (Oxford University Press, 1979), p. 313.

67 PRO, Cab 29/96, f. 195.

68 PRO, Cab 31/1; *DBFP*, pp. 1051–6.

69 157 H.C.Deb., col. 493 (26 July 1922).

70 *DBFP*, pp. 1058 ff.

71 White, *Britain and the Bolshevik Revolution*, pp. 75 f.

72 Shtein, quoted in ibid., p. 76.

73 Lloyd-Greame to his wife, 24 June 1922, quoted in Earl, 'Viscount Swinton', p. 51.

74 *DBFP*, p. 1105.

75 Ibid., pp. 1120 f.; 157 H.C.Deb., col. 502 (26 July 1922). In *I Remember* (p. 25) Swinton ascribes the Russian willingness to make a public statement about referring questions to Moscow to a private conversation he had with Krassin, both men apparently unaccompanied, a few hours before the final plenary session of the conference. This cannot be reconciled with the sequence of events as reconstructed here from the record of meetings in *DBPF*.

76 157 H.C.Deb., col. 501 (26 July 1922). Lloyd-Greame's statement on the conference occupies cols. 491–504.

77 British Library of Political and Economic Science, London, Sir Sydney Chapman's unpublished autobiography (typescript), p. 193.

78 Swinton, *Sixty Years of Power*, pp. 65–7; id., *I Remember*, p. 25.

79 Sir Sydney Chapman's unpublished autobiography, pp. 193 f.

80 Swin. P., 270/2/3: L. Wilson to Lloyd-Greame, 18 May 1922.

81 *Holloway Press*, 4 Feb. 1922, quoted in Michael Kinnear, *The Fall of Lloyd George* (Macmillan, London, 1973), p. 233.

82 Swin. P., 270/2/3: Lloyd-Greame to his wife, 23 Apr. 1922.

83 Lloyd-Greame to Otto Hahn, 30 Dec. 1922, quoted in Earl, 'Viscount Swinton', pp. 58 f. At one time the Government seemed to be contemplating military action against the Turks to prevent complete Greek defeat, and telegraphed to the Dominions to request aid.

84 See, for example, Cross, *Hoare*, pp. 71–82 and the sources there cited. One of the few contemporary references to Lloyd-Greame is in Amery's diary for 13 October, where he is described as being in particularly intractable mood against the Coalition. John Barnes and David Nicholson (eds.), *The Leo Amery Diaries*, i (Hutchinson, London, 1980), 294.

85 Lloyd-Greame to Otto Hahn, 30 Dec. 1922, quoted in Earl, 'Viscount Swinton', p. 59.

86 Ibid.; Lloyd-Greame to Colonel Lloyd-Greame, 24 Oct. 1922, quoted in Earl, p. 62.

87 Swinton, *Sixty Years of Power*, pp. 66 f.

CHAPTER 2. BOARD OF TRADE

1 Middlemas and Barnes, *Baldwin* (1969), p. 126; Stephen Roskill, *Hankey*, ii (Collins, London, 1972), 323; House of Lords Record Office, Bonar Law Papers, Box 115, folder 4: Sir A. Shirley Benn to Bonar Law, 24 Oct. 1922.
2 Swinton, *Sixty Years of Power* (1966), p. 69; id., *I Remember* (1948), p. 30; Gilbert, *Winston S. Churchill, Companion to Vol. V* (1979), p. 41.
3 *I Remember*, p. 28. Cf. *Sixty Years of Power*, p. 68.
4 Lloyd-Greame to Colonel Lloyd-Greame, 6 Jan. 1923, quoted in Earl, 'Viscount Swinton' (MA thesis, Manchester, 1961) p. 29. Another contemporary personal account is in a letter from J. C. C. Davidson to Baldwin, 6 Jan. 1923, reproduced in James, *Memoirs of a Conservative* (1969), pp. 144–6.
5 Barnes and Nicholson, *The Leo Amery Diaries*, i (1980), 319 f. Randolph Churchill, *Lord Derby* (Heinemann, London, 1959), p. 495; James, *Memoirs of a Conservative*, p. 142; Middlemas and Barnes, *Baldwin*, pp. 144–6; Swinton, *I Remember*, pp. 29 f.; Jones, *Whitehall Diary*, i (1969), 228.
6 Swinton, *Sixty Years of Power*, p. 75; id., *I Remember*, p. 30. The detailed accounts in Middlemas and Barnes, *Baldwin*, and Robert Blake, *The Unknown Prime Minister* (Eyre & Spottiswoode, London, 1955) make no reference to Lloyd-Greame's advising Bonar Law. Derby's diary for 31 January 1923 records that in the discussion in Cave's room Novar was 'entirely in Bonar's favour' and Lloyd-Greame was 'sitting on the fence'. R. Churchill, *Derby*, p.496.
7 PRO, Cab 27/206.
8 Cambridge University Library, Templewood Papers, XXI/5: Hoare's unpublished typescript on 'The Bonar Law Government'; India Office Library, Curzon Papers, 286: Crowe to Curzon, 15 Dec. 1922.
9 Curzon Papers 286: McNeill letters to Curzon; ibid., Amery to Curzon, 13 Dec. 1922; Barnes and Nicholson, *Amery Diaries*, i. 311 (entry for 12 Dec. 1922).
10 PRO, Cab 27/206.
11 Maurice Cowling, *The Impact of Labour 1920–1924* (Cambridge University Press, 1971), p. 294.
12 *Sixty Years of Power*, p. 76.
13 Curzon Papers, 320, f. 78.
14 Cambridge University Library, Baldwin Papers, vol. 42, f. 89: Lloyd-Greame to Baldwin, 23 May 1923; Birmingham University Library, Austen Chamberlain Papers, AC 35/3/19: Lloyd-Greame to Chamberlain, 3 Nov. 1923.
15 Voluminous correspondence between them in August 1923 (when Derby was out of the country) is quoted extensively in Earl, 'Viscount Swinton', pp. 73–89. None of this correspondence has survived in the Swinton Papers. See also R. Churchill, *Derby*, p. 517.
16 Baldwin Papers, vol. 126, ff. 241–4: Lloyd-Greame to Baldwin, 30 July 1923; ibid. vol. 128, ff. 150–1: Lloyd-Greame to Baldwin, 24 Oct. 1923.
17 Ian M. Drummond, *Imperial Economic Policy 1917–1939* (Allen & Unwin, London, 1974), pp. 90–2.
18 PRO, Cab 32/23, pt. 1.
19 PRO, Cab 24/161, C.P.355 (23) of 27 July 1923.
20 Barnes and Nicholson, *Amery Diaries*, i. 339 (entry for 2 Aug. 1923).
21 Ibid., p. 347 (entry for 2 Oct. 1923); R. K. Snyder, *Tariff Problems in Great Britain 1918–1933* (Stanford University Press, 1944), p. 138.
22 Swinton, *I Remember*, pp. 31 f.
23 *Sixty Years of Power*, pp. 77 f.
24 Middlemas and Barnes, *Baldwin*, pp. 222–49; Cowling, *Impact of Labour*,

pp. 276–324; James, *Memoirs of a Conservative*, pp. 183–7; Jones, *Whitehall Diary*, i. 250–3.

25 Lloyd-Greame's letters to his wife, 8, 10, and 14 Oct. 1923, quoted in Earl, 'Viscount Swinton', pp. 106 f.

26 Barnes and Nicholson, *Amery Diaries*, i. 349 (entry for 14 Oct. 1923); Middlemas and Barnes, *Baldwin*, p. 222.

27 Middlemas and Barnes, *Baldwin*, p. 227.

28 Ibid., p. 228; Lloyd-Greame to his wife, 4 Nov. 1923, quoted in Earl, 'Viscount Swinton', p. 110; Victor Cazalet's journal entry for 2 Nov. 1923, quoted in Robert Rhodes James, *Victor Cazalet* (Hamish Hamilton, London, 1976), p. 85. Cazalet had joined Lloyd-Greame as his unpaid assistant private secretary in December 1922, and, after his election for Chippenham in the 1924 election, became his parliamentary private secretary for two years.

29 Amery diary entry for 2 Nov. 1923 quoted in Cowling, *Impact of Labour*, p. 313; Barnes and Nicholson, *Amery Diaries*, i. 353, 355 (entries for 31 Oct. and 10 Nov. 1923).

30 Earl, 'Viscount Swinton', p. 111; Middlemas and Barnes, *Baldwin*, p. 231. Most of the Tariff Advisory Committee's brief report, dated 22 Dec. 1923, is reproduced in Ian M. Drummond, *British Economic Policy and the Empire 1919–1939* (Allen & Unwin, London, 1972), pp. 170–3.

31 Curzon to Lady Curzon, 9 Nov. 1923, quoted in Lady Curzon, *Reminiscences* (Hutchinson, London, 1955), p. 184; Middlemas and Barnes, *Baldwin*, p. 237.

32 Cowling, *Impact of Labour*, p. 313, where no source is given for the meeting or what it discussed.

33 Ibid., p. 335; Middlemas and Barnes, *Baldwin*, p. 251.

34 Conservative Research Department, London, Bayford Diaries, ii. 73 (Sanders, created Lord Bayford in 1929, lost his seat in the 1923 election); Barnes and Nicholson, *Amery Diaries*, i. 362 (entry for 13 Dec. 1923); R. Churchill, *Derby*, p. 558.

35 R. Churchill, *Derby*, p. 565; Middlemas and Barnes, *Baldwin*, p. 255.

36 Bayford Diaries, vol. ii, entry for 13 April 1924. The inclusion of Davidson's name in the list throws some doubt on its accuracy, since Davidson, who had temporarily lost his seat, spent much of the period of the first Labour Government abroad, looking after his South American interests. James, *Memoirs of a Conservative*, pp. 192 f.

37 A Gentleman with a Duster [E. H. Begbie], *The Conservative Mind* (1924), pp. 90–2. Edward, Lord Carson, was the leader of the Ulster Unionists before and after the war, a member of Lloyd George's War Cabinet, and later a Law Lord.

38 Baldwin Papers, vol. 42, ff. 192–6. The list also names Neville Chamberlain' for the Treasury and his brother Austen for the Foreign Office.

39 Templewood Papers, V/2: Lloyd-Greame to Hoare, 1 Nov. 1924; Feiling, *Chamberlain* (1946), p. 110; Macleod, *Chamberlain* (1961), p. 111.

40 Baldwin to Lloyd-Greame, 5 Nov. 1924, quoted in Earl, 'Viscount Swinton', p. 123.

41 S. Webb to Lloyd-Greame (Nov. 1924), quoted in ibid., pp. 123–5.

42 Chapman's unpublished autobiography, p. 194.

43 Swinton, *I Remember*, p. 27.

44 Chapman's unpublished autobiography, pp. 164 f.; Sir H. Llewellyn Smith, *The Board of Trade* (Putnam, London, 1928), pp. 231–3.

45 PRO, BT 55/102/198: memorandum dated June 1928 on Board of Trade achievements since November 1924. For Swinton's recollections of the Companies Act and the safety at sea convention see *I Remember*, pp. 55–61.

46 Middlemas and Barnes, *Baldwin*, p. 287. Although he could claim to be the initiator of the Board, Cunliffe-Lister was later felt by Amery to be, with Churchill, distinctly unfriendly to it. Barnes and Nicholson, *Amery Diaries*, i. 573, 583 (diary entries for 28 Nov. 1928 and 23 Jan. 1929).
47 Middlemas and Barnes, *Baldwin*, p. 289.
48 PRO, Cab 24/171, C.P.18 (25) of 14 Jan. 1925.
49 Swinton Papers, 270/2/5, Churchill to Cunliffe-Lister, 15 Jan. 1925.
50 PRO, Cab 27/264.
51 Cmnd. 2327 of 1925; Swinton, *I Remember*, p. 36; Middlemas and Barnes, *Baldwin*, p. 291.
52 Swin. P., 174/2/1; Cunliffe-Lister to Chamberlain, 1 Sept. 1925. See also Baldwin Papers, vol. 28, f. 72: copy of Churchill to Cunliffe-Lister, 10 Sept. 1925, and ff. 67–71, Cunliffe-Lister to Baldwin, 14 Sept. 1925.
53 Middlemas and Barnes, *Baldwin*, pp. 311–6; Swinton, *I Remember*, pp. 36 f.; 189 H.C.Deb., col. 1945 (21 Dec. 1925).
54 Sidney Pollard, *The Development of the British Economy 1914–1967* (Arnold, London, 1969), p. 194. Other protective measures during Cunliffe-Lister's term at the Board of Trade included the ten-year extension, by means of the Finance Act, of the provisions of Part 1 of the Safeguarding of Industries Act, under which 'key industries' such as optical glass, scientific instruments, wireless valves, ignition magnetos, and synthetic organic chemicals were protected by a $33\frac{1}{3}$ per cent duty (waived entirely for empire products); and the permanent reimposition, again through the Finance Act, of the so-called McKenna Duties (with a third remission for empire goods) on motor vehicles, tyres, musical instruments, and cinematograph film, which the Labour Government had allowed to lapse in 1924. Cunliffe-Lister's Cabinet papers on these matters are in PRO, Cab 24/178, C.P.6 (26) of 5 Jan. 1926, and Cab 24/179, C.P.145 (26) of 7 Apr. 1926.
55 PRO, Cab 24/178, C.P.69 (26) of 16 Feb. 1926.
56 Swinton, *I Remember*, pp. 52 f.; 198 H.C.Deb., cols. 2777–8 (3 Aug. 1926).
57 PRO, Cab 24/184, C.P.29 (27) of 28 Jan. 1927; Swinton, *I Remember*, p. 53; 203 H.C.Deb., cols. 2039–2112; 204 H.C.Deb., cols. 237–314.
58 *I Remember*, pp. 53 f.
59 Pollard, *Development of the British Economy*, p. 194; Derek H. Aldcroft, *The Interwar Economy 1919–1939* (Batsford, London, 1970), p. 200.
60 Cmnd. 5320 of 1936.
61 207 House of Lords Debates (henceforth H.L.Deb.), col. 1004 (3 March 1938). Cf. Swinton, *I Remember*, p. 55.
62 Baldwin Papers, vol. 18, f. 83: Cunliffe-Lister to Baldwin, 1 July 1925.
63 Templewood Papers, V/2: Cunliffe-Lister to Hoare, 18 Aug. 1925. Cf. Swin. P., 174/2/1: Cunliffe-Lister to N. Chamberlain, 1 Sept. 1925.
64 See, for example, Baldwin Papers, vol. 16, ff. 16–17; A. Chamberlain to Baldwin, 14 Aug. 1925.
65 Ibid., vol. 18, f. 83: Cunliffe-Lister to Baldwin, 13 Aug. 1925.
66 Ibid., ff. 95–7: Baldwin to Cunliffe-Lister, 15 Aug. 1925. Derby's letter of 12 Aug. 1925 is at ibid., f. 115. Derby was afraid the resignation would set a bad precedent and that anyone who had any association with matters on which the Government had to take action (e.g. cotton textiles, agriculture) would have to resign.
67 Ibid., f. 84: Cunliffe-Lister to Baldwin, 17 Aug. 1925.
68 Ibid., ff. 99–100: copy of Lane-Fox to Cunliffe-Lister, 18 Aug. 1925.
69 Quoted in Swinton, *I Remember*, pp. 40 f.
70 Gilbert, *Churchill, Companion to Vol. V*, p. 530.

71 Swin. P., 174/2/1: Cunliffe-Lister to Chamberlain, 1 Sept. 1925.
72 Baldwin Papers, vol. 18, ff. 85–6: Cunliffe-Lister to Baldwin, 26 Aug. 1925; ibid., f. 102: Baldwin to Cunliffe-Lister, 3 Sept. 1925. Arrangements were subsequently made for Sir Arthur Steel-Maitland, the Minister of Labour, to take over temporarily the supervision of the Mines Department until, in January 1927, Cunliffe-Lister was able to tell Baldwin that the Ackton Hall Colliery Company had been sold and his wife's financial interest in coal-mining was at an end. Ibid., vol. 160, ff. 164–5: Steel-Maitland to Baldwin, 16 Nov. 1925; ibid., vol. 18, ff. 111–12: Cunliffe-Lister to Baldwin, 31 Jan. 1927.
73 Swin. P., 174/2/1: Chamberlain to Cunliffe-Lister, 30 Aug. 1925. A prominent industrialist, Sir Hugo Hirst, chairman of the General Electric Company, also thought Cunliffe-Lister was the right man at the Board of Trade, telling him later in 1925 that under no previous minister in the past forty years had the department 'been so energetic and vitalized as under your leadership'. Hirst to Cunliffe-Lister, 27 Dec. 1925, quoted in Earl, 'Viscount Swinton', pp. 139 f.
74 PRO, Cab 27/316–19; Middlemas and Barnes, *Baldwin*, p. 396.
75 Baldwin Papers, vol. 15, ff. 209–10: Cunliffe-Lister to Baldwin, 27 Apr. 1926.
76 Gilbert, *Churchill*, v. 151; Middlemas and Barnes, *Baldwin*, p. 410.
77 Swinton, *I Remember*, p. 44.
78 Ibid., pp. 42 f.
79 India Office Library, London, Halifax Papers, vol. 17, f. 154: Cunliffe-Lister to Irwin, 19 Sept. 1926; Swinton, *I Remember*, pp. 43–5; G. A. Phillips, *General Strike* (Weidenfeld & Nicolson, London, 1976), pp. 157–9.
80 PRO, Cab 27/358: meeting of the Cabinet committee on unemployment in the coal industry, 2 Dec. 1927, quoted in M. W. Kirby, *The British Coalmining Industry 1870–1946* (Macmillan, London, 1977), p. 110.
81 PRO, Cab 24/184, C.P.10 (27) of 14 Jan. 1927; and Cab 24/202, C.P.57 (29) of 24 Feb. 1929, both quoted in Kirby, *British Coalmining*, pp. 114, 120 f. Rationalization—or, more accurately, the encouragement of industrial mergers—was widely seen in the 1920s as one cure for industrial ills, and Cunliffe-Lister lent his good offices to mergers in textiles, chemicals, and iron and steel.
82 Halifax Papers, vol. 17, f. 370: Cunliffe-Lister to Irwin, 15 June 1927; Middlemas and Barnes, *Baldwin*, pp. 446–52; Swinton, *I Remember*, pp. 47 f.; id., *Sixty Years of Power*, pp. 84 f. His prophecy may be said to have been fulfilled, if only briefly, over forty years later in the ill-fated Industrial Relations Act of 1971.
83 Baldwin Papers, vol. 162, f. 161: Cunliffe-Lister to Baldwin, 20 Dec. 1927.
84 James, *Memoirs of a Conservative*, p. 107.
85 210 H.C.Deb., cols. 1067–84 (16 Nov. 1927); Halifax Papers, vol. 17, f. 478: G. Lane-Fox to Irwin, 23 Nov. 1927; Middlemas and Barnes, *Baldwin*, p. 463.
86 Halifax Papers, vol. 17, f. 188: Irwin to Lord R. Cecil, 20 Jan. 1927; ibid., f. 406: Chamberlain to Irwin, 25 Aug. 1927; ibid., f. 491: Chamberlain to Irwin, 25 Dec. 1927; ibid., vol. 18, f. 48: Hoare to Irwin, 30 Mar. 1928; ibid., f. 159: Chamberlain to Irwin, 12 Aug. 1928; Swin. P., 174/2/1: Chamberlain to Cunliffe-Lister, 8 Jan. 1929; Jones, *Whitehall Diary*, ii (1969), 154, 174. A Yorkshire friend, writing to Cunliffe-Lister on 21 November 1935 to congratulate him on his peerage, told him that he had always thought it was noble of him that 'he did not take the peerage in 1929'. Swin. P., 270/3/11.
87 Baldwin Papers, vol. 30, f. 63: Amery to Baldwin, 22 March 1928: Barnes and Nicholson, *Amery Diaries*, i. 539; Middlemas and Barnes, *Baldwin*, p. 469.
88 Barnes and Nicholson, *Amery Diaries*, i. 560–2; Middlemas and Barnes, *Baldwin*, pp. 473 f.; Gilbert, *Churchill*, v. 294.
89 Baldwin Papers, vol. 19, ff. 11–16: Cunliffe-Lister to Baldwin, 11 Nov. 1928;

90 Gilbert, *Churchill*, v. 253–79; Middlemas and Barnes, *Baldwin*, p. 467 f.; PRO, Cab 24/194, C.P. 105 (28) of 27 Mar. 1928.
91 Templewood Papers, V/3: unpublished typescript by Hoare on the resignation of the second Baldwin Government; Cross, *Hoare*, p. 113; Middlemas and Barnes, *Baldwin*, p. 526.
92 Bridgeman Political Diary (in the possession of Viscount Bridgeman), p. 197 (Nov. 1929).

CHAPTER 3. COLONIAL OFFICE

1 Swinton Papers, 313/1/4: typescript of notes on conversations in Berlin.
2 *The Times*, 10 Sept. 1929 and 27 June 1930.
3 Interview with Lord Brooke of Cumnor, 10 Aug. 1979.
4 *The Times*, 18 July 1929; Middlemas and Barnes, *Baldwin* (1969), p. 555.
5 Baldwin Papers, vol. 31, f. 2: Cunliffe-Lister to Baldwin, 7 Jan. 1930; Middlemas and Barnes, *Baldwin*, pp. 560 f.
6 Baldwin Papers, vol. 104: list attached to a memorandum prepared by Baldwin's staff, 26 July 1930.
7 Middlemas and Barnes, *Baldwin*, p. 575.
8 Swin. P., 174/2/1: Chamberlain to Cunliffe-Lister, 31 July 1930.
9 John Ramsden, *The Making of Conservative Party Policy* (Longman, London, 1980), pp. 52–4; interview with Lord Brooke of Cumnor, 10 Aug. 1979; James, *Memoirs of a Conservative* (1969), p. 322, where the author wrongly attributes the appointment of the committee to Davidson; Middlemas and Barnes, *Baldwin*, p. 552; Swin. P., 174/2/1: Chamberlain to Cunliffe-Lister, 16 July 1931.
10 Baldwin Papers, vol. 104, ff. 79–83; Swin. P., 174/2/2: Cunliffe-Lister to Baldwin, 13 Dec. 1930.
11 Cross, *Hoare* (1977), pp. 118–20; James, *Memoirs of a Conservative*, pp. 557–61; Middlemas and Barnes, *Baldwin*, pp. 585–602; Macleod, *Neville Chamberlain* (1961), p. 144; Bridgeman Political Diary, p. 235; Swin. P., 174/2/1: Chamberlain to Cunliffe-Lister, 26 Mar. 1931.
12 Swin. P., 174/2/1: G. Lloyd to Cunliffe-Lister, 14 Aug. 1931; ibid., Chamberlain to Cunliffe-Lister, 15 Aug. 1931; Feiling, *The Life of Neville Chamberlain* (1946), pp. 190 f.
13 Swin. P. 313/1/5: Cunliffe-Lister to his wife, 21 Aug. 1931.
14 Ibid.: Cunliffe-Lister to his wife, 24 Aug. 1931. The original letter was handwritten, but when Swinton many years later had copies typed the name 'Snowden' was substituted for the 'Thomas' of the original. It is this later, typed, copy which has been followed, for example, in Middlemas and Barnes, *Baldwin*, p. 631.
15 Newcastle University Library, Runciman Papers, W.R.215: Samuel to Runciman, 29 Aug. 1931; Swinton, *I Remember* (1948), p. 160. Gwilym Lloyd George resigned from office after the October 1931 election, on the tariff issue.
16 Swin. P. 313/1/5, Cunliffe-Lister on his wife, 1 Sept. and 8 Sept. 1931.
17 Ibid.: Cunliffe-Lister to his wife, 8 Sept. 1931; ibid., 270/5/6: Swinton to Oliver Stanley, 19 Apr. 1944; Swinton, *I Remember*, pp. 48 f.
18 Swin. P., 313/1/5: Cunliffe-Lister to his wife, 15 Sept. 1931.
19 Ibid.: Cunliffe-Lister to his wife, 8 Oct. 1931.
20 Middlemas and Barnes, *Baldwin*, pp. 653–5; David Marquand, *Ramsay Mac-Donald* (Cape, London, 1977), pp. 703 f.; Lord Snowden, *An Autobiography*,

ii (Nicholson & Watson, London, 1934), 964, 999; Swin. P., 174/12/3: Swinton to Alan Earl, 11 Mar. 1959; ibid.: Chamberlain to Cunliffe-Lister, 2 Jan. 1934, quoted in Swinton, *I Remember*, p. 64; Beaverbrook to Cunliffe-Lister, 6 Nov. 1931, quoted in Earl, 'Viscount Swinton' (MA thesis, Manchester, 1961), p. 233.

21 PRO, Prem 1/97: memorandum for the Prime Minister by H. B. Usher, 26 Sept. 1931; Macleod, *Chamberlain*, pp. 154 f.

22 For a detailed account see Drummond, *Imperial Economic Policy 1917-1939* (1974), pp. 170 ff.; id., *British Economic Policy and the Empire 1919-1939* (1972), pp. 89-120, 186-238. See also Lord Garner, *The Commonwealth Office* (Heinemann, London, 1978), pp. 103-7, for an official's eyewitness account of the Ottawa Conference. There are brief economic analyses in, for example, Aldcroft, *The Interwar Economy 1919-1939* (1970), pp. 285-94, and Sean Glyn and John Oxborow, *Interwar Britain: A Social and Economic History* (Allen & Unwin, London, 1976), pp. 80-2, 137-9.

23 PRO, Cab 27/467: minutes, memoranda, and report of the Cabinet Committee on the Balance of Trade; Swin. P., 313/1/5: Cunliffe-Lister to his wife, 18 Jan. 1932; PRO, Cab 23/70: Cabinet meetings of 21 and 22 January 1932; Middlemas and Barnes, *Baldwin*, pp. 660-2; Marquand, *MacDonald*, pp. 711-3; Macleod, *Chamberlain*, pp. 155 f. It may be noted that the 1975 'agreement to differ' for the Labour Cabinet's dissidents on Britain's continued membership of the European Community did not, at least ostensibly, extend to opposition *inside* Parliament.

24 Cunliffe-Lister to Chamberlain, 27 Jan. 1932, quoted in Drummond, *Imperial Economic Policy*, p. 463, n. 38.

25 Swin. P., 174/2/4: Chamberlain to Lady Cunliffe-Lister, 6 Feb. 1932.

26 Pollard, *The Development of the British Economy 1914-1967* (1969), p. 198.

27 Drummond, *Imperial Economic Policy*, p. 284.

28 Cunliffe-Lister to his wife, 19 Aug. 1932, quoted in Earl, 'Viscount Swinton', pp. 247 f. (the description of Bennett was coined by an Opposition speaker in the Canadian House of Commons). Swinton, *I Remember*, pp. 74 f.; id., *Sixty Years of Power* (1966), pp. 216-20.

29 Middlemas and Barnes, *Baldwin*, pp. 673-84; Feiling, *Chamberlain*, pp. 211-15.

30 Swinton, *I Remember*, p. 73; F. V. Meyer, *Britain's Colonies in World Trade* (Oxford University Press, 1948), p. 92. Meyer points out (p. 27) that agreement was something of a Hobson's choice for the colonies: they either participated or faced the prospect of their exports being subjected to the general tariff rates in the Dominions and India. The Birley portrait presented by Mauritius was the subject of an ill-natured attack on Cunliffe-Lister by a Labour MP, James Milner, in the debate on the Colonial Office estimates in July 1934. Milner claimed Cunliffe-Lister had not himself observed the rule against the acceptance of gifts which he enforced under Colonial Office regulations for colonial governors and officials. Cunliffe-Lister took this to be a reflection on his personal integrity (which Milner denied) and fiercely repudiated it. 292 H.C.Deb., cols. 609-10 (12 July 1934). The portrait is now in the possession of the present Earl of Swinton; a later portrait, by James Gunn, is in the possession of Mr Nicholas Cunliffe-Lister.

31 G. Whiskard to E. Harding, 22 Aug. 1932, quoted in Garner, *The Commonwealth Office*, pp. 106 f.; L. S. Amery, *My Political Life*, iii (Hutchinson, London, 1955), 85; Swin. P., 174/2/4: Gerard Clauson to Lady Cunliffe-Lister, 27 Aug. 1932.

32 Glyn and Oxborow, *Interwar Britain*, p. 139.

33 Sir Charles Jeffries, *Whitehall and the Colonial Service* (The Athlone Press, London, 1972), p. 1.
34 Ibid., p. 3.
35 Swinton, *I Remember*, p. 65.
36 G. L. M. Clauson, 15 Jan. 1937, quoted in D. J. Morgan, *Official History of Colonial Development*, i (Macmillan, London, 1980), 2.
37 Swinton, *I Remember*, pp. 65 f.; interview with Sir Sydney Caine, 7 Oct. 1979; Sir Charles Jeffries, *The Colonial Office* (Allen & Unwin, London, 1956), p. 111.
38 Swin. P., 270/3/2: W. H. McLean to Cunliffe-Lister, 10 Dec. 1931.
39 Swinton, *I Remember*, p. 68. The *Economic Survey* remained an internal office document, although circulated to all the delegates at Ottawa, until it was published by HMSO in 1934 as Colonial No. 95.
40 *I Remember*, p. 71.
41 Ibid., p. 76.
42 PRO, Cab 23/95: Cabinet meetings of 8 and 29 March 1933, quoted in Drummond, *British Economic Policy*, p. 133.
43 Interview with Sir Sydney Caine, 7 Oct. 1979.
44 PRO, Cab 24/248, C.P.106 (34) of 12 Apr. 1934.
45 Swinton, *I Remember*, p. 74; Meyer, *Britain's Colonies in World Trade*, p. 71; Morgan, *Official History of Colonial Development*, p. 10; PRO, Cab 24/250, C.P.201 (34) of 23 July 1934; Drummond, *British Economic Policy*, p. 177.
46 Cabinet meeting of 6 June 1934, quoted in Drummond, *Imperial Economic Policy*, pp. 44 f.; PRO, Cab 24/250, C.P.212 (34) of 19 Sept. 1934, 'The Foreign Trade of the Colonial Empire'.
47 Swinton, *I Remember*, p. 78; Morgan, *Official History of Colonial Development*, pp. 76 f.
48 *I Remember*, p. 66; Jeffries, *The Colonial Office*, p. 111.
49 *I Remember*, p. 67.
50 Interview with Sir Stephen Luke, 30 Aug. 1979; Swinton, *I Remember*, p. 66.
51 Letter from Sir Sydney Caine, 12 Oct. 1979; Swin. P., 174/7/4: Sir Frank Lee to Swinton, 24 Nov. 1959.
52 Sir Robert Watson-Watt, *Three Steps to Victory* (Odhams, London, 1957), p. 150, recounting an interview with Swinton at the Air Ministry, 17 June 1936.
53 Jeffries, *The Colonial Office*, p. 43.
54 PRO, Cab 24/234, C.P.374 (32) of 3 Nov. 1932; Swin.P. 174/2/4: Cunliffe-Lister to his wife, 18 Apr. 1933.
55 Christopher Sykes, *Cross Roads to Israel* (Collins, London, 1965), pp. 166 f.; Nicholas Bethell, *The Palestine Triangle* (Deutsch, London, 1979), pp. 24 f. Of the total Jewish immigration into Palestine between 1932 and 1935 less than an eighth came from Germany, and about 43 per cent from Poland.
56 PRO, Cab 24/248, C.P.95 (34) of 28 Mar. 1934. Cf. Swinton, *I Remember*, pp. 81 f.
57 PRO, Cab 24/229, C.P.124 (32) of 5 Apr. 1932; Cab 27/486: report of the Cabinet Committee on Palestine, 13 Apr. 1932.
58 PRO, Cab 24/234, C.P.374 (32) of 3 Nov. 1932.
59 PRO, Cab 24/251, C.P.256 (34) of 14 Nov. 1934 and C.P.270 (34) of 24 Nov. 1934; Cab 24/253, C.P.25 (35) of 28 Jan. 1935.
60 PRO, Cab 24/253, C.P.36 (35) of 8 Feb. 1935.
61 The account here is based on the voluminous material in C.O.730/177 and 178 in the Public Record Office. Among secondary sources are R. S. Stafford, *The Tragedy of the Assyrians* (Allen & Unwin, London, 1935), and S. H.

Longrigg, *Iraq 1900 to 1950* (Oxford University Press, 1953).
62 Interview with Sir Frederick Pedler, 11 Sept. 1979.
63 PRO, Cab 23/71: Cabinet meeting of 13 June 1932.
64 The brief reference to the incident in Swinton's memoirs is inaccurate in suggesting that, at War Office request, the troops stayed in Iraq until the autumn. They had all left within a month of their arrival. *I Remember*, p. 84. The subsequent history of the Assyrians was not a happy one. They failed to get the League of Nations to back separate status for them within Iraq, and in July and August there were clashes between Assyrians and Iraqi troops which led to the massacre of about 400 Assyrians and the destruction of some twenty of their villages. About 6,000 crossed over into Syria, where they were allowed to settle, and the rest had to come to terms with living in an independent Iraq as ordinary citizens.
65 For an account of his 1933 trip, and the territories involved, see Swinton, *I Remember*, pp. 81-8, and for the problems of Malta, ibid., pp. 88-90.
66 Swin. P., 174/2/4: Cunliffe-Lister to his wife, 11 Jan. 1934; *I Remember*, pp. 91 f. Sir Lee Stack, Governor-General of the Sudan, was assassinated in 1924.
67 Swin. P., 174/2/4: Byrne telegram, 31 Jan. 1934.
68 Ibid., 270/3/8: Byrne to Cunliffe-Lister, 22 Mar. 1934. The two men maintained a continuous correspondence until April 1935. Other letters are in ibid., 270/3/9.
69 Swinton, *I Remember*, p. 99; Swin. P., 174/2/4: Simon to Lady Cunliffe-Lister, 19 Mar. 1934.
70 India Office Library, London, Brabourne Papers, vol. 20: R. A. Butler to Lord Brabourne, 20 Dec. 1934.
71 Neville Chamberlain Papers, N.C.2/2: diary entry for 30 Jan. 1935.
72 Ibid.: diary entries for 11 Dec. 1934 and 3 Feb. 1935.
73 Marquand, *MacDonald*, pp. 764 f.: Brabourne Papers, vol. 20: Butler to Brabourne, 20 Dec. 1934.
74 Neville Chamberlain Papers, N.C.2/2: diary entries for 11 Dec. 1934 and 30 Jan. 1935; Marquand, *MacDonald*, p. 765; PRO, Cab 27/583 and 584.
75 Neville Chamberlain Papers, N.C.2/2: diary entry for 11 Dec. 1934. It is unlikely that Chamberlain would have trusted anyone to succeed him at the Treasury before a replacement became inevitable with his own succession to Baldwin as Prime Minister. In December 1935 he revealingly confided to his sister Ida: 'I know no one that I would trust to hold the balance between rigid orthodoxy and a fatal disregard of sound principles and the rights of posterity.' Quoted in Lord Butler (ed.), *The Conservatives* (Allen & Unwin, London, 1977), p. 369.

CHAPTER 4. AIR MINISTRY I

1 PRO, Air 8/249: memorandum on stages of British Air Rearmament, [May] 1938; PRO, Cab 27/511, ff. 42-52; 286 H.C.Deb., col. 2078 (8 Mar. 1934); 295 H.C.Deb., col. 883 (28 Nov. 1934).
2 Brian Bond (ed.), *Chief of Staff: The Diaries of Lieutenant-General Sir Henry Pownall*, i (Leo Cooper, London, 1972), 71.
3 PRO, Cab 27/518: minutes of the subcommittee on Air Parity; Cab 27/511, ff.175-81: first interim report of the subcommittee; Robert Paul Shay, *British Rearmament in the Thirties* (Princeton University Press, 1977), p. 51 f.

4 Bond, *Chief of Staff*, p. 71. The air intelligence agent may have been F. W. Winterbotham, head of the air intelligence section of the Secret Service. Winterbotham refers to what seems to have been this incident in two of his books, but as the accounts contain obvious inaccuracies (e.g., that the Air Parity subcommittee was set up in July 1935 and included Sir Kingsley Wood as a member) it is difficult to know what credence to give them. See F. W. Winterbotham, *Secret and Personal* (Kimber, London, 1969), p. 66, *The Nazi Connection* (Harper and Row, New York, 1978), pp. 128–31.

5 Baldwin Papers, vol. 1, ff. 182–4, copy of Ellington to Londonderry, 11 May 1935. See also H. Montgomery Hyde, *British Air Policy between the Wars 1918–1939* (Heinemann, London, 1976), pp. 339 f.

6 Neville Chamberlain Papers, N.C.2/23A: diary entry for Friday, 17 May 1935, recording a conversation with Baldwin 'last week' (that is, Saturday, 11 May, or earlier).

7 Winterbotham, *The Nazi Connection*, pp. 128–32, would seem to be referring to this meeting, although the date and circumstances he gives for it are inaccurate.

8 PRO, Cab 27/518: minutes of the subcommittee meetings of 13 and 16 May 1935; Cab 24/255, C.P.103 (35) of 17 May 1935.

9 W. J. Reader, *Architect of Air Power* (Collins, London, 1968), p. 203.

10 PRO, Cab 27/511, ff. 207–12: second interim report of the subcommittee on Air Parity, 17 May 1935.

11 PRO, Air 8/196; 302 H.C.Deb., cols. 367–70 (22 May 1935).

12 302 H.C.Deb., col. 367 (22 May 1935); R. J. Overy, *The Air War 1939–1945* (Europa Publications, London, 1980), p. 22; 96 H.L.Deb., col. 1017 (22 May 1935); Hyde, *British Air Policy*, p. 346; Marquess of Londonderry, *Wings of Destiny* (Macmillan, London, 1943), p. 144.

13 Londonderry, *Wings of Destiny*, p. 145; Swinton, *I Remember* (1948), pp. 101–3; Swinton Papers, 270/3/10: Hore-Belisha to Cunliffe-Lister, 14 June 1935.

14 Robert Rhodes James, *The British Revolution*, ii (Hamish Hamilton, London, 1977), 274.

15 Hyde, *British Air Policy*, p. 350.

16 Interview with Lord Butler of Saffron Walden, 12 June 1980.

17 Swin. P., 270/3/12, Cunliffe-Lister to Blair, 24 Oct.1935. Blair himself replaced Swinton as Conservative candidate and won comfortably.

18 *I Remember*, p. 105.

19 Ibid., p. 112.

20 Chamberlain minute of 25 Sept. 1936, quoted in Shay, *British Rearmament*, p. 123.

21 *Sixty Years of Power* (1966), pp. 88–90, 117 f.

22 Stephen Roskill, *Hankey*, iii (Collins, London, 1974), 201–13; Shay, *British Rearmament*, pp. 67–73; Andrew Boyle, *Trenchard* (Collins, London, 1962), pp. 692–7; PRO, Prem 1/196; Cab 21/424; Cab 24/260, C.P.51 (36) of 20 Feb. 1936.

23 PRO, Prem 1/196 and Cab 24/260: Swinton to Tommy Dugdale (now parliamentary private secretary to Baldwin), 10 Feb. 1936; Middlemas and Barnes, *Baldwin*, p. 912; Gilbert, *Churchill*, v (1976).

24 Shay, *British Rearmament*, p. 297.

25 Charles Evans, an assistant secretary at the Air Ministry, to Trenchard, 7 May 1935, quoted in Boyle, *Trenchard*, p. 689. Trenchard did not give Evans the support he clearly expected. 'You are not going to wreck the efficiency of the air force by doubling it', Trenchard wrote in reply on 8 May, adding: 'I feel

strongly that we are getting into deep waters by setting our face against a quick expansion.' Ibid., pp. 689 f.

26 Cross, *Sir Samuel Hoare* (1977), pp. 87 f., 108 f.

27 *I Remember*, pp. 109, 113. On the Newall succession to Ellington see Sir Maurice Dean, *The Royal Air Force in Two World Wars* (Cassell, London, 1979), p. 142.

28 Cross, *Hoare*, pp. 89 f.

29 The main published references to the Bullock case are in the White Paper Cmnd. 5254 of August 1936, reproduced in *The Times*, 6 Aug. 1936. See also Hyde, *British Air Policy*, pp. 386 f.; G. C. Peden, *British Rearmament and the Treasury 1932–1939* (Scottish Academic Press, Edinburgh, 1979), pp. 53 f.; Roskill, *Hankey*, iii. 209, 360 f. In a letter to *The Times* on 20 May 1972, four days after Bullock's death, Sir William Armstrong, Head of the Home Civil Service, wrote of the 'strenuous' but in the end unsuccessful efforts made after the war to get his case reopened.

30 Swin. P., 270/3/15: Sir Donald Fergusson (permanent secretary of the Minister of Agriculture) to Swinton, 29 Mar. 1938. In Fergusson's opinion Street was the outstanding Civil Servant of his generation.

31 *I Remember*, p. 27.

32 Owen Thetford, *Aircraft of the Royal Air Force since 1918* (Putnam, London, 1979), pp. 28, 289, 521.

33 M. M. Postan, D. Hay, and J. D. Scott, *Design and Development of Weapons* (History of the Second World War, HMSO, London, 1964), pp. 10 f., 489.

34 Weir to Cunliffe-Lister, 10 June 1935, quoted in Reader, *Architect of Air Power*, pp. 203 f.; Swinton to Weir, 4 Mar. 1937, quoted in ibid., p. 275. In May 1936 Weir confessed to Churchill that 'I have no official power and have confined myself to helping by advice in particular directions. Official responsibility covering political exposition would kill me. If we were at war that would not dismay me at all, but we are still at peace, although I grant it is a strained one.' Churchill College, Cambridge, Weir Papers, 9/12: Weir to Churchill, 13 May 1936.

35 Bound volumes of the minutes are in both the Public Record Office (Air 6/23–34) and the Swinton Papers (270/4/1–12).

36 Weir Papers, 19/12: Cunliffe-Lister to Churchill, 12 Aug. 1935, part reproduced in Reader, *Architect of Air Power*, pp. 222 f.

37 PRO, Air 6/23: progress meetings of 17 Sept. and 6 Oct. 1935; letters of Bullock and Cunliffe-Lister, both of 15 Oct. 1935, quoted in Reader, *Architect of Air Power*, pp. 218 f.

38 Shay, *British Rearmament*, p. 56; Hyde, *British Air Policy*, p. 360.

39 PRO, Cab 24/259, C.P.27 (36) of 10 Feb. 1936.

40 PRO, Air 6/24: progress meeting of 6 Feb. 1936.

41 PRO, Cab 24/259, C.P.27 (36) of 10 Feb. 1936.

42 N. H. Gibbs, *Grand Strategy*, vol. i: *Rearmament Policy* (History of the Second War, HMSO, London, 1976), p. 562. See also Hyde, *British Air Policy*, p. 365. Swinton had to reassure Chamberlain, as Chancellor, that the generous reserves provision, outside the yearly estimates procedure, would be administered by the Air Ministry in consultation with the Treasury. PRO, Air 8/204: Chamberlain to Swinton, 11 Feb. 1936, and Swinton to Chamberlain, 12 Feb. 1936.

43 309 H.C.Deb., cols. 1827–53 (9 Mar. 1936). The committee's report also, *inter alia*, recommended the building of an airfield at Gibraltar, apparently on Swinton's urging against considerable Foreign Office opposition. The recommendation was not finally approved by the Cabinet until 11 November 1936. Swin. P., 313/4/3: Swinton to N. H. Gibbs, 2 Dec. 1959.

44 William Hornby, *Factories and Plant* (History of the Second World War, HMSO, London, 1958), pp. 24, 219; Shay, *British Rearmament*, p. 93.
45 PRO, Cab 24/259: Cabinet Paper of 12 Feb. 1936, quoted in Shay, *British Rearmament*, p. 99. Swinton later claimed that he had advocated control of industry in order to achieve the necessary armament production, but had not been able to convince his colleagues. Swin. P., 313/2/2: Swinton to Churchill, 23 Sept. 1947. See also Shay, *British Rearmament*, pp. 129–32.
46 Hornby, *Factories and Plant*, p. 219.
47 See P. W. S. Andrews and Elizabeth Brunner, *The Life of Lord Nuffield* (Blackwell, Oxford, 1955), pp. 219–22; Robert Jackson, *The Nuffield Story* (Muller, London, 1964), pp. 139–56; Reader, *Architect of Air Power*, pp. 255–69; R. J. Overy, *William Morris, Viscount Nuffield* (Europa Publications, London, 1976), pp. 118–21. Relevant correspondence is in PRO, Air 19/1, and Weir Papers, 19/15; some of it was reproduced in the White Paper Cmnd. 5295 of Oct. 1936, *A Note on the Policy of His Majesty's Government in Relation to the Production of Aero-Engines*.
48 PRO, Air 2/23: progress meeting of 3 Dec. 1935.
49 The original site chosen for the Rootes shadow factory had been White Waltham near Maidenhead, but a site in the Lancashire depressed area was substituted as a result of parliamentary pressure. 319 H.C.Deb., cols. 345–6 (21 Jan. 1937) and 753–4 (26 Jan. 1937). See also Hornby, *Factories and Plant*, pp. 289 f.
50 Reader, *Architect of Air Power*, pp. 262 f.
51 PRO, Air 6/25: progress meetings of 21 April and 12 May 1936: Reader, *Architect of Air Power*, p. 263; Swinton, *I Remember*, p. 116.
52 Cmnd. 5295 of Oct. 1936; PRO, Air 19/1; Air 6/27: progress meeting of 27 Oct. 1936; 102 H.L.Deb., cols. 468–86 (29 Oct. 1936); Reader, *Architect of Air Power*, p. 268; Baldwin Papers, vol. 173, f. 132: Swinton to Baldwin [29 Oct. 1936]. Nuffield soon undertook work for the War Office: in January 1937 he formed a company to produce tanks, and, later, another to manufacture Bofors anti-aircraft guns.
53 PRO, Air 19/1; Hornby, *Factories and Plant*, p. 220. The Castle Bromwich factory did not begin to produce Spitfires until May 1940, when it had been taken over by Vickers and thus formally ceased to be a shadow factory. Swinton subsequently claimed that he had arranged for Vickers to build and run the Castle Bromwich factory before he left office and that Kingsley Wood reversed his decision and allocated it to Nuffield instead. Swinton estimated that the production of at least 1,000 Spitfires was lost as a result of Wood's decision. *I Remember*, p. 121; *Sixty Years of Power*, p. 119; Swin. P., 313/4/3: Swinton to N. H. Gibbs, 2 Dec. 1959.
54 Shay, *British Rearmament*, pp. 111 f. The author is under the mistaken impression that the contract was for aero-engines, not airframes.
55 PRO, Air 6/25: progress meeting of 12 May 1936.
56 Ibid., progress meeting of 22 May 1936; Cab 16/136, DPR Committee meeting of 25 May 1936; Shay, *British Rearmament*, p. 112; J. D. Scott and Richard Hughes, *The Administration of War Production* (History of the Second World War, HMSO, London, 1955), pp. 62 f.
57 William Ashworth, *Contracts and Finance* (History of the Second World War, HMSO, London, 1953), p. 151.
58 Hornby, *Factories and Plant*, pp. 202, 222, 254 f.
59 Swinton's own account of the shadow factory scheme is in *I Remember*, pp. 115–17, 119–21.
60 Postan, Hay, and Scott, *Design and Development of Weapons*, pp. 143, 149, 506 f. Production delays at Supermarine meant that the original order for

312   *Notes to pages 168-78*

310 Spitfires, due for completion in March 1939, was not completed until August 1939, when the RAF had about 500 Hurricanes.
61 Shay, *British Rearmament*, p. 113.
62 PRO, Air 6/23: progress meeting of 21 Nov. 1935.
63 Shay, *British Rearmament*, p. 114; PRO, Air 6/25, progress meeting of 24 Mar. 1936.
64 Ashworth, *Contracts and Finance*, pp. 200-2.
65 Ibid., pp. 117 f; Shay, *British Rearmament*, p. 114-25; Swinton, *I Remember*, p. 119.
66 PRO, Air 6/31: progress meeting of 25 Oct. 1937, item 5; minute by A. H. Self, [26] Oct. 1937, quoted in Shay, *British Rearmament*, p. 123. The practice was still going on as late as April 1938. See PRO, Prem 1/236: minute by E. E. Bridges, 12 Apr. 1938.
67 Shay, *British Rearmament*, pp. 115-19, 121-3; Ashworth, *Contracts and Finance*, p. 118 f.
68 270 H.C.Deb., col. 632 (10 Nov. 1932).
69 PRO, Prem 1/236: Swinton to Chamberlain, 12 July 1937.
70 Lindemann to Baldwin, 3 Nov. 1934, quoted in Lord Birkenhead, *The Prof in Two Worlds* (Collins, London, 1961), pp. 175 f.
71 PRO, Prem 1/253: Londonderry to Lindemann, 20 Dec. 1934; J. M. Spaight (Air Ministry) to Lindemann, 30 Jan. 1935.
72 Record of meeting in the Cherwell Papers, quoted in Ronald W. Clark, *Tizard* (Methuen, London, 1965) p. 121.
73 PRO, Prem 1/253: Hankey minutes to Prime Minister, 18 and 22 March 1935; 299 H.C.Deb., col. 1003; Roskill, *Hankey*, iii. 146.
74 Its minutes and memoranda are in PRO, Cab 16/132-4.
75 Baldwin Papers, vol. 47, f. 85: Cunliffe-Lister to Baldwin, 8 June 1935; Winston S. Churchill, *The Gathering Storm* (Cassell, London, 1949 edn., pp. 134 f.
76 Cunliffe-Lister to Tizard, 21 June 1935, quoted in Clark, *Tizard*, p. 124.
77 Robert Rhodes James, *Churchill: A Study in Failure 1900-1939* (Penguin, Harmondsworth, 1970), p. 317; Swinton, *I Remember*, p. 133.
78 Cabinet of 6 July 1936, quoted in Gilbert, *Churchill*, v. 761; PRO, Cab 21/426: Swinton to Hankey, 26 June 1936, quoted in Roskill, *Hankey*, iii. 231 f.
79 PRO, Air 19/26 and Prem 1/253, Churchill to Wood, 9 June 1938. A corrective to Churchill's highly partisan view is provided by A. P. Rowe, joint secretary of the committee under Swinton, who thought that much of its success was attributable to 'the energy and quickness of the Chairman'. A. P. Rowe, *One Story of Radar* (Cambridge University Press, 1948), p. 18, quoted in Roskill, *Hankey*, iii. 146.
80 Roskill, *Hankey*, iii. 233.
81 Swin P., 174/12/6: Sir John Hodsoll to Swinton, 29 June 1964.
82 Watson-Watt, *Three Steps to Victory*, pp. 149 f.
83 PRO, Cab 64/4: Churchill to Inskip, 25 May 1936.
84 Ibid.: Tizard to Swinton, 12 June 1936; ibid.: Swinton to Inskip, 13 June 1936.
85 Clark, *Tizard*, p. 158.
86 PRO, Cab 64/4: Churchill to Swinton, 16 June 1936; ibid.: Swinton to Inskip, 17 June 1936; ibid.: Inskip to Swinton, 18 June 1936; ibid.: Churchill to Swinton, 22 June 1936.
87 Clark, *Tizard*, pp. 144 f.
88 PRO, Prem 1/253: Churchill to Wood, 9 June and 30 Oct. 1938; James, *Churchill*, p. 322. Cf. Roskill's comment: 'The most curious part about this story is that, although as the 1930s advanced it became increasingly apparent

that the Tizard Committee's decision in favour of Radar was absolutely right, Churchill's confidence in Lindemann's scientific judgement was in no way vitiated.' Stephen Roskill, *Churchill and the Admirals* (Collins, London, 1977), p. 85.

89 *I Remember*, p. 129.

90 Clark, *Tizard*, pp. 150-2, 154-6; Gibbs, *Grand Strategy*, i 595; PRO, Air 6/30: progress meeting of 22 June 1937.

91 Quoted in Clark, *Tizard*, p. 169.

CHAPTER 5. AIR MINISTRY II

1 There are accounts in Stephen Roskill,*Naval Policy Between the Wars*,i (Collins, London, 1976), 392-413; Geoffrey Till, *Air Power and the Royal Navy* (Jane, London, 1979), pp. 48-55; Hyde, *British Air Policy Between the Wars 1918-1939* (1976) pp. 397-403. The references in Swinton's *I Remember* (1948), pp. 135 f., 140-2, make no mention of Swinton's own role in the Fleet Air Arm transfer, although there is a brief reference in his *Sixty Years of Power* (1966), p. 241.

2 PRO, Prem 1/282: Baldwin to Monsell, 25 July 1935, and Weir to Baldwin, 20 May 1936.

3 PRO, Cab 64/23: Monsell to Inskip, 21 Apr. 1936; Adm 1/9034: Inskip to Monsell, 1 May 1936; Cab 64/23, Swinton to Inskip, 28 Apr. 1936.

4 Cross, *Sir Samuel Hoare* (1977), pp. 85, 90-7. It seems that both ministerial protagonists were now having to argue against previously held positions, since, according to Hoare, Swinton (then Lloyd-Greame) had in 1923 been in favour of naval control of the Fleet Air Arm. Ibid., p. 95.

5 PRO, Cab 16/151: minutes of the meeting of 17 July 1936.

6 PRO, Cab 64/24: Inskip's report dated 3 Nov. 1936; Inskip to Baldwin, 5 Nov. 1936; Swinton to Inskip, 9 and 26 Nov. 1936.

7 Ibid.: Chatfield memorandum of 16 Nov. 1936; ibid.: Hoare to Baldwin and Inskip, 19 Nov. 1936; ibid.: Inskip to Baldwin, 7 Dec. 1936; PRO, Prem 1/282: Baldwin to Swinton, 16 Feb. 1937.

8 PRO, Prem 1/282: Swinton to Baldwin, 17 Feb. 1937. See also Reader, *Architect of Air Power* (1968), p. 272.

9 PRO, Prem 1/282: Weir to Baldwin, 2 Mar. 1937, quoted in Reader, *Architect of Air Power*, pp. 273 f.

10 *The Times*, 9 Mar. 1937. Several of his Cabinet colleagues wrote to express their sympathy, including Malcolm MacDonald (Dominions Secretary), who told him 'You have worked like a Trojan, with excellent results for this country and the Empire. After a month's rest you will work like two Trojans.' Wigram, the King's private secretary, wrote to convey royal sympathy. Swin. P., 270/3/14: MacDonald to Swinton, 9 Mar. 1937; Wigram to Swinton, 9 Mar. 1937.

11 PRO, Prem 1/283: note on meeting in the Prime Minister's room, 10 Mar. 1937; Cab 64/24, Inskip to Halifax and Stanley, 12 Mar. 1937. Inskip announced the changed inquiry in the Commons on 11 March (321 H.C.Deb., cols. 1331-2). The fact that Weir had threatened resignation was leaked in the *Evening Standard* on 15 March and provoked critical comment from Churchill and Sir Roger Keyes, among others, in the air estimates debate on 22 March (321 H.C.Deb., cols. 2579-652).

12 PRO, Adm 116/3722: Chatfield to Hoare, 12 Mar. 1937, quoted in Till, *Air Power and the Royal Navy*, p. 53.

13 PRO, Cab 53/7.

14 PRO, Air 8/223: Ellington minute to Swinton, 29 Apr. 1937; ibid.: Swinton minute to Ellington, 25 May 1937; Cab 64/24: Ellington to Inskip, 7 May 1937, enclosed with Swinton to Chamberlain, 22 July 1937.

15 PRO, Cab 64/24: Inskip to Duff Cooper, Swinton, and Ellington, 23 June 1937.

16 PRO, Prem 1/282 (and Cab 64/24): Swinton to Chamberlain, 22 July 1937.

17 This paragraph is based on material quoted in Roskill, *Naval Policy*, ii. 402 f.

18 PRO, Cab 24/270, C.P.199 (37) of 21 July 1937, quoted in Roskill, *Naval Policy*, p. 403. Prominent among those briefing Churchill on the naval air question was Lord Louis Mountbatten, who had been posted to the Air Division of the Naval Staff specifically to expedite the transfer of the Fleet Air Arm to the navy. Richard Hough, *Mountbatten* (Weidenfeld & Nicolson, London, 1980), pp. 107–9; Gilbert, *Winston S. Churchill*, v (1976), 852.

19 PRO, Cab 64/24:note of discussion on 26 July 1937; Cab 24/270, C.P.199A (37) of 26 July 1937; Roskill, *Naval Policy*, p. 404; Neville Chamberlain Papers, N.C. 7/11/30/139: Chamberlain to Weir, 1 Aug. 1937; 326 H.C.Deb., cols. 3512–6 (30 July 1937).

20 PRO, Air 8/223: Swinton minute to Ellington, 25 July 1937. Swinton's later recollections of his attitude to the Fleet Air Arm transfer were at variance with the evidence of the contemporary sources. For example, he informed John F. Kennedy (the future US President) in 1950 that he had told the Air Staff that ship-borne aircraft (i.e. the Fleet Air Arm) should be under the navy as long as shore-based aircraft were with the RAF. Swin. P., 174/4/3:Swinton to Kennedy, 18 Apr. 1950. Similarly, sixteen years later he wrote in *Sixty Years of Power* (p. 241) that he 'felt that there was a case for giving the Navy control of aircraft which were actually on board ship, but not of any shore based aircraft. To surrender the latter would have impaired the unity and efficiency of the Royal Air Force and would have been disastrous in practice in a war. As a matter of tactics I opposed all along the line; but then in a spirit of sweet reasonableness I gave way on what I never regarded as essential and got what mattered from a grateful and unanimous Cabinet.' This version is given some credence by the claim that it was Hankey who, in May 1937, suggested the 'compromise' which brought the dispute to an end. Roskill, *Hankey*, iii (1974), 292. But it is difficult to sustain this interpretation from the records, which show Swinton and the Air Staff, like their predecessors in office, to have been as adamantly opposed to the transfer of the Fleet Air Arm (on which the main argument centred) as to the concession of the naval claim to the coastal air units. The enforced Fleet Air Arm transfer was hardly compensated for by the Government's rejection of the more extreme of the navy's demands; and to describe the results as a 'compromise' would seem to strain the meaning of that word.

21 PRO, Cab 64/24: Weir to Inskip, 12 Aug. 1937.

22 PRO, Air 8/223: Newall to Trenchard, 13 Aug. 1937.

23 Rear-Admiral J. H. D. Cunningham, the assistant Chief of the Naval Staff, who was appointed to Chatfield to handle the discussions with the Air Ministry, admitted to Newall that in the past the Admiralty had been 'looking for trouble', but assured him that this would now cease. PRO, Air 8/223: Newall to Swinton, 13 Aug. 1937.

24 317 H.C.Deb., col. 1115 (12 Nov. 1936).

25 PRO, Cab 64/6: Swinton to Inskip, 26 Nov. 1936; Cab 24/267, C.P.18 (37) of 14 Jan. 1937, and C.P.27 (37) of 22 Jan. 1937; Gibbs, *Grand Strategy*, i (1976), 546.

26 PRO, Cab 64/15: Swinton to Eden, 1 July 1936, enclosed with Swinton to Inskip, 1 July 1936; Hyde, *British Air Policy*, pp. 393 f.

27 PRO, Air 8/249: memorandum on stages of British Air Rearmament.
28 PRO, Cab 24/268, C.P.69 (37) of 20 Feb. 1937; Cab 23/87: Cabinet meeting of 24 Feb. 1937; Gibbs, *Grand Strategy*, i. 566.
29 Swin. P., 270/3/13: Chamberlain to Swinton, 24 Dec. 1936.
30 PRO, Cab 23/87: Cabinet meeting of 3 Feb. 1937.
31 Gibbs, *Grand Strategy*, i. 277.
32 Ivone Kirkpatrick, of the British Embassy in Berlin, later reported that General Stumpff had told him that the German mission was 'delighted' with Lord Swinton's 'charm' and 'much impressed' with his humane outlook, keenness, and grasp of his job; on the other hand, it 'had not really taken to' Churchill, whom the mission had met at a dinner given by Trenchard. PRO, Cab 64/18: note by Kirkpatrick enclosed with F. H. Sandford (Air Ministry) to H. H. Sellar of Inskip's office, 30 Nov. 1937.
33 PRO, Cab 24/273, C.P.316 (37) of 15 Dec. 1937, with Swinton's memorandum of 27 Oct. 1937; Gibbs, *Grand Strategy*, i 303 f.; PRO, Air 8/249: memorandum on stages of British Air Rearmament.
34 PRO, Cab 64/30: Inskip to Swinton, 4 Nov. 1937; ibid.: Swinton to Inskip, 4 Nov. 1937.
35 Ibid., Swinton to Inskip, 26 Nov. 1937.
36 PRO, Air 8/226: Inskip to Swinton, 9 Dec. 1937; Cab 24/273, C.P.316 (37) of 15 Dec. 1937; Cab 23/90A: Cabinet meeting of 22 Dec. 1937. See also Gibbs, *Grand Strategy*, i. 547-9, 571 f.; Hyde, *British Air Policy*, pp. 409-12.
37 PRO, Cab 24/274, C.P.24 (38) of 8 Feb. 1938.
38 PRO, Cab 23/92: Cabinet meeting of 16 Feb. 1938.
39 PRO, Cab 23/92: Cabinet meetings of 12 and 14 Mar. 1938; Cab 24/275, C.P.65 (38) of 12 Mar. 1938; Cab 23/93: Cabinet meeting of 22 Mar. 1938; 333 H.C.Deb., cols. 1410-11 (24 Mar. 1938). The interference with 'normal trade' implied by the Cabinet decision of 22 March was the possibility of working day and night shifts in the aircraft industry and of peace-time factories being diverted for war requirements. Gibbs, *Grand Strategy*, i. 582n.
40 Shay, *British Rearmament in the Thirties* (1977), pp. 214, 216f., 223.
41 PRO, Cab 24/276, C.P.86 (38) of 1 Apr. 1938, and C.P.87 (38) of 4 Apr. 1938.
42 PRO, Cab 23/93: Cabinet meeting of 6 Apr. 1938; Hyde, *British Air Policy*, pp. 416 f.; Shay, *British Rearmament*, p. 216.
43 321 H.C.Deb., cols. 1807-15 (15 Mar. 1938); 324 H.C.Deb., cols. 404-14 (28 Oct. 1937); Hyde, *British Air Policy*, p. 433.
44 329 H.C.Deb., cols. 417-79 (17 Nov. 1937), 1218-20, 1242 (24 Nov. 1937), 1979-80 (30 Nov. 1937); Bodleian Library, Oxford, Woolton Papers, Box 8: Swinton to Marquis, 25 Nov. 1937.
45 321 H.C.Deb., col. 1627 (15 Mar. 1937); 326 H.C.Deb., col. 2406 (22 July 1937).
46 330 H.C.Deb., cols. 167-70 (6 Dec. 1937). Fletcher's speech is at cols. 163-7.
47 Neville Chamberlain Papers, N.C. 7/11/30/125: Swinton to Chamberlain, 7 Dec. 1937.
48 Cmnd. 5684 and 5685 of March 1938; PRO, Cab 27/643.
49 Earl Winterton, *Orders of the Day* (Cassell, London, 1953), pp. 231 f.; 333 H.C.Deb., col. 436 (16 Mar. 1938).
50 333 H.C.Deb., cols. 225-372 (during debate on air estimates, 15 Mar. 1938), 433-86 (16 Mar. 1938), 1721-1802 (28 Mar. 1938); 108 H.L.Deb., cols. 193-245 (17 Mar. 1938).
51 Ibid., col. 256 (15 Mar. 1938).
52 Ibid., col. 435 (16 Mar. 1938); Neville Chamberlain Papers, N.C. 7/11/3/261: Swinton to Chamberlain, 16 Mar. 1938.

53 For example, *News Chronicle*, 1 Feb. 1938; *The Times*, 22 Apr. 1938; *Daily Telegraph*, 22 Apr. 1938.

54 Weir Papers, 19/18: Weir's note on a talk with Chamberlain. In January Attlee sent a long and critical questionnaire about air defences to Chamberlain, and Swinton and the Air Ministry had to spend some time in preparing a rebuttal. PRO, Prem 1/238, Attlee to Chamberlain, 11 Jan. 1938.

55 Shay, *British Rearmament*, pp. 204 f. See also M. M. Postan, *British War Production* (History of the Second World War, HMSO, London, 1952), p. 341. In correspondence in 1965 with Lord Stanhope about the reasons for the attacks on him and the Air Ministry in 1938 Swinton mentioned as one factor that 'Some of the inefficient firms resented our concentration on the new types that won the battle and wanted to go on making their unwanted machines.' Swin. P., 174/7/12: Swinton to Stanhope, 22 Apr. 1965.

56 Weir Papers, 19/13: Weir memorandum of 13 Dec. 1937; PRO, Prem 1/236: Bruce-Gardner to Swinton, 20 Apr. 1938. Correspondence and memoranda on Bruce-Gardner's activities are in Prem 1/236 and 251, and Air 19/35.

57 PRO, Prem 1/236: Swinton to Chamberlain, 12 Apr. 1938.

58 Ibid.: statement enclosed with Bruce-Gardner to Swinton, 20 Apr. 1938. As a result of the Weir mission orders were placed in June 1938 for 200 Lockheed Hudsons (of which deliveries began in Feb. 1939) and 200 North American Harvard trainers (delivered from Dec. 1938). Thetford, *Aircraft of the Royal Air Force since 1918*, pp. 387, 415.

59 PRO, Prem 1/236: Wilson minute to Chamberlain [22 Apr. 1938].

60 PRO, Prem 1/252: Fisher to Chamberlain, 2 Apr. 1938; Overy, *The Air War 1939–1945* (1980), pp. 21–3; Roskill, *Hankey*, iii. 664 f. Fisher returned to his vendetta against the Air Ministry in October, but this time Chamberlain sent a copy to Kingsley Wood, Swinton's successor as Air Minister, whose spirited rebuttal included the remarks: 'No responsibility for the present state of our air defences would appear to lie, according to this conception, either with the Treasury or collectively with the Cabinet. I deprecate recriminations, and I am prepared myself to accept the view that decisions were arrived at in the light of the situation then prevailing, and were made in the belief that they were in the best interests of the country.' PRO, Prem 1/252: Fisher to Chamberlain, 1 Oct. 1938; ibid.: Wood to Chamberlain, 14 Oct. 1938.

61 PRO, Prem 1/252: Hankey to Fisher, 5 Apr. 1938; Roskill, *Hankey*, iii. 320. Only two days before, in a letter to his son, Hankey had described Swinton as 'first class' in 'a terribly difficult job'. Ibid., p. 319

62 PRO, Prem 1/236: Bruce-Gardner to Swinton, 23 Apr. 1938, enclosed with Bruce-Gardner to Wilson, 23 Apr. 1938.

63 PRO, Cab 23/93: Cabinet meeting of 27 Apr. 1938. The Treasury official assigned to the Air Ministry was Edward Bridges, whom Swinton later described as a 'good ally' in that capacity. *Sixty Years of Power*, p. 118.

64 Gibbs, *Grand Strategy*, i. 572.

65 PRO, Prem 1/236: Swinton to Chamberlain, 12 Apr. 1938.

66 Gibbs, *Grand Strategy*, i. 573; Hyde, *British Air Policy*, pp. 354 f.; Swinton, *I Remember*, pp. 107 f.

67 Gibbs, *Grand Strategy*, i. 572.

68 Scott and Hughes, *The Administration of War Production* (1955), p. 42. On the advice of Lord Weir (before his resignation) an Air Member for Development and Production was appointed (Sir Wilfrid Freeman, previously Air Member for Research and Development), together with a civilian Director-General of Production, with a seat on the Air Council (E. J. H. Lemon). Both appointments were announced by Sir Kingsley Wood on 27 June 1938 and became

effective in August. Weir Papers, 19/18: Weir memorandum on proposals for Air Ministry supply organization, Apr. 1938; 337 H.C.Deb., col. 1532 (27 June 1938); Scott and Hughes, *Administration of War Production*, pp. 38 f. See also Postan, *British War Production*, pp. 20 f.

69 335 H.C.Deb., cols. 1749-880; 108 H.L.Deb., cols. 1042-103.
70 Winterton, *Orders of the Day*, p. 235.
71 Churchill, *The Gathering Storm* (1949 edn.), p. 208.
72 Neville Chamberlain Papers, N.C. 18/1/1652: Chamberlain to Hilda Chamberlain, 17 May 1938, part quoted in Macleod, *Neville Chamberlain* (1961), p. 261.
73 *I Remember*, pp. 146 f. His subsequent published references to his resignation were even briefer and much less charitable towards Chamberlain. In his *Sixty Years of Power* he claimed that Chamberlain gave him no warning that he would be asked to surrender his post; while in an interview he gave to Ian Colvin in February 1970 he maintained that Chamberlain vouchsafed no reason for the change. Ian Colvin, *The Chamberlain Cabinet* (Gollancz, London, 1971), p. 126. It seems unlikely that after the debate on 12 May, coming on top of all the back-bench criticism of the Air Minister not being in the Commons, Swinton could have been in much doubt that the resignation he had offered to Chamberlain five months before would now be required of him; and it is almost inconceivable that Chamberlain gave him no reason for asking him to step down, especially as his 1948 account had explicitly referred to such a reason.
74 Swin. P., 174/2/1: Swinton to Chamberlain, 16 May 1938.
75 Ibid.: Swinton to Chamberlain, 16 May 1938.
76 Neville Chamberlain Papers, N.C. 7/11/31/263: Swinton to Chamberlain, 20 May 1938. The Chamberlains paid their usual annual Christmas visit to Swinton in 1938, and Mrs Chamberlain was there again at the end of May 1939. There is then a gap in the Swinton visitors' book until August 1947, when Mrs Chamberlain's is the first name to appear. She visited Swinton at least once a year until 1955.
77 They are in Swin. P., 174/2/8-10; some are quoted in Swinton, *I Remember*, pp. 147-9. They include letters from Cabinet colleagues (Halifax, Inskip, Hoare, Hore-Belisha, Elliot, Malcolm MacDonald), senior RAF officers (Ellington, Freeman, Courtney, A. T. Harris), members of the Cabinet secretariat (Hankey, Ismay, Longhurst), industrialists (W. Rootes, Sir Charles Craven of Vickers), and scientists (Tizard, Pye).
78 George VI to Chamberlain, 16 May 1938, quoted in Sir John Wheeler-Bennett, *King George VI* (Macmillan, London, 1958), p. 340.
79 J. P. L. Thomas, MP, quoted in John Harvey (ed.), *The Diplomatic Diaries of Oliver Harvey 1937-1940* (Collins, London, 1970), p. 147.
80 Macleod, *Chamberlain*, p. 260, quoting a contemporary remark by Chamberlain.
81 Swin. P., 174/2/10: Churchill to Swinton, 24 Feb. 1939, quoted in Swinton, *I Remember*, p. 147, and Gilbert, *Churchill*, v. 1042 f. Churchill suggested during the debate on 25 May 1938 that Swinton could have remained Air Minister, continuing 'to discharge the immense task of organizing the Royal Air Force as a fighting service in which he has made great progress', if the Prime Minister could have been persuaded to establish a Ministry of Supply, relieving Swinton of his aircraft production responsibilities. 336 H.C.Deb., col. 1285.
82 Wheeler-Bennett, *King George VI*, p. 340.
83 Dean, *The Royal Air Force in Two World Wars* (1979), p. 85.
84 Brabourne Papers, vol. 226: R. A. Butler to Brabourne, 23 Feb. 1938, reporting

Mark Patrick MP as saying that Chamberlain, Hoare, Wood, and Swinton had been 'gunning' for Eden and had at last 'grassed him'. The diaries of Eden's Foreign Office private secretary, Oliver Harvey, contain several entries recording Swinton's opposition to Eden: Harvey, *Diplomatic Diaries*, pp. 50 (15 Oct. 1937), 56 (3 Nov. 1937), 85 f. (1 Feb. 1938), and 94 (19 Feb. 1938). By contrast, Swinton's recollection of the Eden–Chamberlain split many years later was that 'there were faults on both sides, and the rest of us in the Cabinet found it difficult to bridge the ever-widening gap between them'. *Sixty Years of Power*, p. 116.
85 Neville Chamberlain Papers, N.C.7/11/31/261: Swinton to Chamberlain, 16 Mar. 1938.
86 110 H.L.Deb., cols. 1400-7 (4 Oct. 1938).
87 Ibid., cols. 1519-28 (1 Nov. 1938).
88 Swin. P., 270/3/20: notes for a speech, 27 Jan. 1939. Swinton had changed his mind about Chamberlain and the appeasement policy by the time he came to write *Sixty Years of Power* over a quarter of a century later. On p. 120 he records a conversation with Chamberlain, apparently immediately after Munich and before the Lords debate, which is difficult to reconcile with the speech he made in that debate. 'Chamberlain asked me what line I was going to take over Munich. I said I thought it had been worth while buying a year's grace because in a year much of the air programme would come to fruition. If he would do everything possible to advance rearmament I would support Munich on this count. Chamberlain said: "But I have made peace". At the same time he said rearmament would go full steam ahead. I said on that understanding I accepted Munich but I had no illusions about peace.' He then goes on (pp. 120 f.) to sum up Chamberlain's policy in a markedly different way from his public comments of 1938-9.

CHAPTER 6. WAR SERVICE

1 Swin. P., 270/5/1-3 contain correspondence and memoranda of the committee.
2 122 H.L.Deb., cols. 822-31 (5 May 1942).
3 W. N. Medlicott, *The Economic Blockade*, i (History of the Second World War, HMSO, London, 1952), 243-8.
4 Swinton, *I Remember* (1948), pp. 164 f., 167; Medlicott, *Economic Blockade*, pp. 248, 424 f.
5 PRO, FO 837/288, draft of UKCC's first annual report; Swinton, *I Remember*, pp. 167 f.
6 *I Remember*, p. 165. Pages 164-79 contain a valuable account of the workings of UKCC. See also W. Lionel Fraser, *All to the Good* (Heinemann, London, 1963), pp. 140-4. Fraser was the member of the Treasury staff most closely associated with UKCC.
7 *I Remember*, p. 166; PRO, FO 837/289, Frederick Leith-Ross to Hugh Dalton, 30 May 1940.
8 Peter and Leni Gillman, *'Collar the Lot': How Britain Interned and Expelled its Wartime Refugees* (Quartet Books, London, 1980), pp. 102, 104 f.
9 Interview with Lord Armstrong of Sanderstead, 24 Mar. 1980.
10 364 H.C.Deb., col. 959 (15 Aug. 1940).
11 Swinton, *I Remember*, p. 181.
12 PRO, Cab 65/13: War Cabinet meeting of 28 May 1940; ibid.: interview with Lord Armstrong, 24 Mar. 1980. The official records of the Security Executive

are in Cab 93/2-7, Cab 114, and Prem 3/418/1-3, but none of these will be open before 1991, if then. There is one file in the Swinton Papers—270/6/33—but this is also restricted. The Security Executive is referred to briefly, and not always accurately, in Nigel West, *M.I.5* (Bodley Head, London, 1981), pp. 151, 154-63.

13 363 H.C.Deb., cols. 603-4 (23 July 1940) and 1153-4 (30 July 1940); 364 H.C.Deb., cols. 414-6 (8 Aug. 1940) and 957-64 (15 Aug. 1940).

14 Interviews with Lord Armstrong, 24 Mar. 1980, and Lord Diplock, 4 Oct. 1979.

15 Minute by V. F. W. Cavendish-Bentinck, of the Foreign Office, quoted in Gillman, *Collar the Lot*, p. 234; interview with Lord Armstrong, 7 July 1980; J. R. M. Butler, *Grand Strategy*, ii (History of the Second World War, HMSO, London, 1957), 261. Sir James Butler was comparing the role of Hugh Dalton, Minister of Economic Warfare, in relation to the newly created Special Operations Executive, with that of Swinton in relation to the Security Executive: 'the member of the War Cabinet to whom both these Ministers [sic] would if necessary refer matters of doubt or dispute was to be Mr. Chamberlain'. The Prime Minister's office had proposed that the new Special Operations Executive should be placed under the Security Executive rather than the Ministry of Economic Warfare, but a committee of Halifax, Chamberlain, and Attlee decided in favour of the Ministry. David Dilks (ed.), *The Diaries of Sir Alexander Cadogan 1938-1945* (Cassell, London, 1971), p. 312. When Lord Selborne succeeded Dalton at the Ministry of Economic Warfare in February 1942 it was again proposed, unsuccessfully, that the Special Operations Executive be removed from it and placed under Swinton or Oliver Stanley (at the time without ministerial office). Ibid., pp. 436 f.

16 Interview with Lord Armstrong, 7 July 1980; Swinton, *I Remember*, p. 183, which quotes a minute from Churchill: 'I am much encouraged by all I hear from your sector of the front and of your energy. Press on and keep me informed especially if you encounter obstacles.'

17 Roskill, *Hankey*, iii (1974), 446; F. H. Hinsley, E. E. Thomas, C. F. G. Ransom, and R. C. Knight, *British Intelligence in the Second World War*, i (HMSO, London, 1979), 91; West, *M.I.5*, pp. 151 f.

18 Gillman, *Collar the Lot*, pp. 233 f.; PRO, Cab 65/10: War Cabinet meeting of 7 Nov. 1940; Swinton, *I Remember*, p. 180.

19 Interview with Lord Armstrong, 24 Mar. 1980.

20 Patrick Seale and Maureen McConville, *Philby* (Penguin, Harmondsworth, 1978), p. 206; Swin. P., 174/3/2: Masterman to Swinton, 10 June 1942: 'I want to thank you for all the help you have given to our small section and for the interest you have taken in our work. Everyone in the section feels grateful to you for the personal interest which you took in our operations, and we shall all miss your visits.' Many years later Swinton and Sir John Masterman corresponded over the difficulties Masterman was experiencing in getting official approval for the publication of his contemporary account of the doubt-agent operation. Swin. P., 313/4/4: March–May 1961; ibid., 174/9/16: Masterman to Swinton, 3 Nov. 1967, *et seq*. When eventually published, as *The Double Cross System in the War 1939 to 1945* (Yale University Press, 1972), it was dedicated to 'the Earl of Swinton, amongst whose services to Great Britain the Chairmanship of the Security Executive 1940-42 was not the least'. See also J. C. Masterman, *On the Chariot Wheel* (Oxford University Press, 1975).

21 Hinsley, *et al.*, *British Intelligence*, p. 277; Ronald Lewin, *Ultra Goes to War* (Hutchinson, London, 1978), p. 307. In a debate in the House of Lords in October 1965 Swinton stated that 'for two years in the war I was responsible

for the co-ordination of the whole of security, and that included supervision of all the Secret Services, espionage, counter-espionage and the like'. 269 H.L.Deb., col. 687 (28 Oct. 1965). And in a letter to Masterman in 1967 he remarked that 'our lads took over both M.I.5 and M.I.6'. Swin. P., 174/9/16: Swinton to Masterman, 6 Nov. 1967. On the other hand Lord Armstrong (interview 24 Mar. 1980) was not aware that Swinton had any responsibility for M.I.6., although he recalled that he had a poor opinion of its efficiency and effectiveness. After the war Swinton formed the view, which he communicated to the Labour Prime Minister in the wake of the outcry over the discovery of the atom spy Klaus Fuchs, that 'it was essential to amalgamate M.I.5 and M.I.6 under a single chief'. Bodleian Library, Oxford, Attlee Papers, Box 7: Swinton to Attlee, 6 Apr. 1950.

22 PRO, Cab 65/13: War Cabinet meeting of 27 May 1940; Gillman, *Collar the Lot*, pp. 42 f.

23 PRO, FO 371/29180: memorandum by R. T. E. Latham on the Foreign Office interest in aliens policy, 21 Jan. 1941; Gillman, *Collar the Lot*, pp. 144 f.

24 PRO, Cab 66/13, W.P. 432 (40); Gillman, *Collar the Lot*, pp. 163 ff.; Ronald Stent, *A Bespattered Page?* (Deutsch, London, 1980), pp. 95 f.

25 Interview with Lord Armstrong, 24 Mar. 1980. Twenty-one enemy agents were executed in Britain during the war, four of them British subjects. Others saved themselves from the same fate by agreeing to defect. John Bullock, *M.I.5* (Arthur Barker, London, 1963), pp. 173 f. See also West, *M.I.5*, pp. 244-74, where the number of executions is given as sixteen.

26 Swinton, *I Remember*, p. 181. For Commons criticisms in July and August 1940 see references in n. 13.

27 Swinton, *I Remember*, pp. 182 f.; H. Montgomery Hyde, *The Quiet Canadian* (Hamish Hamilton, London, 1962), pp. 64 f. Stephenson, who attended meetings of the Security Executive on his frequent visits to Britain, had 'the highest regard and friendship' for Swinton. Telegram from Sir William Stephenson to the author, 25 Feb. 1980.

28 Swin. P., 174/3/2: R. Butler to Swinton, 12 June 1942, White to Swinton, 13 June 1942; ibid., 270/5/4, Anderson to Swinton, 4 June 1942; interview with Lord Armstrong, 24 Mar. 1980; Duff Cooper, *Old Men Forget* (Hart-Davis, London, 1953), p. 311. Unlike Swinton, Duff Cooper combined the chairmanship of the Security Executive with ministerial office, as Chancellor of the Duchy of Lancaster.

29 PRO, 554/139, No. 33678: memorandum by K. E. Robinson, 1 Mar. 1944. See also Harold Evans, 'Studies in War-time Organization: (2) The Resident Ministry in West Africa', in *African Affairs*, Oct. 1944, p. 154.

30 PRO, CO 554/133, pt. 1, No. 33800/2: copy of memorandum by Chief of Imperial General Staff, 15 Apr. 1942; ibid., L. C. Hollis, secretary to the Chiefs of Staff Committee, to Sir G. Gater, Colonial Office, 16 Apr. 1942; ibid., Cranborne's record of discussion with General Giffard, 24 Apr. 1942.

31 PRO, Cab 66/25, W.P.201 (42) of 13 May 1942; Cab 65/26: War Cabinet meeting of 18 May 1942.

32 Bodleian Library, Oxford, Crookshank Papers, d.360: diary entries for 19 and 20 May 1942; PRO, Prem 3/502/2: Cranborne to Churchill, 21 May 1942, and undated Attlee note to Churchill; Charles Stuart (ed.), *The Reith Diaries* (Collins, London, 1975), p. 296.

33 PRO, Prem 3/502/2: Cranborne to Churchill, 29 May 1942, which bears a note, in Churchill's hand, 'awaiting Ld. Swinton's reply'.

34 Ibid.: Bridges to Churchill, 4 June 1942. Swinton's acting successor at the UKCC was Sir Francis Joseph, an old friend from his Ministry of National

Service days. Swinton did not formally cease to be chairman of UKCC until December 1944. *The Times,* 9 Dec. 1944.
35 PRO, Cab 65/26: War Cabinet meeting of 8 June 1942; Cab 66/25, W.P.245 (42) of 8 June 1942; Harold Evans, in *African Affairs,* Oct. 1944, p. 155.
36 Roger Makins of the Foreign Office until Dec. 1942, when he was succeeded by W. E. Houstoun-Boswall; K. E. Robinson of the Colonial Office, succeeded by A. C. Talbot Edwards in October 1942; Harold Evans of the Ministry of Information; and Lieut. F. H. Butters of the Royal Navy.
37 A former member of the Resmin staff wrote to Swinton soon after publication of his memoirs: 'Those were happy days at Achimota . . . I have never worked in a more pleasant atmosphere nor where the lead[er] has created such a fine team spirit.' Swin. P., 174/11/1: L. C. Beaumont to Swinton, 6 Feb. 1949.
38 Swin. P., 174/3/3: Swinton to Lady Swinton, 22 July and 9 Oct. 1942.
39 Swinton, *I Remember,* pp. 196 f. The distinguished visitors were the US Admiral King and Field Marshal Sir John Dill, on their way to the Tehran Conference.
40 The correspondence with Cranborne and Stanley is in Swin. P., 270/5/5, and with Lady Swinton, in 174/3/3. In addition, F. H. Sandford kept a detailed diary from July 1942 to February 1944, when he returned to England. Copies have been deposited in Rhodes House, Oxford, and Churchill College, Cambridge.
41 Swin. P., 174/3/3: Swinton to Lady Swinton, 9 Oct. 1944.
42 *I Remember,* pp. 188-248.
43 Swin. P., 174/3/3: Swinton to Lady Swinton, 21 Jan. 1943.
44 Ibid.: Swinton to Lady Swinton, 31 Jan. 1943.
45 PRO, CO 554/132, No. 33712: Swinton's memorandum on 'West Africa: Future Policy', 24 Feb. 1943.
46 Ibid.: minute by G. L. M. Clauson, 28 June 1943. See also John D. Hargreaves, *The End of Colonial Rule in West Africa* (Macmillan, London, 1979), p. 32.
47 PRO, CO 554/132, No. 33718/4: minute by Sir A. Dawe to Sir G. Gater, 9 Feb. 1943; ibid., No. 33729: minute by Swinton to Sandford, 14 July 1943.
48 Swinton, *I Remember,* p. 227; Swin. P., 174/3/3: Swinton to Lady Swinton, 26 Mar. 1943, and following letters.
49 PRO, Cab 95/12: notes of meetings with ministers, 17 Aug.-6 Sept. 1943; *The Times,* 12 Aug. 1943.
50 Swin. P., 270/5/8: Swinton to Stanley, 7 Feb. and 14 June 1944.
51 *The Times,* 24 Nov. 1944, letter from Sir B. Bourdillon.
52 See, for example, Sir Alan Burns, *Colonial Civil Servant* (Allen & Unwin, London, 1949), pp. 189 f.
53 Swinton, *I Remember,* p. 202; Swin. P., 174/11/1: Sir H. Walker to Swinton, 16 Mar. 1949.
54 Swin. P., 270/5/8: Swinton to Stanley, 1 Jan. 1944; ibid., 270/5/4: Richards to Swinton, 8 Oct. 1944; 168 H.L.Deb., col. 1299 (24 Oct. 1950); Swinton, *I Remember,* pp. 228, 247.
55 Swin. P., 270/5/8: Swinton to Stanley, 31 May 1944. On his exasperation with Freetown port development progress see, for example, his letter to his wife of 11 Feb. 1943: Freetown Port Executive 'were being bloody and stupid all afternoon. Knocked their heads together for 3½ hours and left them sore.' Ibid., 174/3/3.
56 Swin. P., 174/3/3: Swinton to Lady Swinton, 13 July 1943. Swinton recommended Sandford for the CMG, which was awarded in the 1944 New Year's Honours List.
57 Ibid.: Swinton to Lady Swinton, 21 June 1944.
58 Swinton, *I Remember,* pp. 228-32, 236 f.

322   *Notes to pages 244-55*

59 Ibid., pp. 246 f.; Swin. P., 174/3/3: Swinton to Lady Swinton, 9 Oct. 1944.
60 PRO, Cab 88/87: Anglo–US informal discussions on civil aviation, 3–6 June 1944; Prem 4/5/9: Sinclair memorandum of 14 Sept. 1944.
61 400 H.C.Deb., cols. 27-9 (16 May 1944).
62 PRO, Cab 65/47: War Cabinet meetings of 2 and 29 Sept. 1944; Cab 65/48: War Cabinet meeting of 5 Oct. 1944.
63 PRO, Cab 66/56, W.P.585 (44) or 23 Oct. 1944.
64 Cmd. 6561 of Oct. 1944, *International Air Transport*; PRO, Prem 4/5/8: Swinton minute to Churchill, 24 Oct. 1944; Cab 65/48: War Cabinet meeting of 26 Oct. 1944.
65 Garner, *The Commonwealth Office* (1978), p. 230.
66 PRO, Cab 87/28. The committee held twelve meetings between 6 November and 1 December, and its thirteenth, and last, on 18 Dec. 1944.
67 Swin. P., 174/3/3: Swinton to Lady Swinton, 23 Nov. 1944; B. B. Bishop and T. B. Jacobs (eds), *Navigating the Rapids, 1918-1971: From the Papers of Adolf Berle* (Harcourt Brace Jovanovich, New York, 1973), p. 503. It is interesting to compare Swinton's published account of the Chicago Conference (*I Remember*, pp. 249-53) with that in Berle's papers (*Navigating the Rapids*, pp. 498-511).
68 PRO, Cab 78/28: meetings of the special civil aviation committee, 20 and 22 Nov. 1944; Cab 65/48: War Cabinet meeting of 22 Nov. 1944; Prem 4/5/9: Swinton telegram to Bridges. 19 Nov. 1944; ibid.: Beaverbrook minute to Churchill [1 Dec.] 1944.
69 PRO, Prem 4/5/9: Roosevelt to Churchill, 24 Nov. 1944 and following telegrams, some of which are reproduced in F. L. Loewenheim, H. D. Langley, and M. Jonas (eds.), *Roosevelt and Churchill: Their Secret Wartime Correspondence* (E. P. Dutton, New York, 1975), pp. 603, 608 f., 612 f., 623.
70 PRO, Prem 4/5/9: Beaverbrook minute to Churchill [1 Dec.] 1944; 134 H.L.Deb., cols. 569-73 (16 Jan. 1945).
71 Stephen Wheatcroft, *Air Transport Policy* (Michael Joseph, London, 1964), p. 69; Bishop and Jacobs, *Navigating the Rapids*, p. 510.
72 PRO, Cab 78/33: Swinton's memorandum of 3 May 1945; Prem 4/5/13: Churchill minute to Eden, 23 May 1945.
73 Wheatcroft, *Air Transport Policy*, p. 70. Cf. Swinton, *I Remember*, p. 254.
74 Swinton, *I Remember*, pp. 256 f. (where the Pretoria Conference is misdated as April 1946); Garner, *The Commonwealth Office*, pp. 231 f.
75 PRO, Avia 2/2751: Swinton minute to W. P. Hildred, 31 Jan. 1945; 409 H.C.Deb., cols. 1897-1934; 136 H.L.Deb., cols. 15-24.
76 *Sixty Years of Power* (1966), pp. 149 f. Cf. *I Remember*, pp. 258 f.
77 PRO, Cab 66/60, W.P.38 (45) of 20 Jan. 1945.
78 PRO, Cab 65/49: War Cabinet meeting of 24 Jan. 1945.
79 Swin. P., 174/3/3: Swinton to Lady Swinton, 27 Jan. 1945.
80 PRO, Cab 65/49: War Cabinet meeting of 8 Mar. 1945; *British Air Transport* (Cmd. 6561 of Mar. 1945); 135 H.L.Deb., cols. 573-640 (15 Mar. 1945).
81 *Sixty Years of Power*, p. 151. Cf. *I Remember*, p. 262.
82 For example, during the second reading debate on the Ministry of Civil Aviation Bill on 11 April 1945. 409 H.C.Deb., cols. 1897-934.

CHAPTER 7. ELDER STATESMAN

1 John Ramsden, *The Making of Conservative Party Policy* (Longman, London, 1980), pp. 102 f., quoting David Clarke. Many years later Sir William Murie recalled Swinton as a 'first class chairman' of the committee. Information from Sir Folliott Sandford.

2 328 H.L.Deb., cols. 507–8 (23 Feb. 1972). Correspondence between Salisbury and Swinton on Lords business is in Swin. P., 174/4/1–2. When Salisbury was installed as Chancellor of Liverpool University in November 1951 Swinton was among the distinguished group awarded honorary degrees to mark the occasion.

3 In 1950 he joined the boards of Lister-Todd Engineering and the Runapples Trust Co.

4 Swin. P., 313/2/2: Swinton to Hutchinson, 12 Sept. 1947. Extracts appeared in the *Sunday Times*, 14 and 28 Sept., and 5 Oct. 1947, and *I Remember* was published by Hutchinson on 2 Dec. 1948. It attracted a good deal of interest, but at least one reviewer (Harold Nicolson in the *Daily Telegraph*, 31 Dec. 1948) regretted that 'such interesting experiences should be presented with so little imagination, with so little light and shade'.

5 Sir Harold S. Kent, *In on the Act* (Macmillan, London, 1979). p. 196.

6 Lord Pakenham, *Born to Believe* (Cape, London, 1953), p. 157.

7 138 H.L.Deb., cols. 984–5 (22 Jan. 1946).

8 137 H.L.Deb., cols. 629–38 (1 Nov. 1945).

9 There is voluminous material on these talks in Swin. P., 174/4/4.

10 Swin. P., 174/4/6: Swinton's typescript note on iron and steel, dated 15 Nov. 1949.

11 Ibid., 313/3/2: Swinton to Salisbury, 1 Apr. 1949.

12 Ibid.: Swinton to Salisbury, 14 Apr. 1949.

13 464 H.C.Deb., col. 373 (28 Apr. 1949); Swin. P., 174/4/2: Salisbury to Swinton, 28 Apr. 1949.

14 Swinton, *Sixty Years of Power* (1966), p. 186. See also Lord Butler, *The Art of the Possible* (Hamish Hamilton, London, 1971), pp. 137 f., and Susan Cunliffe-Lister, *Days of Yore: A History of Masham and District* (Susan Cunliffe-Lister/ The Pitman Press, Bath, 1978), p. 206.

15 The college was closed shortly after Lady Swinton's death in September 1974, on grounds of economy and also its inaccessibility, southern Conservatives apparently disagreeing with Macmillan's maxim about the virtues of going north. The whole of Swinton (apart from two rooms retained by the present Earl for entertaining) was subsequently leased to Lindley Lodge, a charity for training young people in industry.

16 Ramsden, *Making of Conservative Party Policy*, p. 143. The other members were Lord Margesson, Oliver Poole, Marjorie Maxse (from Central Office), and David Clarke, director of the Research Department, with G. Sayers, of the Research Department, as secretary.

17 Swin. P., 174/4/3: Churchill to Swinton, 18 Mar. 1950.

18 Ramsden, *Making of Conservative Party Policy*, pp. 153 f.

19 Ibid., p. 161. Michael Fraser, who had succeeded Clarke as director of the Research Department, took his place on the committee.

20 John Wheeler-Bennett, *John Anderson, Viscount Waverley* (Macmillan, London, 1962), pp. 352 f.; Crookshank Papers, d.361: diary entry for 29 Oct. 1951; Harold Macmillan, *Tides of Fortune* (Macmillan, London, 1969), p. 364; Butler, *Art of the Possible*, p. 159; Ramsden, *Making of Conservative Party Policy*, p. 153.

21 Sir Norman Brook, Secretary of the Cabinet, was sent to prevail upon Swinton

to accept the post, which it was realized would fall below his expectation. Interview with Sir Robert Marshall (then Brook's private secretary), quoted in Anthony Seldon, *Churchill's Indian Summer* (Hodder & Stoughton, London, 1981), p. 79. Lord Chandos (Oliver Lyttelton) has recounted how he was offered by Churchill the post of 'Minister of Materials and Rearmament', apparently in the Cabinet, and, when he expressed some distaste at the prospect, was later offered—and accepted with alacrity—the Colonial Office. Lord Chandos, *Memoirs* (Bodley Head, London, 1962), pp. 343 f. It is possible that Churchill had Swinton in mind as Colonial Secretary, and decided to switch the two men on learning of Lyttleton's attitude to the Materials post.

22 174 H.L.Deb., cols, 167-8 (14 Nov. 1951); 515 H.C.Deb., col. 5 (4 May 1953). The Ministry of Materials was eventually would up in August 1954.

23 G. R. Downes to the author, 30 Sept. 1979. Cf. Macmillan, *Tides of Fortune*, p. 430.

24 Butler, *Art of the Possible*, pp. 158-60. Swinton described 'Robot' (as the plan was known) as a 'dangerous gamble' unless it had full Commonwealth co-operation and was underwritten by the United States.

25 Macmillan, *Tides of Fortune*, pp. 398, 430.

26 Kent, *In on the Act*, pp. 234, 237, 240. Penelope, during the long absence of her husband, Odysseus, at the Trojan War, spent the days making a robe for her aged father-in-law and the nights in undoing her daytime work. Kent enjoyed working with Swinton, whom he found 'agreeable and witty'. Ibid., p. 234.

27 Ibid., p. 236.

28 Seldon, *Churchill's Indian Summer*, p. 96. Swinton was even thought to affect Churchillian verbal mannerisms by some of those who knew him at this time. One of his private secretaries at the Commonwealth Relations Office found that when Swinton was speaking to Churchill on the telephone he could differentiate between them only because Swinton sounded nearer! Interview with R. H. Belcher, 13 Sept. 1979.

29 Interviews with R. H. Belcher, 13 Sept. 1979, and D. J. C. Crawley, 26 Oct. 1979.

30 Lord Egrement (John Wyndham), *Wyndham and Children First* (Macmillan, London, 1968), pp. 146-51; information from Lord Fraser of Kilmorack.

31 Ramsden, *Making of Conservative Party Policy*, pp. 168-70.

32 M. Ogilvy-Webb, *The Government Explains* (Allen & Unwin, London, 1965).

33 Interview with Sir Fife Clark, 9 Aug. 1979; Sir Harold Evans, *Downing Street Diary* (Hodder & Stoughton, 1981), p. 45.

34 Swin. P., 174/5/3; 498 H.C.Deb., col. 2280.

35 500 H.C.Deb., cols. 859-60 (12 May 1952); 502 H.C.Deb., cols. 196-8 (18 June 1952); Ogilvy-Webb, *The Government Explains*, pp. 82 f., 86-8.

36 Quoted in ibid., pp. 190 f.

37 Swin. P., 174/5/3: Churchill to Swinton, 16 June 1952; ibid.: Swinton to Churchill, 20 June 1952; ibid.: Fife Clark to R. B. Marshall, 8 July 1952.

38 Swinton, *Sixty Years of Power*, pp. 138-40; 505 H.C.Deb., cols. 1742-3 (28 Oct. 1952); interview with Sir Fife Clark, 9 Aug. 1979.

39 Swin. P., 174/6/14: E. R. Thompson and E. Spencer Shaw to Swinton, 13 Apr. 1955. Swinton was lunching with the Lobby as late as July 1965. Evans, *Downing Street Diary*, p. 286. See also Seldon, *Churchill's Indian Summer*, p. 61.

40 *Public Relations* (Journal of the Institute of Public Relations), Apr. 1955, p. 17; interview with Sir Fife Clark, 9 Aug. 1979.

41 173 H.L.Deb., cols. 170-204. Swinton's speech is at cols. 170-4.

42 *The Federation of Rhodesia and Nyasaland* (Cmnd. 1948, HMSO, London, Feb. 1963); Sir Roy Welensky, *Welensky's 4,000 Days* (Collins, London, 1964),

pp. 62 f.; Lord Alport, *The Sudden Assignment* (Hodder & Stoughton, London, 1965), pp. 231 f.; 246 H.L.Deb., cols. 1156-242 (18 Feb. 1963).

43 Some years later Swinton told his friend A. L. Geyer, former South African High Commissioner in London, that he had favoured the exclusion of Nyasaland (the one wholly African territory) from the original federation, giving it the option of coming in later when it appreciated the advantages (as Swinton was sure it would). But the Colonial Office, the three governors, Huggins, and the European leaders in Nyasaland 'were all for inclusion'. Swin. P., 174/9/2: Swinton to Geyer, 31 Dec. 1959.

44 Swin. P., 174/7/1: Huggins to Swinton, 4 Feb. 1956; Swinton correspondence with Walter Adams, principal of the University College of Rhodesia and Nyasaland, Oct.-Nov. 1956. See also I. C. M. Maxwell, *Universities in Partnership* (Scottish Academic Press, Edinburgh, 1980), p. 236.

45 Swin. P., 174/9/2-21, contain much correspondence and other material on Rhodesian affairs after Swinton left office. He was frequently consulted on policy questions by Douglas-Home and other Conservative leaders, especially after the Smith regime's unilateral declaration of independence in November 1965. Swinton maintained close personal links with, among others, Sir Humphrey Gibb, the Governor of Southern Rhodesia, and Lord Malvern. See particularly ibid., 174/9/11-20.

46 D. J. Morgan, *Official History of Colonial Development*, V (Macmillan, London, 1980), 57 f., 85; Swin. P., 174/6/12: paper on 'The Future of Commonwealth Membership', Jan. 1955.

47 S. Gopal, *Jawaharlal Nehru*, i (Cape, London, 1979), 168.

48 Swinton, *Sixty Years of Power*, p. 222.

49 Swin. P., 174/6/6: Swinton to Lady Swinton, 20 Oct. 1953.

50 Swin. P., 174/6/4: Clutterbuck to Crookshank, 30 Nov. 1953; ibid.: Swinton to Lady Swinton, 17 Nov. 1953; ibid.: Laithwaite to Crookshank, 30 Nov. 1953.

51 524 H.C.Deb., cols. 171-2; 186 H.L.Deb., cols. 1057-60.

52 529 H.C. Deb., cols 2047-108, particularly cols. 2089-93 (6 July 1954); 190 H.L.Deb., cols. 322-3 (8 Dec. 1954).

53 Swinton, *Sixty Years of Power*, p. 205.

54 Ibid., p. 212; Macmillan, *Tides of Fortune*, pp. 574 f.; Swin. P. 174/10/6.

55 Macmillan, *Tides of Fortune*, p. 573.

56 David Carlton, *Anthony Eden* (Allen Lane, London, 1981), p. 368.

57 James Margach, *The Abuse of Power* (W. H. Allen, London, 1978), pp. 105 f. Margach assisted Swinton with the preparation of *Sixty Years of Power* in 1965.

58 Swin. P., 174/6/3: Swinton to Eden, 7 Apr. 1955, Eden to Swinton, 7 Apr. 1955. Swinton's successor as Commonwealth Secretary was Lord Home, Minister of State at the Scottish Office.

59 The Queen showed her personal appreciation by sending him, through her assistant private secretary, Sir Edward Ford, a signed photograph of herself and the Duke of Edinburgh 'in recognition of your long service as a Minister of the Crown during four reigns'. Swin. P., 174/6/13: Ford to Swinton, 17 Apr. 1955. Three days later Swinton had an audience of the Queen for the conferment of the Earldom. He was reintroduced to the Lords in his new rank on 21 June 1955.

60 Swin, P., 174/6/13: Butler to Swinton, 7 Apr. 1955.

61 Ibid., 174/6/14: Churchill to Swinton, 9 Apr. 1955. This file contains numerous letters to Swinton on his resignation from, among others, Lord Milverton, Llewellin, Home, and Ismay, and Sir Frank Lee.

62 Macmillan, *Tides of Fortune*, p. 583; Lord Boyd-Carpenter, *Way of Life* (Sidgwick & Jackson, London, 1980), p. 126.

63 496 H.C.Deb., cols. 702-3 (25 Feb. 1952); 540 H.C.Deb., cols. 1685-8 (4 May

1955); *The Times*, 5 May 1955; Swin. P., 174/12/3: Swinton to Eden, 28 Apr. 1955, Eden to Swinton, 6 May 1966; ibid., 174/12/4: Brook to Swinton, 12 May 1955, and other correspondence and press cuttings on this file.

64 Swin. P., 174/7/8: Belgian Ambassador to Swinton, 10 Dec. 1962; *The Times*, 7 Feb. 1963.

65 196 H.L.Deb., cols. 8-52 (28 Feb. 1956); 206 H.L.Deb., cols. 977-1020 (10 Dec. 1957); 208 H.L.Deb., cols. 1005-82 (24 Apr. 1958); 210 H.L.Deb., cols. 73-4 (24 June 1958). See also Janet Morgan *The House of Lords and the Labour Government 1964-1970* (Oxford University Press, 1975), pp. 14 f. Up to 19 per cent of peers applied for leave of absence, either for a session or the whole Parliament, in the 1964-70 period.

66 248 H.L.Deb., cols. 265-347 (28 Mar. 1963); 252 H.L.Deb., cols. 126-50 (16 July 1963); Swinton, *Sixty Years of Power*, pp. 190-2.

67 Macmillan spent some days shooting at Swinton towards the end of August and had 'much debate' with his old friend about his personal position as Prime Minister: but this was before ill health precipitated his resignation. Harold Macmillan, *At the End of the Day* (Macmillan, London, 1973), p. 491; Swinton, *Sixty Years of Power*, pp. 188 f.; Swin. P., 174/11/8. As the Conservative leadership crisis developed Swinton was again consulted by Macmillan and also by Home, two days before he became Prime Minister. *Sixty Years of Power*, pp. 188 f., 199.

68 Swin. P., 174/8/1-2, contain much correspondence and other material on the 1968 reform proposals.

69 Ibid., 174/7/3: Douglas to Swinton, 1 Sept. 1958.

70 It was serialized in the *Sunday Times* for several weeks from 17 Oct. 1965 and was published by Hutchinson in April 1966. For correspondence and reviews see Swin. P., 174/11/5-8. Although the book is more crisply written than *I Remember*, the description of it by Iain Macleod as 'a random collection of memories and jottings, without theme or weight' does not seem unfair. The *Spectator*, 29 Apr. 1966. Macleod's review also contained warm praise of Swinton as one of the two men (James Stuart being the other) to whom he, as a young Minister, would often turn 'for criticism or for confirmation of my view. I owe him much.' Macleod was appointed Minister of Health from the back-benches in February 1952.

71 328 H.L.Deb., cols. 507-8.

72 334 H.L.Deb., cols. 1-6 (31 July 1972).

73 *The Times*, 19 Oct. 1972.

74 Cf. the comments of an anonymous reviewer of his *Sixty Years of Power*: 'By the standards of modern image-makers, Philip Swinton has never quite made it. He served in eleven governments, under six different prime ministers, but at no time did he become a household name, an instantly recognizable, cartoonable face. But over some fifty years of active political life, few men have exercised more influence over affairs, particularly the internal affairs of the Conservative party.' *The Economist*, 30 Apr. 1966.

75 Robert Rhodes James has told of the unfortunate American Ph.D. student whose thesis betrayed that he was under the impression that Sir Philip Lloyd-Greame, Sir Philip Cunliffe-Lister, and Lord Swinton were three different politicians. *Swinton Journal*, xviii, no. 3 (Autumn 1972), 11 f.

76 Lord Home, *Where the Wind Blows* (Collins, London, 1976), p. 54.

77 Butler, *The Art of the Possible*, p. 159.

78 Macmillan, *Tides of Fortune*, p. 687; *Swinton Journal*, xviii, no. 3 (1972), p. 6.

79 Interview with Lord Fraser of Kilmorack, 29 Aug. 1979.

80 Swinton, *I Remember*, p. 264.

81 See, for example, Cross, *Sir Samuel Hoare*, 1977), pp. 128 ff. (Hoare was Secretary of State for India from 1931 to 1935.)
82 Baldwin Papers, vol. 104, ff. 79–83; Swin. P., 174/2/2, Cunliffe-Lister to Baldwin 13 Dec. 1930.
83 Seldon, *Churchill's Indian Summer*, p. 599, n. 15; interview with D. J. C. Crawley, 26 Oct. 1979.
84 G. R. Downes to the author, 30 Sept. 1979.

Note on Unpublished Sources

The following are the locations of the various unpublished collections referred to in the notes to chapters:

Attlee Papers: Bodleian Library, Oxford

Baldwin Papers: University Library, Cambridge

Bayford Diaries: Conservative Research Department, London

Brabourne Papers: India Office Library, London

Bridgeman Political Diary: in the possession of Viscount Bridgeman

Cabinet and Departmental Records: Public Record Office, Kew

    Admiralty (Adm)

    Air Ministry (Air)

    Cabinet (Cab)

    Ministry of Civil Aviation (Avia)

    Colonial Office (CO)

    Foreign Office (FO)

    Ministry of National Service (NatS)

    Prime Minister (Prem)

    Board of Trade (BT)

Austen Chamberlain Papers: University Library, Birmingham

Neville Chamberlain Papers: University Library, Birmingham

Sir Sydney Chapman, unpublished autobiography: British Library of Political and Economic Science, London, and John Rylands Library, Manchester

Crookshank Papers: Bodleian Library, Oxford

Curzon Papers: India Office Library, London

Halifax Papers: India House Library, London

Hannon Papers: House of Lords Record Office, London

Runciman Papers: University Library, Newcastle upon Tyne

F. H. Sandford, West African diary, 1942–4: Rhodes House, Oxford, and Churchill College, Cambridge

Swinton Papers: Churchill College, Cambridge (Certain letters no longer available in these papers are quoted in Alan Earl, 'The Political Life of Viscount Swinton 1918–1938', MA thesis, University of Manchester, 1961.)

Templewood Papers: University Library, Cambridge

Weir Papers: Churchill College, Cambridge

Woolton Papers, Bodleian Library, Oxford

Index

leadership, 61-2, 96-7; 1924 view of standing in party, 62-3; wife succeeds to Swinton estate, 63; and defeat of first Labour Government, 64; urges Cabinet post for Churchill, 65; reappointed to Board of Trade, 65-6; work at Board, 66-76, 80-3, 86-90; contemplates resignation, 76-80, 83-6; and General Strike, 80-2; and 1929 election, 90-1; created GBE, 91; political ambition, 93, 267-8; co-operation with Neville Chamberlain on trade policy, 94-6; and formation of National Government, 98-9; at Board of Trade again, 99; and 1931 election, 100-1; appointed Colonial Secretary, 102-3; and Ottawa Conference, 106-9; work at Colonial Office, 110-32, 135; and development of colonial trade, 111-14, 116-17; and Japanese textile quotas, 114-16; working methods, 119-21, 266; and Palestine, 121-3; and mutiny of Assyrian levies, 124-30; serious illness in Kenya, 131; advocates Lloyd George's inclusion in Cabinet, 132-3; chairs committee on Air Parity, 137-42; appointed Secretary of State for Air, 143; work at Air Ministry, 143-4, 145-79, 180-218, 295; accepts peerage, 144-5; and expansion Scheme 'C', 153-4; and aircraft industry, 154-7, 159, 168-71, 205-8, 211; co-operation with Lord Weir, 154-5; institutes weekly expansion progress meetings, 156; and Scheme 'F', 158-9; activates shadow aircraft factory scheme, 160-8; clashes with Lord Nuffield, 160-1, 163-5; negotiates Austin shadow contract, 165-7; presses radar development, 172, 179; and Air Defence Research Committee, 172-9; handles Lindemann–Tizard clash, 175-8; and struggle over control of naval aviation, 180-9; and Scheme 'H', 189-91; and financial limits on defence expenditure, 192; and Scheme 'J', 193-6; dispute on strategy with Inskip, 194-6; and Scheme 'K', 196-7; and Scheme 'L', 198-200; and criticisms of

Imperial Airways, 201-3; and Cadman inquiry, 202, 203-5; defended by Chamberlain, 203, 205; and mounting criticism of Air Ministry, 205; and appointment of Bruce-Gardner, 206; secures Cabinet approval of Scheme 'L', 210; and creation of RAF Volunteer Reserve, 210-11; resignation as Air Minister, 212-18; supports Chamberlain's appeasement policy, 218-19; joins Salisbury's Watching Committee, 220; as Chairman of United Kingdom Commercial Corporation, 221-4, 234; co-ordinates security services, 224-31; work as Resident Minister in West Africa, 231-44; appointed CH, 241; as first Minister of Civil Aviation, 244-55; at Chicago Conference, 247-50; and 'Swinton plan', 252-5; role in Conservative Opposition (1945-51), 256-63; chairs party election briefing committee, 256-7, 263, 285; publishes memoirs, 258; and Swinton Conservative College, 262-3; appointed Chancellor of Duchy of Lancaster and Minister of Materials, 265; and steel supplies, 266; close relations with Butler and Macmillan, 266-7; and steel denationalization, 267; special position in Churchill's 1951-5 Government, 267-8, 283-4; chairs party Liaison Committee, 268-9; co-ordinates home information services, 269-72, 273; and decision to televise Coronation, 272-3; appointed Commonwealth Secretary, 274; work at Commonwealth Relations Office, 274-83; and federation in Central Africa, 275-8; chairs committee on Commonwealth membership, 278-9; clashes with Nehru over Kenya, 279-80; Commonwealth tours, 280-1; decision to close British Council offices in Australia, New Zealand, and Ceylon, 281-3; dropped from office by Eden, 284-5; created Earl of Swinton, 285; Churchill's regret at departure, 285; deals with allegations about his television interests, 286-8; post-